Bound by the City

SUNY series, Insinuations:
Philosophy, Psychoanalysis, Literature

Charles Shepherdson, editor

Bound by the City

Greek Tragedy, Sexual Difference, and the Formation of the *Polis*

Edited by
Denise Eileen McCoskey
Emily Zakin

Published by
State University of New York Press, Albany

© 2009 State University of New York

For information, contact State University of New York Press, Albany, NY
www.sunypress.edu

Production by Ryan Morris
Marketing by Michael Campochiaro

Library of Congress Cataloging-in-Publication Data

Bound by the city : Greek tragedy, sexual difference, and the formation of the
polis / edited by Denise Eileen McCoskey, Emily Zakin.
    p. cm.—(Insinuations : philosophy, psychoanalysis, literature)
Includes bibliographical references and index.
    ISBN 978-1-4384-2711-9 (hardcover : alk. paper)
    1. Greek drama (Tragedy)—History and criticism. 2. Gender identity in
literature. 3. Gender identity—Greece. 4. Literature and society—Greece.
    5. City-states—Greece. I. McCoskey, Denise Eileen,1968– II. Zakin, Emily.

PA3136.B66 2009
882'.0109 353—dc22   2008048482

10 9 8 7 6 5 4 3 2 1

CONTENTS

ACKNOWLEDGMENTS

The editors wish first and foremost to thank our contributors for their energy and persistence in advancing the vision of this volume and bringing it to its final, provocative form. The volume was first conceived when we co-taught an honors course on "Women, Representation, and the State" at Miami University in the fall of 2001; we are grateful to the Honors Program at Miami for that opportunity and to the students in that original seminar. We would also like to offer our gratitude to Miami University for enabling us to host a conference on "Antigone's Dilemma: Gender, Greek Tragedy, and the City-State" in the fall of 2003. For their support of this event we thank, in particular, the departments of Classics and Philosophy; the Harry T. Wilks Leadership Institute; the Sigma Chi/William P. Huffman Scholar-in-Residence Program; the College of Arts and Science; the Center for American and World Cultures; the departments of Comparative Religion, French and Italian, History, Political Science, Theatre, Educational Leadership, and English; the Etheridge Center for Reflective Leadership; the Graduate School and its Office for the Advancement of Research and Scholarship; the Honors Program; the International Studies Program; the Women's Studies Program; the Office of the Provost; and the Women's Center. We are grateful as well to the participants at that conference for their wonderful papers and for the many discussions and conversations that further inspired this work. Publication of this volume would not be possible without the financial support of the departments of Classics and Philosophy, the College of Arts and Science, the Office for the Advancement of Research and Scholarship, and the Graduate School at Miami, so we extend to them our sincere thanks. Finally, we would like to express our deepest gratitude to Charles Shepherdson for his great enthusiasm for this project and his many efforts on our behalf, as well as James Peltz, Jane Bunker, and Ryan Morris at SUNY Press for their stewardship of the volume and Susan Colberg for the striking cover design.

Introduction

DENISE EILEEN MCCOSKEY AND EMILY ZAKIN

The scope of tragedy is such that it carries within itself a kind of knowledge or theory concerning the illogical logic that governs the order of human activities.

—Jean-Pierre Vernant

In characterizing the work of Greek tragedy, Jean-Pierre Vernant acutely captures a contradiction that sustains tragedy at its core: its representation of an irreconcilable impasse between the order of human institutions and the disorder such institutions simultaneously disavow and generate. In apprehending the illogical logic of those political structures that preside over human affairs, tragedy remains inextricably bound by and to the idea of the city-state (the *polis*), the primary site of meaning and value through which the subject assumed its place for the Athenian dramatists. Greek tragedy thereby serves as a potent site for the exploration of anxieties associated with the relation between the body politic and its embodied, especially sexed, subjects. In its dramatic renderings, one finds representations, both metaphorical and phantasmatic, of not only the *polis* at work and in turmoil but also its putative origins and organizing principles. In this volume, we are thus concerned with the Athenian city-state and its mutually formative relation with the citizens and noncitizens who are fashioned within and bound by it.

Situating tragedy within the historical context of its production, many scholars have argued that it displays specifically the transitions in political imagination that accompany the ostensible replacement of an aristocratic form of government with a democratic one, highlighting the passage from aristocracy to democracy as a moment of crisis in Athenian self-conception.[1] While this volume supports and elaborates that view, it also pursues a concomitant scrutiny of the ways in which

1

representations of sexual difference are integral to both this crisis and the political concepts that emerge from it. The authors in this volume treat these emerging political concepts as fundamental to the constitution of sexual difference and vice versa.[2] Sensitive to the crossroads of political and sexual representations in tragic drama, and the dilemmas of citizenship, subjectivity, and justice thereby articulated and revealed, this volume elucidates the ways in which the crises, disquiet, and flawed resolutions portrayed in Greek tragedy continue to inform the metaphors and imagery that structure sexual difference and give shape to political life.[3] The value given to masculine self-mastery as a necessary virtue for the responsibilities of democratic citizenship, and the complementary and enduring ethos that renders feminine citizenship oxymoronic, divulges the thorny manner in which the democratic *polis* simultaneously demands, instantiates, and elides sexual difference, both binding the feminine to it and repressing that bond.

Greek tragedy provides a critical discursive focus of our deliberations for two reasons: first, because of its centrality in ancient Athenian civic life, where it was performed at public religious festivals in front of an audience of citizens; and second, because of its continuing reverberations in later Western philosophy and political practice, both of which almost ritualistically invoke and reinvoke its central tropes. In this volume, our contributors thus pursue contrasting approaches that nonetheless contribute equally to our broader undertaking and arrive at noticeably congruent insights—some authors offer ways of contextualizing the preoccupations of Greek tragedy within the changing tensions and power relations of an Athenian city falling into greater disarray, while others seek to demonstrate the persistent role of Greek tragedy in unveiling and giving voice to the dynamics and deadlocks that still shape the modern city-state and its structures with regard to masculine and feminine subjects and citizens.

In this way, our volume's approach is deliberately interdisciplinary, engaging historical, literary, and philosophical forms of textual analysis in order to draw out the conceptual and political intersections of sexual difference and social order. Seeking to demonstrate the range of ways in which sexual difference and political structure engage with one another throughout Greek tragedy, our chapters cumulatively amplify rather than undermine one another through their different methodologies and interpretations. So, too, given that Greek tragedy has been broadly disseminated in many fields across the academy, one of the challenges and aims of this collection is to foster a rich dialogue between the disciplines of classics and philosophy, to open the canonical field of continental philosophy to a different cultural horizon, that of antiquity, and a different form of knowledge, that of tragic discourse, and to open classical studies, in turn, to the range of intellectual projects that Greek tragedy continues to inspire and illuminate in later historical periods.

In accordance with the concerns that drive this volume, as editors we chose not to examine the genre of Greek tragedy *writ* large, but rather to focus our inquiry on tragedy's engagement with two specific myths or households: the house of Atreus and the house of Laius, both royal households whose dangerous and often violent intimacies seem, at times, to sustain the city and its institutions and, at other times, to undermine or shake their very foundations. The threats posed by and to these households are equally internal and external, implicating in their very lineage the city's fragility and confounding the boundaries between *oikos* and *polis*. The house of Atreus is bound by the city through its murders—father of daughter, wife of husband, children of mother; the house of Laius through its incestuous relations and self-destructive impulses.[4]

Even as we have limited our investigation to only two central myths and the themes they illuminate in tragedy, our volume nonetheless pointedly seeks to consider the divergent ways the three major Greek tragedians (Aeschylus, Sophocles, and Euripides) probe the engagement of sexual difference with civic ordering in each myth. We thus believe the meanings of each tragedy emerge in part via their difference from, and indeed their interplay with, other tragic renditions of the same myth. Whereas in the Aeschylean version, for example, the violent fate of the house of Atreus is resolved only by Athena and the intervention of Athenian law, in the Euripidean, a different god, Apollo, circumvents the demands of the citizen Assembly and establishes harmony only by reinscribing kinship and the demands of aristocratic marriage practice. We have in our volume many Antigones and many Electras, as well as a Jocasta whose use of imagery reveals her repression of her husband's paternity and another Jocasta whose suicide responds not to the revelation of Oedipus' identity, but rather to the mutual destruction of her sons. Finally, many of our contributors view the problems of the *genos* and *polis* pointedly from the position of the other: the unnamed slave who saves Oedipus as a baby and later becomes the primary witness of the patricide at the crossroads; the slave Cassandra whose truthful cry stands outside the reason of the city, marking its exclusions and denials; and the Furies who police the ravages of the *genos* and yet whose domestication by Athena is necessary for the city's order.

Our hypothesis in revisiting these two myths is that sexual difference both supports the foundation of political structures generally, and perhaps democracy specifically, and is also the site of their founding. Our hope when we solicited contributions was that this volume would interrogate this relation from two sides: the formation of sexual difference with relation to the *polis* and the formation of the *polis* with relation to sexual difference. By inviting a series of interdisciplinary readings, we expected to focus attention on a number of different themes: the uncanny aspects of kinship and the *polis*; the conflicting pressures of blood and law; the paternal, patricidal, and fratricidal lineages of citizenship and democracy (and the murderous confusions of origin this entails); the role of marriage and women in the transmission of property; and the establishment or denial of self-mastery and subjectivity via citizenship. The chapters that are included here both fulfill our aims and complicate our hypothesis: cumulatively, they shed light on the myriad ways in which the representations, conceptual and textual structures, and imagery of sexual difference in Greek tragedy have become integral to the fabrication and failings of political institutions.

The first chapter in the volume contrasts two dramatic versions of the fraternal rivalry that brings about the simultaneous deaths of Oedipus' two sons, Eteocles and Polyneices, at one another's hands. In "City Farewell!: *Genos, Polis,* and Gender in Aeschylus' *Seven Against Thebes* and Euripides' *Phoenician Women,*" Peter Burian insists that Euripides' later (and more obscure, at least for modern audiences) play *Phoenician Women* must be read as a response to Aeschylus' *Seven Against Thebes.* Burian argues that, unlike Aeschylus' play, which probes the violent and unsettling intersections of kinship and city inherent in the house of Laius, the royal house of Thebes and its embattled city "are forcibly kept apart" in Euripides in order to highlight the tragic dangers of personal ambition and lust for power engendering political crisis in the Athens of his day. In this version of Thebes, both Jocasta's suicide and Antigone's exile with her blind father follow rather than precede the bloodshed of brothers, suggesting that the source of each woman's primary (albeit troubled) identification with the *genos* and subsequent removal from the domain of the *polis* is dependent as much on fratricide as incest. In contrast to these women's roles, Euripides establishes the mutual slaughter of Oedipus' sons as "an entirely gratuitous act" for the *polis* by inventing a son for Creon, Menoeceus, a child pointedly outside the direct line of Oedipus, whose self-sacrifice alone determines the city's fate. Burian's interest in charting the complex and changing representations of a single myth across two plays and two Greek historical contexts provides an important foundation for the chapters that follow, exemplifying the intricate relay between sexual difference and the *polis* that our volume seeks to document.

Charles Shepherdson's chapter, "*Antigone*: The Work of Literature and the History of Subjectivity," raises fundamental questions regarding the philosophical approach to tragedy. Casting a dim light on the way that philosophical concepts are sometimes imposed on textual schemas, Shepherdson insists on distinguishing the aesthetic features that characterize the literary genre of tragedy and its theatrical form of subjectivity from that posed or proposed by religious, legal, or philosophical discourse. Whatever truths may obtain within tragedy, Shepherdson argues, they cannot simply be translated into the language of the philosophers, nor does the tragic text offer an uncomplicated mirror of the historical, philosophical, or anthropological life of the city. If the world of the theater is distinct and independent from the world of the city, carrying its own language and discourse not readily commensurate even with its own historical context, then any attempt to leap from the "mythic memory" of the former to the rules and parameters of the latter will miss the mark. In Shepherdson's reading of Sophocles' exemplary text, Antigone inhabits and deploys the "I" in a distinctive way; she alone is able to say what she means, and so she embodies a tragic subjectivity that might help us trace shifts in the history of subjectivity and its various configurations.

In "The Laius Complex," Mark Buchan returns to the "primal scene" enacted at the crossroads in Sophocles' *Oedipus Tyrannus* and elaborates not the murderous dynamic between father and son, but rather the position of the unnamed slave who is inserted between the two, refracting the desires of both. While demonstrating the crucial ways in which the slave mirrors Oedipus' own conflicted impulses in the play, not least that of flight, Buchan ultimately uses the slave to provide an interpretation of the play's puzzling insistence on testifying to multiple assailants of Laius at the crossroads. Although Oedipus alone physically strikes Laius down at their meeting, Buchan argues that Oedipus nonetheless remains detached from any pleasure in the act, while the desire for the king's death implicates everyone else: Laius himself, Jocasta, the king's slave, and the entire citizen body of Thebes. As Buchan demonstrates in his conclusion, the surplus of murderous desires inside and outside the *genos* presents a critical backdrop against which the deadly drive of Oedipus' daughter Antigone takes center stage.

Just as Buchan's chapter unravels the myriad meanings attached to the slave's status as eyewitness to the events at the crossroads, the following chapter likewise explores the convoluted processes of sight and desire in Sophocles' play, but in this case focuses specifically on Jocasta's resistance to understanding her own. Developing and distilling Sigmund Freud's notion of the uncanny, David Schur's chapter, "Jocasta's Eye and Freud's Uncanny," highlights the persistent employment of imagery related to blindness and light in Sophocles' *Oedipus Tyrannus*. Schur's reading emanates from a curious line in the play in which Jocasta calls the funeral rites of Oedipus' presumed father, Polybus, "a great eye" (987). By refusing her own knowledge that Polybus is not Oedipus' real father, Schur suggests that Jocasta's use of the image of the (blind) eye signals here not insight, but the distancing of the familiar and familial, a repression that is bound to return. Schur's insights into Jocasta's desire and the force of her repression expose the workings of sexual difference in the ambiguity of maternal birth and the concomitant confusion over death that are at the heart of this drama.

Moving from the repressions of the mother to the claims of the daughter, from Sophocles' *Oedipus* to Sophocles' *Antigone*, the next chapter rethinks the possibilities and meanings of justice. In "Force of Law: The 'Mystical Foundation of Authority,'" Jacques Derrida argues that justice rests on a certain irreducibility of justice to law, and thus an ineradicable violence within the law. Victoria Wohl's chapter on "Sexual Difference and the Aporia of Justice in Sophocles' *Antigone*" demonstrates how such an aporia is at the center of the *agôn* between Antigone and Creon in Sophocles' *Antigone*. Wohl's initial claim is that Creon and Antigone's appeals to different sorts of (self-authorizing) law reflect a conflict that is fundamentally aporetic in structure, an irresolvable crisis that cannot be, as Hegel argues, synthesized at a higher level.[5] But precisely in that *crisis* (the word in Greek also means judgment or court case) lies the possibility of justice, for as Derrida intimates, justice exists only in its difference from law.[6] This chapter thus argues that *Antigone* stages the emergence of the *polis* out of sexual and legal aporia, not as the resolution or transcendence of difference but as the site of its institutionalization in the form of ongoing democratic (legal and political) contest. Such aporetic justice indicates that the democratic city is specifically and structurally tragic.

While continuing to elaborate the theme of tragic contestation, the chapter that follows shifts its theoretical focus from Derrida to Hegel and the latter's readings of the houses of both Laius and Atreus. As with Wohl's chapter, Elaine Miller's chapter, "Tragedy, Natural Law, and Sexual Difference in Hegel," demonstrates that in tragedy sexual difference becomes a structural constituent not just of particular roles within the state but also of the most fundamental ways in which power is articulated. Through a reading of Hegel's often overlooked text, *Natural Law*, the chapter revisits the *Oresteia* as a site of contestation of the very meaning of law, statehood, and ethical life. The chapter goes beyond Hegel, however, in reading these sites of meaning with reference to the salient role played by sexual difference in the trilogy, a role that Hegel ignores. The chapter focuses, in particular, on a comparison between Hegel's treatment of the *Antigone*, on the one hand, and the *Oresteia* trilogy, on the other (and between the characters of Antigone and Electra in his readings), in order to develop the notion that the family and power are imbricated within the state.

Emily Zakin's chapter returns to Freud's notion of the uncanny, in this case to follow its extended political trajectory through Julia Kristeva's reconceptualization in *Strangers to Ourselves*. Kristeva argues that the threat the foreigner poses to political cohesion is fundamentally a threat not of the outsider but the insider: it is the uncanny strangeness within ourselves that renders the *polis* always precarious.[7] In "Marrying the City: Intimate Strangers and the Fury of Democracy," Zakin examines the dynamic of pacification staged in the final scenes of the *Oresteia* and the democratic fantasy of harmony with which she argues it is commensurate, seeing in both something akin to a marital bond that stifles discord. Athena calls the Erinyes strangers; but they also manifest the family curse of the house of Atreus, what is both most strange and most familiar to its members, the element interior to their ancestry that drives their actions and binds them violently together. While Athena would have us believe that the law of the city can absorb aggressions against and within it, fully resolving their collision in unity, this chapter argues that the Eumenides remain as a testament to the fundamental fury of democracy and the political impasse of the uncanny to which it is bound.

Pascale-Anne Brault's chapter resonates with themes introduced earlier in the volume, taking up in concert the language of insight and unconcealment and that of the foreigner. In "Playing the Cassandra: Prophecies of the Feminine in Aeschylus' *Agamemnon*," Brault focuses on the figure of Cassandra who represents prophetic truth as knowledge about the future of the *polis*, even while she is constantly identified as "other," outside the *polis*, both woman and foreigner. Cassandra seems to have access to the future, but unlike her male counterparts, her voice is inarticulate and unheard by those around her, beyond words and reasons, at the limit of the human. At the level of the narrative, however, the marginalized Cassandra becomes central to the development of tragic irony, as her unheeded words provide background for the reinterpretation of past events and the perception and representation of present and future ones. Cassandra embodies both the transformation of the human and the civilized into the inhuman, the barbarian, and the animalistic, and the tension stemming from a "truth" that is at once revealed and concealed. This chapter thus risks the formula that tragedy and the *polis* it represents are essentially related to the feminine, to a certain feminine element that tragedy must suppress or deny but can never totally ignore.

While Cassandra calls attention to the destructive impulses of the city from the outside, Sophocles' *Electra* poignantly dramatizes the violence enacted on Agamemnon's daughter Electra when she moves from a position outside the city into its very center, choosing at a critical moment to embrace the city's destructive logic and demands. In "The Loss of Abandonment in Sophocles' *Electra*," Denise Eileen McCoskey begins by demonstrating the ways in which Electra's isolation and presumed abandonment by her male kin at the play's opening seem to yield an important space not only for impassioned speech and mourning but also for the young woman's fantasies of exercising her own political agency via the assassination of her father's murderers. Yet Sophocles brutally forecloses both openings when Orestes, returning from exile, reunites with his sister and gradually assumes both the central role in the revenge plot and subsequent mastery of his sister and the city. Central to this changing dynamic is the language used to name Electra's passions in the play, for Electra's violent and unrestrained passion at the beginning of the play, encapsulated in the anger or *orgê* that emerges from the death of her father, is strikingly transformed by Electra herself into a very different emotion, pleasure (*hedonê*), when she recognizes her brother. And whereas Electra's *orgê* was once a source of disruption and tragic standing in the play, her sudden embrace of pleasure, in contrast, ominously generates the grounds for Orestes' control over her and her own self-annihilation, since it is precisely on the repression of pleasure and not the necessity of revenge or matricide that Orestes establishes his own ultimate rise to power.

Just as Sophocles epitomizes Electra's diminishment through a shifting vocabulary of emotions, a reading of Euripides' treatment of the intersections between sexual difference and the city in his *Electra*, Kirk Ormand argues, can productively be rooted in the thorny question of how women's relationship to the city was conveyed in ancient Greek. In his play, Euripides' characters rely on two distinct terms for the "city": *polis*, used in reference to men and their affiliations, and *astu*, a term that connotes the city in terms of geographic territory rather than political institutions and is applied in reference to women and their civic bond. Given that such a linguistic gap reinforces men's and women's distinct conceptual and legal status (a distinction complicated by Pericles' citizenship laws in 451/450 BCE), Ormand suggests in "Electra in Exile" that Euripides' use of language continually references that difference in order to call attention to women's peripheral relationship to the city (in which they stand already as a kind of exile), as well as intensify Electra's "double-exclusion," as she lives physically outside the city and awaits her exiled brother's return. Moreover, even after Orestes has returned from his own exile and killed his father's murderers, the two siblings are once again separated via the gendered exigencies of exile: Orestes, deprived of the city of his father, is nonetheless directed to Athens and, eventually, the foundation of his own *polis*, while Electra's farewell to the city (in which she addresses its women with the unusual term *politides*) marks her recognition of a putative female citizenship precisely at its moment of loss.

Although the two *Electras* focus primary attention on what is left for the two siblings after the violence of matricide and political revenge, Euripides in another play broadens his scope to consider the myth's resolution in terms of the children's larger networks of kinship. Euripides' *Orestes* has often been criticized by modern readers for its endless plot twists and its somewhat implausible "happy" resolution in parallel marriages for Orestes and his sister, yet Mark Griffith argues in "Orestes and the In-Laws" that Euripides' play, every bit as much as Aeschylus' *Oresteia*, reveals the interworkings of kinship and its role in structuring Athenian political life. Central to Euripides' approach, for Griffith, is an extension of the notion of kinship to encompass the more extended familial units and the systems of property ownership and transmission that helped structure Greek aristocratic marriage practices. In this way, Euripides presents Orestes' claims to his father's house as predicated not so much on matricide and its consequences (the murder of Clytemnestra notably takes place before the play begins), but rather on the young man's entry into the appropriate political systems and social alliances necessary for the maintenance of aristocratic power. In the final scene, the resolution of the Argive assembly demanding that Orestes and Electra commit suicide is met head-on by the siblings' bizarre and brutal escape plan involving murder of Helen and the kidnap of their cousin, only to have all tension suddenly dissipated by the appearance of Apollo and his proscription of harmony through marriage. In contrast to Aeschylus, then, Euripides powerfully (albeit perhaps ambiguously) situates marriage and not law as the ultimate principle used to establish order in the city and for its citizens.

In all, the disparate trajectories of the readings assembled in this volume attest to the impact of Greek tragedy, its "knowledge or theory," as Vernant calls it, not least its apprehension and representation of the uneasy relationship of sexual difference to political order (as well as disorder, crisis, emptiness, and silence), a relationship whose contours and intersections continue to exert symbolic force today. The chapters contained here focus on different myths, characters, and political processes, and they employ diverse reading and theoretical strategies. Some are more concerned with positions articulated in relation to the *polis* (citizen, other, man, woman, foreigner, slave) and especially with the exclusions written into the tragic dramas themselves as testimony of the exclusions that recur equally in political life; others are more concerned with the political and structural processes by which democracies instantiate and authorize themselves. But all share a conception of the violence and disequilibrium at the heart of the democratic city and the limits of political order. This common thematic perspective exposes the darkness one would expect from tragic discourse: a diagnosis of the city that undoes itself, of a democracy rooted in fraternal and fratricidal origins that cannot be erased or finally excluded and will thus always be haunted by the return of that which, though necessary to its constitution, it represses. This self-annihilating void, generated (produced and reproduced) at the core of the city-state, exposes the inner bond between the impasse of democratic citizenship and the confounding of sexual difference, and the impossibility of harmonious reconciliation between the two: the tragic fate of a city unbound by its own illogical logic.

NOTES

1. See, for example, Jean-Pierre Vernant, "The Historical Moment of Tragedy in Greece: Some of the Social and Psychological Conditions," in *Myth and Tragedy in Ancient Greece*, ed. Jean-Pierre Vernant and Pierre Vidal-Naquet, trans. Janet Lloyd (New York: Zone Books, 1988), 23–28. Peter W. Rose demonstrates the ways in which these two political modes continue to compete with one another in tragic discourse in "Historicizing Sophocles' *Ajax*," in *History, Tragedy, Theory: Dialogues on Athenian Drama*, ed. Barbara Goff (Austin: University of Texas Press, 1995), 59–90. The attempt to apprehend the civic function of tragedy within its broader Athenian context has flourished in recent years; see Paul Cartledge, "'Deep Plays': Theatre as Process in Greek Civic Life," in *The Cambridge Companion to Greek Tragedy*, ed. P. E. Easterling (Cambridge: Cambridge University Press, 1997), 3–35; Christopher Pelling, ed.,

Greek Tragedy and the Historian (Oxford: Oxford University Press, 1997); M. S. Silk, ed., *Tragedy and the Tragic: Greek Theatre and Beyond* (Oxford: Oxford University Press, 1996); Barbara Goff, ed., *History, Tragedy, Theory* (Austin: University of Texas Press, 1995); Ruth Scodel, ed., *Theater and Society in the Classical World* (Ann Arbor: University of Michigan Press, 1993); John J. Winkler and Froma I. Zeitlin, eds., *Nothing to Do With Dionysus? Athenian Drama in Its Social Context* (Princeton, NJ: Princeton University Press, 1990); and J. Peter Euben, ed., *Greek Tragedy and Political Theory* (Berkeley: University of California Press, 1986). Such work coincides with interest in investigating the production of ancient Athenian identity via a range of social and cultural performances. See Simon Goldhill and Robin Osborne, eds., *Performance Culture and Athenian Democracy* (Cambridge: Cambridge University Press, 1999); Paul Cartledge, Paul Millett, and Sitta von Reden, eds., *Kosmos: Essays in Order, Conflict, and Community in Classical Athens* (Cambridge: Cambridge University Press, 1998); and Alan L. Boegehold and Adele C. Scafuro, eds., *Athenian Identity and Civic Ideology* (Baltimore: Johns Hopkins University Press, 1994).
2. Many feminist philosophers have developed this connection, especially with regard to the *Antigone*. These readings have often been worked out on the basis of (though also quite often against or in tension with) the influential interpretations put forward in G. W. F. Hegel, *Phenomenology of Spirit*, trans. A. V. Miller (Oxford: Oxford University Press, 1977); Jacques Derrida, *Glas*, trans. John P. Leavey Jr. and Richard Rand (Lincoln: University of Nebraska Press, 1986); and Jacques Lacan, *The Seminar of Jacques Lacan Book VII: The Ethics of Psychoanalysis*, trans. Dennis Potter (New York: Norton, 1992). See especially Luce Irigaray, "The Eternal Irony of the Community," in *Speculum of the Other Woman*, trans. Gillian C. Gill (Ithaca: Cornell University Press, 1985), 214–26; Tina Chanter, "Looking at Hegel's Antigone Through Irigaray's Speculum," in *Ethics of Eros* (New York: Routledge, 1995), 80–126; Kelly Oliver, "Antigone's Ghost: Undoing Hegel's *Phenomenology of Spirit*," *Hypatia* 12, no. 1 (1996): 67–90; Lisa Walsh, "Her Mother Her Self: The Ethics of the Antigone Family Romance," *Hypatia* 14, no. 3 (1999): 96–125; Judith Butler, *Antigone's Claim: Kinship Between Life and Death* (New York: Columbia, 2000); Mary Beth Mader, "Antigone's Line," *Bulletin de la Société Américaine de Philosophie de Langue Français* 14, no. 2 (2004): 1–31. See also Hélène Cixous and Catherine Clément, *Newly Born Woman*, trans.

Betsy Wing (Minneapolis: University of Minnesota Press, 1986) for a reading of the *Oresteia*. While the present volume invites another look at the *Antigone*, we also seek to situate readings and interrogations of that play within the broader terrain of Greek tragedy—that is, to suggest that the questions feminist scholars have brought to the *Antigone* can also be productively brought to other tragedies. The convoluted intersections of sexual difference and political formation in the *Antigone* are, in fact, not exclusive to that drama but elaborated throughout tragedy.

3. Although we seek in this volume to document the emergence and operations of sexual difference and the *polis* specifically in relation to one another, many scholars have analyzed other critical aspects of gender, sexual difference, and the position of women in Greek tragedy. See Helene P. Foley, *Female Acts in Greek Tragedy* (Princeton, NJ: Princeton University Press, 2001); Laura McClure, *Spoken Like a Woman: Speech and Gender in Athenian Drama* (Princeton, NJ: Princeton University Press, 1999); Karen Bassi, *Acting Like Men: Gender, Drama, and Nostalgia in Ancient Greece* (Ann Arbor: University of Michigan Press, 1998); Victoria Wohl, *Intimate Commerce: Exchange, Gender, and Subjectivity in Greek Tragedy* (Austin: University of Texas Press, 1998); Michael X. Zelenak, *Gender and Politics in Greek Tragedy* (New York: Peter Lang, 1998); Froma I. Zeitlin, *Playing the Other: Gender and Society in Classical Greek Literature* (Chicago: University of Chicago Press, 1996), which collects key essays by Zeitlin from the 1970s to 1990s; and Nicole Loraux, *Tragic Ways of Killing a Woman*, trans. Anthony Forster (Cambridge, MA: Harvard University Press, 1987). There have also been important treatments of individual works and individual authors; see, for example, Simon Goldhill, *Language, Sexuality, Narrative, the Oresteia* (Cambridge: Cambridge University Press, 1984) on Aeschylus; and Kirk Ormand, *Exchange and the Maiden: Marriage in Sophoclean Tragedy* (Austin: University of Texas Press, 1999) on Sophocles. Euripides' representations of gender and sexual difference have attracted particular scrutiny; see Daniel Mendelsohn, *Gender and the City in Euripides' Political Plays* (Oxford: Oxford University Press, 2002); C. A. E. Luschnig, *The Gorgon's Severed Head: Studies in Alcestis, Electra, and Phoenissae* (Leiden: Brill Academic, 1995); Nancy Sorkin Rabinowitz, *Anxiety Veiled: Euripides and the Traffic in Women* (Ithaca: Cornell University Press, 1993); Charles Segal, *Euripides and the Poetics of Sorrow: Art, Gender, and Commemoration in*

Alcestis, Hippolytus, and Hecuba (Durham: Duke University Press, 1993); and Anton Powell, ed., *Euripides, Women, and Sexuality* (London: Routledge, 1990). Charles Segal's interest in the particular conjunction of women and sorrow in Greek tragedy was taken up again by a recent collection of essays published in his honor: Victoria Pedrick and Steven M. Oberhelman, eds., *The Soul of Tragedy: Essays on Athenian Drama* (Chicago: University of Chicago Press, 2005). See also Nicole Loraux, *The Mourning Voice: An Essay on Greek Tragedy*, trans. Elizabeth Trapnell Rawlings (Ithaca: Cornell University Press, 2002). Finally, Linda Kintz utilizes a comparative approach when examining the representation of women in both Greek tragedy and modern drama in *The Subject's Tragedy: Political Poetics, Feminist Theory, and Drama* (Ann Arbor: University of Michigan Press, 1992).

4. The house of Atreus in Greek tragedy most prominently features the murders that result from the homecoming of Agamemnon. Gone for the lengthy duration of the Trojan War, Agamemnon's return to Argos involves resuming his place as head of state and head of household, both of which have been ruled by his wife, Clytemnestra, in his absence. Clytemnestra, unbeknownst to Agamemnon, has long been plotting his murder in revenge for his sacrifice of their daughter Iphigenia. Subsequent to her accomplishment of this act, Clytemnestra herself faces the murderous vengeance of her children, Orestes and Electra. The house of Laius traces the reverberations of familial acts and origins stemming from Oedipus' incestuous relationship with his mother, Jocasta, and murderous replacement of his father, Laius, the former king of Thebes. Following his exile, Oedipus' sons, Polyneices and Eteocles, kill one another in conflict for sovereignty, leading to the ascension of Creon, Jocasta's brother, to the throne. Distraught at Creon's refusal to bury Polyneices, Oedipus' daughter Antigone defies her uncle's edict, an act that will ultimately lead to her death. Our choice of these mythological houses relies specifically on their rich treatment and meaning in Greek tragedy; beyond the demands of tragedy, however, myth has other varied features and functions in Greek cultural and intellectual life. Two important works have considered the role of gender and feminist theory in interpreting classical myth more broadly: Lillian E. Doherty, *Gender and the Interpretation of Classical Myth* (London: Duckworth Publishers, 2001) and Vanda Zajko and Miriam Leonard, eds., *Laughing with Medusa: Classical Myth and Feminist Thought* (Oxford and New York: Oxford University Press, 2006).

5. G.W.F. Hegel, *Phenomenology of Spirit*, trans. A.V. Miller (Oxford: Oxford University Press, [1807] 1977).

6. Jacques Derrida, "Force of Law: The 'Mystical Foundation of Authority'" in *Deconstruction and the Possibility of Justice*, eds. D. Cornell, M. Rosenfeld, and D.G. Carlson (London: Routledge, 1992).

7. Julia Kristeva, *Strangers to Ourselves*, trans. Leon S. Roudiez (New York: Columbia University Press, 1991).

1

CITY, FAREWELL!

Genos, Polis, *and Gender in Aeschylus'* Seven Against Thebes *and Euripides'* Phoenician Women

PETER BURIAN

Two Theban tragedies, Aeschylus' *Seven Against Thebes* and Euripides' *Phoenician Women*, provide one of our rare opportunities to
see ancient dramatic poets shaping the same material in their own ways.[1]
Although these plays share a legendary subject—the rivalry that leads
Oedipus' sons to mutual slaughter before the gates of Thebes—they are
separated by almost sixty years and a totally transformed sensibility.[2] In
this chapter, I propose to analyze that transformation primarily on the
basis of the treatment of themes connected to city, family, and gender.
Comparison of a small but telling detail in the presentation of legendary "background" in the two plays will provide an initial idea of what
is at stake. In *Seven Against Thebes*, the original curse on the house of
Laius is only mentioned three-fourths of the way through the play, after
Eteocles has concluded that he himself must face his brother, Polynices,
in battle and recognizes that he has been caught in the web of his family's fate. The Chorus, whose sole preoccupation has been for the safety
of their city, now see with great clarity how directly Laius' transgression
is connected to their city's, and their own, survival (742–62):

> For I speak of a transgression born long ago, swift in retribution,
> but it lasts into the third generation, ever since Laius, in defiance of
> Apollo ('Απόλλωνος βίᾳ), who thrice told him at Pytho's shrine,
> Earth's very navel, that by dying without offspring he would save

15

his city (σῴζειν πόλιν); yet yielding to his own dear foolish counsel, he begot his death: father-killing Oedipus, who dared to sow
his mother's sacred field, where he himself was nurtured with a
bloody stock.[3] And a sea of evils, as it were, drives on the wave;
one sinks, another rises with triple crest and crashes against the
prow of the city.

Aeschylus' language is typically image-laden but not at all obscure. In
his conception, as R. P. Winnington-Ingram put it long ago, "the destinies of the city and the family" are "dangerously intertwined."[4] Laius'
fathering of a son not only led to his death but also put Thebes at risk.
Without some expiation of his infraction, the danger remains. The offspring of Laius' offspring, the third generation, must perish for the city to
live. The gods have ceased to care for the sons of Oedipus, but they will
not abandon Thebes (as Eteocles reminded us that they do when a city is
captured by its enemies [217–18]). The safety of the city and the slaughter
of the sons are clearly distinguished by the Messenger who brings news of
the battle. Three times he announces that the city is safe, contrasting this
good news with the fate of the princes and expressing the two outcomes
as contiguous but polar results of the war (792–802, 804, 820–21). The
triple juxtaposition, however, strongly suggests that the results are connected. The royal house threatened the city, and its destruction *is* the
salvation of Thebes. Destruction and salvation are not simply differential
results of a difficult struggle; they are causally related at the deepest level:
through the mutually reinforcing wills of gods and men.

Contrast this with the brief presentation of the oracle in *Phoenician
Women*, where the oracle threatens only Laius and his house (17–20):

King over Thebes of the fine horses, do not sow the furrow with
child in defiance of the gods (δαιμόνων βίᾳ); for if you sire a son,
your offspring will kill you and your whole house (οἶκος) will
wade through blood.

Rather than connect the oracle to the decisive moment for the survival of
the *polis*, Euripides weaves it into Jocasta's opening monologue as part of
an exposition of family history, a decisive element in a pattern of blind yet
willful self-destruction within the *genos*. As we shall see, the fate of the
city remains throughout the play deliberately, and at times emphatically,
separate from that of the family. In Euripides' conception, the brothers'
deaths are not essential for the safety of the city; indeed, it is strictly

superfluous. In a bold innovation, he provides a new sacrificial victim who is not a descendant of Labdacus, a son of Creon, as the guarantor of Thebes' survival. And by the time the brothers do meet in fatal combat, the battle is over and the city has already weathered the storm. In *Phoenician Women*, then, "the destinies of the city and the family," far from being "dangerously intertwined," are forcibly kept apart, to produce a startling new interpretation of the meaning of both strife and salvation.

ORACLES AND INTERTEXTUALITY

The differing treatment of the oracle in the two plays not only suggests larger differences in their interpretation of the legendary material but also reveals their fundamentally intertextual relationship. *Phoenician Women*, "this panoramic play," as Froma Zeitlin has called it,[5] is far more expansive in size and scope than *Seven Against Thebes*; indeed it has been criticized since antiquity precisely for refusing to limit itself to the strife of the brothers and the battle of the Seven.[6] Recent criticism has rightly emphasized the status of *Phoenician Women* as an independent creation and has generally been more sympathetic to its inclusive character. Whatever our assessment of this play, however, we must recognize that we cannot fully understand its workings without considering it as a response to Aeschylus' famous tragedy.[7] Indeed, I shall be arguing that its meaning is realized in great measure by its insistent rewriting of themes and tropes from *Seven Against Thebes*. *Phoenician Women* constitutes a rethinking of Aeschylean *mythos* in dramatic and in ideological terms, in essential respects and not just in certain details.

It is not hard to see that Euripides is gleefully playing with precedents.[8] Does the tradition, embodied not only in *Seven Against Thebes* but also in Sophocles' *Antigone*, make Eteocles the high-minded defender of his city against a foreign invasion? Euripides' Eteocles shows no love for his city but only naked ambition for power. In what were apparently the play's most famous lines (Cicero translates them in book 3 of *De officiis* and says that Caesar always had them upon his lips), Eteocles expresses a philosophy worthy of Thrasymachus: "If one must do wrong, it is finest to do wrong for the sake of sole power [τυραννίδος πέρι]," (524–25). Is Polynices, "the man of much strife," a figure of rebellious daring in Aeschylus and the tradition at large? Euripides gives his Polynices a timid entrance, skittish at every noise and movement despite the truce his mother has arranged, and brings out in him a strain of affection for his native place and concern for his family that almost belies his role as would-be sacker of his own city. Is Creon the advocate *par excellence* of the claims of the state over those of the family? Asked to sacrifice his own son Menoeceus to save the state, Creon replies without a moment's hesitation, "I wasn't listening, I didn't hear. City farewell [χαιρέτω πόλις], (919), and goes on to plot his son's escape.

Although it is widely recognized that Athenian tragic drama constantly fashioned and refashioned complex sets of intertextual relations among specific versions of a given tale (and indeed specific versions of different tales),[9] the significance of this kind of operation is perhaps not fully appreciated even now. When challenge to well-known antecedents is as systematic as it appears to be here, and as central in shaping an entire drama, there is surely reason to question whether each instance of it should be treated as an isolated phenomenon, an end in itself. Is Euripides ever concerned simply to criticize his predecessors or to "correct" their telling of the tale, or do his innovations, even where—as in this play—they court a self-conscious and perhaps rather brittle literariness, always serve a larger purpose?

To take an example from *Phoenician Women*, everyone sees that Euripides is responding directly to the famous "shield scene" of *Seven Against Thebes* when he makes his Eteocles specifically reject the opportunity to name each of the Argive attackers and Theban defenders at the seven gates (751–52). This has often been treated, however, as merely a bit of "literary criticism" directed at Aeschylus' supposed lack of realism rather than as a salient feature of Euripides' way of telling his story.[10] But surely more is at stake than a hit at a long-dead and revered predecessor. If we look at Eteocles' refusal in the context of the dramaturgy and thematics of *Phoenician Women*, we see that it is part and parcel of one of the most fundamental alterations that Euripides has made to the Aeschylean model. The preceding dialogue has very clearly shown that this Eteocles, far from being the stout and prudent leader of *Seven Against Thebes*, is a hapless commander, all of whose schemes of frontal attack lead only to *aporia* (734). At this point, Creon brings Eteocles, like some recalcitrant student, to the realization that he must do what the Aeschylean model demands—appoint defenders to meet the enemy captains at each of the seven gates of Thebes. Euripides thus carefully prepares some sort of repetition, only to deny it to us. Crucially, however, Eteocles does not reject the military strategy (he accepts Creon's advice about what to do), but rather the tragic significance of the long and arduous Aeschylean "shield scene" (375–676).

In Aeschylus, Eteocles, intent upon saving his city, appoints captains to the gates, carefully matching each defender to the challenge emblazoned on each attacker's shield, until at last he alone is left to meet the final captain, his brother, Polynices. Only when he realizes to what point his careful military planning has brought him does Eteocles recognize the tragic fate that he is bringing to pass, the control that Oedipus' curse of his sons to mutual destruction now exercises over him. Contrast this with the brief, almost blithe sequence of Eteocles' thought in *Phoenician Women* (748–55):

> Agreed! I'll go to the seven gates and station commanders there, as you suggest. I'll pit an equal number of mine against an equal number of the enemy. It would waste much time to name each one, with the enemy camped beneath our very walls. I'm on my way, so as not be idle when it comes to the fight. May I get my brother opposite me, and destroy him with my sword.

Eteocles' headlong eagerness to confront his brother changes the dynamic of the confrontation utterly. It is not his father's curse (however much that may be supposed to be operating behind the scenes, as it were) that sends Eteocles into battle. Eteocles is, of course, aware that Oedipus has cursed him and his brother to die at each other's hands, but treats his father dismissively and the curse as an annoying contingency (763–65):

> He brings the charge of folly upon himself for having blinded his eyes. I can hardly praise him: he will kill us with his curses, if he gets his way.

What drives Eteocles is the willful, indeed stubbornly self-willed, desire for triumph over his fraternal enemy, and it must be said that it drives Polynices no less. He has already expressed the same intention in a chilling exchange (621–22):

> *Polynices*: Where will you be stationed before the towers?
> *Eteocles*: Why do you ask?
> *Polynices*: I'll take my place opposite.
> *Eteocles*: Desire (ἔρως) for that seizes me, too.

We are free to follow Tiresias' lead and see the brothers as maddened by the family curse (δαιμονῶντας, 888, acting under the influence of daimonic possession),[11] but this text does not encourage us to think in such terms, as that of *Seven Against Thebes* certainly does. No curse seems to excite particular terror in the brothers' breasts, and neither Eteocles in challenging Polynices, nor Polynices in accepting the challenge refers to one at all (1219–37). Self-destruction is not imposed by a force outside; it is an *erôs* that has already made its home in the brothers' souls.

POLIS AND GENOS IN SEVEN AGAINST THEBES

The treatment of *polis* and *genos* themes in the two plays is closely related to the representation of gender and the differential roles played by women in each. Let us begin by considering the two contrasting Choruses. That of *Seven Against Thebes* is made up of Theban maidens, fearful of their city's imminent destruction, who take a vigorous and perhaps surprising part in the action by engaging twice in debate with Eteocles. The Chorus that gives its name to *Phoenician Women*, on the other hand, comes (as did Creon) from far-off Tyre, and thus in a sense also from Thebes' distant past. They only chance to be in Thebes, however, apparently stranded there on their way to Delphi, where they are to enter Apollo's service. These maidens remain well outside the action of the drama, but they have an important function in setting that action in the larger frame of Theban history, about which, on account of the shared descent from Io that links them to Thebes (247–48; cf. 676–82), they can speak with authority.

In *Seven Against Thebes*, individual female characters do not appear until the main action is complete, if at all.[12] The Chorus of Theban maidens, however, are Eteocles' chief interlocutors at the outset of the play and again after he has made his decision to face his brother in battle. The role of these women is extensive and of fundamental importance, their two tense exchanges with Eteocles revelatory. (One feels that these scenes, like several episodes of Aeschylus' *Suppliants*, provide a glimpse of what pre-Aeschylean one-actor drama might have been like.) The first half of *Seven Against Thebes* is almost obsessively concerned with the *polis* and the threat to its survival. *Polis* and *polis* compounds occur some eighty-five times, beginning with the opening words of the play (Κάδμου πολῖται, "citizens of Cadmus") and the close of line 2 (ἐν πρύμνῃ πόλεως, "at the city's rudder"). In particular the first episode

(181–287) effectively constitutes a debate about how best to keep the city safe, with the women of the Chorus expressing their fears and urging the need to propitiate the gods, and Eteocles seeing salvation vested in the military might of the city itself. In this exchange, Eteocles places heavy emphasis upon a stereotypical portrayal of women's timorousness and emotionality, implicitly contrasting their panic with his own steady steering of the ship of state: "Does a sailor who flees from stern to prow find a means of safety when his ship is laboring sea-swell?" (208–10; cf. 2–3, 62–63).[13] He upbraids the women for their public display of fear, which he takes to be subversive of good order and civic morale, and tells the women that men should see to the propitiation of the gods and women should stay at home.[14] In the end, he wrests from them a promise of silence (σιγῶ, 263), and the ode they sing upon his departure, although still terror-laden, is more restrained in expression (288–368; cf. Eteocles' instruction to pray to the gods μὴ φιλοστόνως, "with no inclination to lament," 279).

Despite the easy invocation of such *topoi* as the need for male dominance in the public sphere and the appropriateness of women's invisibility there (e.g., 200–201, 230–32), it is paradoxically the women's fears that make evident the full extent of the peril the *polis* now faces. The initial conflict in *Seven Against Thebes* is, in dramatic terms at least, not between the brothers, as in *Phoenician Women*, but between Eteocles and the Chorus. And in what might be called a further paradox, the women's function is to emphasize that Eteocles' proper role as ruler of Thebes is to save his city from destruction. His point of view dominates the first 650 lines of the play, not necessarily because the justice of his cause is proven or his plan to save the city is clearly the right one, as earlier generations of scholars seem to have assumed. Rather, the exclusive focus on Eteocles as ruler has the effect of minimizing Eteocles as son of Oedipus and inheritor of his curse. Eteocles guides the ship of state, sees to its good order and preparedness, and in the shield scene symbolically counters the Argive threat. Only with Eteocles' discovery that he must face his brother at the seventh gate does the theme of the family curse and self-destruction become a central issue.

When the debate resumes (677–719), the roles of the Chorus and Eteocles are reversed. The Chorus Leader answers Eteocles' announcement that he will meet his brother in battle with a short speech in trimeters, pointing out the special *miasma* (682) that would result from the shedding of fraternal blood. In the following exchange, similar in form to the preceding debate (a lyric exchange [*amoibaion*] followed by a line-for-line spoken exchange [*stichomythia*]), the Chorus tries and fails to persuade Eteocles to change his purpose and give up his plan to fight Polynices. The new and shocking situation has changed Eteocles' perspective, and Aeschylus brings this out by changing his role vis-à-vis the Chorus.[15] He is now conscious of the looming, ineluctable presence of the Erinys, and his eagerness to fight his brother may bespeak in some way its influence upon him, but he shows no sign of a changed character. His acknowledgment and acceptance of his fate reflect rather a fundamentally unchanged position. His masculine desire to dominate and his belief in the honor of battle have been on view since the beginning of the drama, and they have now brought him to this point. He acts to fulfill his fate in accordance with his beliefs. In this context, the question of his freedom of will does not sound at all like an Aeschylean question to me. (Consider Agamemnon confronted, in the play that bears his name, with the need to sacrifice Iphigenia.) Eteocles does what he does because he must *and* because he will.

The Chorus, too, is entirely coherent in its advice to Eteocles. Their feminine fear of the consequences of violence and their religious scruples continue what we saw in the first episode. Ironically, however, the Theban maidens have misunderstood the underlying situation. They see Eteocles' combat with his brother according to traditional moral law as the shedding of "unlawful blood" (αἵματος οὐ θεμιστοῦ, 694), and express the belief that the Erinys (that is, the enforcer of Oedipus' curse) "will leave the house when the gods receive sacrifice from your hands" (ὅταν ἐκ χερῶν θεοὶ θυσίαν δέχωνται, 700–701). But, as Eteocles seems at least momentarily to know, the only acceptable sacrifice will be the blood of Oedipus' sons (which is, of course, a sinister meaning already lodged in the Chorus' words that I just quoted). He answers them by saying, "We have ceased to be of concern to the gods; the service from us that is admired is our dying" (χάρις δ' ἀφ' ἡμῶν ὀλομένων θαυμάζεται, 702–3). In the following stasimon, the Chorus will provide the means to understand that the brothers' deaths at last fulfill the oracle given to Laius long ago and save Thebes from destruction. Ironically, then, the Chorus, when they urged Eteocles not to meet his brother in battle, were threatening the survival of the city for whose safety they prayed.

And yet, the language of the Chorus as they lament the fallen brothers provides a clue to the ineluctable madness of the brothers' mutual slaughter by connecting the "defiant/disobedient decision" (βουλαὶ δ' ἄπιστοι, 842) of Laius with "this defiant/incredible deed you have done" (τόδ' εἰργάσασθ' ἄπιστον, 846), the brothers' mutual slaughter. (Note also the description of the brothers as "defiant/faithless to their loved ones," (φίλων ἄπιστοι, 876). All along, even when trying to bring order to the disorder he finds within his city so that he can face the enemy without, Eteocles can be seen as fighting an enemy within himself. And, as Helen Bacon shrewdly observed, that enemy seems always to take the form of women:

> The engulfing passion, the danger which breaks out from inside, is incestuous rivalry—of Oedipus with Laius, of Eteocles and Polyneices with Oedipus and with each other—over the city, the land, the woman who is the source of their life....For the house of Laius the female is destruction. It is where three ways meet, in the sphere of Hecate, the goddess...of all dark incomprehensible female functions, that Oedipus committed the act of violence against his father that led to his incestuous marriage....The sphinx also is a female and destroyer of men, as is the fury.[16]

Whether one reads the initial encounter of Eteocles and the Theban women from a psychoanalytic perspective or symbolically, with Bacon, it seems clear that Eteocles' fear of what he sees as the women's wild, disordered, and subversive terror, a force that can turn the men of the city into cowards (191–92, 237) and slaves (254), is deeply overdetermined. Eteocles the statesman and soldier works with all his might to contain the women's force, to keep them inside where they can do no harm. In the harshness and horror he displays to the women, Eteocles the accursed son of his accursed father will out.

POLIS AND GENOS IN PHOENICIAN WOMEN

The Chorus of *Phoenician Women* could hardly be more different from that of *Seven Against Thebes*. These maidens, as I noted above, have no share in the Theban *polis* or its tribulations, although their distant kinship gives them the requisite knowledge to provide through their songs a cycle of history that connects the action of the drama to a long and violent past.[17] Nevertheless, they do not take a stand in opposition to the continued bloodletting. But the play does offer a female figure who takes that role emphatically, though in the end just as ineffectively. That figure is, of course, Jocasta, who, in her role as convener and moderator of the debate between Eteocles and Polynices (443–637), is the voice of balance and moderation in a world ruled by unbridled lust for power. Jocasta plays a role analogous to that of the Chorus of *Seven Against Thebes* by attempting to head off the war and the fatal duel of her sons but with a crucial difference: whereas the Chorus of Theban maidens act (even though they are women) as the representatives of the city in all its hopes and fears, Jocasta is emphatically the representative of her accursed *genos*, intervening, above all, out of concern for both her sons and the desire to reconcile them before they risk their lives in battle.

This is not to say, of course, that the possible destruction of the *polis* is entirely ignored in this scene, only that it is thoroughly subordinated to the dispute between Jocasta's sons, the feuding brothers. Inevitably, Jocasta uses arguments that touch on aspects of contemporary political ideology, and this may well have been part of the pleasure of the scene for the original audience. Most obviously, Jocasta extends the Athenian political catchword of ἰσότης (equality) into a cosmic principle of equality (538–48) in order to persuade both her sons that they should share power. This is an argument congenial to supporters of democracy in which offices and duties shared among citizens in succession have a central role.[18] This does not, however, make Jocasta a theorist of democracy any more than the scorn for oracles of Sophocles' Jocasta in *Oedipus Tyrannus* makes her a systematic skeptic.[19] Nor is she in some way disqualified by her love for her sons from concern for her city. In this scene, however, Jocasta's use of the language of what we may call public discourse is aimed, above all, at meeting the philosophical and political arguments of her sons head on. She acts as the arbiter (cf. κοινὰς βραβείας, "impartial arbitration"; 450) of a dispute in which the welfare of the *polis* is evidently at stake, but her concern is all for the survival and well-being of both her sons, and the fate of the city enters her argument in relation to its effects on them.

Even before the debate begins, we see this tendency clearly in Jocasta's lyrical greeting of Polynices, divided between her joy for his return finally from exile (301–17) and her laments for the sorrows of the house, increased by his absence (318–53). Her solicitous questioning of her son in their subsequent dialogue skirts the issue of his attack on Thebes until her final question (426): "How did you persuade an army to follow you here?" Polynices' answer puts forward the claim that his own family (τοῖς φιλτάτοις [434], i.e., his brother), has imposed the necessity to attack his city on him and places on his mother's shoulders the responsibility to find a solution "by reconciling kin of common birth[20] to stop the suffering of me, yourself and the whole city" (436).

As the debate begins, Jocasta tells her sons not to glare in anger at each other, stressing their relationship (brother: ἀδελφόν [456], κασίγνητον [457]; kin: φίλος...φίλῳ [461]) as the key to the desired behavior. When they have both made their cases in terms that leave no opening for compromise, Jocasta appeals successively to each to consider his own interest in deciding whether to fight (528–85). Eteocles, by allowing ambition to overshadow justice, seeks wealth and power at the cost of his city's welfare. Polynices, whatever the outcome, wins only dishonor, whether he destroys his own city or the army he has brought to sack it. Jocasta's final words decry "the most hateful thing of all: the folly of two people who strive for the same thing" (584-85). The sufferings that will beset the city are expressed only insofar as they convey the folly from which a mother is intent upon dissuading her sons: Would Eteocles really rather be sole ruler (τυραννεῖν) than save the city (560)? Would Polynices really be willing to sack his own city and dedicate its spoils as trophies to Zeus (570–74)? Jocasta's argument and the entire debate scene present the impending crisis as depending neither on fate, nor on divine will, nor on fear of divine retribution, but rather as the result of Eteocles' refusal to give up absolute power and Polynices' mad willingness to destroy what he claims to love most, his own fatherland (πατρίς [405–6; cf. 388–89]).[21]

This focus on the familial at the expense of the political is part and parcel of what I take to be the central point of this scene. Jocasta's truce, by bringing her sons together in debate, illustrates their intransigent unwillingness to compromise and constitutes an essential stage in the dramatic action as Euripides conceives it, above all as the moment in which personal ambition eradicates any serious concern for the well-being of the *polis* or, indeed, of politics in the strict sense of the term. Both brothers assert instead their own right, and their own overwhelming desire, to rule. Eteocles is more blatant, praising sole rule (τυραννίς) as "the greatest of gods" (506), but Polynices' claim of justice is fundamentally a matter of recovering "what is mine" (τἀμαυτοῦ, 484)[22] with the city left to suffer as it must. Jocasta, in refuting both her sons, castigates them equally for their self-centeredness.

Jocasta provides *Phoenician Women* with a female interlocutor who, although clear-sighted about the disastrous consequences of the impending action, inevitably sees it from the perspective of her family attachments. Whereas *Seven Against Thebes* starts with Eteocles' address to the citizen body (πολῖται), Jocasta begins *Phoenician Women* with a monologue that sets out the history of the Labdakids in some detail, right down to the truce she herself has just arranged in hopes of persuading her sons of making peace. It is typical of Euripides' way of working in this play, and of its focus on the family, that not only has Jocasta survived Oedipus' downfall, but also he himself is still alive and at home (ζῶν δ' ἔστ' ἐν οἴκοις, 66) while his sons fight over his inheritance. And Euripides' "restaging" of Jocasta's suicide (which takes place in Sophocles' *Oedipus Tyrannus* as soon as she has understood his and her own horrible pollution) as the despairing response to her sons' mutual slaughter (1455–59) is a clear sign of her complete identification with family: Jocasta, "overwhelmed with grief (ὑπερπαθήσασ') seized a sword from the corpses," killed herself, and lies in death "among those dearest to her" (ἐν τοῖσι φιλτάτοις), embracing both her sons. Coming where and as it does, Jocasta's demise is also significantly a part of the separation of the destruction of the *genos* from the city's salvation.[23]

Beyond such considerations, of course, Jocasta is important as a feminine voice of opposition to the rigidly military masculine ethos embodied by her sons. Again, however, the point is elaborated in familial rather than political terms. The scene of a mother castigating both sons equally for their mirror-image hostility, and the sons' equal unwillingness to listen and learn from her feminine wisdom, is a kind of dramatization of the failure of the sons' maturation process, their inability to achieve full individuation. There are two related issues here: the problem of separation from the father, which they mutually attempt only to be drawn fatally back into his orbit by his curse and their own ambition, and the need of each to differentiate himself from his brother in order to claim the father's position. Unable to share, they remain, in their total hostility, paradoxically inseparable, inextricable. Further evidence in Euripides is the alarming symmetry of their final duel as described by the Messenger.[24] Even more striking is the Chorus' comment in *Seven Against Thebes* (937–40): "Their enmity has ended, but their life has been mingled in the blood-drenched earth. They are indeed of one blood" (ὅμαιμοι). And, as has often been noted, the laments in *Seven Against Thebes* treat the brothers as equal, even identical, in every way.

ANTIGONE TRANSFORMED

In *Phoenician Women*, women play a far more varied role than in *Seven Against Thebes*. Antigone, whose role in Aeschylus is limited to the final hundred lines of the play,[25] in *Phoenician Women* cuts an arresting figure. To a considerable extent, it is she who binds the various phases of the play together. Her role in the *exodos* of the play moves beyond the legendary material with which this chapter is primarily concerned, and is beset as well by substantial questions about its textual integrity.[26] Suffice it to say that in her final appearance Antigone promises to disobey Creon's decree forbidding the burial of Polynices, like her Sophoclean counterpart, and that she refuses marriage with Creon's son—by threatening to kill Haemon should she be forced to wed him (1657–75). Faced with this threat, Creon immediately acquiesces to her plan to accompany Oedipus into the exile he has ordained for the blind old man.[27]

For our purposes, the earlier appearances of Antigone hold special interest, for in their course we see her transforming herself under the pressure of circumstances from a shy, sequestered maiden into the Antigone we know from Sophocles—a self-reliant and powerful agent in the world of men. We meet the Sophoclean heroine (or, for that matter, the Antigone of *Seven Against Thebes*) only at the moment when she begins her resistance to the ban against Polynices' burial. Euripides has chosen to show her first as a girl who has fully internalized the accepted ideas of maiden propriety and women's proper place, and then to dramatize the change as it takes place. Immediately following Jocasta's prologue speech, Antigone appears on the roof of the stage building, led by her old Tutor. He speaks first, informing us both that Antigone's absence from the maidens' quarter (παρθενῶνας, 89) is an exceptional privilege granted by her mother and that Antigone herself had begged for it in order to see the Argive army (στράτευμ᾽ ἰδεῖν Ἀργεῖον ἱκεσίαισι σαῖς, 91).

Antigone's viewing of the enemy army is functionally the counterpart of the Chorus' entry song (*parodos*) in *Seven Against Thebes*: both make us vividly aware of the enemy at Thebes' gate.[28] In terms of tone, however, the two could hardly be more unlike. The Chorus burst onto the scene with a cry (θρεῦμαι, "I shriek" [78]—a verb always used of women), and they alternate outbursts of fear and fervent prayers for salvation throughout the entire song. The maidens report what they see and hear as fraught with sudden danger if not disaster, conveying the confusion of an attack and their own terror with great immediacy (note, for example, the striking synesthesia of κτύπον δέδορκα, "I see the noise" [103]). At the end of the *parodos*, Eteocles excoriates the women for damaging the city's morale with their screaming and howling and for offending those with self-control by their excess (181–86).

By contrast, the scene in *Phoenician Women* is a model of decorum. The Tutor has Antigone wait until he can discover whether any citizen (τις πολιτῶν, 93) is approaching the palace, thus causing both him, a slave, and her, his mistress (ἀνάσσῃ, a word which denotes royalty [95]) to incur reproach. For Antigone, appearing in public might itself cause censure; she has left her chambers but is hardly appearing in public. When she is allowed to emerge onto the roof, her excited responses to the sights she sees show a mixture of childlike wonder and fear, but neither in excess. Appropriately for a maiden, her prayers are addressed to virgin goddesses.[29] Her questions and responses to the Tutor's answers run the gamut of emotions: fear (expressed in an apotropaic invocation of Hecate) and wonder at the sea of gleaming bronze armor below (109–11); astonishment and dread at the gigantic stature of Hippomedon (217–30, a detail borrowed from *Seven Against Thebes*, 488–90) and excitement at the youthful Parthenopaeus, of the flowing locks and fierce glance (cf. *Seven*, 537), followed immediately by a corrective prayer that Artemis slay him for coming to sack her city (145–53); the wish to be able to fly to embrace her long-absent brother Polynices, gleaming like the dawn in his golden armor (163–69); and so on. Antigone is not uninformed or naïve about what is happening; the dialogue concludes with Capaneus, whom she asks the Tutor to point out to her. She has heard that he boasted he would enslave the women of Thebes to the women of Mycenae, and she therefore prays to Artemis that she may never endure slavery (179–92). But her fears are tempered by hope, excitement, and simple curiosity. "You have had gratification of the desire (πόθου...τέρψιν) for what you wished to see (194–95), says the Tutor, ushering the maiden back to her chambers as the women of the Chorus approach, a mob (ὄχλος, 196) naturally inclined, in his view, to spread censorious gossip.

Antigone's next appearance makes evident how fully she has internalized the ideology of women's invisibility and silence. When Jocasta has wrested from a reluctant Messenger (1207–22) the news that Eteocles and Polynices have decided to face each other in single combat, she calls Antigone outside, significantly telling her that her normal pattern of life is about to change (1265–90):

The fortune set down for you by the gods does not proceed now with choral dancing or maidenly pursuits, but with your mother you must prevent two heroes (ἄνδρ' ἀρίστω), your brothers, bent on death, from dying at each other's hands.

A clarion call, and from her mother, but Antigone still hesitates to leave her maiden quarters (παρθενῶνας, 1275) and hesitates to appear before the army. "I feel shame amidst a mob" (αἰδούμεθ' ὄχλον), she tells her mother. "Your situation does not allow shame," replies Jocasta (1276), and with continued exhortation marches her off to the battlefield.

Antigone's transformation takes place offstage. A second Messenger reports the brother's mutual wounding, the arrival of mother and sister in time just to witness and mourn their pathetic deaths, and Jocasta's subsequent suicide. He then tells us that Antigone withdrew when the armies renewed their battle (1465) and that she is returning, now that Thebes has prevailed, with the soldiers who bear her brothers' corpses (1476). This hardly prepares us, however, for her entrance leading that procession as a self-proclaimed "bacchant of the dead" (1489). Antigone's transformation is, in effect, acted out in the opening of her aria. The formerly demure maiden now throws off her headdress, saying that she feels no shame in exposing her maiden's blush to view, and opens or removes her outer robe (1485–91).[30] She acts as the "greatly groaning leader for the corpses" (1492),[31] suggesting that she is now performing a kind of funeral song and dance for her mother and brothers. Antigone caps her laments for the destruction of her house (1494–1507) and for her own fate (1508–29) with a peremptory call to her blind, old father to come from the palace; he appears reluctantly to hear news of the three deaths (1530–50).

Antigone, who at the beginning of the play was allowed to leave her maiden chambers only under strict supervision to prevent her from being seen in public, and who later resisted her mother's urging to appear before the assembled armies in an attempt to save her brothers' lives, has overcome any such inhibitions after her brothers' deaths. Now it is she who orders her father into the open, and it is she who will insist on leading him into the exile to which Creon condemns him, leaving the city and her marriage behind. Indeed, to Oedipus' objection that it is "shameful for a daughter to wander in exile with a blind father," Antigone can reply, "Not if she is prudent, but rather it is noble" (1691–92).

To the extent that Antigone becomes an actor in the larger world of men, the transformation reflects devotion to her *genos* rather than further engagement in the affairs of the city.[32] Like Jocasta, Antigone can use the tools of public discourse to assert her will—and, indeed, she is more successful than Jocasta at changing the course of events. But she is also now deeply resistant to the claims and demands of the *polis*. She returns from the battlefield as a kind of bacchant, freed by the extremity of her grief from the control of men and the restraints of city life, no longer part of the *polis* that she soon will leave. Although ready to engage the city by defying the ban on her brother's burial, and quite capable of disputing its validity with Creon (1643–57), Antigone—even more emphatically than Jocasta when she attempted to mediate her sons' dispute—acts with the interest of her *genos* at heart. She does not hesitate to sacrifice her marriage and the prospect of a normal woman's life to tend her father.[33]

The forcefulness of her rejection of marriage stuns Creon (1673–80):

> *Antigone:* Do you really think I will marry your son? I'd rather die![34]
> *Creon:* You have to, for where could you go to escape the marriage?
> *Antigone:* Then night will make me one with the Danaids.[35]
> *Creon:* Did you see the daring with which she hurls insults?
> *Antigone:* Let steel bear witness, and the sword by which I swear.
> *Creon:* But why are you so eager to be free of this marriage?
> *Antigone:* I will go into exile with this most wretched father of mine.
> *Creon:* There is nobility in you, but also some kind of folly.

With this exchange, Antigone does more than turn her back on the life that the *polis* offers its women—marriage, in this case, with a man "who would ordinarily have been deemed an excellent catch"[36]—she turns her back on the *polis* itself. She has moved from total conformity to her society's gender regulation to a dangerous outspokenness and beyond in her appropriation of *parrhesia* (the free, frank speech of the male citizen).[37] She has threatened the integrity of the state by threatening the life of the ruler's son and heir.

Antigone's oath by the sword (presumably the actual sword of Polynices that she picks up from beside his body, where she has been kneeling)[38] suggests that her newfound self-possession and independence have endowed her with an aura of masculinity. Creon obviously takes her threat seriously; rather than try to correct her outrageous

misbehavior or to punish her for it, he tells her that she will not kill his
son and orders her to leave Thebes (1682), precisely what she has just
said she wants to do. And at this point Creon withdraws, either leaving
the stage or at least retreating to the background. Antigone's raising of
her brother's sword as witness both to her oath and her threat also suggests an implicit contrast with Jocasta, who (as the Messenger reported)
took up the sword from beside her dead sons to kill herself. Antigone
does not yield either to despair or to power that would ordinarily be
far beyond her own. Indeed, there is in the emergence of this new and
powerful Antigone a curious dynamic at work. It is as if when Jocasta
dies, Antigone is able fully to come to life.

This sense of Antigone's new-won agency and independence should
not, however, obscure the fact that she is making an enormous sacrifice
by renouncing marriage and Thebes. Oedipus himself underlines this
fact in his initial hesitations to accept his daughter's offer to accompany
him into exile (1683–86):

> *Oedipus:* Daughter, although I praise your concern...[39]
> *Antigone:* What if I married and you went into exile alone,
>   father?
> *Oedipus:* Stay here and be happy (εὐδαίμονα). I will put up
>   with my own woes.
> *Antigone:* And who will care for you, blind as you are,
>   father?

Antigone will freely sacrifice *eudaimonia* (happiness) to dedicate her
life to this blind and difficult old man, her father and brother, all that
remains to her of those she loves, her dreadful and compelling *genos*.

MENOECEUS AND THE SURVIVAL OF THE *POLIS*

The battle for Thebes in Euripides' version exacts, in perfect contrast
to Antigone's sacrificial gesture, the sacrifice of a male victim who gives
up life itself for his city. To sever the deaths of Eteocles and Polynices
as clearly as possible from the salvation of the *polis*, Euripides links
the outcome of the battle to an older strand of Theban history. Tiresias
makes his seemingly obligatory appearance in a Theban drama to
deliver an unwelcome prophecy—but its content is anything but
traditional and involves an entirely marginal figure, a son of Creon
called Menoeceus, apparently invented *ad hoc* by Euripides.[40] Tiresias

explains to the astounded Creon that Ares has suddenly demanded
the sacrifice of a pure victim from among the descendants of the Sown
Men to expiate Creon's slaying of Ares' dragon at the time of Thebes'
founding. Only the unmarried Menoeceus qualifies. Creon, appalled,
responds that he will never sacrifice his son to ransom his city (964),
a remarkably frank statement of the preference for *genos* over *polis*
that characterizes this play. Menoeceus himself, however, is equally
clear about his course. Shrewdly pretending to acquiesce in his father's
plan for escape, he tricks him into leaving by artful dissimulation, then
announces his true intention. Rather than go into shameful exile, he will
offer his life to save the city. It is noteworthy that for him alone of all
the characters in the play, there is no disharmony between the claims of
state and family: he refuses to betray his city *and* his kin (πατέρα καὶ
κασίγνητον προδοὺς πόλιν τ᾽ ἐμαυτοῦ, 1003–4).

It is worth noting that Menoeceus plays a role usually reserved for
maidens, chosen precisely because he is a male *parthenos*.[41] But Euripides has further complicated the nexus of family relations here. Jocasta
is Creon's sister, and she nursed Menoeceus after his mother's death
(986–89), so that the kinship relations are—not surprisingly for this
tribe—involuted. Precisely why Euripides introduces this singularly intimate bond between Jocasta and her nephew is uncertain, but in the
context of Menoeceus' deception, it emphasizes that Jocasta, like her
brother Creon, could be expected to do whatever possible to spare a
member of her *genos*. Creon and Jocasta love their children; both are
called *philoteknoi* (965 and 365, respectively), both strive mightily but
unsuccessfully to save their sons. Menoeceus has picked the perfect ruse
(presumably invented for this scene) to free himself from his father.

Menoeceus' unexpected sacrifice is not simply another twist in a play
notable for plenitude and innovation; it shows the main action of the
play in an unexpected and unsettling light. Menoeceus is not a descendant of the house of Laius, and his willing self-sacrifice, the one truly
disinterested act of the drama, offers a complete contrast to the utter
self-interestedness of both Polynices and Eteocles. Menoeceus reclaims
the possibility of genuine patriotism. As a descendant of the Sown
Men, he can speak of "the fatherland that gave me birth" (πατρίδος ἥ
μ᾽ ἐγείνατο, 996) in a more or less literal sense that conjoins *genos* and
polis in a way otherwise unseen in this play. Menoeceus undertakes to
set this fatherland free with the gift of his own death (1011–14). In complete contrast, whatever love of country Eteocles and Polynices may feel
is emphatically subordinated to their insistence on ruling it, insistence on
retaining or recapturing what they see as *theirs*. Polynices, for example,

enters the scene saying that "all men of necessity love their fatherland" (ἀναγκαίως ἔχει πατρίδος ἐρᾶν ἅπαντας, 358–59), but we soon hear that for him there is a higher necessity: his allies have rendered him a "bitter but necessary service" (λυπρὰν χάριν, ἀναγκαίον δέ, 431) as he marches against his own city, regardless of the consequences for its welfare. Both sacrifice their lives as well, but not for their city.

That brings us to a second, related, and equally important point: Menoeceus' self-sacrifice makes the brothers' duel irrelevant to the issue of Thebes' safety, since safety has quite astoundingly been guaranteed before the battle even begins. Scholars over the years have given the sacrifice both positive and ironic interpretations, but when we take into account the fundamental reassessment it requires us to make of the mutual slaughter of the sons of Oedipus, it emerges as a particularly cogent example of Euripidean reshaping of a myth for the purposes of shaping a characteristically complex tragic plot. When we then look more broadly at the play, we see that the distinction between the fate of Thebes and the deaths of Polynices and Eteocles has been reinforced again and again by characteristic Euripidean choices. Not the least of these is the fact that the battle narrative leads to an Argive withdrawal from the walls without requiring the brothers even to meet, much less fight.

The Messenger, a soldier who brings news directly from the field, answers Jocasta's most urgent questions immediately: the Argive attack has failed, and both brothers have survived (1075–85). Only after this, in the Messenger's description of the Argive forces moving upon Thebes (cf. 1098–1102), does Euripides (assuming it is he)[42] introduce his version of the "shield scene" describing the emblems carried by each of the Argive captains (1104–40), although, unlike the Aeschylean original, it does not pit them against their Theban counterparts, or even culminate with Polynices. The general consensus that the Messenger's descriptions are far less coherent and effective than those of Aeschylus has seemed, to many, to argue for interpolation. However, in the context of Euripides' intertextual play with themes and dramatic procedures from *Seven Against Thebes*, it is worth considering whether this passage is not effective in doing something quite different from what Aeschylus did, whose effectiveness is partly lodged in that emphatic difference.[43] Euripides may well present the Argive opponents in no obvious order and deliberately confuse the Aeschylean signs as a way of showing the Argive attack as a threat already leaderless and defeated.

In the battle scene itself, vignettes of various moments of the fighting at several gates culminate in the traditional picture of Capaneus scaling the wall with the mad boast that not even Zeus can prevent him from taking the city. When a lightning bolt strikes him down, however, what follows is Euripidean innovation. Adrastus, the Argive king, reading Capaneus' downfall as a sign of Zeus' hostility to the expedition, orders his troops to withdraw from the walls, and the Thebans, treating it as a favorable omen, pursue them and cause sufficient carnage to assure the city's safety (1187–97). That this divine favor is brought about by Menoeceus' sacrifice rather than anything Eteocles has done is at least suggested when Jocasta responds to the Messenger's account with the comment that through Menoeceus' death, poor Creon is "bereft of his son—happily for the city" (1206). We have briefly glimpsed Eteocles going from gate to gate, entering the fray where he is needed (1163–64, 1168–70); we have heard Polynices urging on his men (1144–47). Neither man, however, makes a decisive contribution, and we never see them pitted against one another during the fight for Thebes at all. Only when pressed by Jocasta to reveal her sons' further plans does the Messenger reluctantly reveal that Eteocles has proposed to fight his brother in single combat and that Polynices has accepted (1207–41). This way of presenting the duel as an entirely gratuitous act is as un-Aeschylean as possible, the very antithesis of the response of a brother who discovers that he must face his brother in the battle to save his city, and accepts his doom. It has, however, been extensively (if perhaps misleadingly) prepared by the statements that we examined earlier, in which both brothers express the desire to meet and kill the other on the battlefield (621–22, 748–55). The Aeschylean story of a fated fall is thus transformed into a story of self-destruction through the passionate pursuit of selfish ends—from the perspective of the brothers' motives and actions, at any rate, for as the Chorus keeps reminding us, the history of Thebes is a seemingly endless and inexorable succession of horror in expiation of earlier horror.

DRAMA AND HISTORY

I have been focusing largely on dramaturgy and the different ways in which the plays we are examining configure the personal and the political, the demands of kinship and the needs of the city, and the conventional roles of men and women in Athenian society and their distortion in the extreme situations of tragic legend. I close with an attempt to relate the differences we have been observing to specific strands of contemporary Athenian politics. I do not wish by any means to return to the old fashion of reading tragedy as a kind of political allegory, but I do think that the happy circumstance that we have two such distinctive imaginings of a famous swathe of legendary history, separated by more than half a century of turmoil and radical change, inevitably raises the question of the ways in which each play can be said to reflect its particular moment. In the case of *Seven Against Thebes*, Winnington-Ingram long ago proposed what I think is the essential connection for a play so deeply concerned with the salvation of a city endangered by disordered family relations.[44] He points out that the reforms of Cleisthenes, designed to lessen the power and influence of the great Athenian *genê* by strengthening the specifically civic attachments and loyalties of the citizen, began a process that was still going on in Aeschylus' own lifetime. It seems to me extraordinarily helpful to understand the *polis-genos* thematics so prominent in *Seven Against Thebes* as a kind of reflection on the tensions between the old aristocratic family structure and the new order of citizen governance. Eteocles is depicted as operating between the worlds of dynasts preoccupied with privilege and wealth that threaten the state and that of a *polis* that owes its survival to the selfless devotion of its citizens. He is finally a figure of contradiction, not only dying as a member of a doomed family, but also fighting as the leader of his city, which he implicates in his family's disastrous feud but saves by his own and his brother's death. Thus through bloody struggle is the curse of the *genos* lifted at last from the *polis*.

Just as *Phoenician Women*'s thematics are different, so too is its political context. Jocasta herself, in the great debate scene, offers a key to political interpretation in her condemnation of the one son's *philotimia* (unbridled ambition; 531–35) and the other's willingness to sack his own city in order to rule it (569–77). If one thinks of the political climate in Athens circa 410 BCE, it lies to hand that Euripides shapes the old tale of the fall of the house of Laius to dramatize the factional strife and the ruthless jockeying for power that were to prove so disastrous for Athens. This was the season of Alcibiades' defection to Sparta and subsequent return from exile. It is fascinating to read the words that Thucydides puts into the mouth of the brilliant renegade in a speech to the Spartans, and to realize that, recast in verse, they could be spoken by the Polynices of *Phoenician Women* (*Peloponnesian War*, 6.92.4): "I have no love for my city when it does me wrong, but only when it gives me my rights. Indeed, I do not consider myself to be attacking my own country, but rather to be rewinning a country that is mine no longer. The man who really loves his city, if he loses it unjustly, will not refrain from attack; on the contrary, desire will lead him to do anything to get it back." This is not to say that *Phoenician Women* is about Alcibiades or the struggle of Athenian factions, or that it is designed to further the policy of reconciliation of exiles or to oppose it. Rather, this play seems to share with Thucydides' *History* the sense that at the root of the Athenian political crisis was the loosing of civic ties, the replacement of public interest with the interests of factions and ambitious individuals. Thus, when Euripides replaces the contrast of *genos* and *polis* as the key to representing the legendary conflicts of this myth with themes of self-seeking and self-destruction, he gives powerful dramatic expression to the most urgent civic concerns of this moment in Athenian history.

NOTES

1. The best known, of course, is the case of Aeschylus' *Choephoroi* (*Libation Bearers*), Sophocles' *Electra*, and Euripides' *Electra*, and we also have a comparison of Sophocles' *Philoctetes* with the lost ones of Aeschylus and Euripides in Dio Chrysostomus' *Orations* 52, along with a summary of the Euripidean prologue in *Orations* 59. In any case, that this sort of intertextual relation among multiple tragedies should not be regarded as exceptional but rather as part of the way Greek tragedy works is clear from surviving lists of titles that permit us to deduce a very large number of cases of multiple adaptations of the same legendary subjects for the tragic stage. See Burian 1997, 183–84. For an overview of the complex transmission of the story of the Seven, see Cingano 2002.

2. *Seven Against Thebes* was produced in 467 BCE; the date of *Phoenician Women* is uncertain but is most likely to fall between 411 and 409; see Mastronarde 1994, 11–14. Apart from the intertextual dynamics of the genre mentioned in the preceding note and differences in the artistic profiles of the two playwrights, consideration of what went on in Athens during the intervening years—the regime of Pericles and the growth of the Athenian empire, the Peloponnesian War with its vicissitudes and periods of internal strife, the presence in Athens of the Sophists, just to mention the most obvious developments—can go some way toward explaining the very different character of the two dramas. See the final section of this chapter for possible reflections of contemporary issues in the two plays.

3. The text at this point presents some difficulties. This translation follows the suggestion of Hutchinson 1985, 169–70.

4. Winnington-Ingram 1983, 51.

5. Zeitlin 1990, 133.

6. It is precisely the profusion of incident in *Phoenician Women* that so many critics have found unsatisfactory, at least as early as the late antique critic whose complaint of "overfull and episodic construction" found its way into the *hypothesis* that prefaces this play in the manuscripts. Even those, however, who believe that the Euripidean original has been considerably expanded by interpolation must admit that Euripides' strategy here was not to concentrate on a single event or issue but deliberately to include a large number of well-known characters and incidents and even to add some of his own making.

7. That the play was well remembered at the end of the fifth century is clear from the character Aeschylus' proud mention of it in Aristophanes' *Frogs* of 405 BCE as an example of a play properly "full of Ares" (1021). It should be added that Euripides may well have been responding not only to *Seven Against Thebes* but also, explicitly or implicitly, to the other plays of Aeschylus' victorious tetralogy, now alas vanished almost without trace. The loss of Aeschylus' *Laius* and *Oedipus*, as well as the satyr play *Sphinx*, affects the certainty of interpretations of *Seven Against Thebes* and limits our ability to establish the intertextual relations of *Phoenician Women* with Aeschylus' treatment of Theban material.

8. I limit myself in this paragraph to a few of the most obvious examples of divergence from Theban plays known to Euripides and his audience, but Zeitlin 1990, 143, is right to point out the particular contribution that *Phoenician Women* makes to Theban tradition on the Athenian stage by "draw[ing] all the various strands together and play[ing] them off one another." Euripides indeed makes of this play an especially elaborate exercise in intertextual relations altogether: epic reminisce and reflections of the lyric tradition are featured alongside responses to theatrical predecessors.

9. I have elsewhere tried to suggest what one might call a systemic or institutional basis for such a claim (Burian 1997). Tragedy as an institution was wedded to a restricted repertoire of subjects and embedded in the resources of a particular theater and the ritualized framework of Dionysiac festival. At the same time, the regular demand for new dramas presented in a competition of great civic importance produced an ever-renewed impetus for novelty—that is, for innovation in the presentation of the old tales. This innovation served not only to differentiate repeated enactments of myth but also permitted poets to push to the limit the search for truth in myth, for the relevant cultural meanings to be found in tales

hallowed—but not fixed—by tradition. And given the civic importance of the festival, it is not surprising that the repeated stagings
of the conflict between male and female, parent and child, rival
siblings, individual and community, even god and mortal, would
provide the occasion for ideological comment and questioning.

10. See Mastronarde 1994, 751–52, for the range of earlier interpreta-
    tions, and notice that even this recent commentary sees the intertex-
    tuality in terms of criticism of Aeschylus that is "captious at best,"
    and allows only "local meaning" for the refusal (such as demon-
    strating Eteocles' impatience with details of military planning).

11. The use of this word here may be a kind of reminisce of *Seven
    Against Thebes*, where the phrase δαιμονῶντες ἄτᾳ ("possessed
    by ruin," 1007) is used of the brothers after their mutual slaughter.

12. There is a long-standing dispute about the authenticity of the end-
    ing of *Seven Against Thebes* as transmitted in our manuscripts,
    which brings Antigone and Ismene on at line 861, attributes to
    them the lyrics at line 961 mourning the fallen brothers, and goes
    on to a scene (1005–78) in which a herald announces the banning
    of Polynices' burial, and Antigone replies that she will bury him
    despite the prohibition; the Chorus divides on the issue as well.
    Both Thalmann 1978, 137–41 and Hutchinson 1985, 202–3,
    209–11, eliminate Antigone and Ismene from the play entirely,
    giving the lyrics to members of the Chorus and eliminating the
    final scene completely as a later fifth-century (Thalmann) or post-
    classical (Hutchinson) interpolation. Both provide the essential
    earlier bibliography on the issue.

13. *Pace* the comment of Hutchinson 1985, on 208–10, who notes that
    the "sailor" in these lines must be the helmsman who guides the
    ship and finds it surprising that this important figure should implic-
    itly be compared to women who "can only sit in their homes." He
    attributes this apparent oddity to Aeschylus' desire to evoke the fla-
    vor of Eteocles' prologue speech, in which the figure of the helms-
    man guiding the ship of state has an important role. The contrast,
    however, seems to be precisely calculated to underline the differ-
    ence between the calm resolve of the (male) leader and the women's
    dangerous surrender to fear.

14. Foley 2001, 45–55, and McClure 1999, 45–46, emphasize the
    inherence in the Chorus of *Seven Against Thebes* both of the resis-
    tance to masculine authority made possible by women's lament and
    societal efforts to contain its threatened eruption into the political
    realm.

15. I am here passing over one of the central questions in interpretative history of *Seven Against Thebes*, the significance of the change that comes over Eteocles when he decides (or discovers) that he must face Polynices in combat. Many interpretations that have been offered since Wilamowitz-Moellendorff 1914 picked up his suggestion that Aeschylus was combining two different traditions in *Seven Against Thebes* (see especially pp. 64–68). One tradition, Wilamowitz-Moellendorff believed, depicted Eteocles as his city's defender; in the other, his role was to be the victim of the family curse. In his view, Aeschylus joined the two imperfectly. A more influential version of "the two Eteocleses" was put forward by Solmsen 1937, who suggested that Aeschylus deliberately staged a sudden and dramatic reappearance of the curse, which must have dominated the preceding plays of the trilogy. Solmsen argued that Eteocles' recognition of the curse transformed him and his motivation completely after line 652. This view of an Eteocles transformed from the provident commander to a daemon-driven agent of his family curse reappeared in a number of significantly divergent interpretations, including the well-known essays of Wolff 1958 and Patzer 1958. In more recent times, the "transformation" view of *Seven Against Thebes* has yielded some ground to a more sophisticated version of the *Opfertod* theory Wilamowitz-Moellendorff had rejected. This view accepts that Eteocles is and remains the defender of the city to the death, even when he recognizes and accepts his role as fulfiller of the family curse. Unlike the earlier and rather simplistic formulation that imagined an Eteocles who consciously accepted his fate to experience mutual fratricide in order to save the city, the later formulations, propounded in essays such as Kirkwood 1969 and von Fritz 2007, suggest an Eteocles who recognizes with horror that he is fulfilling the curse, but as defender of Thebes has no other choice than to persist. My own view coincides to a degree with Gagarin 1976 and Thalmann 1978 in regarding the emphasis in much earlier scholarship on the character of Eteocles, as opposed to the nature of his dilemma, as excessive. See Zeitlin 1982, 161-68, for a cogent argument that the play's fundamental *anagnorisis*, the recognition that Eteocles is not after all the man who represents the interests of the city, but rather the last in the accursed line of Laius, makes a truly sacrificial role impossible. Zeitlin further points out that, if the creation of character requires "a nexus of significant human relations," Eteocles can only be regarded as a

"negative exemplar of character precisely because he has nothing that would allow him to be a character" (190).

16. Bacon 1964, 31.

17. See the brilliant exploration of the Chorus' role in Arthur 1977.

18. Foley 2001, 281–82. Mastronarde, 1994, 528–85, points out that, effective as Jocasta's speech is rhetorically, it fails to achieve the results it aims at.

19. See *OT* 707–25, and notice that Jocasta begins the following episode with a prayer to Apollo, god of prophecy (911–23).

20. ὁμογενεῖς φίλους, the intensifying adjective reminding us of the convoluted closeness of the family.

21. In this context, the word must at some level evoke the lurking presence of father (πατήρ) Oedipus.

22. The ruler's identification of self and state as a mark of the tyrant (in the modern sense of the word) can be paralleled, for example, in Sophocles' *Oedipus Tyrannus* 625–30. Oedipus has summarily condemned Creon to death for his role in an imagined plot to seize power. Creon says, "I see you are not well disposed to me," and Oedipus answers, "I am well disposed to my own interest" (τὸ γοῦν ἐμόν). "What if you understand nothing?" asks Creon. "None the less, I must rule," Oedipus replies. And Creon, "Not if you rule badly." To Oedipus' exasperated outburst, ὦ πόλις πόλις—something like "do you hear that, my city?"—Creon answers, "I, too, have a share in the *polis*, not you alone." For Oedipus, as for Polynices, ἡ πόλις and τὸ ἐμόν have become one and the same thing.

23. Mastronarde 1994, on 1427–79, points out the density of kinship terms in this passage (twenty-four instances in thirty-one lines).

24. See Girard 1977, 44–45.

25. And contested even there; see n. 12, above.

26. There are, as with the *exodos* of *Seven Against Thebes*, intractable questions concerning the authenticity of much of the final scenes of *Phoenician Women*. Diggle 1994 excises 1582–1766 in their entirety, as well as making numerous smaller cuts throughout the *exodos*. There are numerous problems, but this probably goes too far. See Mastronarde 1994, 591–94, for judicious comments and a survey of views on this problem, and 39-48, for general principles. Among the difficulties is the oddity that Antigone insists that she will bury Polynices, but facing Creon's intransigent opposition, she appears to shift ground and departs with Oedipus without any indication whether she will indeed bury Polynices or not. In regard to Antigone's refusal and Creon's rejection of her marriage with Haemon, we should recall that

Euripides' own Antigone offered an alternative version of the legend in which she secretly married Haemon (who was charged by Creon with her execution) and bore him a son. We must always bear in mind that versions of myths that seem entirely canonical to us need not have had that status in the fifth century.

27. For arguments designed to show that this scene directly influenced the putative interpolator of the final scene in *Seven Against Thebes*, See Hutchinson 1985, on 1005–78.

28. From a literary standpoint, of course, the scene in *Phoenician Women* evokes the *teichoskopia* in *Iliad* 3.161–242, where Helen, standing on the battlements of Troy, identifies the leaders of the Greek army to Priam.

29. Hecate (109–10), Artemis (151–53, 191–92), Selene (175–76), and Nemesis together with the thunder and lightning of Zeus (182). These goddesses can all be seen as one and the same, since Hecate and Nemesis are often treated as manifestations of Artemis, who is goddess of the moon. Selene (the personification of the moon) is otherwise known for her liaisons with various gods, as well as the eternally young Endymion. In this context, however, it is easy to associate her with the virginal Artemis. See Craik 1988, on 109.

30. It is not clear whether Antigone at this point exposes her breast (see Mastronarde 1994, on 1490–91, for instances in which that gesture is implied elsewhere in tragedy) to beat it in mourning, or simply discards an outer garment (Craik 1988, on 1490–91). Seaford 1987, 124, usefully sees Antigone's unveiling of her head out of grief as an ironic reference to a bride's unveiling as part of the wedding ritual.

31. For the unusual phrase, see Mastronarde on 1492. Seaford 1987, 124 n. 185, finds its point in a contrast with the bridal procession ("She...sheds her veil, but is not led in a bridal procession but by the dead"). This, he believes, necessitates giving ἀγεμόνευμα a passive sense ("one being led"), but that contradicts Antigone's forceful self-assertion in this passage (and presumably the stage picture of her leading in the corpses with a dance as "bacchant of the dead," 1489). The implied contrast will rather be between being led in a wedding procession and leading a procession of the dead.

32. In what follows, I implicitly dispute the claim made in Saxonhouse 2005 that Antigone becomes a "political actor" when she breaks away from normative constraints on her speech. From my point of view there are a number of problems with Saxonhouse's argument, including a very odd equation of Antigone's emergence from seclusion with the effects of the "political and epistemological

dissolution" embodied in Eteocles' praise of injustice. Here, however, I would just emphasize that Saxonhouse, in asserting that Antigone enters the "political arena," neglects a fundamental fact about her trajectory. She engages with the state only to defy it and depart. She has nothing to offer it, and it has nothing to offer her, since her attachment to her *genos* comes, through the same extremity of loss that forced her to abandon maidenly shame and appear in the public sphere, to outweigh any other possible attachments.

33. *Genos* here refers to the family into which Antigone was born. In other circumstances, of course, a maiden such as herself would pass through marriage into her husband's *genos*. But the example of Jocasta, who passed from her father's family to that of Laius and then that of her new husband (and son) Oedipus, reminds us how the marriage laws that regulate the normal *genos* within the *polis* could never encompass, much less sanction, this family's incestuous bonds. Moreover, Antigone rejects marriage because the *polis* has denied her the right of her paternal *genos* to bury its own, and the marriage she rejects is a dynastic marriage to the ruler's son, and therefore of political as well as familial consequence. Along with marriage, Antigone rejects any role in the *polis* (including, at the most basic level, obedience to its ruler) and leaves the city behind in order to care for her father in his wanderings, remaining a daughter without a *polis* rather than taking a place in the *polis* as wife and mother. Antigone's choice of *genos* over *polis* could hardly be more emphatic.

34. Literally, "while (I am) still alive" (ζῶσα). Fraenkel 1963, 110, thought this line might have stemmed from an interpolator's recollection of similar phraseology at Sophocles' *Antigone* (750), where Creon says to Haemon, "There is no way you will marry that woman [Antigone] while she is still alive" (ἔτι ζῶσαν). As Mastronarde 1994, on 1673, points out, however, if there is such an allusion here, it is a "clever and meaningful reversal" more likely to be Euripides' own than the work of an interpolator.

35. Such an allusive line is not usually found in stichomythic exchanges. Antigone refers to the daughters of Danaos, unwilling brides all but one of whom killed their grooms on their wedding night. There may be a second sinister allusion: because the only couple to survive gave birth to the royal line of Argos, Argives can also be called Danaids (in this play, 466, 860, 1245) or Danaans (430, 1226), so that Antigone also figuratively declares herself an enemy of Thebes.

36. Mastronarde 1994, on 1676.

37. Cf. 391–92, where not to have *parrhesia* is said by Polynices to be the greatest evil of exile, and by Jocasta to be the equivalent of enslavement.

38. Line 1661 implies that she is actually clinging to the corpse, and there is nothing to suggest that she moves away until Creon accedes to her request to accompany her father.

39. See Mastronarde 1994, on 1683, for the adversative force of the Greek.

40. See Mastronarde 1994, 28, with further references.

41. Even Haemon is unsuitable, because betrothed to Antigone, 944–45. Elsewhere in Euripides, the sacrifice of "Macaria" (the traditional name of the maiden in *Children of Heracles*) and that (probably voluntary also) of one of the daughters of the king in the fragmentary *Erechtheus* are both designed to save besieged cities. In *Iphigenia at Aulis*, the heroine transforms herself into a voluntary victim whose death will permit the Greek expedition to sail against Troy. Alcestis, in the play that bears her name, though not a maiden, also willingly gives up her life that her husband may live; Evadne, in *Suppliants*, chooses to join her husband in death. For the plot type, see Schmitt 1921, O'Connor-Visser 1987, Wilkins 1990.

42. The authenticity of this passage has often been challenged, but for a convincing defense with full bibliography, see Mastronarde 1978 and Mastronarde 1994, on 1104–40.

43. The fullest and richest analysis of the Aeschylean "shield scene" is provided by Zeitlin 1982. Regarding the description of the shields in *Phoenician Women*, interesting and partially contrasting approaches can be found in Saïd 1985, 506–09; Foley 1985, 128; and Vidal-Naquet 1988, 299–300—all emphasizing deconstructive indecipherability; and Goff 1988, the most detailed and demanding interpretation, in which reading the signs and discovering how they turn against their bearers is a way for the spectator to elaborate, rather than resolve, the complex relation of this scene to the central concerns of the play.

44. Winnington-Ingram 1983, 51–52.

REFERENCES

Arthur, Marilyn B. 1977. The curse of civilization: The choral odes of the *Phoenissae*. *Harvard Studies in Classical Philology* 81: 163–85.

Bacon, Helen H. 1964. The shield of Eteocles. *Arion* 3 (3): 27–38.

Burian, Peter. 1997. Myth into *Mythos*: The shaping of tragic plot. In *The Cambridge companion to Greek tragedy*, ed. P. E. Easterling, 178–208. Cambridge: Cambridge University Press.

Cingano, Ettore. 2002. *I nomi dei Sette a Tebe e degli Epigoni nella tradizione epica, tragica e iconografica*. In *I Sette a Tebe. Dal mito alla letteratura*, ed. A. Aloni et al., 27–62 (Atti del Seminario Internazionale, Torino 2001). Bologna: Pàtron Editore.

Craik, Elizabeth M. 1988. Euripides, *Phoenician Women*, ed. with Translation and Commentary. Warminster: Aris & Phillips.

Diggle, J., ed. 1994. *Euripidis fabulae*. Vol. 3. Oxford Classical Text. Oxford: Clarendon.

———. 1994. *Phoenissae*. Ed. D. J. Mastronarde. Cambridge: Cambridge University Press.

Foley, H. P. 1985. *Ritual irony: Poetry and sacrifice in Euripides*. Ithaca, NY: Cornell University Press.

———. 2001. *Female acts in Greek tragedy*. Princeton, NJ: Princeton University Press.

Fraenkel, Eduard. 1963. *Zu den Phoenissen des Euripides. Sitzungsberichte der Bayerischen Akademie der Wissenschaften*, Phil.-Hist. Kl., Heft 1.

Fritz, Kurt von. 2007. The character of Eteocles in Aeschylus' *Seven against Thebes*. In *Oxford readings in Aeschylus*, trans. and ed. M. Lloyd, 141–73. Oxford: Oxford University Press. German publication 1962.

Gagrin, Michael. 1976. *Aeschylean drama*. Berkeley and Los Angeles: University of California Press.

Girard, René [1972] 1977. *Violence and the sacred*. Trans. P. Gregory. Baltimore: Johns Hopkins Press.

Goff, Barbara E. 1988. The shields of *Phoenissae*. *Greek, Roman and Byzantine Studies* 29: 135–52.

Hutchinson, Gregory O. 1985. Aeschylus, *Septem contra Thebas*, ed. with Introduction and Commentary. Oxford: Clarendon Press.

Kirkwood, Gordon MacDonald. 1969. Eteocles *Oiakostrophos*. *Phoenix* 23: 9–25.

Mastronarde, Donald. J. 1978. Are Euripides' *Phoinissai* 1104–1140 interpolated? *Phoenix* 32: 105–28.

———. 1994. Euripides, *Phoenissae*, ed. with Introduction and Commentary. Cambridge: Cambridge University Press.

McClure, Laura K. 1999. *Spoken like a woman: Speech and gender in Athenian drama*. Princeton, NJ: Princeton University Press.

O'Connor-Visser, E. A. M. E. 1987. *Aspects of human sacrifice in the tragedies of Euripides.* Amsterdam: B. R. Grüner.

Patzer, Harald. 1958. Die dramatische Handlung der *Sieben gegen Theben. Harvard Studies in Classical Philology* 63: 97–119.

Saïd, Suzanne. 1985. Euripide ou l'attente déçue: l'exemple des Phéniciennes. *Annali della Scuola Normale Superiore di Pisa*, Cl. di Lettere e Filosofia, Series 3. 15, no. 2: 501–27.

Saxonhouse, Arlene W. 2005. Another Antigone: The emergence of the female political actor in Euripides' *Phoenician Women. Political Theory* 53: 472–94.

Schmitt, Johanna. 1921. *Freiwilliger Opfertod bei Euripides.* Giessen: A. Töpelmann.

Seaford, Richard. A. S. 1987. The tragic wedding. *Journal of Hellenic Studies* 107: 106–30.

Solmsen, Friedrich. 1937. The Erinys in Aieschylos' *Septem. Transactions of the American Philological Association* 68: 197–211.

Thalmann, William G. 1978. *Dramatic art in Aeschylus's "Seven against Thebes."* New Haven: Yale University Press.

Vidal-Naquet, Pierre. 1998. The shields of the heroes. In Jean-Pierre Vernant and Pierre Vidal-Naquet, *Myth and tragedy in ancient Greece,* trans. Janet Lloyd, 273–300. New York: Zone Books.

Wilamowitz-Moellendorff, Ulrich von. 1914. *Aischylos Interpretationen.* Berlin: Weidmann.

Wilkins, John. 1990. The state and the individual: Euripides' plays of voluntary self-sacrifice. In *Euripides, women and sexuality,* ed. A. Powell, 177–94. London: Routledge.

Winnington-Ingram, R. P. 1983. *Septem contra Thebas.* In *Studies in Aeschylus,* 16–54. Cambridge: Cambridge University Press.

Wolff, Erwin. 1958. Die Entscheidung des Eteokles in den *Sieben gegen Theben. Harvard Studies in Classical Philology* 63: 89–95.

Zeitlin, F. I. 1982. *Under the sign of the shield: Semiotics and Aeschylus' "Seven against Thebes."* Rome: Edizioni dell' Ateneo.

———. 1990. Thebes: Theater of self and society in Athenian drama. In *Nothing to do with Dionysos?* ed. John J. Winkler and Froma I. Zeitlin, 130–67. Princeton, NJ: Princeton University Press.

2

ANTIGONE

The Work of Literature and the History of Subjectivity

CHARLES SHEPHERDSON

> *O sweet spontaneous*
> *earth how often have*
> *the*
> *doting*
>
>   *fingers of*
> *purient philosophers pinched*
> *and*
> *poked*
>
> *thee*
> *,has the naughty thumb*
> *of science prodded*
> *thy*
>
>   *beauty   .how*
> *oftn have religions taken*
> *thee upon their scraggy knees*
> *squeezing and*
>
> *buffeting thee that thou mightest conceive*
> *gods*

—e.e. cummings

EPIC, TRAGEDY, AND PHILOSOPHY

W orks of literature have been increasingly read in recent years, not in their capacity as literature, but as historical or quasi-anthropological evidence of the broader social milieu that gives rise to them, by scholars in "cultural studies" who seek to show how literature contributes to the historical formation of subjectivity and participates in the broader institutional and discursive organization of culture. These are worthy aims, but it is sometimes forgotten that literature has its own peculiar characteristics and its own unique demands, which cannot be inscribed in the broader "social text" without considerable difficulty, as if there were no difference between the literary work and the horizon from which it emerges, or as if literature did not stand apart from its social context, to the point of questioning and even disrupting the conventions and modes of truth that surround it.

Lest these theoretical issues appear too remote from the field of tragedy, consider the relation between Antigone and Achilles. In "A Beautiful Death," Jean-Pierre Vernant has written eloquently about the layers of significance that surround the treatment of the dead warrior in Homer and the way in which Achilles reclaims the body of his beloved friend (*philos*) Patroclus, washing the mangled corpse in order to beautify it as much as possible, so that the image and unity of the body will make Patroclus recognizable when he makes his passage into the underworld, and so that the spirit of his friend will not wander for eternity.[1] Vernant does not extend his argument beyond epic, but one might venture to wonder whether Antigone asks to be compared to the heroic Achilles in her care for the similarly ruined body of Polyneices, mangled by birds and dogs, with only his "friend" (*philos*) to care for him ("Friend shall I lie with him, yes friend with friend, when I have dared the crime of piety" [73–74]).[2] Indeed, given her renowned desire for glory or *kleos* ("How could I have gained greater glory than by placing my own brother in the grave?" [502]), one might wonder whether she seeks not only to provide a "beautiful death" for Polyneices but also to die such a death herself, in the manner of an epic warrior, as she suggests in saying, "I shall bury him! It is honorable [*kalon*, "beautiful"] for me to do this and die" (72).

Without overplaying these hints, the relation of tragedy to epic must be considered here, in the way tragedy "remembers" epic values, but we must be cautious here, for tragic memory is not mere repetition, and all these "heroic" values are transformed by the tragic context, not simply because *the social horizon* has altered (transforming the aristocratic "desire to be first," as Vernant puts it, into an emerging democratic desire to be "one among equals"), but because *the literary frame* submits these majestic figures to new conditions of existence, producing imaginative and conceptual forms of subjectivity that are distinct not only from epic but also from the conditions that prevail in the city at large.[3]

Of course, any mention of the "esthetic" today is likely to draw fire from critics who will raise the cry of "formalism," or condemn the "estheticizing of politics"; but this convenient opposition is far too simple, for the peculiarities of the esthetic work invariably affect any conclusions about politics or ethics or the history of subjectivity that we may seek to draw from the literary text. One simply cannot reach the politics of the work of art "directly," so to speak, without confronting the protocols of the esthetic domain, which have their own demanding and sometimes technical features. Historicism and cultural studies today have tended to avoid this problem, weaving the tangled threads of the literary work without hesitation into the broader fabric of the "social text." But *Antigone*, as a literary work, confronts the reader with a daunting series of literary considerations, formal and esthetic details that are not simply embellishment of a "message" that could be extracted and rendered in philosophical discourse without significant loss. These literary features cannot be circumvented in our eagerness to produce a thesis on G. W. F. Hegel's philosophy or Lacanian psychoanalysis, on the social formation of gender or the politics of ancient democracy.

The tragic hero (Antigone, for example, but we will have to return to this question) inherits epic values but reorganizes them according to different principles, which are those of the genre as much as they are of the city beyond the theater. Thus, if Antigone loves her brother, this "love" cannot immediately be plucked from its tragic context, by a psychoanalytic reading bent on discovering "incestuous desire," or by a general anthropology that aims at a thesis on kinship relations; nor can it be immediately equated with the "love" that one finds in epic, or with the Romantically "purer" love that Hegel and his contemporaries idealized in the relation of brother and sister, which still influences a number of contemporary readings of this play.[4] Neither should guilt and responsibility, honor and shame, or law and crime be removed from the literary formation they acquire in epic or tragic discourse and inserted into a general ethical discourse on justice or virtue, or immediately inscribed in the broader "social context," as if there were no difference between the imaginative forms of life that are possible in the literary universe and those that exist in the field of social practice.

Translation becomes especially important in this regard: *philē met'*
autou keisomai, philou meta (73), Sophocles has Antigone say, which
David Grene rightly renders, "Friend shall I lie with him, yes friend
with friend, when I have dared the crime of piety" (161), and which F.
Storr translates using "brother" and "sister," which are not in the text
here but which are nevertheless introduced, and then further figured
with an incestuous emphasis that is closer to Hegel's reading than to
Sophocles' work: "How sweet to die in such employ, to rest,—Sister
and brother linked in love's embrace" [73–74]).[5] Indeed, if we were
to look more closely at this comparison in which two exposed bodies,
Polyneices and Patroclus, are recovered, mourned, and "beautified" by
friends who "love" them, it would be necessary to look at the differences that emerge with every word, across a number of fundamental
concepts, from the body and friendship to love and death, including
even beauty, as a few all too cursory examples will suggest.

Homer and Sophocles use the same language of *Atē*—"passionate
folly" or "catastrophic delusion" (the English "atrocity" is a current
derivative)—to describe these two unyielding heroes, both driven to
recover the body of a beloved *philos*, both haughty, implacable, and
isolated in their pursuit of honor, both persisting to a point of excess
that puts the justice of their claims in touch with madness, even as they
both protect the values and the modes of human recognition on which
their communities are based. If Antigone reanimates the epic ideals of
individual *kleos*, then, this hardly means that she represents the women
of her time, but it does mean that Sophocles keeps alive within the city,
in the protected and perhaps quarantined space of the theater, a form
of subjectivity that is not available elsewhere. Nor does it mean that
the position of the epic hero is simply repeated in this literary memori-
alization (on genre and memory there is more to be said).[6] For even if
we find a trace of catastrophic *Atē* in both Antigone and Achilles, "in
tragedy," as Ruth Padel reminds us, "the word *Atē* loses most of its
Homeric meaning," to which we add that this shift in meaning cannot
immediately be assimilated to shifts in the fields of law or religion that
are operative beyond the theater, which likewise deal with crime, guilt,
and pollution, and make use of the same vocabulary.[7]

A similar caution would have to be exercised around all the terms
we have just so lightly touched in broaching the question of the relation between Antigone and Achilles. When we speak of the "body"
of the fallen friend, Bernard Williams reminds us that the word philosophers will soon use to designate the "body" (*sōma*), conceived by
Plato as distinct from the soul (*psuchē*), in Homer designates not the

living body but the *corpse*.[8] Likewise, the soul is not a rational faculty charged with regulating unruly passions or animal appetites, much less the "thinking substance" of Descartes, but something quite different. As Williams notes, "the word that came to mean something like 'soul' by the time of Plato, *psuchē*, stands in Homer for something that is mentioned only when someone is fainting, dying, or dead....The other half of the dualism is also missing. The later Greek word for the body as opposed to the soul, *sōma*, means a corpse in Homer" (23). So strong was this association, Williams observes, that it led the eminent Bruno Snell wrongly to conclude that the early Greeks had no concept of the body as such, but only of its parts ("the early Greeks," Snell writes, "did not, it seems, either in their language or the visual arts, grasp the body as a unit" [23]), until philosophy advanced and provided a proper concept. Williams is critical of this view for the same reasons Christopher Gill is critical of Snell, namely that such a view of the early Greeks as primitive (lacking a concept of the body, or the will, or the moral law in a properly universal sense) presupposes a developmental model of rationality and scientific progress in which archaic thought appears ethically inferior and conceptually lacking (judged by roughly Cartesian and Kantian standards) rather than being regarded as a different conceptual system.[9] Here again, the question of vocabulary would have to be pursued more carefully, including the distinctive language of tragedy. The "body" (*sōma*) in epic is neither "extended substance" nor the site of appetite and desire that the virtuous man will regulate by his reason, but the physical remainder that lies on the earth once the warrior's spirit has left it. Vernant's "A Beautiful Death" keeps this in mind in its original French title, "*La belle mort et le cadavre outragé*" ("A Beautiful Death and the Desecrated Corpse"). And obviously, the concept of the "soul" (*psuchē*) whose history one can trace across epic, tragedy, and philosophy (and with it the "history of subjectivity" from *psuchē* to *anima* to *spiritus*, and from Latin formations to the Christian "soul," to Teutonic "*Geist*" and the Anglo-Saxon "mind," and then to the "brain" and "consciousness" and the Freudian "ego") will shift alongside these changing conceptions of the "body."[10] But once again, the principle point is that the "body" as it appears and is imagined and conceived in tragedy is not to be immediately equated with the body that one finds in the philosophical or medical or psychological or religious discourses of the time, even if these discourses may be cited and momentarily put into play within the more peculiar discourse of tragedy.[11]

Similarly, we might consider the act of "burial" itself, not only because death in tragedy is quite different from death in epic—as Nicole Loraux has shown in *Tragic Ways of Killing a Woman*—but also because every nuance is caught in this literary frame, right down to the most scrupulous detail.[12] Consider, for example, the famous dust that Antigone, constrained by necessity, uses to cover the body of Polyneices (a theme Carol Jacobs has discussed productively in "Dusting Antigone").[13] This act, in *Antigone*, allows the heroine to provide a slender barrier that protects Polyneices from exposure, at least a visual veil, if not a proper burial rite, to cover the corpse of Polyneices. Sophocles has the Messenger famously elaborate, explaining to Creon how her act was undone as soon as the burial was discovered, only to find the body suddenly covered once again, by a god-sent cloud of dust, a "trouble in the sky" (*ouranion achos*) that could also be rendered as "a celestial grief," as Charles Segal observes:[14]

> After those terrible threats of yours, we swept away all the dust that covered the corpse, carefully stripped the mouldering body... and then suddenly a whirlwind on the ground raised up a storm, a trouble in the air, and filled the plain...and we shut our eyes and endured the godsent affliction...And when after a long time this went away, we saw the girl: she cried out bitterly, with a sound like the piercing note of a bird when she sees her empty nest robbed of her young; just so did she cry out, weeping, when she saw the corpse laid bare....At once she brought in her hands thirsty dust, and from the well-wrought brazen urn that she was carrying she poured over the corpse a threefold libation. (407–31)

Compare with this the numerous instances in which dust covers the body in Homer: "A cloud of dust rose where Hektor was dragged, his dark hair was falling about him, and all that head that was once so handsome was tumbled in the dust" (Il 22.401–3, cited in Vernant, 70). As Vernant points out, dust is pollution or desecration in Homer: "One kind of cruelty consists in defiling the bloody corpse with dust and in tearing his flesh, so that the enemy will lose his individual appearance, his clear set of features, his color and glamour; he loses his distinct form along with his human aspect, so that he becomes unrecognizable" (70). "Earth and dust defile the body because their contact pollutes it," Vernant says, and this is why mourning women, simulating the catastrophe that has befallen the beloved, "inflict on their own bodies a kind of fictive outrage by defiling themselves and tearing their hair, by rolling in the dust, by smearing their faces with ashes" (70–71). Williams likewise recalls "the death of the hero Kebrides, for instance, one of many, around whose body the battle raged on," and of whom Homer says, "but he lay in the whirling dust, mightily in his might, having forgotten all his horsemanship" (Il 16.775–76).[15]

Or again, consider the much more daunting and complex question of law as it emerges in the context of tragedy. *Antigone* is, no doubt—like the *Oresteia* and many other tragedies—deeply engaged with questions of justice, law, and punishment, and even stages before the audience scenes and modes of argumentation and defense that imitate the courtroom (one thinks of the first encounter between Antigone and Creon in which he asks her, first, if she did the deed, and then, on her defiant confirmation, asks whether she knew such action had been prohibited, to which she even more defiantly replies that of course she knew and that this "announcement" or mere "proclamation" [*kerugma*] meant nothing to her); but Sophocles' thinking operates in a genre, a discursive space, a region of imaginative and esthetic specificity, and moreover within the institutional frame of the dramatic festival, which does not coincide with, and indeed often suspends or contradicts, the legal practices that are at work in the city at the same moment. The universe of tragedy cannot simply be inserted into the broader horizon of "Greek culture" or "Greek thought" without considerable difficulty. Danielle Allen has acknowledged this difficulty in *The World of Prometheus: The Politics of Punishing in Democratic Athens*, and the problem arises precisely when the broader history of punishment opens a chapter that turns to tragedy for evidence:

> The tragedians were quirky playwrights who imposed idiosyncratic linguistic patterns and ideas on their native language. To some extent, however, they had to leave in place the category structures bequeathed them as raw material by their language regardless of how brilliant and unconventional each may have been. Linguistic patterns and repetitions of usage do appear across the texts of Aeschylus, Sophocles, and Euripides. I use their tragedies to find a "grammar of punishment" for Athens but only by drawing on expressions that are repeated across tragedians and across several plays. Nor do I take the language of tragedy, not even the conventional language of tragedy, as representing the day-to-day language of the Athenians. The playwrights could have been deploying a set of conceptual conventions restricted wholly to the genre of tragedy.[16]

Indeed, an enormous problematic opens here regarding not only the complex *historical* shifts that take place in a number of fundamental terms and concepts from Homer to Sophocles to Plato but also—and more importantly from our current perspective—concerning the way those shifts are differently organized by the particular *literary* forms in which they are inscribed.

On *philia*, to take yet one more example, we can certainly inquire into the history of friendship and the ancient codes of honor and recognition that bound one aristocratic man to another, such that they were obligated by laws of hospitality to take in another aristocratic man, offering food and protection in "friendship," even if the two had never met before (an ethical relation to the friend that is quite different from the affective bonds that we assume to underlie modern "friendship" relations, which we regard as freely chosen and based on emotional inclinations rather than being built on ethical obligations established by status or rank).[17] And we can certainly see that the debate between Antigone and Creon on "friends" and "enemies" has some relation to the broad historical and political change by which bonds of blood uniting the aristocratic *genos* are replaced by bonds of political allegiance that unite the *polis*, such that the city can begin to assert a higher ethical claim on the "friendship" of the individual, according to obligations based on the name, understood not merely as the notorious "name of the father," but as the group name that (as Sigmund Freud also argues in *Totem and Taboo* when he speaks of the totem animal ancestor) replaces the actual father with an identity that binds families in unities at the level of the "city" or "nation" (making them "Thebans," or "Athenians," for example). These broader anthropological considerations are surely relevant, but this social, political, and philosophical analysis of the history of the "friend" (the passage from aristocratic *genos* to the democratic *polis*) cannot ignore the peculiarities of the tragic universe.

Still more complex are the arrangements of *philia* in this text when we recall that Creon himself, beyond the framework of "blood" and "city," or "family" and "state," which governs so much contemporary commentary, belongs to a *mythical genos* that is distinctively tragic. For, in fact, Creon is a "dragon-man," the last of the archaic Thebans, the autochthonous line of men sown by Cadmus from the dragon's teeth and referred to by the Chorus in the opening lines of the play when they tell of the rout of Polyneices and his Argive soldiers, vanquished by "his dragon-foe, a thing he could not overcome" (125–26).[18] If we follow this line of thought, we soon recognize that the death of Creon's only sons, Megareus and Haemon, both mentioned by Eurydice before her suicide, means that Creon is now the last remaining male member of the original "Sown Men." How then can we suppose that *"philia"* or "family" or "kinship" in the modern biological sense can be imposed on this ancient "race" to which Creon belongs? As Froma Zeitlin has said, tragedy points to "a double and valid principle: parentage itself may be a fictive category, an 'as if,' and ties of blood, although essential to one's genetic identity, are not the only relations that count."[19]

This also affects any notions of "guilt" or "crime" that we might wish to impose on this text, together with notions of "justice," "responsibility," "agency," and "will." Indeed, as Hugh Lloyd-Jones has shown in his analysis of *Oedipus*, a story of pollution is very prominent in this text, which is clearly dominated by references to divine vengeance, not in pursuit of Oedipus himself, whatever his crimes or errors may have been, but in pursuit of Laius, who dared to ignore Apollo's prophesy, which warned him not to have children, a prophesy Laius sought to circumvent, foolishly thwarting the will of the god, having children in spite of the oracle's warning, and then sending his son away to adoptive parents, as if this could conceal the child from Apollo's sight. Such offenses do not go unrequited, and from this perspective, Oedipus is not punished for the quasi-anthropological crime of incest, nor for the ethical crime of murder, nor even for his alleged *hubris*, but simply because he is the son of Laius, whose entire line, according to Lloyd-Jones, including Polyneices, Antigone, and the rest, should never have existed and is simply destined to be expunged, so that the will of the god will be established.

Creon is, no doubt, as Martha Nussbaum has suggested, the very model of (a certain figure of) *phronesis*, "the king who makes a bad decision," and he is, no doubt, held ethically responsible for this mistake and even punished as a result.[20] One need not negate the operative values of these terms in order to recognize an entirely different tangle of threads that have equal importance in the tragic text. As the last of the monstrous "Sown Men," Creon is simply being cut down, expunged from the city—and here we follow yet another mythical thread in the complex tapestry of literary memory—in order to prepare for the arrival of Theseus and his Athenian army, who will now take control of Thebes on behalf of the dead Polyneices and all the other fallen warriors whose bodies have likewise been abandoned on the battlefield and refused a proper burial. Creon is, no doubt, punished for this extreme outrage— a fact that is mentioned in Sophocles' version when Tiresias speaks of the "mangled warriors who have found a grave i' the maw of wolf or hound, or winged bird that flying homewards taints their city's air" (Storr, 1082–83). This is the pollution of the altars for which Tiresias holds Creon responsible, the desecrated bodies of all these abandoned soldiers raining down on the city's altars in a horrifying manner from the mouths and in the excrement of birds. Can this catastrophic image simply be reduced to a "metaphor" that is meant to illustrate Creon's "mistaken judgment"? Can we really translate such a universe into the discourse of rational deliberation, as if these literary embellishments were only the "metaphorical dressing" that should actually be read as a discourse on Aristotelian *phronesis* and the virtues of moderation, and as if we were situated in the world of the *Nicomachean Ethics*? The language of inherited pollution and the broader mythical references to the inexorable defeat of Thebes, together with a divinely sanctioned ascendancy of Athens that goes well beyond any personal error or individual punishment, is not so easily circumvented. We are no longer in the universe of *phronesis* and human self-determination here. This larger, impersonal, and mythical horizon is interwoven with the individual punishment of Creon, as the "disaster" that Tiresias predicts in his famous speech near the end: "There lie in wait for you the doers of outrage who in the end destroy, the Erinyes of Hades and the gods," he says, and "all the cities are stirred up by enmity" (1074–80). At this level, *Antigone* is not the story of an individual mistake or blindness (whether Creon's or Antigone's), but the story of the collapse of the dragon-men and of divinely sanctioned Athenian supremacy over Thebes—an ambiguous supremacy, because Thebes is the "other," which simultaneously serves as a mythical origin for Athens itself.[21] Creon, from this mythic perspective, is merely one of the pawns that is sacrificed in this process—and his "bad decision" as a "psychological individual" with "free will" and "ethical commitments" is simply a bone that Sophocles throws to the philosophers who wish to chew on the concepts of "responsibility" and "individual agency," but which cannot capture the truth of the grander divine purpose by which Thebes is surpassed by Athens. We need not enter, with René Girard, into any grand and questionable thesis about scapegoating and religious ritual in order to recognize that Creon is being brought to ruin not for any individual or personal decision but because the entire "race" or *genos* to which he belongs is being extinguished by the gods for their own inscrutable reasons. This mythical "race" cannot be inserted into contemporary debates about "family" and "state" without considerable complication.

Whatever else one may wish to say about Antigone's typically Sophoclean rashness, stubbornness, and wild or untamed (*ōmos*) inflexibility of temper, or indeed her "personal character," her virtue, or the justice of her claims, it is clear that the punishment and "guilt" that afflict her—as with Oedipus, the unwilling and ignorant "outlaw"—include a dimension of inherited family *Atē*, and cannot be made to fit neatly with the idea of a "crime" committed in violation of some general law, moral or otherwise, that she has personally and willfully transgressed, or even with its opposite, the idea of "unjust punishment" by a tyrannical king (even if this is *also* part of the texture of the play). This, as Lloyd-Jones says, is especially true of Sophocles (see pp. 113–19). Speaking of Antigone's *Atē*, set in the context of the pollution that runs through the house of Labdacus, which extends far beyond Oedipus himself, Lloyd-Jones recalls the choral ode that follows her condemnation by Creon: "The Chorus sing an ode of great beauty in which they reflect on the history of the house of Labdacus," and he stresses "the leading metaphor of the opening pair of stanzas, the comparison of the afflicted family to a beach struck by successive waves." In the end, "even these last surviving members of the house of Oedipus are now to be cut down. Their executioners will be the usual ministers of *Atē*, 'foolishness in thought and the Erinyes in the mind'" (113). One simply cannot collapse such a perspective into the "psychological" model of "personal subjectivity" that is so often presupposed by modern readers when they speak of "character," or "guilt," much less "sin" or "pride" as they are understood today. Such is the importance of the family curse or "*Ate*," inherited and passed across generations, such that one can be "punished" (if this is the right word) or pursued by the Erinyes without having committed any crime, as Antigone herself is punished, according to the Chorus: "You have run against the high pedestal of Justice with your foot," they tell her as she is led away to the cave, and "you are making atonement, I think, with an ordeal come to you by inheritance" (853–55).[22] What "Justice" has Antigone stumbled on here, so far from the petty "pronouncement" (*kerugma*) of Creon's edict? Can we really say, then, that tragedy belongs within the framework of "crime," "responsibility," and "punishment" in the legal and ethical sense?[23] And can we suppose that the modern biological form of the family, in opposition to the state, governs tragic thinking on the *genos*? Tragedy thinks in conjunction with myth, and it would be a mistake to hold the play hostage in the city of philosophy and expect it to reveal its secrets there.

BEYOND HEGEL

The relation between esthetics and politics or philosophy is thus more complex than the familiar charges of estheticism and formalism might suggest. Attention to considerations of genre is not a detour from broader social concerns, or a retreat into esthetics. The very opposite is the case: any route to the political or social dimension of art that seeks to bypass the peculiar demands of literary work, regarding them as "merely esthetic," actually diminishes the possibility of any politics of art.

Some caution is therefore advisable when we approach all the words that Sophocles deploys concerning law and justice, family and state, gender and kinship, man and woman, the living and the dead. These words cannot simply be extracted from their tragic horizon and placed in the "external" social milieu that contemporary historicism so frequently presupposes today, but must rather be situated in their "context," which is that of literary discourse, as much as it is of the city. "Gender" is only one of many terms that is implicated in these considerations of genre, but here too, it should be clear that we cannot immediately pass from the figure of Antigone to "woman" in general, or even to the conceptions of woman that are operative in the city-state at Sophocles' time.

One cannot pass so quickly from the discourse of tragedy to legal or philosophical discourse without sacrificing something essential. How then can Hegel and so many contemporary readers in his wake move from Antigone to "woman" in general, not only leaping from the theater to the world of ancient Greece, as if there were no discontinuity between the language of tragedy and the languages of medicine and religion, law and philosophy, that organize "gender" in the ancient city, but also passing even from this historical culture to "woman" as such, now generalized as the "eternal irony of the community" (*die ewige Ironie des Gemeinwesens*), a formula that sweeps us along from the dense and meticulous formations of tragic art to the cultural milieu of the ancient city-state, and then to pronouncements on "womankind"?[24] How indeed can we so easily accept and allow ourselves to be inscribed in a history of determinations that lead to the discourse of "gender" that now dominates so many discussions of this play—as if no one dared to break the law or emerge from the shadow of Hegel, and venture forth to pay respects to the abandoned body of this text?

Carol Jacobs, one of the very few contemporary readers to have broached the literary aspect of this issue, reminds us, "The role woman plays is certainly not simple nor ever completed. Not in Hegel and not in Irigaray. All the less so in *Antigone*. And yet...[u]ntil now we have looked to the philosophers rather than to Antigone. Both Hegel and Irigaray glide unproblematically from the figure of Antigone to the role of ‚woman in general. Would a return to the specificity of the Greek heroine accomplish a redefinition?"[25] The etymological link between gender and genre is not an accident: figurations of femininity, as Loraux, Vernant, Zeitlin, Kirk Ormand, and many others have shown, cannot be detached from the specific discourse that organizes them, and the discourse of tragedy is quite different from what one finds, for example, in Aristotle's notorious and often-criticized pronouncements on women.[26]

Philosophers who offer to read tragedy for us have therefore entered this domain at their peril. Defending Aristotle against Plato's critique of tragedy (*against Plato*, which means we are already in the philosophical city from the very outset, as if tragedy itself were a thing of the past, forgotten or translated into the discourse of the Academy, with its debates about the dangers of "rhetoric"), or entering the fray of post-Hegelian thought with all its consequences for the "family" and the "state," many philosophical readers have recently returned to *Antigone* for their own purposes, whether they be in the arena of gender studies, as with the work of Judith Butler, or in the domain of moral philosophy, as with that of Nussbaum. Having buried *Antigone* alive beneath the heavy weight of their own preoccupations—*which are those of the city and its self-regulation, including a quite classical philosophical care for the well-being of the citizen*—philosophers may find, in the end, that they are sacrificing something essential, indeed *something of their own*, something that could be called truth, if it were only recognizable as such, after being thus transported like a slave into foreign land, or married off into the house of philosophy, where it is forced to do the productive labor of the concept and can no longer speak in its own tongue.

PLOT AND CHARACTER

Obvious as these points may be, they bring us to some very fundamental difficulties that contemporary criticism has tended to avoid regarding the literary dimension of tragedy and the distance that separates it from the languages of the city that surround it. And yet, if one returns to the simplest of terms in traditional literary study—terms such as "plot" and "character"—one immediately encounters a host of difficulties that cannot easily be circumvented. Consider "character" first. A "hero" in epic poetry is quite obviously distinct from a tragic hero and is not made in the same way, or according to the same procedures, values, and representational codes. The slow and painful sequence of events that make up the "plot" or *mythos* of tragedy, culminating in the acquisition of knowledge by the hero (what Aristotle calls *anagnoresis*), whose experience and artistic presentation is confined within the narrow circuit of the city and generally contained within a short span of time, is very different from the sweeping action of the hero in epic, exercised in cunning, with the courage of the warrior, and accomplished beyond the reaches of the city-state; nor would we expect the same virtues or beliefs, or the same confrontation with problems (of law or justice, gods or monsters, friendship or enmity), or even the same form of subjectivity from the one that we immediately anticipate from the other.

What Nussbaum has called the "practical wisdom" (*phronenis*) of the tragic hero, the political judgment that informs his or her action as a ruler—Oedipus' attempt to discover the truth, Pentheus' effort to resist the influence of "foreign" religious mysticism, Creon's search for a response to the aftermath of civil war—and the sequence of events that exposes that hero's decisions to forces that *phronesis* cannot master, is very different from what Marcel Detienne and Vernant have called the "cunning intelligence" or *metis* of a figure like Odysseus.[27] If Achilles is not Oedipus, the difference between them cannot be attributed to their "character" in the abstract sense of the term, and certainly not in the sense that a moral philosopher might use when speaking of "character" in reference to the "psychological person" in the modern sense, or in reference to philosophical standards of virtue.[28] In the space of literature, "character" is, first of all, a matter of the genre in which these figures emerge and become possible for us, as tragic or epic figures. Nor would we confuse the "hero" celebrated in lyric songs of praise—the heroic victor of the Olympic games, for example, or the military general returning home in victory—with the grand and solitary figures of Sophocles, who are not the monumentalized objects of veneration and nationalistic aggrandizement that the lyric poet describes for his contemporaries, but exiled, furious, catastrophic, or woebegone figures who nevertheless command our attention as "heroes" in a very different sense.[29]

Moreover, to touch briefly on only the most obvious points emphasized at the very outset of Aristotle's *Poetics*, tragic characters are not figures whose actions are *related to us through narrative*, as in the case of epic, but figures who appear onstage and *speak in their own voices, in propria persona*. This means, in turn, that the audience has to decide—each time, with every speech, at each instant in the unfolding of the tragic action, where characters no longer act on the field of battle but appear in dialogue, in constant interchange with those who converse with them, agreeing or disagreeing—how to estimate what the hero of tragedy is saying, without relying on the interpretive framework that is afforded by the medium of epic and lyric discourse, which situate and explain the hero's position for us. This unfolding of "character" is unintelligible if one simply refers to the "social context," in the hope of extracting a political or philosophical message without attending to the discourse in which it is framed. It would be foolish to pretend that tragedy has no bearing on philosophy or that Sophocles was not in considered dialogue with the discourses of what we now call the "public sphere." Nor is it my intention to isolate literature within the confines of the "esthetic" domain, as if it could not challenge and respond to the languages of philosophy, law, and religion that surround it. My point is much rather that we will never understand tragedy's response to those languages—or literature as a form of thinking and critique—if we translate it from the very outset into the discourse of the city.

A "character" in literature is thus shaped by the formal constraints of the literary work, constraints of genre that allow us to distinguish what we might call the "forms of personhood" that appear in epic poetry from those we find in tragedy or lyric—and even, more importantly, from the accounts of personhood that we may find in philosophical discourse, like Aristotle's treatise on the soul. As Sheldon Sacks showed with magisterial clarity and precision years ago, in *Fiction and the Shape of Belief*, we do not expect, and will not find, in an apologue like *Rasselas* or *Candide*, the same kind of psychological depth, or even the same kinds of narrative situations (with greater degrees of interpersonal complexity, greater concern with psychological interiority or "personal development," greater space within the linguistic medium for the elaboration of a character's "internal thought") that we find in the history of the novel, beginning with the *Bildungsroman*, which, for its part, is very different from epic or tragic discourse, as it is different from the types of "personage" we encounter in Chaucer's *Canterbury Tales*, whose moral and psychological character is very attentively drawn but in accordance with a mode of literary discourse that is found neither in ancient epic nor in the modern novel.[30] One can certainly develop a *relationship* between Chaucer's presentation and the Medieval theory of the four humors, together with Christian doctrines on the vices and their typology, as the cultural, medico-religious background against which Chaucer's personages (and their physiognomy) should be understood, but such an account cannot avoid the literary genre in which these characters are presented, with its distinctive narrative frame, its comic mode of presentation, and the games of requital that link each speaker to the next, in a strictly literary field of invention, one that is quite different from what we would expect to find in the religious or medical discourse of the same period. Given the enormous complexity of these formal inventions in which "character" emerges, each time in a different literary genre, it should be clear that "character" in the ethical or philosophical sense of the term cannot simply be transported into the literary domain without considerable difficulty.

Similar difficulties would emerge from a consideration of "plot," and here again considerations of genre are more decisive than recent critical procedures would lead us to believe. A plot (*mythos*) is not simply the narrated sequence of "events" that can be reduplicated or paraphrased by critical commentary. One recalls Claude Lévi-Strauss' famous method, in his structural analysis of myth, which consisted in writing down on a separate card each distinct "event" of a mythic narrative, reduced to a single sentence—"Oedipus kills the Sphinx," "Oedipus marries Jocasta," and so on—as if the essence of the myth could be captured by this quasi-logical reduction. But one should not forget his additional observation that this "infinite translatability" of myth should be contrasted with the absolute untranslatability of poetry, whose syntax, style, and formal organization is constitutive and irreplaceable.[31] Tragic drama, of course, is poetry, and if it inherits and "remembers" myth, it reconstitutes the "mythic memory" that it preserves, and does so in a genre that cannot be ignored. Poetry, moreover, is not the only genre in which such formal considerations are relevant, as the "story-discourse" distinction of structuralism has made clear.[32] Indeed, the same "story" can be told (put into "discourse") in very different ways, from multiple perspectives, in various time sequences, with flashbacks, repetitions, allegorical configurations, degrees of reliability, and so on, or with certain events foregrounded while others remain submerged (as happens, in fact, with the legend of *Antigone* itself).[33] Even the genre of history, as Hayden White has shown, is different from mere chronicle—the bare listing of individual, dated events ("Pope died," or "Caesar crossed the Rubicon")—precisely to the extent that history inexorably entails narration, with generic styles and plot formations that cannot be ignored and that have a decisive impact on the "content."[34]

What thinking takes place in the genre of tragedy, then, and can we really reduce this tragic form of thought, tearing it from the womb in which it was conceived and holding it hostage in the house of philosophy, where it is forced to speak in a different tongue, and generate conclusions for the dialectic of Spirit, or for political debates about kinship and the conflict between "blood" and "state" in the modern sense? In its current and eminently philosophical reception, Sophocles' *Antigone* would appear to be like the Erinyes, buried beneath the Acropolis, and allowed to speak only through the mouth of the Eumenides, which speak of peace and justice, their original voices silenced or forgotten.

THE TRAGIC HERO

To make these remarks more concrete, let us consider the opening speech of Creon, to take only a brief example. We cannot say how Sophocles' work may intervene in debates about political authority in fifth-century Athens, about ancient democracy, the status of women, or any ethical views we may wish to find in the work, unless we are able to grasp the position assigned to Creon by this play, and this requires a knowledge of both the historical and the literary domain. On the one hand, it may well be, as Vernant has pointed out, that Creon's decision not to bury Polyneices represents the standard judgment that would be required of any ruler *from a legal point of view* at that time: "Of course Creon, as a chief of state, is right in not wanting to allow the burial of an enemy who is a traitor. 'Why is he right?' one may ask. I would say 'He is right from the Greek point of view' because he acts according to the laws of the Greek City-State. In Athens, the traitor or the sacrilege who dies or is executed must not have a tomb."[35]

Thus, although contemporary readers may not like it, Creon cannot be made into a simple tyrant from the outset and charged with excess and "pride" (by the moralists), or with egotism and self-aggrandizement (by the psychoanalysts); nor would Antigone attain her stature of severe and majestic isolation from the community if her antagonist could be so easily dismissed.[36] Creon's speech must have sufficient standing, legally and ethically, apart from his personal assertion of authority, to allow him to represent the community and to make his betrayal or degradation of its larger claims moving and important for the audience. On the other hand, however, and *from the standpoint of tragedy*, this historical fact about the legal arrangement of Sophocles' time must be balanced, in turn, by an understanding of Creon as a tragic figure who, whatever may be his legal "correctness" from a *historical perspective*, stands within the *tragic context* as a figure of human wisdom exposed to its own catastrophic blindness and violence (for, indeed, *hubris*, so often translated as "pride" by a Christianizing reception, means "violence," the disruptive force of a power that oversteps its bounds). This tragic positioning of the hero in the literary sphere, so different from the formation of the hero in epic poetry, is a fact that cannot be drawn from the sociohistorical context of the play but only from other tragedies, which form the context against which Sophocles and his audience would expect the drama to be understood. Creon's position is, indeed, that of a ruler set in the historical context of Athenian democracy and its emerging legal order, but it is, at the same time, that of a tragic hero, and these two dimensions do not necessarily coincide. What we call "the standpoint of tragedy" is thus explicitly at odds with the "historical context" of Sophocles' cultural moment.

The same discontinuity could be followed across almost every line of Sophocles' text. Consider, for example, only one word, *amēchanon*, which appears in Creon's opening speech. Let us first set this word in its "context." A champion of plain speaking who does not tolerate any indirection from his soldiers, who threatens them with punishment for hesitating to deliver bad news, and who suspects even Tiresias' prophetic discourse of being motivated only by profit (1055, 1061), Creon appears for the first time onstage and explains to the city elders—who do not know him well, the new ruler that he is—that "talk is cheap" and that he will show his character through action.[37] Speech is insufficient in revealing the "soul" and "mind" of a man (his *psuchē*, *phronēma*, and *gnōmēn*), but decisions made in ruling (the edict prohibiting Polyneices' burial, which he is about to announce) will reveal who he is: "'Tis no easy matter to discern the temper of a man, his mind and will, till he be proved by exercise of power" (175–77). This platitude (and Creon's speech is full of philosophical formulas, like the speech of Polonius in *Hamlet*) will be repeated by Aristotle in *Nicomachean Ethics* (1130a1) as a moral truism (*archē andra deixei*, "rule will reveal the real man"). But tragedy is not philosophy, and the meaning of this sentence is almost entirely lost when it reappears as a proposition in Aristotle's *Ethics*. Consider: Creon means to say, of course, that he holds the city dear, that it is the best of friends, and that he will reveal who he is and show by his action that he is prepared to protect it above all else: "Anyone thinking another man more friend than his own country, I count him nowhere" (202–3). This is what he means to say, but for a tragic audience, even before the prohibition is announced, Creon's words already "reveal the real man," not by expressing any philosophical truth or any principle concerning friends and enemies, family and state (a warning to Hegelian readers), but rather by showing that Creon does not know himself, his own "soul" or "temper," or even understand what he is saying, for he is already declaring, without intending to do so, that (like Oedipus) he is not the person he thinks he is: *egō kratē dē panta*, or "I hold all the power" (173), he says, meaning that he is now responsible for the city. But also, "I will show you who I am through my exercise of power," he says in effect. This tragic irony, as it is called, hangs over his entire opening speech, positioning Creon in a context that is entirely lost whenever his language is removed from this literary universe and translated into the discourse of philosophy, as if it were simply a statement of "principles" or "laws."

Given this sentence—*egō kratē dē panta*—and without opening a very long parenthesis on the language of the play, we should at least note the very different use that Creon and Antigone make of the word "*egō*" in this play, for this tragic deployment of the "I" is crucial to whatever we may say about *Antigone* in the history of subjectivity, and we cannot circumvent the literary usage of this "I" that Sophocles explores here. Consider Antigone first. In their opening exchange, Antigone and Ismene are tightly joined, from the "common womb" (*autadelphon*) of the opening lines and the series of linguistic duals that link them as one, until the moment Antigone breaks away, as the *only one left* to perform her solitary act. At this point, as Segal has stressed, she clearly "takes things personally."[38] At first, she presents Creon's edict to Ismene as something that aggravates the long series of "your sorrows and mine" (*tōn sōn te kamōn...kakōn*; 5–6), to which Ismene replies that she has heard nothing "since we two were robbed of two brothers, each at the other's hand" (13–14). But once Ismene has withdrawn in fear, and even before this point, Antigone's solitude emerges in the way she takes this "general law" of Creon's to be *aimed at her personally*. Creon uses the abstract and universalizing language of law in this edict ("anyone who..."), but Antigone takes it as aimed at herself, saying, "This is the proclamation which they say the good Creon has made to you and me (*soi kamoi*)," only to take it solely on herself, and adding, "yes, to me, I tell you" (*legō gar kame*; 31–32). And then, in a peculiar locution that some editors have tried to emend (since her formulation appears to suggest there are two distinct brothers involved, which is, in fact, close to the truth), "I will bury my brother, and yours too, if you will not (*ton goun emon, kai ton son, ēn su mē thelēs*; 45). And finally, as their separation becomes extreme, "Be the kind of person you have decided to be, but I shall bury him! It is honorable (*kalon*, beautiful) for me to do this and die. I am his own and I shall lie with him who is my own" (71–73).[39] She thus speaks from a point of absolute individuation or isolation, marked elsewhere by the term "*autonomos*" (giving herself her own law), a word that, as Mark Griffith observes, appears in Sophocles' text as the first extant usage of this term in Greek.[40] But we must grasp this "taking things personally" in the right way, so as not to confuse it with Creon's narcissism, as has sometimes been done with this "stubborn girl."

We must not oppose Creon and Antigone as two counterparts, symmetrically opposed, each stubborn and single-minded, each devoted to a particular "principle" or "law," which they apply with inflexible rigidity, as Nussbaum and others have argued, for this furious, solitary, devoted, intransigent, and fatefully exiled figure uses the word "I" in a way that is quite different from Creon's usage. When he says, "I have all the power," or "authority rests with me," he is setting himself, in a way that is conspicuously undemocratic, at the center of a power that he identifies with his own person. This is what psychoanalysts would rightly call "narcissistic," as opposed to inhabiting the lawful position of one who is responsible for ruling and for assuming the symbolic position of the king who protects the community. It is this betrayal of his symbolic role that becomes progressively more evident in the play, until the point when his deployment of this "I" no longer has any bearing on the general law, but only on his own person ("No woman will rule me while I live," etc. [678]). Antigone's use of the first person pronoun, by contrast—and with this the entire figuration of her status as a subject— is not narcissistic in the same way, and if she indeed "takes personally" the edict Creon has announced, she does so not as an assertion of her own "person," for she rather speaks as one who has been captured by circumstance, claimed by a situation that makes her responsible and implicated in a way that she will not try to avoid.[41] It is not that she is passive, or simply "fated" by circumstance. Indeed, Ismene is the "disciplined" subject in Michel Foucault's sense, the one who has submitted to being a "woman" in the sense the city requires of her—"Remember we are just women," she says (according to what theorists today like to call "interpellation," though this vocabulary is not precise enough to capture the differences we are delineating here). Neither captured by her own ego, like Creon, nor passive like Ismene, Antigone rather has a "heroic" status and even the desire for "glory" (*kleos*), not for "herself," but as befits one who is capable of responding to her situation with the greatest honor. This capacity is what makes Ismene call her "mad," and it gives Antigone, no doubt, a certain "inhuman" dimension, as has often been noted, exiling her from the usual understanding of the human community.[42] The edict is something "personal," then, in the sense that it is "up to her" to act and to take responsibility for the situation she has been handed—even at the cost of her own life, which is to say that she renounces the more recognizably "human" defense of her "personal interests." This is what Creon's use of the word "I" shows him incapable of doing. In place of honor, he only has his own ego. In place of a capacity to act in relation to the world and the situation that he has been thrown into (the disaster of civil war and its aftermath), Creon can only substitute "himself."

In tracing the function of the "ego," then, we cannot be content with the generalized appeal to "shifters," those personal pronouns that appear to pass neutrally from one speaker to the next, first when Antigone says "I," figuring Creon as "you," only to be reversed as the dialogue proceeds. Such a generalized linguistic model is insufficient, and indeed, Foucault, Emile Benveniste, Wayne Booth, and many others have discussed the functioning of "shifters," not merely as linguistic forms, but as the conjunction of subjectivity and language, a conjunction that is especially important and complex in literary discourse.[43] We will not develop these issues here, but on the basis of these two deployments of the "I," on the part of Creon and Antigone, two modes of inhabiting the position of a subject, it would be possible to elaborate a very important issue, namely, the question of who is the tragic hero in this play, and all the implications this has for the history of subjectivity, as it is configured in this unique genre.

Antigone is indeed challenging from a technical point of view with respect to the question of the tragic hero. In one sense, it is clear that Creon is the tragic hero in this play. He is the king who makes a bad decision, who in blindness and arrogance persists in that decision despite being warned in progressively more emphatic scenes (as the construction of the tragic plot warrants), first by the city elders, then by his son, and finally even by Tiresias, until it is too late to correct his mistake. He is the one, moreover, who is forced in the end to "subjectify" this experience, to undergo a reversal of fortune and recognize his guilt. Antigone, by contrast, makes no such error and exhibits no blindness, but only a lucid clarity about what she has to do. She assumes her position at the outset of the play, in full awareness of the consequences it will entail, and while she suffers, she makes no "tragic error" in the technical sense and undergoes no reversal of fortune in the course of the play (being dead from the start, as she herself says). And given her death, she cannot experience any "moment of recognition," unlike Creon, who is forced to continue living as the plot proceeds, until the truth is subjectively registered, and he is brought to see his blindness. The attempt to cast Creon and Antigone as "opposites" or "counterparts," both stubborn, both devoted to a single "rational principle," as so many philosophers following Hegel have done, completely ignores this tragic asymmetry, which is also the problem of the tragic hero, a figuration that separates the two figures absolutely. Interpretations that reduce or obliterate this difference, grasping these two figures only in terms of "opposing principles," are able to maintain this symmetry, dialectical or not, only by lifting these characters out of their tragic context, as if

they were speaking the language of philosophy and as if the "ethics" of
their positions could be grasped without stumbling over the irreducible
fact that the text is a tragedy, with all that this entails.

In perfect conformity with the classical analysis of Oedipus given by
Aristotle, then, Creon is the one who exhibits all the technical features
of the tragic hero. And yet, this does not keep Antigone from being the
"heroine" of the play. We have not paused over this peculiarity enough.
But from a technical point of view, it could be said that in this play,
Sophocles is inviting us to consider the very function and position of
the "tragic hero" as such, the very form of subjectivity that defines such
a figure. I am stressing here a configuration of subjectivity that is intimately intertwined with tragedy as a literary genre, its unique capacities
for figuration and thinking, which are quite different from those that
are possible in the legal, medical, religious, and philosophical discourses
of the city that surround the theater. As I have argued elsewhere, it is as
if Sophocles passes off all the "traditional" features of the tragic hero
(*hamartia, anagnoresis, peripeteia,* etc.) onto a surrogate, in the figure
of Creon, so that Antigone can now stand out as the hero in even more
supreme isolation and magnitude.[44] This is why there is some truth in
the position of those who wish to say that Creon is a mere bureaucrat,
a petty tyrant who is rightly held in contempt, and who does not rise to
the sublime level that is reached by Antigone, who—beyond all merely
narcissistic care for herself—now stands as the equivalent of Ajax or
Achilles, as a warrior whose *kleos* or honor must be protected at all
cost and whose memory will be preserved for posterity in the play that
bears her name. It is clear that Antigone is the "heroine" of the play,
then, but we should not reach this conclusion too easily, since Creon's
status absorbs into itself most of the canonical features of this figure.
What then is Sophocles inviting us to think, and what intervention is he
making in the history of subjectivity, in this figuration of the "hero"?

With this "context" in mind, let us now return to Creon's opening
speech. "Tis no easy matter to discern the character of a man" until
he shows himself in action, Creon says, and yet the character of a man
is more evident in words than Creon supposes, and whatever he may
wish to say about justice, human or divine, whatever philosophical or
ethical position he may wish to set forth with this generalized discourse
about principles and laws, the Chorus clearly hears Creon's message
for what it really is, a violation of democracy, including a conspicuous
disregard for their own traditional role as advisers to the king: "I have
summoned you," Creon says, because "you always honored the power
of Laius's throne...and you remained reliable advisors" (168–69), but

following his pronouncement he dismisses these advisers without the slightest consultation, and the Chorus, "usually bland and inconsequential," as Griffith says (162), in this case, makes Creon's position quite clear: "Son of Menoikeus, *it pleases you to do as you wish* to him who bears ill will towards the city *and him who's friendly*. No doubt *you have the power* to use any law in dealing with the dead *or us the living*" (211–14; emphasis added).[45] Much of Creon's language is filled with "undemocratic terms," Griffith notes, and *kratos*, "power," a root of "democracy," which Creon deploys here (*egō kratē dē panta* [I hold all the power]; 173), is a double-edged sword, as has often been pointed out, meaning both "legitimate rule" and "brute force."

This tragic ambiguity, so conspicuous to the Chorus and the audience, is lost whenever one takes Creon's discourse out of its tragic context, as though it were merely the expression of a "principle" or "thesis," the representative of a clear philosophical stance, opposed in turn to the "counterthesis" so often attributed to Antigone, who for her part would be drawn into the same philosophical discourse, as if this could represent her, one general law opposed to another law. How then can Hegel simply extract a "message" from Creon's speech, converting it into a rational discourse about justice or "rights" and "obligations," as if his language could be rendered in philosophical discourse without significant loss? Such ambiguity hangs over every word of Creon's opening lines, resounding for the audience but ignored by the man himself, which only shows all the more what Aristotle calls his *hamartia* or blindness. So also did Croesus resolve ambiguity, consulting the oracle at Delphi. "If Croesus goes to war, he will destroy a great kingdom," Apollo told him, but Croesus only heard words that sent him out against the Persians, with disastrous consequences. The analogy is instructive, since, for a tragic audience, the generalized platitude that aims at an empty universal can always recoil on the speaker in the exact opposite sense from the one he intends. So it is with Creon's discourse in its relentless universality (so different from Antigone, who says, "It's up to me, then"): "Any man who [*hotis*, "anyone," 178], guiding the city, fails to take the best council for her, but keeps silent for fear... seems to me the worst of men," Creon proclaims, and we already know, though he himself does not, that he will begin by failing to take the best council—from the Chorus and his son—and proceed to silence others in fear, finally ending as the worst of men. Or again, generalizing about "whoever" puts a friend higher than the city (*hotis*, "anyone who," 182), Creon proclaims, "I count him nowhere," with all the violence of one who is prepared to punish his enemy even beyond death, expelling him from the city, and even from his resting place in Hades itself, exiling him to "nowhere"; but while he speaks of his enemy ("I count him nowhere"), he foretells his own destiny with these very words: "Lead me away," he says in the end, "me who am no more than nothing" (1321–25).

From his very first words, Creon's language enacts in its smallest details the entire structure of the plot, which will reverse his fortune, reveal his blindness about his own identity, and show him to be the "enemy" of the city. How then can we circumvent this language, as if Creon were speaking a legal or purely philosophical discourse, setting forth a "position" that would purportedly be given its "antithesis" in Antigone's counterdiscourse, supposedly rendering an "opposite" point of view in which family would be set above the state, the values of friends and enemies reversed—especially if one considers that Antigone's discourse, unlike Creon's, is prey to no such tragic ambiguity? When she speaks, she says exactly what she means. This difference and asymmetry between the characters is fundamental, but it is entirely lost the moment their language is dislocated, torn from the tragic womb in which it was conceived, transported out of the tragic universe, and held hostage by the concept.

At last we come to Creon's word *amēchanon*, which Storr renders here as "no easy matter," but which is translated more precisely by Grene as "impossible" ("It is impossible to know the mind of any man") (175). This word, which issues from Creon's mouth (as he denounces language in favor of action), is the very word the Chorus famously explicates for us in the "Ode to Man," saying that man is very clever, having techniques to master everything (*sophon ti to mēchanoen technas* [365]), but being unable to master death. "From Hades," the Chorus says, "escape is impossible," *amēchanōn* (363). Without knowing it, Creon has thus announced to the Chorus and the audience that he is already fatefully situated among the three famous contradictions or "aporias" that the Chorus elaborates, three variants of man's character as "*deinon*," uncanny and self-undoing: *hypsipolis apolis* (high in his city and citiless; 371), *pantaporos aporos* (having many ways, and no way out; 360), and *amechanon mechanoen* (armed with many devices but defenseless against death, or "without refuge" despite his "skilled invention"; 363–65). This is indeed the very word Ismene has already used in the opening scene to tell Antigone that she is "in love with the impossible" (Grene's translation for *amēchanōn erais*; 90).

The discourse of tragedy does not function like the discourse of philosophy. Creon's edict, however "correct" it may or may not be from a legal standpoint, and however much his speech may be repeated as a truism in philosophical treatises on ethics ("rule will reveal the real man"), or construed as a general thesis on "friends and enemies" and redeployed by Hegelian dialectic, reappears in the language of tragedy as a manifestation of man's "character" (*ēthos*), which is to be *deinon*, "too clever for his own good," inventive and disastrous at the same time. The language of tragedy is not philosophical or legal language, and Creon's proclamation is rendered in words that he himself does not understand. It is all the more striking, therefore, that Demosthenes could quote Creon's speech, as Griffith points out, taking it "as a model of civic leadership, with no trace of irony intended" (29), thus sharing with contemporary cultural theory a disregard for the difference that separates the language of tragedy from the discourses of the city that surround it.

Every line of Sophocles' text would bear similar scrutiny, and we cannot simply pass from the discourse of tragedy to legal, political, and philosophical discourse—with their familiar oppositions between family and state, man and woman, all deployed at the level of the concept—without significant loss. This problem bears on all the words that tragedy sets in motion around kinship and justice, family and state, man and woman, the living and the dead. Is this not what Creon learns in the end after hearing of Eurydice's suicide, when he appears onstage lamenting in the tones of a woman? "It is a dead man you kill again," he says (1288), singing in this scene in dochmiac lyrics for the first time, his voice now accompanied by the *aulos*—the song of the flute that was craftily invented by Athena when she took the gruesome gift of Perseus, the horrifying head of the Gorgon with all her snaky hair, and transformed the screams of the Medusa into music, which she called "the many-voiced song."[46]

NOTES

1. See Jean-Pierre Vernant, "La belle mort et le cadavre outragé," in *L'individue, la mort, l'amour* (Paris: Gallimard), 41–79; Vernant, "A 'Beautiful Death' and the Dis-figured Corpse in Homeric Epic," in *Mortals and Immortals: Collected Essays*, ed. Froma Zeitlin (Princeton, NJ: Princeton University Press, 1991), 50–74. See also Charles Segal, *Tragedy and Civilization: An Interpretation of Sophocles* (Norman: University of Oklahoma Press, 1981), 157.

2. I have used several translations throughout (with occasional small changes of my own), principally Hugh Lloyd-Jones (unless otherwise noted). Line numbers vary, mostly as a result of a few contested speeches, and I follow Lloyd-Jones throughout. See *Sophocles*, trans. and ed. Lloyd-Jones (Cambridge: Harvard University Press [Loeb Classical Library vol. 21], 1994); and *The Complete Greek Tragedies, Sophocles, Vol. 1: Oedipus the King, Oedipus at Colonus, Antigone*, trans. David Grene (Chicago: University of Chicago Press, 1991). See also *Sophocles*, trans. F. Storr (Cambridge: Harvard University Press [Loeb Classical Library], 1962). I have consulted the extensive annotations in *Antigone*, ed. Martin L. D'Ooge (New York: Ginn and Co., 1885), and the more recent French translation with useful notes by Nicole Loraux in *Antigone*, trans. Paul Mazon, with introduction, notes, and postface by Loraux (Paris: Les Belles Lettres, 2002). For another useful recent translation with good notes, see *Sophocles Antigone*, trans. Reginald Gibbons and Charles Segal (Oxford: Oxford University Press, 2003). Finally, and above all, see the indispensable critical edition of the Greek text, *Sophocles Antigone*, ed. Mark Griffith (Cambridge: Cambridge University Press, 1999), with comprehensive and detailed notes from which I have drawn extensively.

3. Jean-Pierre Vernant, "Greek Tragedy: Problems of Interpretation," in *The Structuralist Controversy: The Languages of Criticism and the Sciences of Man*, ed. Richard Macksey and Eugenio Donato (Baltimore: Johns Hopkins University Press, 1970), 273–89.

4. For G. W. F. Hegel's emphasis on the Romantic and, in my view, revisionist fascination with the supposedly "purer" love that is possible between brother and sister—shared by Percy Bysshe Shelley and others—see George Steiner, *Antigones* (Oxford: Oxford University Press, 1984).

5. The motif of the friend, concealed by Storr beneath "brother" and "sister," nevertheless emerges once more at the end, as Antigone stands on the verge of her descent: "Unwept, friendless, unwedded [*aklautos, aphilos, anumenaios*], I am conducted, unhappy one... lamented by no friend [*oudeis philōn stenazei*]" (876–82).

6. Memory (Mnemosyne) is the mother of the muses, but each genre has its muse, as well as its music. See Jean-Luc Nancy, *The Muses*, trans. Peggy Kamuf (Stanford: Stanford University Press, 1996). For further remarks on memory in different discourses, see Marcel Detienne, *Masters of Truth in Archaic Greece*, trans. Janet Lloyd (Cambridge: MIT Press, 1996); and Pietro Pucci, *Hesiod and the*

Language of Poetry (Baltimore: Johns Hopkins University Press, 1977).

7. Ruth Padel, *Whom Gods Destroy: Elements of Greek and Tragic Madness* (Princeton, NJ: Princeton University Press, 1995), 249; see also Padel, *In and Out of the Mind: Greek Images of the Tragic Self* (Princeton, NJ: Princeton University Press, 1992).

8. Bernard Williams, *Shame and Necessity* (Berkeley: University of California Press, 1993), 23. See especially "Centres of Agency," 21–49.

9. Christopher Gill, *Personality in Greek Epic, Tragedy and Philosophy: The Self in Dialogue* (Oxford: Oxford University Press, 1996).

10. Michael Frede, for example, has provocatively argued that Aristotle's *De Anima* provides an account of the "body" that is not only quite far removed from the Cartesian concept of "extended substance," as opposed to "thinking substance" (a point that has often been made), as well as removed from the broader Christian framework of "body" and "soul," but also that Aristotle's notion is profoundly anti-Platonic, and gives Aristotle's work a much more foreign character than many modern readers suppose, such that emotions, desires, and dispositions, as aspects of bodily life, are understood as part of the activity of the soul itself and not opposed to it, as reason is opposed to appetite or passion. Bodily phenomena in Aristotle are thus understood in ways that—and this is the connection I wish to stress here—bring Aristotle's thought far closer to the discourse of tragedy and make him far more capable of articulating (as he does in his *Rhetoric*) what the role of emotion is in the experience of tragedy. See Frede, "On Aristotle's Conception of the Soul," in *Essays on Aristotle's De Anima*, ed. Martha C. Nussbaum and Amélia Oksenberg Rorty (Oxford: Oxford University Press, 1992), 93–107. On the issue of the body and emotion in relation to ethics, see also Christopher Gill, "The Personality Unified by Reason's Rule," in *Personality*, 240–320. Thanks to Alexandrine Schniewind for some remarks in an unpublished paper on the history of the "soul" that helped me to see this more clearly.

11. In fact, the "corpse" in *Antigone*, in contrast with Williams' epic references, is more often "*nekron*." For further remarks on the "body" in this regard, see Adriana Cavarero, "On the Body of Antigone," in *Stately Bodies: Literature, Philosophy, and the Question of Gender*, trans. Robert de Lucca and Deanna Shemek (Ann Arbor: University of Michigan Press, 2002), 13–97.

12. Nicole Loraux, *Tragic Ways of Killing a Woman*, trans. Anthony Forster (Harvard University Press, 1987). For further discussion of death in connection with femininity, as it is figured in different discursive or (as I prefer here) generic contexts, see Jean-Pierre Vernant, "Figures féminines de la mort en Grèce," in *L'individue, la mort, l'amour*, 131–52; Vernant, "Feminine Figures of Death in Greece," *Mortals and Immortals*, 95–110.

13. Carol Jacobs, "Dusting Antigone," *Modern Language Notes* 111, no. 5 (December 1996): 889–917.

14. Segal, *Tragedy and Civilization*, 167.

15. Williams, *Shame and Necessity*, 49.

16. Danielle Allen, *The World of Prometheus: The Politics of Punishing in Democratic Athens* (Princeton, NJ: Princeton University Press, 2000), 76.

17. As Suzanne Stern-Gillet explains, the word *philia* does not correspond to what we think of today as "friendship," and in Homer's time, laws of *philia* and hospitality required that a man of a certain rank could claim the right to stay at the house of another "equal," even if the two had never met before, with the result that the host could, in turn, claim such a right of others, when passing through unknown territory. These are laws of aristocratic *philia* that have little resemblance to what we think of today as the intimate emotional bond that links two "friends" to each other on the basis of "free choice" or "affection," a framework that we may take too quickly for granted for explaining the discourse of *philia* and friendship in *Antigone*, or Antigone's tie to Polyneices. Stern-Gillet, *Aristotle's Philosophy of Friendship* (Albany: SUNY Press, 1995), 6–7. The point is still more complex if we note that Creon's discourse on "friends," apparently tied to the logic of the city (which, like hospitality laws, would legislate over friendship obligations automatically), is given in a language that suggests quite strikingly that one can "choose" one's friends (see Griffith, 159).

18. I cite Antigone from Grene's translation, line 142; but see also Griffith, where the line in question is given as 126.

19. Froma Zeitlin, *Playing the Other: Gender and Society in Classical Greek Literature* (Chicago: University of Chicago Press. 1996), 334. On "blood" (*haima*) in connection with the gods, whose role in parentage has been overlooked in some recent analysis (consider the Chorus' remark that Antigone is *theogenes*), see Giulia Sissa and Marcel Detienne, *The Daily Life of the Greek Gods*, trans. Janet Lloyd (Stanford: Stanford University Press, 2000), 28–33.

On incest, family, kinship, and *philia*, see Jean-Pierre Vernant and Pierre Vidal-Naquet, *Myth and Tragedy in Ancient Greece*, trans. Janet Lloyd (New York: Zone, 1988), 102–11; and Nicole Loraux, *Born of the Earth: Myth and Politics in Athens*, trans. Selina Stewart (Ithaca, NY: Cornell University Press, 2000), 18–27. On *philia*, see also Judith Butler, *Antigone's Claim: Kinship between Life and Death* (Stanford: Stanford University Press, 2002).

20. Martha Nussbaum, "The Antigone: Conflict, Vision, and Simplification," in *The Fragility of Goodness: Luck and Ethics in Greek Tragedy and Philosophy* (Cambridge: Cambridge University Press, 1986), 51–82.

21. See Loraux, *Born of the Earth*, 30–31, 58–59.

22. Hugh Lloyd-Jones, *The Justice of Zeus* (Berkeley: University of California Press, 1971), 115.

23. Compare Lloyd-Jones' perspective with that of Nussbaum, whose reading of Antigone begins with this astonishing sentence, which transports the entire universe of Sophocles' play into the arena of Aristotelian ethics, judgment, and moderation: "The Antigone is a play about practical reason" (*The Fragility of Goodness*, 51). And later, "the play is about Creon's failure" (60). For some excellent developments of "punishment" in antiquity, see Allen, *The World of Prometheus*.

24. Jacobs quotes G. W. F. Hegel, *Phenomenology of Spirit*, trans. A. V. Miller (Oxford: Oxford University Press, 1977), 475, 288. See also Hegel, *The Phenomenology of Mind*, trans. J. B. Ballie (London: Allen and Unwin, 1910). "Since the community gets itself subsistence only by breaking in upon family happiness, and dissolving [individual] self-consciousness into the universal, it creates its enemy for itself within its own gates, creates in what it suppresses, and what is at the same time essential to it—womankind in general. Womankind—the everlasting irony of the community–changes by intrigue the universal purpose of government into a private end, transforms its universal activity into a work of this or that specific individual, and perverts the universal property of the state into a possession and ornament for the family." Quoted from *Hegel on Tragedy*, ed. Anne Paolucci and Henry Paolucci (New York: Doubleday [Anchor Books], 1962), 284.

25. Jacobs, "Dusting Antigone," 895.

26. Kirk Ormand, *Exchange and the Maiden: Marriage in Sophoclean Tragedy* (Austin: University of Texas Press. 1999); Victoria Wohl, *Intimate Commerce: Exchange, Gender, and Subjectivity in Greek*

Tragedy (Austin: University of Texas Press, 1998); Rush Rehm, *Marriage to Death: The Conflation of Wedding and Funeral Rituals in Greek Tragedy* (Princeton, NJ: Princeton University Press, 1994).

27. Marcel Detienne and Jean-Pierre Vernant, *Cunning Intelligence in Greek Society and Culture*, trans. Janet Lloyd (Chicago: University of Chicago Press, 1991).

28. This is not the place to elaborate the point, but a prolonged engagement would be valuable here regarding Aristotle's claim that tragedy is not about the presentation of character (in contrast to the novel), but rather about plot, since tragedy concerns happiness and unhappiness, which depends not on the person's virtue alone but on events or actions in which that character's destiny is unfolded. This is one reason why Aristotle says the better tragic hero is a good man who suffers, since this shows unhappiness coming to one who does not deserve it (a point that is requisite for pity on the part of the audience as well, since pity is not felt for a bad man who suffers). Nussbaum has explored this usefully in her account of "luck" or fortune. See "Interlude 2: Luck and the Tragic Emotions," in *The Fragility of Goodness*, 378–94. See also Elizabeth Belfiore's careful treatment of "character" in *Tragic Pleasures: Aristotle on Plot and Emotion* (Princeton, NJ: Princeton University Press, 1992). Also on luck and ethics in ancient thought see Bernard Williams, *Moral Luck* (Cambridge: Cambridge University Press, 1981).

29. On the lyric, see Christopher Gill, *Personality in Greek Epic, Tragedy and Philosophy*; Helene Foley, ed., *The Homeric Hymn to Demeter: Translation, Commentary and Interpretive Essays* (Princeton, NJ: Princeton University Press, 1993); on funeral lament, see Nicole Loraux, *The Invention of Athens: The Funeral Oration in the Classical City*, trans. Alan Sheridan (New York: Zone Books, 2006).

30. Sheldon Sacks, *Fiction and the Shape of Belief* (Berkeley: University of California Press, 1964).

31. Claude Lévi-Strauss, "The Structural Study of Myth," in *Critical Theory Since 1965*, ed. Hazard Adams and Leroy Searle (Gainesville: University of Florida Press, 1986), 809–23.

32. Gérard Genette, *Narrative Discourse. An Essay in Method*, trans. Jane E. Lewin (Oxford: Blackwell, 1980); Seymour Chatman, *Story and Discourse: Narrative Structure in Fiction and Film* (Ithaca, NY: Cornell University Press, 1978).

33. For a brief but very helpful discussion of the legend and some variants, see Griffith, 5–12.
34. See Hayden White, *Tropics of Discourse: Essays in Cultural Criticism* (Baltimore: Johns Hopkins University Press, 1985); Edward Hallett Carr, *What Is History?* (New York: Random House, 1961).
35. Vernant, "Greek Tragedy: Problems of Interpretation," 281. Vernant adds, "I think that when you read this tragedy you agree with Antigone about unwritten laws. Unfortunately this interpretation is indefensible in the organization of the text" (281). Creon follows the laws of the actual city at Sophocles' time, Vernant claims, but he adds that tragedy introduces yet another dimension: "Neither the *nomoi* of Creon nor the *nomoi* of Antigone are sufficient. They are both but aspects of the *nomos* of Zeus. I would point out right away, to indicate my disagreement with the Hegelian position, that this *nomos* of Zeus cannot be mediation because it is absolutely incomprehensible from the human viewpoint" (281). On the question of burial laws, Vernant's position has been contested, and Griffith points out that the extant evidence "is by no means clear-cut or self-evident" (Griffith, 29). Burial within the boundaries of the polis was denied to traitors and violators of temples, but this does not mean that the burial owed to the chthonic gods could be simply overlooked. We should note, moreover, that Polyneices is not the only one to have been denied a burial. As Griffith also observes, the legend of Antigone, and the house of Labdacus, generally, includes the arrival of Theseus with an Athenian army, following Creon's catastrophic decline, and the eventual burial of all the Argive dead, who have been left *ataphos*, without a tomb, like Polyneices—a fact that is mentioned briefly by Tiresias in Sophocles' version when he speaks of the pollution of the altars. As Griffith ultimately and rightly notes with respect to the question of the legal validity of Creon's edict, however, "It does not seem to have been S[ophocles'] purpose to provide a systematic analysis of, and solution to, these issues; instead, he has composed a tragedy" (32). It is this difference between legal and tragic discourse that we wish to underscore here.
36. In this respect, it is tempting to agree with Jacques Lacan when he insists—though readers with less experience of psychoanalysis might be surprised—that Creon's fault is not a "personal" or "psychological" one, a failure of judgment, or a vaguely Christianized "sin of pride," or a "fear of femininity" (which is not to say that ancient Greece was not a misogynistic culture or that such psychological issues are entirely irrelevant to tragic drama). Rather

than emphasizing Creon's individual psychology and his conspicuous egotism ("I won't be beaten by a woman," etc. [525, 578–79,
678, 740, 746]), as one might expect the psychoanalyst to do,
Lacan insists that Creon's mistake is to impose a law at the level of
universality, what Lacan calls a "good that would rule over all,"
legislating over "friends and enemies," in contrast to Antigone's
radical adherence to a form of singularity, her "irrational" attachment to the "unsubstitutable" Polyneices, who (unlike a husband
or children, as she says) is singular and "irreplaceable," which is to
say, outside any general law, outside "writing" and the discourse of
universals, detached from the level of the "concept" that governs
so many Hegelian and post-Hegelian readings, dominated as they
are by "family" and "state," "man" and "woman." Lacan thus
claims, rightly in my view, that Antigone cannot be positioned in
the usual Hegelian way as representing a principle or law that is
dialectically opposed to Creon's law, but rather that her desire is
of another order from the level of the concept and universality that
captures Creon's position. This critique of the Hegelian frame is
extremely useful, especially insofar as it detaches Antigone from
the position of "protest" commonly ascribed to her, in which one
law (family or blood) is opposed to another law (that of the state
and universality), as I have argued elsewhere, but the opposition
between "universality" and "singularity," which has been central
to Lacanian readings of the play (largely guided by Lacan's account
of sexual difference in *Encore*, where the universal law of masculinity is contrasted with a feminine refusal of totality), in that
it construes Creon's position from the standpoint of the Kantian
universal, is also dubious. Lacan is much too quick in applying an
explicitly Kantian formula to Creon's position on the "moral law,"
for it is quite clear, as Stephen Gill has pointed out in convincing
detail, that the Kantian notion of a moral will determined by a
universal law is simply nowhere on the horizon of Greek culture.
Such an emphasis on moral universality obscures not only Creon's
self-aggrandizement but also the entire horizon of ethical thought
that distinguishes the ancient world from that of Kantianism. See
Lacan, *The Ethics of Psychoanalysis*, ed. Jacques-Alain Miller,
trans. Dennis Porter (New York: Norton, 1992). For the critique
of Kantianism as inappropriately imposed on ancient thought, see
Gill, *Personality in Greek Epic, Tragedy and Philosophy*, and Williams, *Shame and Necessity*. For Lacanian readings of *Antigone*,
see Alenka Zupancic, *Ethics of the Real: Kant, Lacan* (New York:

Verso, 2000) and Joan Copjec, *Imagine There's No Woman: Ethics and Sublimation* (Cambridge: MIT Press, 2003), 12–47. See also Charles Shepherdson, "Of Love and Beauty in Lacan's Antigone," in *Lacan and the Limits of Language* (New York: Fordham University Press, 2008), 54–86.

37. As Samuel Weber has said, it is difficult to read this play today without thinking of other rulers who speak loudly of "democracy" but show themselves to be committed to a very different form of power. See Weber, "Antigone's 'Nomos,'" in *Theatricality as Medium* (New York: Fordham University Press, 2004), 121–40.

38. Segal, *Tragedy and Civilization*, 161–66.

39. Griffith has noted the strangeness of Antigone's formulation, "I'll bury my brother, and I'll bury yours too, if you won't," as if she were speaking of two different people, which, in a sense, she is, since Polyneices, and indeed perhaps the meaning of "brother," to her is (now) different from what it means to Ismene. The phrasing is so strange that proposals have been made to reformulate the construction or construe it differently, and thus "escape the strangeness," as Griffith says (131).

40. Griffith, 268.

41. Indeed, the fact that it is not something "she wants" is evident in her lament, when she acknowledges the loss of everything she might have wished for "in person," as it were, and "for herself." Readers who have seen this lamentation as contradicting the "unity of her character," which has been otherwise so apparently cold, so steadfast and unrelenting, do not capture the careful delineation by which Sophocles separates her "personal" interest (her "care for herself") from her action as a heroic figure, which is precisely the separation Creon cannot accomplish.

42. This difference between, on the one hand, Creon's contradictory assertion of "himself" into the very language of universality that he takes himself to be using even as his speech subverts it (a point Lacanian readers have missed, with their emphasis on Creon's purported Kantianism), and, on the other hand, Antigone's use of the "I," or, more precisely, the way her very different "subjectivity" enters into or inhabits the language she uses, goes well beyond the difference between the "public" and "private" that Segal has used to characterize their two distinct ways of speaking (*Tragedy and Civilization*, 161–65), just as it goes beyond the alternative between "masculine" universality and "feminine" particularity or relationality that organizes Foley's reading of the play, oriented as it

is by Carol Gilligan's thesis on the "ethics of care" (Carol Gilligan, *In a Different Voice: Psychological Theory and Women's Development* [Cambridge: Harvard University Press, 1982]). The intersection of subjectivity and language here, it seems to me, has not yet been sufficiently elaborated.

43. Michel Foucault, "What is an Author?" in *The Essential Foucault*, ed. Paul Rabinow and Nikolas Rose (New York: New Press, 2003), 377–91; Emile Benveniste, "Subjectivity in Language," in *Critical Theory Since 1965*, 728–33; Wolfgang Iser, "Toward a Literary Anthropology," in *Prospecting: From Reader Response to Literary Anthropology* (Baltimore: Johns Hopkins University Press, 1989), 262–84; Wayne Booth, *The Rhetoric of Fiction* (Chicago: University of Chicago Press, 1961). For a Lacanian elaboration of the difference between the shifter and the proper name, see Wilfred Ver Eecke, "Translator's Introduction" to Alphonse de Waehlens, *Schizophrenia* (Pittsburgh: Duquesne University Press 1978), 1–25.

44. For an elaboration of this point in relation to Hegelian readings, see Shepherdson, "Of Love and Beauty in Lacan's Antigone," 54–86.

45. I cite from *Sophocles Antigone*, trans. Gibbons and Segal.

46. On the music of these lines, see Griffith, 341–46; on the *aulos* and Medusa, see Belfiore, 9–39; on the cry and its transformation into song, which is something quite distinct from lament in general (i.e., outside the theater of Dionysos), see Nicole Loraux, *The Mourning Voice: An Essay on Greek Tragedy*, trans. Elizabeth Trapnell Rawlings (Ithaca, NY: Cornell University Press, 2002), 54–65.

3

The Laius Complex

MARK BUCHAN

Criticism of the *Oedipus Tyrannus* (hereafter, *OT*) has often foundered on an old and well-known problem. There are the conflicting reports of the drama's most crucial and opaque event, the action at the crossroads where Laius, the ruler of Thebes, meets his death. This antiscene is available to us only through the garbled reports of two witnesses. As Oedipus hears that Laius' death occurred at a crossroads, he will remember his own actions at a crossroads, and therefore the possibility opens up that Oedipus is the murderer of Laius and his entourage. Much of the play's momentum depends on the way that this account of the murder replaces an earlier, apparently contradictory, account. Laius' slave had insisted that he saw many robbers at the crossroads: ληστὰς ἔφασκε, (he kept saying 'robbers'; 122).

Most agree that the second account is correct. But the discrepancy has come into focus in recent years. Sandor Goodhart suggested that the gap between the account of Oedipus and the slave means that Sophocles is interrogating the process of mythmaking itself, a process that we are complicit in insofar as we identify with Oedipus.[1] For Frederick Ahl, the play is not about Oedipus' objective guilt (according to Ahl, if we pay careful enough attention to the evidence provided by the play, he is innocent) but about his subjective guilt, his desire to be found guilty.[2] Once more this tells us something about our own psyches as watchers and theatergoers. Driven by an unconscious *horror vacui*, we prefer a knowing guilt (an identification with Oedipus as criminal) to a more terrifying, abstract sense of guilt (perhaps an identification with the plague-ridden and lost community of Thebes, who seem not to know who did it), and therefore construct Oedipus as parricide.[3] Oedipus, and whoever identifies with him, is in the same position as the famous subject hailed in the Althusserian process of interpellation: in response to the tale of murder, Oedipus prefers to see himself as the murderer than to confront the abyss of a lack of knowledge of what happens at the crossroads, a lack to which he is nevertheless drawn.[4]

But such theories bring problems. They fly in the face of the obvious: the overall coherence of the plot so revered by Aristotle, the accepted status of Oedipus in myth as a parricide, and also the "basic narrative contract" between playwright and assumed audience, not to mention the power of the Freudian tradition that takes the peculiar and problematic power of the desire for incest and parricide for granted.[5] So how can we accept this and yet continue to recognize some of the critical power of these Ahl and Goodhart readings and the problematic aspects of the story that they linger over? They have surely shown us something. Indeed, many infelicities are present in Sophocles' plot, neatly summed up by Charles Segal:

> We also have to accept the facts that the sole survivor and witness simply lied about how many attackers there were (118–119) and that Oedipus is mistaken in thinking that he killed "all" the men escorting Laius (813). And we have to admit that Sophocles has left vague the amount of time that had elapsed between the killing of Laius and this witness' return to Thebes to find Oedipus already in place as king (758–62). During this unspecified interval (see 558–61), Oedipus has managed to defeat the Sphinx, marry Jocasta, and become installed as king of Thebes.[6]

Are there not too many facts for us to accept?

Critical progress can be made, but not by delving into the psyche of Oedipus. More interesting possibilities open up when we read the play through the eyes of a crucial secondary figure, the slave of Laius who both witnesses the events at the crossroads and receives the condemned baby Oedipus from Laius. When we break with the temptation to identify with Oedipus, we can begin to reimagine the play and Oedipus' role in it. But far from an anti-Freudian polemic, this reading will elaborate on, and defend, the readings of Sigmund Freud, for it is in the characters around Oedipus, not Oedipus himself, where we learn the most about the Oedipus complex. The slave functions as a test case of the way the Oedipal problematic haunts the psyches of those around him. This journey into the life of the slave will ultimately produce an answer to our central question: why does this slave, the one eyewitness to the scene at the crossroads, keep insisting that there were "many robbers," not the solitary Oedipus? The slave's dilemma—to kill or not to kill, to flee or not to flee—doubles that of Oedipus himself, whose own life is a curious mixture of murder and flight.

By ignoring Oedipus in a search for the Oedipus complex, I am already on the path of Freud, for where did Freud find evidence of the Oedipus complex? Certainly he found it not in Oedipus himself, nor in any actor on the stage, but in us, in our reactions to him, and in the persistent attraction to the drama shown by its audience:

> If *Oedipus Rex* moves a modern audience no less than it did the contemporary Greek one, the explanation can only be that its effect does not lie in the contrast between destiny and human will, but is to be looked for in the particular nature of the material on which that contrast is exemplified....His destiny moves us only because it might have been ours—because the oracle laid the same curse on us before our birth as on him. It is the fate of all of us, perhaps, to direct our first sexual impulse toward our mother and our first hatred and our first murderous wish against our father....Here is one in whom these primaeval wishes of our childhood have been fulfilled, and we shrink back from him with the whole force of the repression by which those wishes have since that time been held down within us. While the poet, as he unravels the past, brings to light the guilt of Oedipus, he is at the same time compelling us to recognize our own inner minds, in which those same impulses, though suppressed, are still to be found.[7]

In the play, Oedipus runs away from the oracle that tells of his parricide and incest, but he eventually stops running, first at the crossroads, where he kills his father, and later at Thebes, where he marries Jocasta. But, for Freud, it is at the very time that Oedipus stops that we start running. Even as we are stuck to our seats, we consciously turn away from Oedipus in horror. But this horror is checked by an unconscious enjoyment, an enjoyment repeated each time we drag ourselves to the play. We get off on Oedipus' crimes through Oedipus.[8] Freud relentlessly implicates us in every reading and viewing of the play. What if all our reactions to the play, whether critical, academic, or aesthetic, are part of an ongoing effort to keep at a proper distance from this underground, obscene enjoyment? Our critical vocabularies keep us from getting too close to the terrifying content of the action even as they allow us to approach, circuitously, this forbidden fruit.[9] This could be one definition of the Oedipus complex: a structure that gives us access to a regulated economy of pleasure and pain (the interlocking domains of the reality and pleasure principle), on condition that we obey a shared prohibition, the taboo on a traumatic mixture of pleasure-pain that the fantasy of incest keeps at the proper distance.

So if Freud looks not to Oedipus but to the audience to help us understand the play, and thereby removes Oedipus from center stage, I want to perform a more modest act of decentering, by seeing the play first through the eyes of the slave and only then, via the slave, through the eyes of the other Thebans, and finally on to us, for though there is a marked disjunction between Oedipus' incest and our own conflicting feelings of attraction and revulsion, the slave can be used to bridge that gap and also to mediate between clashing critical interpretations. If the audience flees Oedipus in horror as Oedipus begins to stay in one place, Oedipus' slave runs away as much as Oedipus himself, until his flight stops, with great violence, in the torture scene at the end. Having summoned the slave from the mountains, Oedipus forces him to tell the truth, swapping physical pain for psychic pain. So what follows is a (psycho) analysis of this ongoing flight.

Let us isolate the life story of the slave, as the play presents it. We find out that he was not purchased but brought up in the house.[10] This seems to emphasize a good relationship to his master, the closeness of his ties, and to provide evidence of a quality that is later confirmed: he is loyal to house and master.[11] But this loyal slave is entrusted with an unusual task. There has been an oracle, though the slave refers simply to a *logos*, the meaning of which is significantly indeterminate: "Κτενεῖν νιν τοὺς τεκόντας ἦν λόγος [There was a *logos*, predicting enmity to the death between parents and child]" (1176).[12]

This *logos* relates to the earlier oracle that Laius and Jocasta (as Jocasta tells us earlier) interpreted to mean that the father would die at the hands of his son. Because of it, the slave is entrusted with killing the child. But, through pity, he chooses to spare the baby, giving him instead to a Corinthian shepherd. After this, we have no information about his life; we do not know, for example, whether he knows what happens to the baby Oedipus. But he reappears later as a witness to a killing at a crossroads. He flees back home to Thebes, where rumor has it that he made a claim about brigands at the crossroads: "ληστὰς ἔφασκε" (He kept saying many robbers). There is a presumption that he went to the crossroads as a member of Laius' party, but the evidence for this is shaky, mired in the general darkness surrounding the numbers of Laius' party.[13] Further, his initial return to Thebes is also shrouded in rumor. Only the phrase "ληστὰς ἔφασκε" is to be relied on. What is clearer is that, when he finds out Oedipus has returned to Thebes to become the new ruler, he immediately asks Jocasta for permission to flee once more, which he promptly does. He is later retrieved from the mountains and forced to confess. It was he who failed to kill Oedipus, but instead handed him over to a Corinthian shepherd, with the well-known consequences.

Let us begin our interpretation with the torture scene at the end. Dragged back from the mountains, Oedipus demands that the slave tell him the truth about his origins. With Freudian hindsight, it is easy to view this scene as a fundamental perversion of the clinical situation in psychoanalysis. The slave is forced to articulate a traumatic scene, an injunction to kill a child. His response to that injunction will determine his subjective existence, for his evasion of the order that constituted the first scene, Laius' command to kill the child, is linked to his flight from the second traumatic scene that he is not asked to talk about by Oedipus, the events at the crossroads. The slave lives a life defined by his response to this command of the master, and it is this that Oedipus forces him to recount. In the clinical situation, too, a subject agrees to talk about and around the traumatic events that determine his or her behavior. Psychoanalysis explores the traumatic scene that causes the analysand's everyday behavior, but it is central to psychoanalytic ethics that the analysand be willing to undergo such a process.[14] The analysand takes responsibility for the trauma that plagues him or her by transferring the problem over to the analyst. In the slave's case, he is forced to talk by Oedipus who remains oblivious to the slave's suffering.

So we have two scenes, and both involve attempts on Oedipus' life. In the first, Laius orders Oedipus to be killed, in the second he confronts him at the crossroads. On both occasions, the slave exhibits a curious mix of activity and passivity. At the crossroads, he chooses to witness at least part of what happens, but then flees. At the birth of Oedipus, he seems to obeys his master Laius' injunction to kill (passivity) but then subverts it by not killing the child (activity), but only by feigning that he has killed it (a strange mixture of the two). The scenes both relate to the slave's role in the near killing of Oedipus. In the first, the slave runs away from Laius' order to kill Oedipus: he escapes the situation by pretending to kill him. He has his cake of obeying Laius and eats it by not killing Oedipus either. In the second, a violent conflict spontaneously breaks out between father and son. In the first scenario, the slave acted as a bridge between Oedipus and his father, acting as the link that Laius hoped would result in Oedipus' death; as it turns out, he becomes the unreliable human link whose pity allows Oedipus to live. In the second the slave watches the encounter between father and son, but this time without his own mediation. He witnesses what happens when he is absent from the scene.

Critics commonly refer to the encounter at the crossroads in Freudian vocabulary as a "primal scene," but for whom? The prime watcher of this scene is the slave. But it traumatizes only because it is linked to Laius' earlier command to kill the child. The scenario of deadly rivalry between father and son at the crossroads is the scenario the slave tried to avoid; he had hoped to remove the baby Oedipus from danger. But if at Thebes he had a choice, at the crossroads he simply watches. So his is a strange sort of impotence, since he is directly responsible for the situation that causes it. Without his decision to spare Oedipus, the scene at the crossroads could not have happened. The prophecy, which the slave had hoped to subvert, returns, in the actions at the crossroads.

What exactly did the slave see at the crossroads? One clue might lurk in the slave's later report of the prophecy, as he explains how he received the child:

OI. ῍Η γὰρ δίδωσιν ἥδε σοι; ΘΕ. Μάλιστ᾽, ἄναξ.
OI. Ὡς πρὸς τί χρείας; ΘΕ. Ὡς ἀναλώσαιμί νιν.
OI. Τεκοῦσα τλήμων; ΘΕ. Θεσφάτων γ᾽ ὄκνῳ κακῶν.
OI. Ποίων; ΘΕ. Κτενεῖν νιν τοὺς τεκόντας ἦν λόγος.

[Oed. What? Did this woman give it to you?
Slave. Absolutely, my lord.
Oed. For what purpose?
Slave. That I should destroy it.
Oed. She, the bearer of the child, had the heart?
Slave. From her fear of evil oracles.
Oed. Of what kind?
Slave. There was a *logos*, predicting enmity to the death between parents and child.] (1173–76)

There was a *logos*. A *logos* that said what? We take it for granted that the oracle reports the death of the father at the hands of the son, as the sequence of the events that follow (Oedipus kills Laius) and the former interpretation of it given by Jocasta suggest, for she claims that it prophesied Laius would die at the hands of his son. A worry here is the disjunction with the reading of the oracle as provided by the slave, which speaks of the plurality of those to be killed: "τοὺς τεκόντας" (There was a logos that he would kill the *parents*). But the Greek has a more fundamental ambiguity. Does it refer to the death of the parents at the hands of a son, or the death of the son at the hands of the parents? That is, should we take "νιν" or "τεκόντας" as the subject of the infinitive?[15] If the latter, then by killing his child together with Jocasta, Laius would directly bring about this *logos*: the parents would kill the child.

The word *logos* itself highlights the way that the authoritative oracular predictions are trapped in words, subject to all the ambiguity of language, with the constant need for further exegesis to ensure clear meaning.[16] It is as if in the very phrase "Κτενεῖν νιν τοὺς τεκόντας

ἦν λόγος" that the oracle predicts its immediate effects, as the threatened death of the parents is overtaken first by parental fear, and then
the desires of the parents to kill the child, relayed back to us through
the words of the slave. This perfectly fits with the dramatic moment
described; Jocasta vacillates as she is caught up in the ambiguity of
this *logos*. Neither child nor parents are yet dead. We are trapped in
a moment of hesitation before the polysemy of these words will be
fixed by an act of murder. For now, let us merely note the difficulty of
translating this *logos*, which marks a slippage from the authoritative
(but absent) discourse of the oracle and its problematic articulation in
words: "Word on the street had it that parents and child would always
hate each other *until one or the other died.*"

But consider now how this ambiguity impacts our slave, for the oracle's authority alone does not haunt him, but only by its peculiar relationship to a second discourse of authority. Laius has put the slave in a
peculiarly powerful, and uncomfortable, position: he can now choose
between the life of the father and the life of the child. The slave is caught
between the command of the father and the command of the oracle,
thoroughly implicated in this enmity to the death between parents and
child that now rests in his hands. And what does he do? He tries to
defuse that enmity by opening up a space between parents and child
by sparing the son, and then sending him to the Corinthian shepherd.
Might it not be that initial, still-to-be-decided enmity that returns at the
crossroads? And is this not the first thing that the slave sees?

Here is Oedipus' own brief account of the meeting at the crossroads:

Καί σοι, γύναι, τἀληθὲς ἐξερῶ. Τριπλῆς
ὅτ᾽ ἦ κελεύθου τῆσδ᾽ ὁδοιπορῶν πέλας,
ἐνταῦθά μοι κῆρύξ τε κἀπὶ πωλικῆς
ἀνὴρ ἀπήνης ἐμβεβώς, οἷον σὺ φής,
ξυνηντίαζον· κἀξ ὁδοῦ μ᾽ ὅ θ᾽ ἡγεμὼν
αὐτός θ᾽ ὁ πρέσβυς πρὸς βίαν ἠλαυνέτην.
Κἀγὼ τὸν ἐκτρέποντα, τὸν τροχηλάτην,
παίω δι᾽ ὀργῆς· καί μ᾽ ὁ πρέσβυς ὡς ὁρᾷ
ὄχου παραστείχοντα, τηρήσας μέσον
κάρα διπλοῖς κέντροισί μου καθίκετο.
Οὐ μὴν ἴσην γ᾽ ἔτισεν, ἀλλὰ συντόμως
σκήπτρῳ τυπεὶς ἐκ τῆσδε χειρὸς ὕπτιος
μέσης ἀπήνης εὐθὺς ἐκκυλίνδεται·
κτείνω δὲ τοὺς ξύμπαντας.

[And to you, lady, I will tell the full truth. When as I went along I was near this junction of three roads, there I was met by a herald, and a man riding in a horse-drawn coach, such as you describe; and both the leader and the old man himself were for driving me forcibly from the road. I angrily struck the man who was pushing me aside, the driver of the carriage, and when the old man saw this, he watched from the carriage till I was going past, and came down full on my head with his double goad. I tell you, he more than paid for it. In an instant, hit by the staff in this hand of mine, he immediately rolls out of the middle of the carriage on his back; and I kill every man of them.] (800–813)

Rather than imagining the scene through the eyes of Oedipus, what happens if we imagine it through the eyes of Laius? A king and his entourage meet a helpless young man, and rather than step aside, they embark on violence. So a second, unmediated encounter between Laius and an innocent man repeats the first imaginary scene that Laius' command forced the slave to contemplate. What if the slave fled at this point, with Laius and his entourage about to confront Oedipus?

If this complicates matters at the crossroads, it does so by returning us to Laius' order to kill the child. What is at stake in this order? First, to disobey his master is to defy his symbolic identity as faithful slave. His refusal is overdetermined: it would result in the destruction of his own identity as faithful slave of Laius, through his betrayal of his master's order, as well as the physical destruction of the master with whom he identifies. A symbolic death (his very self-conception) is belatedly followed by a real one, the death of the master who himself provides a prop for the slave's identity. But to obey Laius means incurring the guilt of killing a child. We thus have the horrifying ethical situation of being given a forced choice between two evils, where part of the evil lies in being directly responsible for the death that ensues. The ethical horror is linked to the way it is impossible to avoid guilt, a guilt directly linked to one's own act.[17]

But if Sophocles' play raises this ethical dilemma, the slave fails to face it squarely.[18] He refuses to obey his master's command, resists his authority, but only by a pretense: he feigns killing Oedipus. He saves the child, but he refuses to take any responsibility for his failure to kill it. Again, compare this to the situation of Oedipus, whose flight from the oracle attempts to evade its authority, but only brings about what he intended to avoid: "One knows in advance one's destiny, one tries to evade it, and it is by means of this very attempt that the predicted destiny realizes itself. Without the prophecy, the little Oedipus would live happily with his parents and there would be no 'Oedipus complex.'"[19]

We can say the same thing about the slave. By sparing the child, he destroys both the child and the master. If he had killed Oedipus, Laius would live; if he had told Laius that he would not kill the child, Laius himself would have another opportunity to kill Oedipus. For the greatest catastrophe to occur, the destruction of both parents and child, we need the slave to flee the choice.[20]

Let us turn to the final flight of the slave, away from Thebes and to the mountains when he hears of Oedipus' victory. An analogy with the psychoanalytic situation can again be of help,[21] for what does the arrival of Oedipus at Thebes signify to the slave? That Oedipus has defeated his old master Laius at the crossroads and is his new master. But it returns him to the choice he made to spare Oedipus. The problem is not his desire to avoid the taint of killing a child, but that he feigns killing the child, and therefore continues to appear before his master as a good servant. The play centers on a double betrayal. The slave not only betrays Laius, but he also betrays his desire to betray him. He flees the consequences of the betrayal and, in so doing, preserves a certain image of himself, but at the price of compromising his desire. The consequence will be his master's death. His refusal of his master was always colored by his knowledge of the prophecy of his death, a prophecy he knew well, even as his actions sought to deny the zero-sum logic that the oracle articulated: to spare the child will destroy the parents. So might not this be the true horror, for the slave, of the appearance of Oedipus? He is forced to confront his own responsibility for the death of his master. In Lacanian terms, the Symbolic returns to him his own message, but in inverted form. The sparing of the child hides the desire to harm the master, and the return of Oedipus to Thebes tells him this: "*You* wanted the death of Laius, didn't you? You didn't kill the child, and you *knew* this would mean the master's death, the master who made you what you are! That's what *your* reading of the prophecy signified."[22] The slave's desire to appear as a good slave is corrupted from the beginning with this desire for his master's death, though this knowledge is only consciously available to the slave with hindsight.[23] Given that this desire is incompatible with his own symbolic identity as Laius' faithful servant, it is not surprising that he flees it.[24]

All this untangles during the torture scene, where Oedipus' self-destruction uncannily coincides with his destruction of the ego of the slave. Oedipus' ego, his basic self-conception, dissolves progressively as he discovers his unwitting transgressions. But the slave simultaneously loses his symbolic identity. We are left with a tragic remainder of the selves of both, with all positive symbolic support for their identities gone. They are not so much selves as a leftover of the self, an empty shell with all meaning removed.[25] Oedipus and the slave are mutually compromised, caught up

in each other's desires. The slave falls foul of Oedipus' desperate desire to
know his origins, a desire that causes him to ignore any effect his words
have on any others, in this case, the psychic torture he inflicts on the slave.[26]
But the reverse is equally true. Oedipus is a child of the slave's desire. He
owes his existence to the slave's vacillation in the face of the command of
his master. Oedipus is a living symptom of this double betrayal. He exists
only because of this compromise. Much recent criticism on Oedipus can
be understood as an extended exegesis of Jacques Lacan's dictum that we
are born into the Other's discourse. Oedipus' own name is a sign of this
otherness.[27] But related, and no less crucial, is the way in which Oedipus'
desire is the Other's desire. For Oedipus, the slave crystallizes the desire
of the Other, the mixture of the desire of the oracle for his murder of his
father, and the desire of his father for his own murder. The torture scene
then stages the moment when Oedipus confronts the enigma of the Other's
desire. He tortures the slave in order to find out what the Other wants from
him, to ascertain his position in the cosmos. But instead of finding some
definite desire of his parents, he encounters only their doubts about him.
The certainty of his origins (he finds out he really is the baby cast aside on
the hillside) is in tension with his discovery of the uncertainty of his parents
from the very beginning. They simply did not know what to do with this
Oedipus-child-thing, whether to kill it or spare it. He discovers his incestuous origins, but simultaneously discovers that the Other lacks, that there is
no answer to the problem of the Other's desire.

So let us return to the problem of the "many robbers." If most attention has focused on the slave's suggestion that "many robbers" were
responsible for the death of Laius, there is a second, related discrepancy
that is just as serious. For the oracle, a source with greater authority
than the slave, also refers in the plural to the killers of Laius:[28]

ΚΡ. Τούτου θανόντος νῦν ἐπιστέλλει σαφῶς
τοὺς αὐτοέντας χειρὶ τιμωρεῖν τινας.

[With him dead, Apollo now clearly commands us
to punish the murderers with our hand, whoever they may
   be.] (106–7)

We have two problems: who are the "brigands" spotted at the crossroads
by the slave and repeated in hearsay at Thebes, and who are the multiple
murderers of Laius referred to by the oracle? The play clearly is a
detective story. Oedipus seeks the perpetrator of a crime, but he remains
ignorant that he seeks himself. But why the narrative misdirection? As

Oedipus later says, if the slave sticks to his story, he can never be judged
the killer of Laius, because one can never equal many. Yet, when the
slave appears, Oedipus never asks this question. The puzzling narrative
detail sticks out: ληστὰς ἔφασκε. It has brought a series of critical
responses. Ahl's literal reading takes it a face value, which, in turn,
produces skepticism as to Oedipus' guilt.[29] More metaphorical readings
emphasize that Oedipus, as committer of parrincest, is always already a
"plural figure."[30] Or, following Segal, we can dismiss it as an irrelevant
detail,[31] for the play never explains this misdirection.

Let us look in detail at Creon's report of the flight of the slave.

> ΟΙ. Οὐδ' ἄγγελός τις οὐδὲ συμπράκτωρ ὁδοῦ
> κατεῖδ' ὅτου τις ἐκμαθὼν ἐχρήσατ' ἄν;
> ΚΡ. Θνῄσκουσι γάρ, πλὴν εἷς τις ὃς φόβῳ φυγὼν
> ὧν εἶδε πλὴν ἓν οὐδὲν εἶχ' εἰδὼς φράσαι.
> ΟΙ. Τὸ ποῖον; ἓν γὰρ πόλλ' ἂν ἐξεύροι μαθεῖν,
> ἀρχὴν βραχεῖαν εἰ λάβοιμεν ἐλπίδος.
> ΚΡ. Ληστὰς ἔφασκε συντυχόντας οὐ μιᾷ
> ῥώμῃ κτανεῖν νιν, ἀλλὰ σὺν πλήθει χερῶν.
> ΟΙ. Πῶς οὖν ὁ ληστής, εἴ τι μὴ ξὺν ἀργύρῳ
> ἐπράσσετ' ἐνθένδ', ἐς τόδ' ἂν τόλμης ἔβη;
> Δοκοῦντα ταῦτ' ἦν· Λαΐου δ' ὀλωλότος
> οὐδεὶς ἀρωγὸς ἐν κακοῖς ἐγίγνετο.
> ΟΙ. Κακὸν δὲ ποῖον ἐμποδών, τυραννίδος
> οὕτω πεσούσης, εἶργε τοῦτ' ἐξειδέναι;
> ΚΡ. Ἡ ποικιλῳδὸς Σφὶγξ τὸ πρὸς ποσὶν σκοπεῖν
> μεθέντας ἡμᾶς τἀφανῆ προσήγετο. (116–31)

[Oedipus. And was there no one to bring word, no
  companion of his journey, who saw (the murder), whose
  evidence someone could have listened to carefully and used?
Creon. (No), for they died; except one man who, fleeing
  in fear, about what he had seen, except one thing, had no
  certain information to give.
Oedipus. What thing? One thing could discover many
  things for us to learn, if we could seize a small beginning
  for hope.
Creon. He said that bandits fell in with him and killed him,
  not with a single strength, but with a large number of
  hands.[32]

Oedipus. Then how could the bandit—unless there was
some business with money from here—have reached that
degree of daring?
Creon. This was surmised; but Laius was dead, and no
champion was forthcoming in our troubles.
Oedipus. And what trouble stood in your way to prevent a
full inquiry, when royalty had thus fallen?
Creon. The riddling Sphinx induced us to look at what lay
before our feet, neglecting mysteries.]

Was there no fellow traveler or messenger who gave an eyewitness
report of the murder, asks Oedipus? Creon offers an oracular utterance
at a point in the play where his own language blends into the riddling
discourse of the oracle.[33] "All perished, except for one, who fled in
fear, and of the things he saw could speak knowledgeably about one
thing" (118–19). This one thing will turn out to be the "many robbers."
What is most striking about these lines is that they seem to apply most
naturally not to the slave but to Oedipus. Oedipus flees from fear. He
knows his destiny from the oracle, he tries to evade it, and by means of
the flight itself, he brings it about. He flees to the crossroads, and the
later death of Laius gives him further reason for flight.[34] We need take
only one more step to solve our problem, for if we stop to think about
what Oedipus saw at the crossroads, the answer is "many robbers,"
a series of men who invade his person. This is the one thing he is sure
of and believes will ultimately guarantee his innocence.[35] Creon's own
lines at 122–23 foreshadow how Oedipus himself will remember the
incident. Oedipus happens upon some men, who "fell on him with
not one strength, but with a mass of hands," the herald's and Laius'
hands and strength at the very least. The identification with Oedipus
continues with Oedipus' reply. How could a man dare to kill the king,
unless he had cash? As many have noted, the question of hard cash
and ties to the city raises the specter of tyranny. This is, after all, what
Greek tyrants do; they create alliances, raise funds, and use these funds
to disrupt traditional authority in a *coup*. So, once more the answer
to the question lies in Oedipus' own person. How can a man become
tyrant without cash? Well, imagine a man who is peculiarly intelligent,
meets a Sphinx just after he has unwittingly killed the previous tyrant,
and so on. The irony continues in the last pair of lines by Creon. He
claims there was no champion for the city after Laius' death. But, of
course, there was. Or rather, there is—Oedipus. It is worth emphasizing
that he is the only champion, since, as Oedipus himself makes clear, all

of the citizens of Thebes are characterized by their failure to help Laius. The play begins with Oedipus moving into the role of Laius' helper at the moment he finds out about the plague, a role that has remained conspicuously unfilled up until that moment.

What are we to do with this reading? The play sets up the possibility of a different and much neater plot. In this alternative plot, it would be Oedipus who is the only witness to the crime he commits and Oedipus who gives himself away because of the lack of control over his own language, exhibiting an unconscious compulsion to confess: he kept talking of robbers, thus giving himself away. Oedipus will eventually self-convict in this way, at the moment Jocasta mentions Laius' death at the crossroads. In this other play, the answer to the problem of "ληστὰς ἔφασκε" would be the conventional one: It is Oedipus himself. Oedipus looks for an objective eyewitness who saw many robbers, missing the fact that he is the witness, and that he saw many robbers. But this is not our play. In our play, the slave doubles Oedipus' report. Why?

The problem is not the one suggested by Ahl's book. Ahl makes much of the contradictory nature of the reports from the murder scene and suggests that there is no compelling evidence for Oedipus' guilt. But rather than relying on the all-importance of a positivistic discourse of the law-courts that somehow comes to dominate other, formal aspects of Greek tragedy (rather than legal language simply influencing the language of tragedy, which seems certain), it is better to see the evidence in relation to what the plot requires. Since there are two accounts of the crossroads, there is *too much* evidence, not too little.[36] So what did the slave see, and why is there such certainty about the "many robbers"? When we listen to the eyewitness report of the slave, we presume that he is one of the party who go to Delphi and, as such, a faithful slave of Laius. We also presume that he sees the event from the perspective of Laius and his followers. We trust in the closeness of the slave to his master. But should we? The slave has already betrayed Laius and betrayed him for Oedipus. So might he see the events of the crossroads not through the eyes of Laius, but through the eyes of Oedipus? If so, he would see a group of robbers attack a young man. Neither for Laius, nor wholly against him, he is outside the scene entirely, though thoroughly implicated in it because of its relationship to his previous injunction to kill Oedipus. It is quite reasonable, in this scenario, to believe Oedipus when he says he kills the entire party, for the slave was never a part of the party Oedipus saw.

This reconstruction of what is seen at the crossroads has interesting symbolic connotations, for Oedipus remains structurally blind to this figure who has controlled his destiny, the slave who is neither with Oedipus nor with Laius, but an impotent watcher. The slave sees from the same position as Oedipus, even as his distance from him allows him to see exactly what Oedipus must remain blind to. Their different knowledge colors what each of them see at the crossroads.[37] It is only at the torture scene that the two men are so fatefully brought together, a mutual destruction of people forced into knowing too much. If we accept that the slave watches "many robbers" approach Oedipus and flees at this moment, then the reconstruction of his story is effortless. He returns to Thebes, frantically screaming out what he has seen: ληστὰς ἔφασκε. He presumes, quite reasonably, that Oedipus has died, though perhaps he does not yet know this. But when Oedipus arrives at Thebes, he realizes the truth; it is his master, Laius, who has died, and because of his own act. His pity hid a murderous aggression, and so he flees once more to the fields.

There is more to be said. First, it is worth emphasizing how the fleeing slave takes over the role allotted to Oedipus until the crossroads. Oedipus flees from fear until the slave replaces him. The slave flees the parrincest that he is responsible for, even as Oedipus is allowed to stay in the same place and enjoy it. Retroactively, we should question why we are so ready to identify slave with master, to refuse to see a gap open up between their interests. The play stages the "political unconscious" of Athenian society, skirting around class antagonism, a slave betraying a master.[38] If such a political analysis of the play has been missed, it is perhaps because, like a well-known police force searching for a purloined letter, we look for its "political unconscious" in some fantasized depth of the play, whereas it hides itself by its obviousness, in the structure of the plot. We should also go a step further than any sociological analysis, which locates the problem of ideology in a mapped out, relational class tension between slave and master. That tension is certainly there, but it spills over into a more general inquiry into the fragility of social links, for the breakdown of the relationship between master and slave is simultaneously a glimpse into the tentativeness of all social bonds. Questions of class antagonism leak into the problem of the reliability of communicative systems that manage this antagonism: in this play, the fundamental stories people tell each other about themselves and their social identity—that is, their shared ideology—begin to fall apart. Broader allegorical readings are also possible. To what extent is the impossible situation of the slave, confronted with a choice that necessarily entails a fundamental guilt, a choice that he tries to flee but only runs into more danger because of this flight, applicable to subjectivity as such? This is a question that, certainly, psychoanalytic theory has explored most fully.[39]

One final thought. I have spoken of the slave's aggression, the retroactive knowledge of his implication in his master's death, but where does that desire come from? Is it his, or is it already an interpretation of what his master wants? Laius is given an order to kill his child. But he does not kill his child; he passes it over to the slave. The vacillation of the slave is already set up by the vacillation of the master who opens up the possibility of what? Here, I think, we need to follow the advice of Joan Copjec, and imagine the slave reading not what the master says, "Kill the child," but what the master desires. Laius asks to have the child killed, hands him over to Jocasta, who hands him over to the slave.[40] But if he really wanted Oedipus killed, why did he not kill him directly? Is it not the implication that he wants his own death, as he transfers over to someone else the son who will kill him? In the last resort, the actions of the slave may be less a betrayal than an act of fidelity, and to something that sets the whole play in motion, Laius' desire for death.

This may allow us to understand why the oracle, as reported by Creon, speaks of the plurality of murderers of Laius, because a plurality desired his death. We can begin with Jocasta and the slave. As Jocasta passes the baby Oedipus, presumably received from the hands of Laius, into the hands of the slave, what exactly is being passed around? Surely, they are passing around Laius' death, failing to take responsibility for killing Oedipus, but thereby putting Laius himself in danger. But where exactly does the responsibility stop? If Jocasta and the slave are implicated in the death of Laius, and thus can be said to show a desire for Laius' death, who at Thebes is not compromised? What stops the plurality of murderers from turning into a universal desire for the death of Laius? Let us recall the contrast between the plague-ridden Thebans and the plague-free Oedipus at the play's beginning. The contours of the plot, as told by Sophocles, are quite simple; after the death of Laius, no one seemed to care about his death because, according to Creon, the Sphinx appeared, forcing them to pay in gradual loss of life for their failure to answer its riddle. But we can link these events. Doing nothing about the death of Laius, they render their collective guilt bearable by a gradual self-murder, as they turn citizen after citizen over to the Sphinx. The loss of the Sphinx, just as much as Oedipus' victory, provides a crisis: how are the Thebans to manage their collective guilt after the death of Laius? The death of the king is significant for them, because it retroactively triggers an awareness of their desire for his death. But it is not so much the loss of symbolic ties that is on show as the way the people are united in their guilt, their unconscious awareness of their complicity in the death of the master. In Freudian terms, we have traveled from the myth of the foundation of the Oedipus complex to the myth of *Totem and Taboo*. The Theban population provides the contours of a dark reading of the Freudian picture of a community linked by the collective guilt for the killing of a mythical master. This makes the contrast with Oedipus even stronger. In a sense, Ahl is right that Oedipus is literally innocent of the crime of patricide, even if for the wrong reasons, for Oedipus is the only person at Thebes not compromised by this desire for Laius' death. He may be the efficient cause (he pulled the trigger), but he is innocent at a far more fundamental level. Herein lies precisely the point of Oedipus' accusation of Teiresias: "Know that in my opinion you actually helped to plot the deed, and carried it out, *short of killing with your hands*; if you had sight, I would have said that even the doing of it was yours" (346–49).

Oedipus accuses Teiresias when he is himself the murderer, and the reversal is exact: Teiresias is accused of guilt of everything except the act itself because of his physical blindness, whereas Oedipus is innocent of everything except the act because of his epistemic blindness. But everyone else is guilty in precisely the way Oedipus is innocent. The people remain at Thebes, and pay with their lives for the guilt they feel, while Oedipus enjoys the death of the master without any such guilt. The slave bridges the gap by fleeing both the guilt *and* the enjoyment.

But this process is set in motion by Laius himself, by a lurking desire for his *own* death. The guilt of the population, a lurking aggression, is parasitic on Laius' own vacillations. But what is at stake in this choice? The choice is between his own obliteration as a living individual and the loss of any possibility of family continuity, a *symbolic* death—in short, an expanded version of the famous choice of Achilles, but now spanning two humans instead of one. Achilles, famously, was given a choice by his mother between a long, peaceful life at home but without fame, and a short life with undying fame at Troy. For Laius, the short life for himself is compensated by the continuation of his family in the life of his son, while a long life involves no hope of the continuation of his name. In both choices, the idiocy of a purely biological existence, of life itself, divorced from any symbolic attempt to explain or understand it, is contrasted with the belief in a meaning that transcends such a temporal existence. And, following in the path of Achilles, it is a choice that Laius finds himself unable to make. Well before Antigone's "no" to

Creon, at the very heart of the *Oedipus Tyrannus*, we find that a desire for death already insists within the Labdacid family.

NOTES

1. Sandor Goodhart, "Leistas Ephaske: Oedipus and Laius' Many Murderers," *Diacritics* 8, no. 1 (1978): 55–71.

2. Frederick Ahl, *Sophocles' Oedipus: Evidence and Self-Conviction* (Ithaca, NY: Cornell University Press, 1991).

3. For the play as a critique of forms of "knowingness," see Jonathan Lear, *Open Minded: Working out the Logic of the Soul* (Cambridge, MA: Harvard University Press, 1998), chap. 3.

4. For the importance of this "abstract," primal sense of guilt as constitutive of subjectivity, and as central to what the Althusserian theory of interpellation misses see Mladen Dolar, "Beyond Interpellation," *Qui Parle* 6, no. 2 (1993): 75–96. Ahl has simply given this reading a positivist twist, trading in the unknowability of this primal scene for a legalistic attempt to establish what we do, circumstantially, know about the crime. If we follow Ahl and imagine the guilt or innocence of Oedipus in line with the rules of an Athenian law court, there is evidence for Oedipus' innocence mixed with his desire to self-convict. Of course, the price to be paid for this interpretation is the implicit recognition that the positivistic world of the law-court is the one that truly matters for Greek tragedy—a recognition that we need not, and should not, make.

5. The sensible point made by Simon Goldhill in his review of Ahl, "East Coast Oedipus: Suspicious Readings," *Arion* 4, no. 2 (1996): 155–71. As with most other reviews of Ahl's work, there is an open tension between much of the critical ingenuity of Ahl, which is recognized, and the general failure of the overall theory.

6. Charles Segal, *Oedipus Tyrannus: Tragic Heroism and the Limits of Knowledge* (New York: Oxford University Press, 1993), 56.

7. Sigmund Freud, *The Interpretation of Dreams*, trans. J. Strachey (New York: Basic Books, 1965), 295–96.

8. I borrow the phrase "get off" as a nice translation of what Lacan means by "jouissance" from Bruce Fink. See Fink, *The Lacanian Subject: Between Language and Jouissance* (Princeton, NJ: Princeton University Press, 1995).

9. Parrincest is the useful term, coined by Pietro Pucci, to refer to the double aspect of Oedipus' crimes: patricide and incest. See Pucci,

Oedipus and the Fabrication of the Father (Baltimore: John Hopkins University Press, 1992).

10. Oedipus asks, "Did you ever belong to Laius?" to which the slave responds, "Yes, a slave not bought, but nurtured in the house" (*OT* 1123).

11. See *OT* 1118ff.

12. The translation here is my own. In general, I follow the self-consciously "literal" translation of Philip Vellacott in *Sophocles and Oedipus: A Study of "Oedipus Tyrannus" with a New Translation* (London: Macmillan, 1971).

13. There is some confusion over the number killed by Oedipus and the number of people who were part of the party. See *OT* 802ff., and the discussion *ad loc* in the commentary of Richard Jebb. Jebb, *The Oedipus Tyrannus of Sophocles* (Cambridge: Cambridge University Press, 1958).

14. On this aspect of the "ethics of psychoanalysis," see the useful comments by Russell Grigg, "Signifier, Object and the Transference," in *Lacan and the Subject of Language*, ed. Ellie Ragland-Sullivan and Mark Bracher (New York: Routledge, 1991), 100–115.

15. I provide two equally possible translations: (1) there was a *logos* that the son would kill the parents, and (2) there was a *logos* that the parents would kill the son. It is this ambiguity that my translation tries to keep.

16. That is, in Lacanian terms, the words produced in response to the enigma of the oracle are thoroughly *phallic*, signifying their own impotence. On the problems produced by oracles in general, see the interesting study of Michael Wood, *The Road to Delphi: Oracles and Their Afterlife* (New York: Farrar, Strauss and Giroux, 2003).

17. The situation of the slave can perhaps be clarified by the contemporary story that dramatizes this "forced choice" best: "Sophie's choice," from William Styron's well-known novel. Sophie, given the choice by the Nazi guard to choose between the deaths of her children, is forced to choose one. Should she refuse to choose, she is told that both will die. If we develop the situation that Laius' slave faces, the formal contours are strikingly similar (though, of course, the content of the general ideological parameters are quite different): a symbolic authority (the master, himself justified by his obedience to the oracle in the *Oedipus Tyrannus*, the order of the Nazi guard representing Nazi ideology in *Sophie's Choice*) outlines a necessary evil (death of father or son, death of sister or brother), which becomes worse if it is avoided. On the ethical significance

of this choice, I am indebted to an unpublished paper by Alenka Zupancic, given at the University of Michigan in the fall of 1998.

18. That is, unlike Sophie, whose heroism lies in accepting the inevitable guilt by making the choice, the slave runs from the choice itself.

19. Slavoj Žižek, *The Sublime Object of Ideology* (London: Verso, 1989), 58.

20. Do we not have a simple false alternative here, one that the slave rejects? I think not. The attempt to subvert the command while feigning obedience is a sign of his tacit acceptance of both the master's authority and the authority of the oracle, for he could choose skepticism, refuse to believe in either discourse of authority. Instead, he enters into the terms of this game and will pay the price for thinking he can outwit master and oracle alike. That is, his attempt to find a third way is a sign that he believes.

21. Freud, famously, linked the events of the play to the ongoing revelations at work in psychoanalysis. But what if it is the slave, not Oedipus, for which this analogy works best?

22. Compare the famous message of Thetis to Achilles, after the death of Patroclus, where a similar reading is possible. Thetis consoles Achilles, because he has lost Patroclus. But this is not the true source of horror—it is, quite simply, that Achilles *wanted this* and cannot escape this.

23. We should not try to explain the slave's motivation in terms of simple self-preservation, for just as he is never dealing with a simple child but instead the tissue of signs and prophecies that are already attached to this child, so too his attachment to his own life is never simply biological, but rather to the meaning he attaches to it, his *symbolic* identity.

24. Can we not use this knowledge to reread the oracle given to Laius, at least as reported by Jocasta.

χρησμὸς γὰρ ἦλθε Λαΐῳ ποτ', οὐκ ἐρῶ
Φοίβου γ' ἄπ' αὐτοῦ, τῶν δ' ὑπηρετῶν ἄπο,
ὡς αὐτὸν ἕξοι μοῖρα πρὸς παιδὸς θανεῖν
ὅστις γένοιτ' ἐμοῦ τε κἀκείνου πάρα. (711–14)

You will die at the hand of a "*pais*," whose existence was the result of me and him. Born into the household, he lacks any form of otherness. Child. Or slave? Oedipus, or the slave into whose hands the boy Oedipus is given? In short, isn't the slave the person who replaces Oedipus in the affection of the parents—Jocasta, retroactively at least, loves the slave, even as she rejects Oedipus. This is part of the strange sorts of exchange happening in the play—not only that Oedipus is transferred from one household, that of his biological parents, into the loving hands of Polybus and Merope, but also that the slave replaces him in the affection of his biological parents.

25. I owe this formulation to Jim Porter.

26. Oedipus' crime, as emphasized by Lacan, is his desire to know, and this desire makes him oblivious of all others around him throughout the play—the concerns of Jocasta and Creon.

27. This was explored, for example, in Pucci, *Oedipus and the Fabrication of the Father* (n. 9 above).

28. This destroys any efforts at explaining the discrepancy merely as a lie of a slave in panic.

29. This is the shared belief of Ahl, *Sophocles' Oedipus* (n. 2 above), and Goodhart, "Leistas Ephaske" (n. 1 above).

30. This is the ingenious solution of Froma Zeitlin, "Thebes: Theater of Self and Other in Athenian Drama," in *Nothing to Do with Dionysos*, ed. John J. Winkler and Froma I. Zeitlin (Princeton, NJ: Princeton University Press, 1990), 101–41, though clearly influenced by work done on the significance of counting in the play by Segal.

31. So concludes Segal, though with some despair (*Oedipus Tyrannus*, n. 6 above, 77ff).

32. Note again the ambiguity in the accusative and infinitive construction, one that previews the slave's later report of the oracle. Did the bandits kill him, or did he kill the bandits?

33. On this, see Ahl, *Sophocles' Oedipus* (n. 2 above), ch. 2.

34. Note the emphasis on his flight at lines 796 and 823.

35. Also, if we follow the useful discussion of *leistas* by Ahl, who emphasizes the etymology of thief in *leia*, that which belongs to the people, we can see a further point to the slave's description. Laius steals the future of the people, the *laos* when he both tries to kill Oedipus and when he meets him at the crossroads—the "brigand" is a stealer not just of what belongs to the people, but insofar as Oedipus, the legitimate heir of the king, stands for the people, the theft at the crossroads is of the people itself. Does this not also help us make more out of the weapon at the crossroads? Laius uses a goad, Oedipus a scepter to kill him: the narrative is written as a

reclaiming of authority, a return of the scepter to Thebes against the man who tried to prevent its use.

36. I in no way wish to undermine the value of Ahl's book, *Sophocles' Oedipus* (n. 2 above), which, following Goodhart (n. 1 above), has done a great service in making much of what we take for granted in the play problematic and puzzling. This remains the case, even if its central thesis is incorrect.

37. In Lacanian terms, does not the slave function here as a sort of stand-in for Oedipus' unconscious, for the kind of knowledge that simply can not be assimilated into Oedipus' world? Oedipus remains oblivious to the discourse of the Other, the scene that determines him, and so he acts. The slave sees the split between Oedipus' conscious and unconscious self collapsing, and is thus a witness to the moment when ideology no longer functions as a barrier to the horror of the Real of one's desire.

38. This kind of reading has been offered by Edith Hall, "The Sociology of Athenian Tragedy" in *The Cambridge Companion to Greek Tragedy*, ed. P. E. Easterling (Cambridge: Cambridge University Press, 1997), 93–126.

39. Psychoanalytic attempts to come to grips with modern subjectivity in turn continue to make use of the subjectivities of tragedy. On this, see Alenka Zupankic, *The Ethics of the Real* (New York: Verso, 2000). See also Joan Copjec, *Imagine There's No Woman: Ethics and Sublimation* (Cambridge, MIT Press, 2003).

40. The agency here is blurred. Jocasta at first gives no hint of who kills the baby, only that it is passed into the hands of others by Laius. The slave later will tell us that those hands belonged to Jocasta.

4

JOCASTA'S EYE AND FREUD'S UNCANNY

DAVID SCHUR

When the young Oedipus portrayed by Sophocles runs away from Corinth to Thebes by way of Delphi, he is both foreign and secretly familiar. Thebes is secretly his true birthplace, so Oedipus has been going toward the place from which he began. This is "an extraordinary paradox....For once Oedipus discovers that he has found his true home in Thebes, he also discovers to his or our horror that he has been only too much 'at home.'"[1] In essence, Thebes is secretly familiar because Jocasta is secretly family—she is the one who placed and then displaced the birth of Oedipus. From a Jocastan perspective, Oedipus is *her* secret, long repressed and now agressively returning to the home that should have been his. Something of a blind spot in Sigmund Freud's interpretation of the myth, the paradox of this secret's return has the dynamic of Freud's uncanny. Oedipus' return to Jocasta becomes increasingly *unheimlich*—that is, "uncanny, unhomelike, unconcealed."

This chapter is ultimately concerned with a word uttered by Jocasta in the middle of *Oedipus Tyrannus*. When the Corinthian Messenger arrives with news that he thinks may cause sorrow as well as pleasure, Jocasta says, "What is it? What kind of double power does it have?" (938). The doubleness of the situation has thus been made explicit; simultaneous, contradictory reactions are expected. The Messenger says that Polybus, the supposed father of Oedipus, lies "buried" (*en taphois*; 942). Jocasta welcomes the father's death because it seems to contradict Apollo's fearful prophecies and counter Oedipus' fear of patricide. But Oedipus is still afraid of sleeping with his mother. Jocasta tries to comfort him, saying, "And yet surely the burial [*taphoi*] of the father is a great eye [*megas ophthalmos*]" (987). The problem of interpretation I wish to focus on is largely a matter of translation. How are we to construe the word *ophthalmos*? Translators usually (and understandably) seek readability, so they normalize the semantic opacity of the sentence, and *ophthalmos* tends to be (justifiably) replaced by something metaphorical like "comforting light."[2] I say "replaced" rather than "rendered" because, when this *ophthalmos* is read as an ordinary metaphor, we lose the antithetical meaning—the vivid, haunting placement of a physical eye that ominously shadows whatever metaphorical comfort it may offer. Translation has effectively been preempted by the lexicon, as though a different lexeme had been substituted for *ophthalmos*, and then, in turn, translated.[3] But still, how can a literal, physical eye represent or describe a burial? Only uncomfortably. Freud's uncanny provides a helpful framework for discussing this eye's unsettled place in its Sophoclean context.

Most of the following chapter will be spent preparing for an interpretation of Jocasta's *ophthalmos* as an example of uncanny language. Charles Segal has laid the groundwork for such an interpretation in an essay called "Freud, Language, and the Unconscious" (1995). Stressing Freud's relevance to contemporary study of *Oedipus Tyrannus*, Segal advocates a salutary shift of focus from the action-based plot of the drama to the realm of language, calling "language itself the field that most fully enacts the play between the hidden and the obvious" that is so central in Sophocles' work.[4] Although he does not link the hidden with the burial or the obvious with the eye, Segal does find Jocasta's remark especially creepy: "As we move close to the revealing of unconscious fears, and fears of the unconscious,...the dialogue takes on an eerie, phantasmagoric quality."[5] This part of the play, he observes, is generally characterized by a growing sense of fear—in part created by the repetition of the words "fear" (*phobos*) and "terrible" (*deinos*)— that signals the Freudian uncanny: "The literary effect of 'the uncanny' here takes the form of the simplest words' becoming vehicles of the 'fearful' or 'the terrible' that surfaces from repressed knowledge, from the unspeakable."[6] For Segal, the uncovering of Oedipus' identity is a dynamic unconcealment of unconscious truth.

Segal (like Pietro Pucci) also connects the play's treatment of truth with Greek notions of *alêtheia*, translatable as "un-forgetting" or "the unforgetting of truth," as well as "truth" itself.[7] Although Freud's uncanny certainly differs from Greek *alêtheia*—and from *alêtheia* as understood by Martin Heidegger and Karl Reinhardt—these concepts share an unstable structure of negated concealment, or of discovery, that makes them germane to the reading of Sophocles.[8] Since the German adjective *heimlich* ordinarily means "secret, concealed," *das Un-heimliche* (the not-concealed) resembles *alêtheia* when the latter is construed etymologically as *a* + *lêthê* (not + forgotten). The resemblance is more pronounced when one takes into account Heidegger's use of *Unverborgenheit* (unconcealment) for *alêtheia*. And while Freud's interpretation of *das Unheimliche* also stresses the word's paradoxical relation to *Heim* (home), so does Heidegger's, when he connects *unheimlich* with *heimisch* (of the home) in analyzing Friedrich Hölderlin's translation of Sophocles' *Antigone*. The Sophoclean word that Heidegger translates as *unheimlich* is *deinos* (terrible), one of the key words that signals the uncanny in Segal's interpretation of *Oedipus Tyrannus*.[9]

The uncanny, in Freud's wide-ranging essay of that name (published in 1919), is "that class of the frightening that leads back to what is known of old and long familiar" (Freud, *Standard Edition,* 17:220, hereafter cited parenthetically as *SE*). Rather than a pure, immediate fear, it is a fright caused by the possibility of recovering or discovering a once-active fear that has been overcome. The uncanny is primarily a feeling, a psychological phenomenon, which an astute interpreter can theoretically trace back to hidden sources. Causes of this feeling may be found in real life and in literary fiction, and Freud uses the adjective "uncanny" to describe such events or works. The uncanny either involves the return of something (an instinct or complex) that was repressed, or it "proceeds from forms of thought that have been surmounted" (*SE* 17:251); but "these two classes of uncanny experience are not always sharply distinguishable" (*SE* 17:249). Freud has in mind seemingly impossible, eerie occurrences, whether in real life or in the understood confines of a fictional world. Unbelievable coincidences, for instance, can make us doubt our modern rationality and confront primal human beliefs in superhuman forces, beliefs that we usually think we have surmounted.

There are many possible approaches to Freud's wide-ranging and elaborate essay on the uncanny. Freud's first example of the uncanny is the word *unheimlich* itself, however, which underscores the importance of language for any understanding of the phenomenon. So this is where I will concentrate my attention. Freud uses etymological analysis to introduce his topic, and his method proves remarkably metaphorical and suggestive in certain respects. His investigation is prompted by a desire to understand the special sense of the adjective *unheimlich* that takes it beyond "frightening." "The German word *'unheimlich'* is obviously the opposite of *'heimlich'* [homely], *'heimisch'* [native]—the opposite of what is familiar," suggests Freud, "and we are tempted to conclude that what is 'uncanny' is frightening precisely because it is *not* known and familiar" (*SE* 17:220).[10] A crucial twist in Freud's ensuing analysis is the claim that this obvious opposition (the focus of an earlier study by Ernst Jentsch) conceals hidden depths.

Freud resists the temptation of the obvious by setting a dizzying cascade of antitheses into motion. For example, whereas the familiar view of *unheimlich* construes the word as an opposition between familiar and unfamiliar, Freud's unfamiliar, opposing view is that the unfamiliar of *unheimlich* is secretly familiar because an opposition between familiar and unfamiliar already exists in the word's familial history. That *unheimlich* developed from a coincidence of familiar and unfamiliar implies, for Freud, that the experience of the uncanny does as well, setting off a chain of semantic doublings and coincidences. But the coincidences are by implication not coincidental. Is it an uncanny coincidence that the word *uncanny* itself comes to seem so uncanny? In Freud's analysis, the linguistic form *unheimlich* is not arbitrarily linked with its meaning(s); on the contrary, the word reflects its meaning in a *mise en abyme* of conceptual mimesis.

Rather than try to untangle every turn in Freud's complicated sequence of oppositions, it may be wiser to consider the procedure and results of Freud's uncanny etymology. In accord with general psychoanalytic practice, Freud here treats something familiar as a manifestation or symptom, a façade concealing the latent realm of the unconscious. Analysis in this sense then becomes a technique of continuous defamiliarization. A word—*unheimlich*, for instance—is examined until it grows estranged. Any sort of analysis will ultimately involve some kind of metalanguage, and talking about words necessarily estranges them. For us, notions about doubling in language, including metalanguage, metaphor, and homonymy, may offer a working (if inadequate) vocabulary with which to discuss these matters. For Freud, the metalanguage of etymology is a neat tool for the psychoanalysis of a word—as though a word's origins provided a family album suited for the reconstruction of unconscious primal scenes, and as though the synchronic lexicon had a (diachronic) unconscious. But when Freud's method of defamiliarization is brought to bear on the topic of defamiliarization, the metalanguage and the so-called object language fold back into each other semantically, graphically, and at times uncannily.

Using everyday language to talk about everyday language forms a metalanguage that makes the usual distinction between literal and metaphorical usage untenable. In practice, metalinguistic words have split identities. Confusion can arise from the use of homonyms or homographs, so that typographical indications (italics, quotation marks) are often needed to clarify when an everyday word is being used in a metalinguistic sense. A casual look at the complicated nature of metalinguistic metaphors in English may demonstrate this. When we talk about a family of related words in English, *family* is a metalinguistic term. Let us say that this special meaning of *family* is linguistic and different from the everyday sense, "parents and offspring." (In fact, the sciences of linguistics and biology each have specific technical meanings for the word *family*, meanings that must remain beyond the scope of this chapter.) Metalinguistic usage creates a literal version of the everyday word *family* for its specific purposes. Yet the linguistic use of *family* would usually be considered a metaphorical extension of the everyday *family*. Such an extended member of the *family* family, when it has become familiar enough and no longer seems figurative, may be called a *dead metaphor*.[11] A dead metaphor is, usually yet paradoxically, a literalized metaphor, which is not strictly the same as either a literal term or a metaphor. Meanwhile, the everyday *family*'s life has died only from the perspective of the linguistic term. The metaphorical framework of *dead metaphor*, hinging on life versus death, grows even harder to maintain upon recalling that everyday *family* never really died. If we concede it a certain death at all, the dead word lives as a linguistic doppelgänger, a ghostly double or counterpart of a living word.

Familiarization supposedly wipes out linguistic *family*'s figurative, metaphorical origins; the metalinguistic word's metaphorical quality is forgotten, like a family secret, letting the new word live on with a literal meaning. The neologism is a seemingly identical counterpart. But as long as the biological meaning of *family* persists somewhere, the linguistic term *family* will never entirely escape its everyday conception. Indeed, a metalinguistic discussion of the dead, metalinguistic metaphor *family* will, as linguists put it, revive it.[12] Metalanguage can bring a metaphorical quality back to life by defamiliarizing it, even though metalanguage is the process of literalization that killed the metaphor in the first place. And if we use a metalinguistic term *family* to talk about the word *family*, as I have done here, our enterprise becomes excessively reflexive.

The theoretical difference between homonymy and polysemy offers another way to expose these complications. As Jean-Pierre Vernant writes, when considering Sophoclean language, "Ambiguity...translates the tension between certain values felt as irreconcilable in spite of their homonymy."[13] Etymology has traditionally been a serviceable way to distinguish homonymity (understood as the existence of unrelated but identically written or pronounced words) from polysemy, in which single words have multiple meanings.[14] Freud's etymological view of the word *unheimlich*, however, essentially denies the existence of homonymy.

Phenomena that look alike—at least insofar as they are uncanny—will be meaningfully related, even if only through unconscious paths of association. The processes of condensation and overdetermination that Freud finds in the dreamwork, as well as the acceptance of coincident contrary meanings, inevitably lead the interpreter to polysemy. The simultaneity of meanings found in *unheimlich* suggests that the word has undergone a linguistic process comparable to dreamwork. Most importantly, the diachronic development of the word, the history of coincident contraries, has not been overcome. Freud instead takes an anachronistic or synchronic view in which the dead or forgotten meaning of the word remains a ghostly counterpart in the present. One might even call the Freudian perspective oracular because it predicts the return of what was hidden.

A revitalized metaphor could also be called an *undead metaphor*, and this model fits Freud's treatment of both the concept and the linguistic form of the uncanny—the return of the repressed is the revival of a dead (but not gone) and forgotten secret. Freud observes that two radically different meanings of the German word *heimlich* may be found in dictionaries; *heimlich* has at times meant "belonging to the house or the family" as well as "secret, concealed, hidden from sight." Because the concealed meaning of a word meaning "concealed" is at issue, Freud's own prose becomes tricky, providing an example of metalinguistic ambiguity. In several of Freud's sentences about the words *heimlich* and *unheimlich*, it is ambiguous whether the words function metalinguistically—representing themselves as words—or adverbially—describing themselves. One way to highlight this is to compare the standard English translation with the original. Unlike the German text, in which Freud soon eschews the typographical signals that indicate words used as words, the *Standard Edition* disambiguates the words in question by italicizing them within single quotation marks, as in this part of a larger sentence: "the word '*heimlich*' exhibits." In the English, *heimlich* is clearly not an adverb here.

But if we read *heimlich* and *unheimlich* as adverbs in the larger sentence just mentioned, we see a different meaning in Freud's initial response to a lengthy dictionary entry on *heimlich*: "What interests us most in this long extract is to find that, among its different shades of meaning, the word secretly exhibits one which is uncannily identical with its opposite" (*SE* 17:224, modified). (*Aus diesem langen Zitat ist für uns am interessantesten, daß das Wörtchen heimlich unter den mehrfachen Nuancen seiner Bedeutung auch eine zeigt, in der es mit seinem Gegensatz unheimlich zusammenfällt.*)[15] This ambiguity betrays a collapse or coincidence of opposite meanings, a kind of coincidence that happens to be central to Freud's process of discovering the uncanniness of the uncanny. That is, Freud uncannily identifies the uncanny in the word *uncanny* itself. A good part of the word's riddling character comes from our assumption that *unheimlich* could not simply mean "not secret" (*un-heimlich*). But it could not simply mean "not familiar" (*un-heimisch*) either. "In general we are reminded that the word secretly [*heimlich*] is not unambiguous [*nicht eindeutig*]," remarks Freud (*SE* 17:224). In other words, the word is insistently polysemous. Freud's etymological analysis suggests that irresolvable ambiguity, rooted in radical polysemy, is a fundamental characteristic of the uncanny.

This view is in accord with remarks made in *The Interpretation of Dreams* (1900): "There is no need to be astonished at the part played by words in dream formation. Words, since they are the nodal points of numerous ideas, may be regarded as predestined to ambiguity" (*SE* 5:340). Freud also explicitly explores an etymological model of self-contradiction in "The Antithetical Meaning of Primal Words" (1910).[16] There, he draws on a philological theory to understand why dreams "show a particular preference for combining contraries into a unity or for representing them as one and the same thing" (*SE* 11:155). The theory, as reviewed by Freud, holds that ancient languages, particularly early Egyptian, contained single words that expressed double, antithetical meanings; some such words later developed into two distinct words with single meanings. Although Freud does not do so in his essay on antithetical meaning, we may adduce the modern example of *heimlich* ("homey" and "secret," later *heimisch* and *heimlich*).[17] Freud believes that the account of linguistic development out of antithesis affirms his theory of "the regressive, archaic character" of distortion in dream formation, and he wonders whether translators of dream language should not learn more about the origins of language (*SE* 11:161).

With all this in mind, let us return to *Oedipus Tyrannus*. In its general outline, the Sophoclean version of Oedipus' return to Jocasta could be read as an extended metaphor—an allegory—of Freud's uncanny. Or perhaps it could be read as a drama literalizing human fears of the uncanny (somewhat like Franz Kafka's story "The Metamorphosis," in which a salesman who feels lousy literally wakes up as a louse). In any case, as Segal suggests, "Oedipus' life parallels the struggle of language in the play."[18] Each uncanny defamiliarization of this primal story will revive some of the forgotten metaphors and subsumed literalisms that have haunted it since birth. If the uncanny, like the Oedipus complex, is truly a human experience, the tragedy and the uncanny should illuminate each other. A strange hermeneutic chronology can be justified by a work that is, to some extent, timeless, and a theory that foresees the past returning to haunt the future.[19]

While citing uncanny doubles, ghosts, coincidences, and various forms of involuntary repetition, Freud's essay on the uncanny pays special attention to fears about the loss of eyes, fears that frequently emerge, he says, in dreams, fantasies, myths, and literature. In the essay, however, Freud seems to take the figure of Oedipus for granted. Oedipus is mentioned for the sake of an example: his self-blinding readily takes the place of castration (SE 17:231). Freud here may take a literary gesture a bit too literally, or may read a physical act too metaphorically. In any case, a striking number of blind eyes inhabit Sophocles' drama, and an unobvious one belongs to Jocasta. As indicated earlier, Jocasta is central to the uncanny trajectory traced by Oedipus. His emergence from her maternal womb in Thebes is the event that defines the terms of his life. Jocasta, who never leaves Thebes, is the fixed marker of home and family, familiarity and genealogy. She embodies "the inert pull of lêthê," like a collapsing supernova of forgetfulness.[20]

Oedipus himself, plagued by a family history of transgressions and cover-ups, unknowingly conceals an uncanny genealogy when he arrives in Thebes, the same genealogy that Jocasta has tried to forget. Having become nearly disconnected from its past, an uncanny phenomenon is never entirely at home in its present identity. And just as the etymology of unheimlich leads us back to an identity of home and concealment, Oedipus' past makes him homeless and unplaceable in the present. Because his birth parents sent him away from his birthplace, he is neither a native nor a son, not when in Corinth and not when in Thebes. The initial act of infanticidal misplacement, in addition to the crimes of parricide and incest, dooms him to remain an outcast forever. As tyrant of Thebes, Oedipus is—manifestly—in the right place at the right time. Yet latently he is neither entirely at home in the family nor entirely hidden from sight, neither a murdered baby nor a banished murderer. What makes this uncanny is the threatened exposure of the hidden genealogical instability. The dynamic of the uncanny is seen in the manifestation of this latent familial displacement. From Jocasta's point of view, the person who has become Oedipus is supposed to be dead. Having returned from this maternally wished-for death, Oedipus is a ghost, a revenant, a double.[21] To put it another way, Oedipus would not be his own doppelgänger were he not supposed to be dead.

Finally, the hidden genealogy and contextual displacement of the uncanny correspond to a peculiar temporal dynamic. Retrospective foreboding, a cumbersome but useful locution for the repressed that is returning, is another component of the uncanny I wish to point out. The uncanny indicates a forbidden past that threatens to return in the future. With this sense of foreboding in mind, we may note that genealogy, alienation, and foreboding correspond roughly to past, present, and future perspectives. The uncanny, constantly pointing backward and forward, lacks a stable presence. While the full disclosure of frightening unconscious thoughts would eliminate the uncanny, the process is more likely to be interminable and plagued by subsequent amnesic roadblocks and deferrals.[22] Yes, Oedipus, as the first and only figure to fulfill the wish to kill the father and sleep with the mother, has perhaps left the Oedipus complex behind for the rest of us. And a similar claim could be made about the uncanny Oedipus: he is the living disclosure of his family secret. But, in general, the uncanny fear of the forgotten is unlikely ever to be entirely dispelled or exhausted, not even through the cathartic screening of artworks. Even within the world of Sophocles' Theban plays, Thebes cannot give Oedipus a funereal home. A hidden funeral at Colonus is the only way to dispose of his body, leaving us with not only closure but also the buried secret of a secret burial.

And now I would like to confront Jocasta's buried eye. To repeat, Jocasta tries to allay Oedipus' fear of having committed parricide as predicted by the oracle of Apollo. Relieved that Oedipus' putative father Polybus has died, she says, "And yet surely the burial [*taphoi*] of the father is a great eye [*megas ophthalmos*]" (987). Commentators explain that *ophthalmos* is, in this instance, metaphorical, meaning "bright, comfort."[23] And the word undoubtedly conveys these meanings, just as the comfort offered by Jocasta's mistake is powerfully ironic, gaining doubled meaning through dramatic irony. Still, the familiar reading is complacent. As translators, we are compelled to take comfort in the accepted reading, and we invariably cut out the eye, replacing it with something more familiar. In doing so, we repeat Jocasta's own withdrawal toward familiarity, comfort, and forgetfulness. Let us take a closer look at this sentence and its eye. Instead of a relatively familiar, univocal, and stable metaphor, *ophthalmos* is a semantically unstable homologue of the complacent repression that is haunted and then overturned by the disclosure of Oedipus' identity.

The sentence in question links two elements, the singular eye and the burial or funeral rites (plural in the Greek). Although the sentence has the form of a declarative statement, it functions like a question. With the adversative combination "and yet" (*kai mên*), Jocasta seeks to direct Oedipus' attention.[24] He is missing something of magnitude, she suggests. So the sentence has an implied interrogative tag: the burial is a great eye, is it not? "[Yes,] I understand," replies Oedipus. He agrees that the burial (and the eye) is indeed "great" (*megas*). Rather like *deinos* (fearful, terrible, powerful), which Heidegger translates as "*unheimlich*," the word *megas* can have both good and bad senses, awesome and awful aspects. Oedipus is the first to interpret Jocasta's eye, and he seems to have no trouble doing so. He does not find it strange. But as we know, Oedipus is blind to his blindness when it comes to matters of identity. Passing by the great and awful eye, he continues to fear the threat posed by his living mother, even though he is speaking eye-to-eye with her all the while.

The combination of joy and bereavement in a bright burial is oxymoronic, an awkward combination of feelings anticipated by the Messenger who announces Polybus' death (936–37). Besides the tragic irony occasioned by the woeful ignorance of the dramatic characters, we should also sense the ominous significance of an eye whose presence seems so established (overdetermined) yet out of place (arbitrary). As readers, we may readily recognize the significance of an eye within the Sophoclean poetics of unconcealment and concealment, a network of themes and diction especially prominent in *Oedipus Tyrannus*. Key words concerning eyesight, knowledge, blindness, and ignorance have their linguistic nexus in the common Greek verb for seeing (*horaô*), and its perfect tense, used of knowing (*oida*). The etymological significance hidden in the name Oedipus (swollen foot, knowing foot) makes it a comparable nodal point. Hence the eye's overdetermined character; it is a condensed, extraordinarily polysemous sign, fundamentally associated not only with brightness but also with seeing and knowing.[25] Opthalmic imagery is a major nexus where these themes converge.[26] And this puts *ophthalmos* in a different relation to the darkness implied by burial in the sentence. Burial (the crucial part of the funeral rites referred to here) is not only sorrowful but also concealing. By casting a bright eye on the burial, Jocasta, whose name seems etymologically to indicate brightness (but is related to the English verb *cast* only through homonymy), happens to be concealing or repressing the horrible truth about Oedipus' origins. In this sense, the *ophthalmos* is blind, a misplaced sign or *sêma*, marking the tomb of the stepfather, not the father.[27] The eye buries the truth, but it does so conspicuously, covering it up in the manner of the familiar–unfamiliar uncanny.

In addition to misplacing the father's death, the *ophthalmos* seeks to replace the truth of Apollo's oracle at Delphi. A basic meaning conveyed by Jocasta is that Polybus' death proves the oracles false. She prays to Apollo when anxious (911–23), but she appears, as does the Chorus (498–501), to distinguish between divine power and humanly mediated prophecy, which she disparages (708–9, 723–25, 857, 946). Her own utterance serves as a tragically parodic double of oracular discourse.[28] First, the sentence in question exhibits several oracular features. It is itself cryptic and oracular, steeped in double meanings. Second, the utterance discerns a (positive) omen in the death of Polybus. Here, we may recall Creon's return from the oracle early in the play, when Oedipus hopes for good news from Apollo and looks for Creon to appear "bright like an eye" (*lampros hôsper omma ti*; 82). Oedipus' eye (*omma*) occurs in an explicit simile and refers to a person, which is a typical metaphorical usage for the word. As a replacement for Tiresian prophetic vision, Jocasta's *ophthalmos* specifically bears comparison with the Delphic *omphalos* (navel), the rock considered the center of the earth and the seat of Apollo's oracle (464, 480, 899). Pindar gives us a parallel image in *Nemean* 7, calling the rock a "great *omphalos*" (*megan omphalon*; 32; see also *Pythian* 4.74). Jocasta's great eye signals an attempt to assume control over her family. The Delphic *omphalos* has distorted Oedipus' path from birth, displacing him from Thebes and then from Corinth, vying with Jocasta for centrality in Oedipus' geographical and familial disposition. Having replaced the omphalic *sêma* with an ophthalmic substitute, Jocasta believes that the oracular version of events has been replaced and overcome, and this belief makes her susceptible to the return of the repressed.

Comparing Jocasta's *ophthalmos* with Apollo's *omphalos* also gives us the interpretive advantage of considering her maternal failure against the foil of a paternal navel. In terms of Freud's Oedipus complex, Jocasta's reassurance, which neglects and fails to name the father, is a strikingly wishful formulation, preserving the eye from castration while burying the father. Apollo's prophetic truth, in contrast, represents a paternal law, but one with the navel of mother earth at its center. This is the ultimate displacement of gendered parenthood that betokens Jocasta's failure, Apollo taking precedence as the ultimate father, occupying the very first place, in this story. Through foreknowledge of Oedipus' conception, crimes, and punishment, the oracle at Delphi is the father of the story, an eye of the sort identified in Mark Griffith's essay "The King and Eye" as a figure for supremacy in Greek tragedy: "the Father as the symbol, or representative, or embodiment…of social and aesthetic, as well as familial, Order."[29] It should come as no surprise that Apollo's oracular brilliance outshines Jocasta's.

A final uncanny aspect of Jocasta's eye deserves special mention. In his description of ambiguous discourse in Sophocles, Vernant emphasizes the doubleness and the oracular tenor of utterances that seem to exceed Oedipus' own knowledge and insight: "Oedipus does not hear the secret discourse which is established, without his knowing it, at the heart of his own discourse."[30] In Vernant's view, Oedipus represents a special kind of ambiguity in Sophocles' *Oedipus Tyrannus*, a confrontation between human and divine discourses—and the divine dimension of Oedipus' speech is oracular, corresponding to Delphic truth and correctly describing events as they unfold.[31] This kind of discourse has much in common with Freud's uncanny, expressing itself without the knowledge or consent of the speaker and making him or her act as the medium of superhuman ventriloquism. But Jocasta too says things that go beyond the scope of acceptable possibility within the fictional drama; she can know nothing about Sophocles' ophthalmic diction and his thematic focus on insight, yet she confronts us with a pregnant eye. Even more uncanny is the way that her eye seems to say things about itself. With the uncanny quality of endless reflection, the *ophthalmos* turns out to be a sign of foreboding, signaling its own oblivion.

NOTES

1. Zeitlin (1990, 132); cf. Vernant (1982, 23); Segal (2001, 62).
2. Compare the following translations of *ophthalmos*: Lloyd-Jones (1994): "source of light"; Grene (1991): "light of comfort"; Bollack (1990): "lumière"; Jebb (1885): "bright, sudden comfort."
3. See Liddel, Scott, and Jones (1940) (hereafter cited as *LSJ*), s.v. *ophthalmos*.
4. Segal (1995, 162).
5. Ibid., 165.
6. Ibid., 167.
7. Ibid., 164, 168–69 with notes; Pucci (1992, 27–28) with notes.
8. See Heidegger ([1927] 1996), section 44; Reinhardt (1979, 100–101); see also Detienne (1999), especially chap. 2.
9. Heidegger (1953, 112–26; 1959, 146–65); Segal (1995, 167). On Heidegger's view of *unheimlich*, see Weber (2000, 21–31).
10. My quotation preserves the *Standard Edition*'s italics, single quote marks, and glosses in square brackets. That Freud initially treats *heimlich* as synonymous with familiar (listing *heimlich, heimisch,*

vertraut), even though it commonly means "concealed," adds an extra wrinkle to his presentation.

11. On dead metaphors, see Cruse (1986, 41–45); cf. Nietzsche (1999); Culler (1981).

12. In discussing the semantics of dead metaphors, Cruse initially puts the terms *dead*, *live*, and *revive* in quotation marks, thereby typographically indicating their peculiar metalinguistic status (1986, 41–42).

13. Vernant (1983, 189); cf. Segal (1986, 68): "The very subject of the *Oedipus Tyrannus* is polysemicity."

14. In this chapter, I focus on graphical rather than phonological identity but prefer to use the term homonymy rather than homography; the theoretical distinction here concerns either form of doubling. See Lyons (1977, 2:550–69). Lyons calls absolute homonymy a "theoretically ideal notion" (569). See also Cruse (1986, 80–81); Greenbaum (1996, 428–30).

15. This is the German text in Freud's *Gesammelte Werke* (1952 12:235).

16. *SE* 11:155–61. On Freud, language, and literature, see Orlando (1978); Segal (1995, 163n6); Lacan (1977, especially 59).

17. However, we must share Freud's awareness that the meanings of *heimisch* and *heimlich* are mutually foreign (*fremd*) rather than strictly antithetical (*SE* 17:224).

18. Segal (1981, 242).

19. "The process of reading Sophocles through Freud's eyes can also be reversed, to cast light on Freud's processes of intellectual discovery" (Segal 1995, 176). But also compare Segal on Freud's limited approach to literature: "A Freudian reading is often unhistorical and inattentive to esthetic form and tends to disregard cultural differences" (2001, 41); see also Segal (1995, 177–79).

20. Wohl (2002, 254).

21. See Vernant (1983, 191): "Oedipus is double." See also Segal (1981, 241–44); Pucci (1992).

22. Cf. Chase (1979, 65).

23. See note 2. Citing parallels in which *ophthalmos* seems to mean "highly prized," Dawe (1982, 196) notes that none provides a suitable meaning for this context, and he regards emendation favorably. Kamerbeek (1967, 13) does not find the received text suspicious; as he puts it, "the sentence is at the same time a terrifying oxymoron and a terrible tragic irony."

24. On this combination of particles, see Denniston ([1934] 1950, 357); see also Jebb (1885, app. A).
25. See Segal (1986, 68): "Oedipus is a constellation of opposites where the ambiguity of the individual's primal word, his name, implicates the entire denotational, differentiating system of language itself." Cf. Pucci (1992, 66–78).
26. On visual symbolism in Sophocles generally, see Segal (1986, 113–36).
27. On the semantics of *sêma*, see Nagy (1990).
28. Vernant (1983) attributes this sort of doubled, oracular discourse to Oedipus in particular.
29. Griffith (1998, 77). See also Pucci (1992); Wohl (2002, especially 251).
30. Vernant (1983, 192).
31. Ibid., 191–93.

REFERENCES

Bollack, Jean. 1990. *L' "Oedipe roi" de Sophocle: Le texte et ses interprétations*. 4 vols. Lille: Presses universitaires de Lille.

Chase, Cynthia. 1979. Oedipal textuality: Reading Freud's reading of Oedipus. *Diacritics* 9: 53–68.

Cruse, D. A. 1986. *Lexical semantics*. Cambridge: Cambridge University Press.

Culler, Jonathan. The turns of metaphor. In *The pursuit of signs*, 188–209. Ithaca, NY: Cornell University Press.

Dawe, R. D., ed. 1982. *Sophocles: Oedipus Rex*. Cambridge: Cambridge University Press.

Denniston, J. D. [1934] 1950. *The Greek particles*. A facsimile of the first edition, rev. K. Dover. Indianapolis, IN: Hackett.

Detienne, Marcel. 1999. *The masters of truth in archaic Greece*. Trans. Janet Lloyd. New ed. New York: Zone Books.

de Man, Paul. 1984. *The rhetoric of Romanticism*. New York: Columbia University Press.

Freud, Sigmund. 1952. *Gesammelte Werke*. Ed. A. Freud et al. 17 vols. London: Imago.

———. 1953–74. *The standard edition of the complete psychological works of Sigmund Freud*. Trans. and ed. J. Strachey et al. 24 vols. London: Hogarth.

Greenbaum, Sydney. 1996. *The Oxford English Grammar*. Oxford: Oxford University Press.

Grene, David., trans. 1991. *Oedipus the King*. Vol. 1 of *Sophocles*. 2nd ed. Chicago: University of Chicago Press.

Griffith, Mark. 1998. The king and eye: The rule of the father in Greek tragedy. *Proceedings of the Cambridge Philological Society* 44: 20–84.

Heidegger, Martin. [1927] 1996. *Being and time*. Trans. Joan Stambaugh. Albany: State University of New York Press.

———. 1953. *Einführung in die Metaphysik*. Tübingen: Niemeyer.

———. 1959. *An introduction to metaphysics*. Trans. Ralph Manheim. New Haven, CT: Yale University Press.

Jebb, Richard C., ed. 1885. *Sophocles: Oedipus Tyrannus*. Repr., Bristol: Bristol Classical Press, 1981.

Kamerbeek, J. C. 1967. *The Oedipus Tyrannus*. Part 4 of *The plays of Sophocles: Commentaries*. Leiden: Brill.

Lacan, Jacques. 1977. *Écrits*. Trans. A. Sheridan. New York: Norton.

Liddel, H. G., R. Scott, and S. Jones, eds. 1940. *Greek–English Lexicon*. 9th ed. Oxford: Oxford University Press.

Lloyd-Jones, H., ed. and trans. 1994. *Sophocles*. 3 vols. Cambridge, MA: Harvard University Press. Oxford: Clarendon.

Lyons, John. 1977. *Semantics*. 2 vols. Cambridge: Cambridge University Press.

Nagy, Gregory. 1990. *Sêma* and *Noêsis*: The hero's tomb and the "Reading" of symbols in Homer and Hesiod. In *Greek mythology and poetics*, 202–22. Ithaca, NY: Cornell University Press.

Nietzsche, Friedrich W. 1999. On truth and lying in a non-moral sense. In *"The Birth of Tragedy" and other writings*, ed. R. Geuss and R. Speirs, trans. R. Speirs, 141–53. Cambridge: Cambridge University Press.

Orlando, Francesco. 1978. *Toward a Freudian theory of literature*. Trans. C. Lee. Baltimore, MD: Johns Hopkins University Press.

Pucci, Pietro. 1992. *Oedipus and the fabrication of the father*. Baltimore, MD: Johns Hopkins University Press.

Reinhardt, Karl. 1979. *Sophocles*. Trans. H. and D. Harvey. New York: Barnes & Noble.

Segal, Charles. 1981. *Tragedy and civilization: An interpretation of Sophocles*. Cambridge, MA: Harvard University Press.

———. 1986. *Interpreting Greek tragedy: Myth, poetry, text*. Ithaca, NY: Cornell University Press.

———. 1995. Freud, language, and the unconscious. In *Sophocles' tragic world: Divinity, nature, society*. Cambridge, MA: Harvard University Press.

———. 2001. *Oedipus Tyrannus: Tragic heroism and the limits of knowledge*. 2nd ed. Oxford: Oxford University Press.

Vernant, Jean-Pierre. 1982. From Oedipus to Periander: Lameness, tyranny, incest in legend and history." *Arethusa* 15: 19–38.

———. 1983. Ambiguity and reversal: On the enigmatic structure of Oedipus Rex. In *Greek tragedy: Modern essays in criticism*, ed. E. Segal, 189–209. New York: Harper & Row.

Weber, Samuel. 2000. *The legend of Freud*. Expanded ed. Stanford: Stanford University Press.

Wohl, Victoria. 2002. *Love among the ruins: The erotics of democracy in classical Athens*. Princeton, NJ: Princeton University Press.

Zeitlin, Froma I. 1990. Thebes: Theater of self and society in Athenian drama. In *Nothing to do with Dionysus? Athenian drama in its social context*, ed. J. J. Winkler and F. I. Zeitlin, 130–67. Princeton, NJ: Princeton University Press.

5

SEXUAL DIFFERENCE AND THE APORIA OF JUSTICE IN SOPHOCLES' *ANTIGONE*

VICTORIA WOHL

In G. W. F. Hegel's influential gloss on Sophocles' *Antigone* in *Phenomenology of Spirit*, the dialectic between the human law of the state and the divine law of the family is made manifest in sexual difference, the dialectic of man and woman. The coming together of the sexes represents the possibility of synthesis or mediation between the two realms and laws: "The union of man and woman constitutes the active middle term of the whole and the element which sunders itself into these extremes of divine and human law" (§ 463). Harmonizing divine law and human, family and state, the sexual relation effects the equilibrium that Hegel identifies with justice (§ 462).[1]

But Sophocles' play, like many Greek tragedies, illustrates the truth of the Lacanian dictum, "there is no sexual relation." In a world where man and woman are antagonists and *erôs* is bound up with incest and death, sexual difference resists the synthesis or transcendence of an ideal union. That impossibility entails another, the irresolvable conflict between two antithetical and mutually exclusive laws, each with its own claim to and definition of justice. These two laws are gendered in *Antigone*, and their conflict is charted onto the conflict between the sexes, but the convergences between sexual difference and legal difference are far from straightforward. A gender transgression engenders a legal crisis: two sexes breed two laws. Creon tries to resolve this legal crisis by articulating it with gender hierarchy, the obvious priority of male over female. But instead of the certainties of gender clarifying legal confusion, the impasse of sexual difference opens a space of difference within the law itself, exposing the irreducibility of justice to any specific law, male or female. The play does not try to resolve this aporia between law and justice, male and female, but instead institutes this

119

impasse as the law of tragedy and the grounding condition for democratic deliberation.

In this play, legal conflict and gender conflict are inseparable. Antigone disobeys Creon's specific *nomos* (law), burying her brother Polyneices in direct contravention of his command; she also transgresses the *nomoi* or conventions of Athenian gender relations. Women were not legal or political subjects in democratic Athens. They did not vote or speak in the assembly or law courts. Ideally, they did not speak or act in the public sphere at all. Their realm was the household, and when their interests extended beyond it, they were represented by a male *kyrios* (master, guardian), typically a husband or male kinsman.[2] Sophocles' play (again, like much tragedy) dramatically inverts this state of affairs. Antigone acts and speaks in public, challenging the king in front of the elders of the city and justifying her action in front of a (presumably male) audience of Athenian citizens.[3] What could be interpreted as a typically female act of familial piety, honoring her dead brother in accordance with the obligations of kinship, is simultaneously a political act, committed in knowing defiance of the law (*Ant.* 447–49). This reversal of gender norms is all the more remarkable in that Antigone is not just a woman, but an unmarried daughter, typically the most subordinate member of the family; Creon is not just a man, but the king of Thebes and, as her uncle and closest male relative, her *kyrios*. Her action is thus a crime not only against civic law but also, ironically, against the family and the patriarchal authority vested within it.

The legal implications of this gender transgression are apparent from the first scene of the play, where Antigone's sister Ismene equates obedience to the law with feminine submission. We will be killed, she warns Antigone, "if in violation of the law we go beyond the vote and power of tyrants. But we must recognize that we were born women, so as not to do battle against men; then, too, because we are ruled by people more powerful than ourselves we must obey this or even worse" (59–64). Ismene's language, which conflates law with both autocratic power (*tyrannôn kratê*) and democratic process (*psêphon*), ignores the question of justice: right or wrong, the law compels (*biazomai*, 66) obedience. The law's power over its subjects is as incontrovertible, in Ismene's mind, as the power of men over women, of stronger over weaker. The law is masculine and its obedient subjects are docile daughters. Antigone's disobedience does violence to the law (*nomou biâi*, 59) and presages a war between the sexes (*pros andras...maxoumena*, 62). This thinking is echoed in Creon's horrified reaction to Antigone's act. She has committed one violent transgression (*hubris*) by going beyond the established laws and another in exulting over her deed in public (480–83). "Now I am not the man but she is the man if with impunity the power in this affair will lie with her" (484–85). Antigone's act simultaneously threatens masculinity and law; it threatens precisely the masculinity of law and the legal dominance of masculinity.

This in itself might not be catastrophic: the law, after all, needs its outlaws and a masculine law might particularly welcome the opportunity to prove itself by punishing a female transgressor; this is, in fact, a common tragic plotline. But Antigone not only breaks Creon's law; she propounds another law of her own.[4] Her burial of her brother, which she wishes to be publicly announced to the city (*kêrukseîs*, 87), is a proclamation to counter that issued by Creon (*ekkekêrukhthai*, 27; *kêruksant'*, 32; *prokêruksonta*, 34). As Sophocles represents it, their two laws are as different, as irreducible, unmediable, and mutually exclusive, as male and female. Each grounds itself on a different and equally valid basis; each has an equal claim to authority and justice; each has strong support within the play. Creon's is the law of the city: it aims at and is authorized by the ideal of civic order. With his ship of state metaphor, his promotion of the city's interests over the individual's, and his echoes of the popular contemporary statesman Pericles, Creon stakes his law on the hallowed soil of Athenian civic ideology.[5] "I would never take as my friend an enemy of this land, knowing that she is our salvation and only when she sails upright can we have friends at all. This is the law by which I will make this city great" (187–91). The city's good is both the grounds and the goal of his proclamation banning the burial of Polyneices; it is the foundation of his personal authority and the authority of his law (*toioisd' egô nomoisi*, 191). The gods, to the extent that Creon is concerned with them, surely support his position (288). This legal philosophy of course begs many thorny questions (including the definition of the civic good) to which we will return later. In its broadest outlines, however, it probably would have been compelling to an Athenian audience. Its general principles—the primacy of the city over the individual, the foundation of law's authority in the *polis*—underlie much political rhetoric of the fifth and fourth century. It may have seemed particularly valid here, in the mouth of a general (*stratêgon*, 8) in the wake of a civil war. A measure of its legitimacy is the strong endorsement of the Chorus of elders who represent the Theban political community. Their response to Creon's statement of his principle of law (178–91) suggests that to them the principle authorizes not only this, but any law based on it: "It is your prerogative to enact every law" (213; cf. 681–82). Although it is possible, as Antigone later suggests

(504–9), that fear silences their opposition, it seems that at least for the first three-quarters of the play the Chorus of Theban elders support the fundamental philosophy and claim to legitimacy of Creon's position.

The law Antigone expounds is antithetical, although equally valid, based on the unwritten law of the gods that dictates that kin must be buried. She, too, has an unimpeachable authority behind her: Zeus, his daughter Justice, and the gods of the underworld (450–52). Zeus is the supreme power and source of legitimacy in the world of tragedy and in contemporary Athens. Creon himself calls on Zeus to witness and legitimate both his particular law (304–5) and his legal philosophy (184). Antigone's divinely authorized unwritten laws, like Creon's civic laws, would have been familiar to, and no doubt resonated positively with, an audience of Athenian citizens who prided themselves on their piety and their attention to ritual prescriptions.[6] Again, her specific claims can be debated (what exactly did the laws of burial require?), but the underlying principle of divine authority is indisputable and is strongly supported within the play by Tiresias, the blind seer of Apollo, a figure who, with his unerring prophetic ability and direct access to the gods, carries a good deal of moral weight in Sophoclean tragedy. His revelation of the gods' displeasure at the dishonored corpse and his prediction (proven true at the end of the play) of the suffering that will result seem unambiguously, if belatedly, to endorse the divine law on which Antigone bases her action.

Ideally, these two laws should and did coexist within the *polis*.[7] Like male and female, or city and household, they were seen as compatible and complementary; both had to be respected for the *polis* to be strong. So says Pericles in Thucydides' Funeral Oration: "We Athenians obey those who are currently in office and we obey the laws, especially those which are established for the benefit of victims of injustice and those unwritten laws whose breach brings undisputed shame" (Thuc. 2.37.3). This ideal of civic and divine laws in harmony is echoed in *Antigone*'s first stasimon (the famous "Ode to Man"), where man's "civic-minded, law-abiding temperament" (*astunomous orgas*, 355–56) is part of what makes him *deinos* (wonderful, terrible, awesome): "Honoring the laws of the land and the sworn justice of the gods, he stands high in his city; but citiless is the man who for the sake of daring dwells with evil" (368–71).[8]

But that harmony between the two laws—like the ideal of cooperation between male and female—is not borne out in the rest of the play. While Athens honored both laws and regarded them as mutually reinforcing, tragedy puts them into conflict, representing them as mutually exclusive and mutually invalidating. If the law Antigone champions is valid (as Tiresias and the catastrophic end of the play suggest), then Creon's law is criminal not only in its results (the death of an innocent girl) but also in its very claim to justice: the proclamation that instantiates Creon's law is, in fact, a breach of law. If, on the other hand, Creon's law is valid (as the Chorus seem to think and the audience is led to believe for the bulk of the play), then Antigone's law is illegal, a mere excuse for criminality. By their very conflict, the two laws are set up as absolutes: the polarization of the sexes has its legal corollary in the contest between these two antithetical laws.[9] So the play brings us to an impasse, trapped between two irreducible and equally legitimate versions of justice, with no possibility of adjudicating between them—legal and hermeneutic aporia. The situation also yields civic aporia, for the city of Thebes cannot take a step without breaking a law on one side or the other: it is faced with a nonchoice between ritual pollution and political anarchy.

Moreover, Antigone and Creon's laws not only stand on different ground but also show each other to be groundless. Each declares the other law outlaw from its own perspective; it also shows the other law to be illegal in its own terms. Antigone's resistance reveals the arbitrary and illegitimate violence within Creon's law, a violence that his law cannot itself legislate or guard against. Forced by Antigone's transgression to defend and justify his position publicly, Creon exposes its weaknesses in the very speech intended to prove its strength (640–80). Speaking to Haimon, Creon sets his legal theory in the context of paternal authority: filial obedience is likened to military (*opisthen hestanai*, 640) and political (*katêkoous*, 642) obedience, and the father-son relation, with its loving authority and willing submission, becomes a model for the bond of civic *philia*: the law-making ruler is a benevolent father and the law-abiding citizen a loyal son.

Domestic order is the model and basis for civic order. Both are threatened by woman and the desires she arouses. A "wound" within the house (652), a bad wife is the paradigmatic enemy (*philos kakos*, 652; *dusmenê*, 653), just as the good son is the ideal ally. Disrupting the bond of loyalty between father and son, she creates chaos in the household. The fear of this disorder prompts Creon's most explicit exposition of his political philosophy:

> If I nurture disorder within my family
> certainly I will have it outside as well.
> For whoever is a good man in the household

will show himself to be just in the city too.
I am confident this man
would rule well and be willing to be ruled in turn
and would keep to his post in the storm of spears,
a just and noble comrade.
But whoever transgresses the laws and does them violence
or thinks to command those who rule him
will never get my approval.
Whomever the *polis* appoints must be obeyed
in matters big or small, just or the opposite.
There is no greater evil than anarchy.
This destroys cities; this overturns houses;
this makes allied spears
break out in flight. Obedience
saves many souls of those who are set straight.
Therefore order must be preserved
and I must never be beaten by a woman.
It is better, if I must, to fall at a man's hand
and not be called worse than a woman. (659–80)[10]

Creon represents Antigone's action as a crime not only against himself but also against masculine authority and the natural order of gender,
and its violent enforcement as a restoration of proper gender relations:
his punishment of Antigone will be a lesson to women not to be "wandering free" (579; cf. 525). This is a depressingly familiar strategy in
Greek tragedy: otherwise irresolvable conflicts can be resolved by charting them onto gender difference, with its unambiguous and seemingly
incontrovertible hierarchy of male over female.[11] Creon tries to cut the
knot of legal conflict with the sword of sexual difference, tying his law
to the "unwritten laws" of male superiority. But this misogynist strategy
in fact cuts both ways, for even as it asserts the power of masculine law
over female disorder, it also makes the former dependent on the latter.
Displacing the just citizen (661) from city to household, it grounds Creon's civic justice in the familial realm that is properly Antigone's own.

Moreover, the exact shape of the civic order he imagines is obscure
and shifting. At first we seem to have a democracy, with citizens ruling
and being ruled in turn (a virtual definition of democracy) and standing
shoulder-to-shoulder in hoplite battle. But in the next lines we move from
legitimate democratic authority (*kalôs arkhein, eu arkhesthai*) through
the rule of law (*nomous*) to the powerful individual whose word must
be obeyed in every instance, whether it is just or "the opposite" (667).

The civic good has become the will of the powerful individual (though still imagined as appointed by the city, 666). This shift from democracy to autocracy reveals a fundamental weakness in Creon's law. It is authorized by the notion of civic order, but the definition of that order is not fixed or obvious; instead it must be negotiated through political contest. Again the authority of Creon's position is deferred, this time not to the domestic realm but to the political. Once there, in the absence of the institutional safeguards of democracy, it easily collapses into the will of the stronger: the powerful define the civic good.[12] Pushed to its extreme, as it is by Antigone's resistance, Creon's law becomes tyranny: the city belongs by law and custom to its ruler, Creon will later tell Haimon (*tou kratountos hê polis nomizetai*, 738). This signals a third displacement of the foundation of Creon's law—onto himself.

With no reference to anything beyond itself, Creon's law of the civic good (a law, I suggested above, that would have resonated positively within Athenian democratic ideology) is transformed into its and democracy's inverse, a tyranny.[13] Under this regime, the good citizen, no longer a loyal son, becomes a broken horse, a slave, a woman (473–85). Masculine law becomes the law of one man, and the male dominance on which Creon tried to prop his power instead illuminates its oppressive and antidemocratic asymmetry. This tyrannical strain in Creon's position is, to be sure, implicit from the beginning of the play: it is hinted in Ismene's reference to the "vote and power of tyrants" (60) and even in the Chorus' approving response to Creon's first speech ("It is your prerogative to enact every law," 213); it is also displayed in Creon's overbearing dealings with the guard (280–331). But it is Antigone and her transgression that really bring it to the surface; it is she who, by forcing him to articulate and enact the autocratic violence within his power, turns him into a tyrant and transforms his law into murder. She does this quite literally at the end of the play. Creon has had Antigone locked up without food in the hopes of avoiding religious pollution, but the violence his law would deny is laid bare by the scene of her actual death: her suicide by hanging, along with Haimon's and Eurydice's bloody deaths by the sword, all laid explicitly at Creon's feet.[14] Thus Antigone brings out the tyrannical force implicit in Creon's law—the reducibility of the civic good to power politics and civic law to the will of the strongest—and shows that the law founded only on masculine authority and civic order ultimately destroys both the city and the man.

At the same time, the law Antigone puts forth, which claims a different and more elevated authority than Creon's, seems unable to shake the traces of that other law it calls illegality.

> For me it was not Zeus who made this proclamation
> nor did Dikê, who dwells with the gods below,
> define these laws among mortals.
> Nor did I think your pronouncements so strong
> that you, a mortal man, could overrun
> the unwritten and unfailing laws of the gods.
> For they live not just now or yesterday
> but forever, and no one knows their origin.
> I am not about to pay the penalty for these laws
> in a court of gods, out of fear of any man's will. (450–60)

Antigone's law is authorized by Zeus and Dikê, the divine personifications of justice: her law, in her view, *is* justice. She draws an absolute distinction between the eternal, unwritten laws of the gods and the pronouncements of man. But that distinction is hard to maintain: the gods' laws are unwritten (*agrapta*), but so apparently are Creon's, which are referred to here and throughout the play as *kêrugmata*, pronouncements. Moreover, Zeus' law, the antithesis of Creon's, is also a *kêrugma* (*kêruksas*, 450). The distinction between written and unwritten, which for Antigone shores up the divine law (*agrapta k'asphalê*, 455), is not black and white in this passage. Indeed, the distinction was hazy in Athenian legal discourse more generally: written laws in Athens were, for the most part, known in oral form[15] and, conversely, "the unwritten laws" were a category within actual Athenian legal practice. Aristotle advises that if a litigant is composing a defense speech and the written laws do not support his case, he should appeal to the unwritten laws and their timeless and self-evident justice; he even cites this speech of Antigone's as an example (although perhaps an ill-chosen one, since she loses her case).[16]

Antigone's speech ends, as it began, with Dikê, but whereas Dikê at the beginning is the deified abstraction Justice, *dikê* appears at the end of the speech in its most terrestrial form, meaning to pay the penalty in a court of law (*dikên dôsein*). This shift is explicable if, as Helene Foley argues, Antigone tailors her arguments to their specific audience: responding to Creon, this speech mirrors his legal language and logic.[17] But the effect is that her divine law collapses back into his civic law: the law of the city and its courts is displaced but not radically altered. Antigone's *dikê* is elsewhere but not clearly other.[18] Her law, too, like its earthly counterpart, is masculine and paternal, based on the supreme authority of Zeus, and the personification of Dikê as her father's loyal daughter merely reiterates in inverse the logic that makes a disobedient daughter the quintessential criminal.[19] Even as her law challenges and undermines Creon's, it supports its fundamental premise of the masculinity of power.

Antigone's charge that Creon is overstepping divine law (*huperdramein*, 455) chimes with his similar charges against her (*huperbainein*, 449, 481; cf. 663). The boundaries may be different, but the diction of transgression is the same and makes divine law no less bounded than human. Both can be gone beyond. This spatial idiom is echoed by the Chorus later: "Reaching the extreme of daring, you [Antigone] have tripped on the lofty seat of Dikê" (853–55). Antigone's relation to justice seems to be more equivocal than her initial appeal to Dikê suggests, and if this is true, then it means that the divine laws are no less open to interpretation and debate than are mortal laws: they, too, are ultimately a matter of politics. And while Antigone's position would appear to be reaffirmed at a higher level by Tiresias toward the end of the play, this comes too late to help Antigone, who goes to her death wondering if the law for which she is dying is really *dikê*: "What justice [*dikê*] of the gods did I transgress? Why in my misery should I still look to the gods? What divine ally should I invoke, since I who am pious have been charged with impiety?" (921–24).[20]

Moreover, Antigone's law, too, like Creon's, has its violence. A law regulating death, emanating from death ("Hades desires these *nomoi*," 519), it commits her knowingly to death.[21] This, as she says, is her own choice and desire, but it takes others in her wake, including her fiancé and nearly her sister. A violence against the laws (59) and the citizens (79, 907), it ultimately does, as Creon warns, bring devastation to the city. Further, there are hints that Antigone's actions may enact a violence against the gods as well. Creon notes that, in honoring Polyneices, she is committing an impiety by dishonoring Eteocles (512–16). She is forced in response to admit that no one knows what is holy in the underworld (521), a confession that reveals the force within her own interpretation of the laws of burial.[22] The Chorus, too, perhaps imply that Antigone commits violence against the gods when they compare her to Lycurgus (who was punished for his opposition to Dionysus), although the exact purpose and meaning of their comparison is obscure.[23] Like Creon's law, Antigone's is shown to be violent in its own terms and destructive of its own authorizing principles.

Not only does the conflict between the two laws starkly illuminate the differences between them, but it also reveals an internal difference within each law, a difference of the law from what it claims to be and from justice. On the one hand, the conflict sustains both laws: each posits the other as its own exterior, the "outlaw" it needs to prove its power. On the other hand, each is internal to the other: Creon's civic law is predicated on domestic order; Antigone's divine law contains traces of the political. Each is thus, like Creon and Antigone themselves, the other's "in-law," an internal counterlaw that works to expose the other's inner contradictions and inherent violence and to corrode the foundations of its exclusive authority. Set in polar opposition, each criminal to the other, they cannot be synthesized or mediated; intimately entangled, they refuse hierarchal ordering or definitive choice. They are simultaneously outlaws and in-laws to one another, a legal kinship that delegitimates both and produces aporia within each and in the relation between them.

This legal aporia is thematized in the play by that other seminal aporia, sexual difference. But is it, then, resolved through sexual union, as Hegel proposes? Love, both *erôs* (sexual desire, passion) and *philia* (fondness, nearness), is fraught in *Antigone*, ambivalent in itself and in its relation to *nomos*, bound up with death and unable to free itself from the pull of incest. "I was born to join in love [*sumphilein*] not in hate," says Antigone in justification of her act (523). But what is her *philia*? Not love for Haimon, toward whom she expresses no sentiment at all, as many scholars have noted. Theirs is a missed connection not only at the emotional level but also at the institutional: this marriage of a virgin heiress to her cousin, which would have seemed an ideal arrangement to many Athenians, is forbidden by her *kyrios*, who instead ultimately consigns both his ward and his son to sterility and death.[24] The nonlove story at the center of the play indicates at the most obvious level the failure of sexual union: Haimon and Antigone are united neither in love nor in marriage and Creon's house fails to reproduce itself in the next generation.

Instead, her *philia* leads Antigone back toward her natal family. The incestuous overtones of Antigone's devotion to her brother are subtle but pervasive.[25] She imagines in death "I will lie with him, dear to him who is dear to me, committing a pious crime" (73–74; cf. 898–99); she seeks to please her "dearest brother" in the grave (75, 81, 89). Repeating the generational introversion of her parents, Antigone is pictured both as Polyneices' bedmate in death (73) and as his mother, mourning him like a nightingale crying over her nest "orphaned" of chicks (424–25).[26] This incestuous *philia* replaces sexual *erôs*: her devotion to her brother has left her, as she laments repeatedly, "without marriage bed or hymeneal, with no share in marriage or motherhood" (917–18). In the play's allusive aural punning, she rejects Haimon and the hymeneal in favor of *haima* (blood) and *ho sunhaimos* (he who shares her blood).[27] The result is sterility: the generations turn back on themselves as Antigone's hanging repeats that of her mother. Rejecting sexuality, she fulfills the prophecies implicit in her own name (*anti-gonê*): instead of reproduction, she takes the place of her own parent and gives her life in exchange for her birth.[28]

This impossible, destructive desire metaphorizes Antigone's status as outlaw, playing out in an erotic key the theme of her repudiation of both the gender norms and the laws of the city. Her desire to please the dead, says Ismene, is a "lust for the impossible" (*amêkhanôn erâis*, 90); her disobedience, as Creon puts it, is "a lust to die" (*thanein erâi*, 220). Her rejection of Creon's law is represented as a rejection of the incest taboo along with the corollary mandates to marry and reproduce; conversely, it is her criminal ancestry that drives her to break Creon's prohibition: her crime "manifests the wild breeding of the daughter from a wild father" (471–72); her suffering "pays the penalty for some paternal ordeal" (856). But while her incestuous desire may represent her transgression of Creon's law, it also grounds her own law. Her justification of her divine mandate boils down to this: she will not leave unburied the "man from my mother" (*ton ex emês mêtros*, 466–67). This vague and compressed circumlocution evokes the complexities of her family relations, where all derivations are overdetermined (Polyneices is "from" Jocasta both as son and grandson). It places incest at the root of her act and her law. The Chorus characterizes her in her living descent to Hades as *autonomos*, making or obeying her own law (821). The intensive *auto-* root ("self," "same"), which recurs so many times in this play, connotes not only the isolated self but also the reflexive self-sameness of incest. Antigone not only transgresses Creon's law but also establishes an incestuous counter-law all her own.[29]

The incestuous logic of Antigone's (*auto*)*nomos* and its implications are laid out with disturbing clarity in a famous and much-debated speech:[30]

> For not if I were the mother of children
> nor if my husband had died and lay rotting
> would I have taken on this task in defiance of the citizens.
> In consideration of what law [*nomos*] do I say this?
> My husband dead, I could have another,
> and a child from another man, if I lost one.
> But with my mother and father both buried in Hades,
> no brother might ever be born again.
> By this law [*nomos*], brother, I honored you above all
> and in Creon's eyes committed
> a crime of terrible daring. (905–15)

Antigone's law rejects the substitutive economy of marriage and reproduction (husband replaces father, one generation replaces another) that makes all husbands and children theoretically replaceable. Instead, her law honors her unique and irreplaceable brother, born from unique and irreplaceable parents. These parents are also, of course, her own: he is, she said, "the man from my mother [*ton ex emês mêtros*]" (466–67); change the grammatical gender and he is she.[31] Polyneices is unique, then, in his birth from her own unique origin, from the mother and father who are both two and one (note the dual, 911) and whose mysterious union is barred ("buried") by their death. This is the sexual relationship in its purest form: a union of two that produces a third, a mysterious synthesis inaccessible to the child it generates.

It is precisely this buried origin that Antigone aims to reach with her act. Death will return her, she says, to the "madness of the maternal bed and the incestuous lying with my father of my unfortunate mother" (863–65). She imagines returning to this incestuous scene as both its native offspring (*hoiôn egô ephun*, 866) and an alien (*metoikos*, 868). Antigone projects herself back to the moment of her inception and before, entering into her mother's mind (*atê*) and her incestuous, self-generating (*autogennêta*) bed. At the same time, she acknowledges that she can never occupy that position: she will always be a metic at the imagined scene of her own birth.

This is what Polyneices represents for her, the impasse of the sexual relation from which she was born, a place to which she cannot return but from which she will not move on. This, she says, is her law. True to its incestuous foundations, this law, too, is impossible, an impasse. One of the many objections to Antigone's speech at 905ff. is that it seems to contradict the universal divine mandate to which she appealed earlier and to posit a law that applies in one, and only one, instance.[32] Is a law that cannot be generalized still a law? If law is predicated on the same logic of replaceability as marriage (in that its mandates and punishments apply indiscriminately to all), then what is a law founded on the immobility, the constant return-to-the-same, of incest? Just as incest often defies the logic of crime and punishment in tragedy (as each crime, even as it is punished, breeds more crime), so, too, incest seems to resist the universalizing imperative of law. The aporia at Antigone's origin generates an aporetic law, an *autonomos* (self-law, incest-law) unable to reproduce itself as law.[33]

In theory, Antigone's impossible desire and the legal impasse it creates would seem to strengthen the position of Creon and his own law. Precisely because they are the children of Oedipus, Ismene implies, they must obey the law (49–60). Indeed, Creon's law is a sort of incest taboo, inasmuch as incest is the most extreme manifestation of the domestic and civic disorder he fears and aims to prevent. His speech of self-justification (659ff., quoted in full above) starts from the terror of incest: "If I nurture disorder within my family [*ta g'engenê phusei akosma*] certainly I will have it outside as well" (659–60). *Ta g'engenê phusei akosma* is a virtual family motto for the Labdacids. Its most recent manifestation, and the target of Creon's legislation, is fratricide, the death of Polyneices and Eteocles at each other's hand. The play treats this mutual murder in the same overdetermined language that characterizes the incest of the previous generation. Ismene first draws the connection (49–60), linking the crime of her brothers to that of her parents in its constant confusion of singleness and doubleness (one hand blinds two eyes, one woman is both mother and wife, two brothers share a single fate on a single day) and painfully intense reflexivity (in the repetition of *auto-*).[34] This family legacy culminates in the simultaneously single and double, reciprocal and reflexive deaths of the two brothers: "The two brothers killed each other, accomplishing together, the two wretches, a common fate by one another's hand" (55–57).[35] Creon tries retroactively to undo their incestuous death. The duals that Antigone and Ismene use in speaking of them give way in Creon's decree to the polarizing *men/de* construction (on the one hand/on the other hand). Eteocles died fighting for the city and deserves a hero's burial; Polyneices, although he shares his blood, attacked his homeland and will be left unburied (194–206). His law divides the bad from the just (*hoi kakoi tôn endikôn*, 208) and, by apportioning praise and blame, divides the two brothers whom Oedipus' curse had united.

Seeing Creon's law as an attempt to outlaw the *engenê akosma*, the incest and fratricide, of the Labdacids also explains the misogyny that marks his position, for incest is here represented (as Jacques Lacan, in particular, has emphasized) as a crime of female desire, the "madness of the maternal bed and the incestuous lying with my father of my unfortunate mother" (863–65).[36] Creon imagines woman and her pleasure as a force of chaos in the house and family: "Never jettison your good sense, son, for the sake of a woman under the influence of pleasure," Creon warns Haimon. "Realize that this is a chilly embrace, to have a bad wife as a bedmate in your house" (648–51). The Chorus later echo Creon's warning in their Hymn to Eros: Eros "draw[s] aside the minds of just men, making them unjust to their ruin" and "rake[s] up kindred strife [*neikos xunhaimon*] between men" (791–94). Desire threatens to draw Creon's house back into the Labdacids' violent cycle of incest.

His solution is a cruel exogamy. To Ismene's incredulous query whether he will really kill his own son's fiancée, he answers, "Yes, for others have fields for him to plough" (569).[37] With jarring vulgarity (especially addressing the virginal Ismene), Creon voices the logic of substitution that Antigone rejected in her own *erôs*, the economy that replaces the forbidden mother with an infinite string of equivalent wives. And while to Haimon he enjoins the indifferent ploughing of matrimony, his exogamous mandate to Antigone is "to marry someone in Hades" (654; cf. 575).[38] Here, Creon's misogyny and Antigone's incestuous death drive converge: "I was born to join in love [*sumphilein*] not hatred"; "Go, then, if you must love, and love [*philei*] the dead" (523–24).

Creon's law would banish incest, along with Antigone, to Hades. But, as his own words reveal, that outlawed incest is already inside the law that bans it:

> Spit her out like an enemy; release
> the girl to marry someone in Hades,
> since I caught her manifestly disobeying me,
> she alone out of the whole city.
> I will not prove myself a liar to the city,
> but I will kill her. In the face of this let her sing hymns
> to Zeus of Kin [*Xunhaimon*]. For if I nurture
> disorder within my family, certainly I will have it outside as
>   well. (653–60)

Antigone's imagined hymn to Zeus Xunhaimos sums up in a single, overburdened word the incestuous sexuality Creon fears in her and seeks to marry safely to death. Zeus Xunhaimos (literally, Zeus of shared blood) is the god who protects kin but also, in this play's bad domestic economy, the god of incest, patron of the blood shared between Oedipus, Jocasta, and their children and the shared blood spilled between Polyneices and Eteocles. Antigone's wedding hymns for Haimon are songs of incestuous *haima*. This sarcastic line also evokes Antigone's appeal to Zeus and Dikê, the ultimate authorities behind her law (450ff.). Her Zeus, Creon implies, is an incestuous father, and her law the Labdacid familial violence. Summed up in this epithet is all that Creon's law seeks to banish and the banishing of which sustains his law. But Creon's own language betrays him, for the word order enjambs Antigone's bloody, inbred hymeneal into the domestic space Creon hopes to put in order: the chaos he fears—the chaos of shared blood—is already inside his house and city, and he himself is "nurturing" it.[39]

Shared blood also links Creon's civic law to the incestuous murder it tries to outlaw, the *neikos xunhaimon* (793–94; cf. 198) of the sons of Oedipus. Creon claims the authority to rule Thebes in the first place by his kinship with the family of Oedipus. He has called the Chorus to witness his proclamation, he says in his first speech of the play, knowing that they honored "the power of the throne," first of Laius, then of Oedipus, and following his death remained loyal advisers to his sons. Creon himself is the heir to that power after the deaths of Oedipus' sons: "I hold all authority and royal power by virtue of my close kinship with the dead" (173–74). The incestuous legacy Creon hopes to end is the source of his own power.[40] By way of justifying the proclamation he is about to reveal, he sets out his theory that the city must take precedence over the individual: "These are the laws by which I will make this city great. And now I have issued to the citizens a proclamation concerning the children of Oedipus that is the brother [*adelpha*] of these" (191–93). The diction of kinship insinuates itself within Creon's law, which becomes another brother to the children of Oedipus, Polyneices and Eteocles, Ismene and Antigone.

That kinship comes out in the end as Creon repeats the crimes of Polyneices. Shared blood is spilled in a death represented as the posthumous consummation of the marriage Creon forbids: "Still conscious he [Haimon] clasped the maiden in his weak embrace, and panting spurted a sharp stream of bloody drops on her white cheek" (1237–39). Lying corpse upon corpse, the Messenger concludes, "The wretched man has completed his marriage rites in the house of Hades" (1240–41). This ejaculatory death draws Haimon into the trajectory of Antigone's death drive, but it also repeats in a new and horrible form the incestuous murders of the previous generation, as Nicole Loraux (1986) shows. Haimon's spurting blood is the result of a suicide that is also a simultaneous parricide and infanticide. Haimon had tried to stab his father but missed and, "angry at himself," thrust the sword into his own side (1231–36). Creon takes responsibility for this death (1319–20, 1340; cf. 1173, 1260): he has killed the son who killed himself after failing to kill his father. This overdetermined death is summed up in the Messenger's initial announcement: "Haimon is dead: his blood is on an intimate hand" (*Haimôn olôlen; autokheir d haimassetai*, 1175). Haimon becomes the meaning of his name, *haima*. *Autokheir* can mean by one's own hand or by a kinsman's, hence the Chorus' follow-up question, "By his father's hand or by his own?" (1176). The *auto-* prefix leads us back again to the reflexive violence of the house of Labdacus, to the brothers' mutual murder (*autktonounte*, 56; cf. 172), Oedipus' self-blinding (*autos autourgôi kheri*, 52), and Antigone's burial of her brother (*autokheir*, 900). Creon's law attempts to banish the violence and chaos of incest, but those are its ultimate results, "kindred murderers and victims" (*ktanontas te kai thanontas...emphulious*, 1263–64), generations collapsed on themselves.

For both Creon and Antigone the sexual relation, far from signaling the hope of harmonious resolution, suggests the impossibility of any mediation or transcendent union between the two sexes or the two laws. As in the involuted arithmetic of incest, two cannot become one, nor unite to produce a viable third. *Erôs* stands in equivocal relation to *nomos*. Haimon's eroticized death occurs in opposition to Creon's law but also inside the prison cave that enforces it. Is *erôs* inside the law or outside it? This question and its ramifications come to the fore in the Chorus' third stasimon, the "Hymn to Eros":

> You draw aside the minds of just men,
> making them unjust to their ruin.
> You have raked up kindred strife between men.
> Radiant desire sits victorious
> on the eyelids of the happy
> bride, fellow counselor in the magistracy
> of great decrees. Aphrodite
> plays, irresistible goddess. (791–800)

Following immediately upon the confrontation between Creon and Haimon, the ode seems to confirm Creon's view that *erôs* has turned his son against him. Eros derails sense and justice: it leads the mind astray, as Creon warned Haimon at line 648–49, and draws men back into the incestuous mire of "kindred strife" (*neikos xunhaimon*). It is a force that opposes law and good order. But then the ode swerves: "Radiant desire sits victorious on the eyelids of the happy bride, fellow counselor in the magistracy of great decrees." Is love the outlaw or the judge? The text here is almost certainly corrupt,[41] but as they stand these lines reinstall *erôs* in the very place from which the previous lines (and the previous scene) tried to exile it: sexual desire sits alongside the law, between the magistrates and their decrees (*tôn megalôn paredros en arkhais thesmôn*). Does *erôs* destroy the law or preserve it, generate strife or resolve it? Neither the ode nor the play seems able to answer these questions or to situate *erôs* securely in relation to the law.[42]

That failure leaves in doubt not only the status of *erôs* in relation to *nomos* but also the status of *nomos* in relation to *erôs*, a significant irresolution given that Antigone's law is based on her *erôs* and Creon's on his opposition to it. Wandering Eros (781–90) destabilizes the law built on it. Far from an equilibrium, as Hegel suggested, *erôs* generates disequilibrium within the law.[43] The Hymn to Eros ends with the lines quoted above, but the effect of Aphrodite's play continues in the Chorus' opening words of the next scene: "Now I myself am also carried outside the decrees" (*nun d'êdê' gô k'autos thesmôn exô pheromai*, 801–802). Singing about *erôs*, they too (*egô k'autos*) have come to feel its destabilizing effect: they too take up an equivocal position in relation to the laws. But what carries them beyond the law is not in fact Eros, but instead the action of the drama: "I am no longer able to hold back the stream of tears when I see Antigone here approaching her chamber of eternal rest" (803–5). Throughout the play the Chorus have supported Creon's law and will continue to do so up until Antigone's death (e.g., 853–56, 872–75). But the piteous spectacle of Antigone brings them up against the limits of this law, allows them to be "carried" (if only metaphorically) beyond it. Tragic pity works like love upon them. *Erôs* opens an aporia within the law, an aporia marked here as particularly tragic.

And yet perhaps it is in this aporia and not in equilibrium that the play stakes its hopes for justice. In his essay "Force of Law: The 'Mystical Foundation of Authority,'" Jacques Derrida argues that justice is precisely the experience of the aporia within the law.[44] The undecidabilities that exist structurally and inevitably within law—the violence that founds the law but stands outside its legislation, the tension between the particularity of justice and law's universality, the temporary suspension of past laws in the creation of new laws—ensure that justice is never reducible to a single specific law. Instead, justice is the remainder or trace left by the law's indeterminacies; it is what the law, by virtue of its internal self-difference, always defers.[45] It is only by holding open these aporiai, then, that we can retain the possibility of real justice, a justice that is always to come, unattainable in itself but vital as a political and legal demand.

That horizon of future justice can perhaps be glimpsed—though obscurely—in Antigone's final exchange with the Chorus. Carried beyond the law by erotic ambivalence and tragic pity, they become a new jury that she implores to try not her crimes but the laws that have condemned her (842–49). But this case, too, goes unresolved, and Antigone goes to her death uncertain in the end about the justice of her position: "If these things are pleasing to the gods, then through suffering I will know that I was wrong; but if Creon is in the wrong, may he suffer nothing worse than the injustice he is doing me" (925–28). The final judgment on her act is deferred—justice itself is deferred, to be decided at some always future moment elsewhere.[46]

This is the justice that tragedy offers us. Tragedy sets up conflicts that it cannot and does not resolve, but in the very nonresolution it offers some hope of wisdom through suffering, justice through aporia.[47] *Antigone* does not define the shape of this future justice—it cannot if it is to be truly futural and thus truly just—but it does imagine its outlines; in this dim shape, justice appears as both civic and tragic. The Chorus, brought into an aporetic relation to *nomos* through the tragic spectacle, are called on to witness Antigone's suffering explicitly as citizens (*politai*, 806; cf. 842–43, 937–39). The civic dimensions of this aporetic justice emerge particularly clearly in the play's increasing insistence on *euboulia*, good counsel, as a remedy to legal conflict and a foundation for justice.[48] Tiresias, in particular, endorses the virtue of good counsel, under which he includes correct observance of divine law (1026, 1050). Accordingly, Creon's *peripeteia* is represented as a move from *atê* (blindness, folly, madness) to *euboulia* (1097–98). *Euboulia* denotes individual good sense or prudence. To the Athenian ear it also had a civic, indeed democratic, ring, recalling the good counsel forged in Athens' central legislative council, the *Boulê*. This political connotation resonates with the apparent optimism of the first stasimon, where justice in the *polis*, the harmony of divine law and human, is the hoped-for result of man's "voice and windy thought and civic-minded, law-abiding temperament" (355). Thanks to this, the ode continues, man goes resourceless (*aporos*) toward no future except death (360–362). *Euboulia* is his greatest resource (*poros*) and path (*poros*) toward a secure future.

But that apparently optimistic message is belied by the tragic world in which human action is defined by nothing more than its aporia toward the future. The second stasimon is a negative answer to the first: "nothing in human life proceeds entirely outside of *atê*" (613–14).[49] Mortals are deceived by "foolish desires" (*kouphonoôn erôtôn*, 617) and do not see what is coming until they have burnt their feet on the fire. "Bad seems good to the man whose mind the god leads into *atê*; he acts only briefly outside of *atê*" (622–25). *Atê* makes *euboulia* impossible; it undermines man's resourcefulness and diverts him from the path toward justice, leaving him in aporia. The ode attributes this law of *atê* (*nomos hod'*, 613) to Zeus, but this is also the law of tragedy itself. At the very end of the play, Creon laments his miserable fate: holding his dead son in his arms, he cries, "You are dead, released from life by my own bad counsels (*dusbouliais*)." The Chorus respond, "Alas, you seem to see justice (*dikên*) too late" (1268–70). Justice is wisdom, but wisdom in tragedy always comes too late.[50] If the play proposes *euboulia* as a tentative solution to its legal *aporiai*, the genre's aporetic law seems to undercut that solution, trapping *euboulia* in the impasse of *atê*.

But tragedy's law of *atê*—man's aporia in the face of the future—does not completely invalidate the play's calls for *euboulia*. Instead, it argues for the necessarily communal nature of that wisdom. If every individual is liable to the blindness that confuses right and wrong, and spends little time free from *atê* (622–25), then the only hope is collective deliberation of the sort the Athenians themselves practiced in their democratic *Boulê*. Only such civic and, especially, democratic institutions prevent the *atê* of one powerful man from being established as law, as seems to happen with Creon, whose civic *eunomia* quickly collapses into tyranny. Likewise, only the collective deliberation of the *polis* (as Antigone hints before her death) can judge what justice lies within her violent, anarchic *autonomos*. The optimism of the final strophe of the first stasimon is warranted, then, only within the civic framework of that strophe, in which man's resourcefulness stands in clear responsion to the prosperity of his city (*pantoporos, aporos*, 360; *hupsipolis, apolis*, 370): the *polis* is the *poros*.[51] Individual *atê* thus becomes an imperative toward communal deliberation. At the same time, *atê* guarantees that that deliberation will always be open and ongoing. Because wisdom comes always too late, the definition of the good (*to eu*) can never be determined once and for all; it must be constantly revised through communal deliberation (*boulê*). *Atê* is thus a vital supplement to *euboulia*, for it alone saves *euboulia* from the ossification the play stages in its conflict of laws. It guarantees that *euboulia* is not a transcendental value but a finite and engaged process, a path (*poros*) to justice not as a Platonic Form but as a contested political possibility. If *boulê* is necessarily provisional, always susceptible to deception and derailment, to "foolish desires" and aporia, then no Creon or Antigone can ever claim to know the single meaning of *to eu*; no single definition of law can be definitively equated with justice.

Tragedy, in staging the conflict of laws as an aporia, a conflict without resolution, itself becomes the enactment of justice, as the play seems to suggest in its final ode to Dionysus as patron god both of the city of Thebes and of theater (1115–52).[52] But the justice it enacts is itself aporetic. It cannot be fixed or localized in a simple moral. It is a possibility that emerges out of the experience of irresolution, but a possibility always deferred, a wisdom that will come (with suffering) too late. I have argued that in *Antigone* one force behind that deferral is the aporia of sexual difference, which maintains the two laws in a perpetual and irreducible conflict without hope either of a happy equilibrium or of a final victory of the one over the other. *Erôs*, the sexual relation that is so impossible in this play, is one of the forces of *atê* that blinds mortals to their future (*kouphonoôn erôtôn*, 617) and guarantees that *euboulia* will always come too late. Both inside and outside *nomos* (as the Hymn to Eros suggests), it destabilizes the boundaries of *nomos* so that even a Chorus of elders might occasionally be carried "outside the decrees" (801). Confounding law and outlaw, it disrupts the law's claims to justice and, in this way, transforms justice into the law's longing, its "love of the impossible" (90).

This hope of justice, however, is bought at the expense of women, who were barred from participation in political institutions like the *Boulê* partly because of their perceived incapacity for *euboulia*. The legal aporia that for the male citizen opens the path toward future justice traps women at the impasse of sexual difference; if the road forward is (as I have suggested) political, it is barred to them. On the one hand, by representing sexual difference as irreducible, the play resists Creon's attempt to resolve it into a fixed hierarchy, and thus at least saves women from a dialectic in which the man will always be master and the woman slave. On the other hand, by predicating the possibility of civic justice on that irreducibility, it suggests that the just city requires the constant reproduction of *Antigone*, with its endless *agôn* between male law and female. If in the process the possibility of sexual justice is also reproduced, so are the political obstacles that prevent women from moving toward it. The play may ultimately eschew the closure of Creon's prison cave and point toward the open horizon of a democratic future to come, but for Athens' disenfranchised women, that open expanse may still be a dead end.[53]

NOTES

1. Hegel ([1807] 1977, 263–96); cf. Hegel in Paolucci and Paolucci (1962, 73–74, 132–33); Irigaray (1985, 214–26; 1993, 116–29); Chanter (1995, 80–126); Conklin (1997); Butler (2000, 31–39); Copjec (2002, 13–19). On Hegel's theory of drama, see Gellrich (1988, 23–93), who argues that Hegel's imposition of an orderly teleology and ultimate unity on tragedy's contradictions not only requires him to exclude everything that would disrupt such unity

(such as, in *Antigone*, the internal instabilities of Antigone's and Creon's ethical positions [44–71]) but also ignores the subversive potential of tragic agonism.

2. Pericles in Thucydides famously asserts that a woman's greatest glory is to have no reputation, either good or bad (Thuc. 2.45.2), and it was a commonplace that virtuous women were known by name only to their male relatives; one courtroom speaker can even claim (no doubt hyperbolically) that his sister and nieces were so modest they were ashamed to be seen even by their kinsmen (Lysias 3.6). On the gendered division of space, see Xenophon *Oikonomikos* 7–10.

3. Whether women were allowed to attend the tragic festival is still debated: see Henderson (1991) and Goldhill (1994). For tragedy's ubiquitous reversals of house and city, inside and outside, see Foley (1982) and Zeitlin (1996).

4. Butler (2000) shows how modern readings of *Antigone* (particularly those of Hegel and Lacan) posit Antigone at and as the limit of law and deny Antigone a counterlegality that might critique the law (including the laws of kinship based on the incest taboo). See also Irigaray (1985, 214–26). My reading attempts to identify that counterlaw and its effects within the play.

5. Knox (1964, 84–86). See Griffith (1999 at 162–210) for the resonances of Creon's character and position with contemporary political discourse. That Demosthenes quotes the speech in support of his own case (18.246–47) indicates its normativity.

6. On the unwritten laws, see, for example, Lysias 6.10–11; Dem. 18.275, 23.70; Pl. *Laws* 793a; Arist. *Rhet.* 1368b, 1373b, 1375a–b; Xen. *Mem.* 4.4.19–20 (who includes under this heading honoring the gods and obeying the incest taboo). See also Guthrie (1971) 117–31), de Romilly (1971, 25–49), Ostwald (1973), Carey (1996, 40), Thomas (1996, 16–19), and Foley (2001, 288–90; with further bibliography).

7. Harris (2004, 27–31).

8. Santirocco (1980, 182). Even this, ostensibly the most optimistic ode in the play, has its ambiguities and opens itself to much more negative readings: see Griffith (1999, 180–81), Segal (1981, 152–206; 1986, 146–61), and Oudemans and Lardinois (1987, 123–31).

9. This conflict is signaled in the competing meanings of the word *nomos* in the play: see Santirocco (1980, 183–86), Vernant (1988, 42–43), and Segal (1981, 168–70; 1986, 140–41). Goldhill (1986,

88–106) tracks similar semantic shifts in the play around the terms *philos* and *ekhthros*.

10. Following Seidler's reordering of the lines: see Griffith (1999 ad loc).

11. The end of the *Oresteia* is the most notorious example; there, the traumatic legal and political crises of the first two plays are finally resolved by appeal to the manifest priority of the father over the mother.

12. Compare the circularity in Demosthenes 21.223, where the laws authorize the democratic jury and the jury the laws. Thebes is not a democracy, of course, but even in democratic Athens the reduction of law to politics with no reference to an external notion of justice seemed problematic. In Aristophanes, for example, the courts are often imagined as instruments of mob rule, open to manipulation by unscrupulous demagogues (see especially *Wasps, Knights*). Cf. Arist. *Ath. Pol.* 9.

13. On Creon as tyrant, see, for example, 60, 506–7, 690–91, 1056; Podlecki (1966); Lane and Lane (1986, 169–71); and Euben (1997, 153–64).

14. This dynamic is anticipated at line 36, where Antigone rejects Creon's attempt to legitimate the violence of his death sentence (by spreading the guilt through a public stoning, *dêmoleuston*) by calling the act murder (*phonon*). See further Santirocco (1980, 185–86).

15. In fifth-century Athens, the laws were inscribed on *stelai* distributed throughout the city but were also read aloud during court cases, and it is probably in the latter form that most citizens became familiar with them. See Svenbro (1993, 109–22), and on this passage, Knox (1964, 94–98).

16. Arist. *Rhet.* 1375a–b. Even the dicastic oath, sworn by all jurors, may have made some provision for unwritten law in the form of the jurors' own sense of justice. One plausible reconstruction of the oath has jurors vow to vote according to the laws and decrees of the Athenian *dêmos* and "in matters about which there are no laws I will decide by most just opinion" (Dem. 20.118, 23.96, 39.40).

17. Foley (2001, 182); cf. Butler (2000, 10–12). For the translation of *en theois* as "in a court of gods," see Jebb (1902 ad 458–59).

18. Cf. 520–22: Creon asserts with confidence that the laws below are the same as those above; Antigone's answer ("Who knows if these things are holy below?") is hesitant: perhaps the law she obeys is no different from Creon's after all.

19. Johnson (1997). As Griffith (2005, 111) argues, there is an "intimate connection in Antigone's mind between her father, Zeus-the-Father, and the idea of a supreme law or authority that completely defines her own existence and potential for action."

20. Cf. Douzinas and Warrington (1994, 199–200).

21. See, for example, 95–97, 220, 460–64, 555–60. Thus, for Lacan (1992, 270–83), Antigone's action is situated between two deaths, her corporeal death (which she already lives as her life) and the total annihilation of the symbolic toward which her action aims. On Lacan's Antigone, see Miller (2007, 61–99).

22. On the force inherent in legal interpretation, see Cover (1986), Fish (1989, 503–24), and Derrida (1992).

23. For the difficulties of the fourth stasimon, see Benardete (1975 § 50), Griffith (1999 ad loc), and Oudemans and Lardinois (1987, 150–51). Antigone also compares herself to Niobe (823–33), another mythic figure punished for insulting the gods.

24. Athenian marriage relations, at least among the elite, tended to be relatively endogamous, designed to keep property within the family; an *epiklêros* (heiress) like Antigone would be adjudicated (along with her father's estate) to her nearest male kin. See Just (1989, 40–104), Sealey (1990, 25–36), and Foley (2001, 61–105). On marriage in this play, see Ormand (1999, chap. 4).

25. See especially Johnson (1997, 388–95); Griffith (2005, 94–96, 110–22) collects and discusses the relevant passages. Contrast Hegel, who considers the brother-sister bond the purest relation between male and female, an "equilibrium of the blood and...a relation devoid of desire" ([1807] 1977, 274–75).

26. The verb *keisthai* (to lie, 73) may have sexual connotations: see Benardete (1975 § 9.6). Maternal associations may also be evoked in Antigone's comparison of herself to Niobe, a famous mythical mother (823–33).

27. See 512–13, 658–59, 1175; cf. 486, 488, and Loraux (1986, 177–78).

28. On Antigone's name, see Benardete (1975 § 8) and Hamilton (1991, 95). On Antigone's death and the parallels with her mother, see Loraux (1986, 191–95; 1987, 31–32).

29. Cf. Butler (2000, 57–82). The road that Antigone takes, *autonomos*, to the underworld leads her to the *autogennêta* (self-begotten) bed where she was born (864–65); as the Chorus say, her "self-willed temper" (*autognôtos orga*; 875) has destroyed her. On the prefix *auto-* see Loraux (1986), for whom it encapsulates the whole

incestuous, murderous history of the Labdacids. Further examples occur at 1, 51–56, 172, 306, 503, 696, 900, 1175, and 1315.

30. See especially Benardete (1975 § 48.6–7), Murnaghan (1986), Neuburg (1990), Johnson (1997, 393–94), Griffith (1999 ad loc), Foley (2001, 175–80), and Copjec (2002, 40–47).

31. Cf. 503 (*autadelphon*), 511 (*homosplankhnous*). Perhaps this also helps explain Antigone's harsh rejection of Ismene, who, after all, also shares the same birth (1). The difference of gender is key because it replicates the sexual difference at Antigone's origin, even as her incestuous relation to her brother repeats that between her parents. For related explanations, see Chanter (1995, 102–3) and Johnson (1997, 390–91). Eteocles, of course, would be indistinguishable from Polyneices on these terms, but that is precisely Antigone's point. Finally, there is a fourth sibling from this same womb: Oedipus.

32. Butler (2000, 10, 52–53). Foley (2001, 172–96) examines the tension between a generalizing (masculine) and particularizing (feminine) ethics in the play.

33. This problem within the play marks for many of its modern interpreters the fold between law's universality and ethics' obligation to a particular other. See, for example, Lacan (1989, 55–104; 1992, 179–203), Irigaray (1993, 185–217), Derrida (1992, 17), Douzinas and Warrington (1994, 206–207), Ziarek (1997), and more generally the debate in Butler, Laclau, and Žižek (2000). The font of the issue is Freud's discussion of the impossibility of the commandment to "love thy neighbor as thyself" in Freud ([1930] 1961, 62–70).

34. Loraux (1986, 180–84). Zeitlin traces this "unstable arithmetic of the self" throughout the Oedipus cycle (1990, 139–40).

35. See Jebb (1902 ad loc). Incestuous collapse is pushed even further in the first choral ode, where the two brothers (again in the dual), "two hateful men born both from one father and one mother, having planted doubly-victorious spears against themselves [*kath'hautoin*], held both a share of a common fate" (144–47). The reflexive *kath'hautoin* (against themselves) replaces the expected reciprocal *kath'allêloin* (against one another). See Loraux (1986, 182).

36. Lacan (1992, 282–83), and on Lacan's reading see Leonard (2003, 144–46). See also Loraux (1986, 194–95).

37. While the metaphor is traditional, the sentiment's crassness is emphasized by Ismene's response ("But none as well suited to him and her," 570). Note too the aural echo of *arôsimoi* (to be

ploughed) at the beginning of 569 with *hêrmosmena* (suited) at the end of the following line.

38. This is a twist on the trope in which dead virgins are imagined married to Hades himself; cf. 575, 806–16; Seaford (1987); Rehm (1994).

39. Lines 659–60 read, *xunhaimon; ei gar dê ta g'engenê phusei / akosma threpsô*. Cf. Segal (1981, 189–90).

40. Rosivach (1979, 21–22). Cf. Zeitlin (1990, 149): "The desire on the political level to rule alone in autonomy is also equivalent in the family domain to the desire for an autonomous self-engendering, which the acts of patricide and incest imply."

41. Jebb (1902); Lloyd-Jones and Wilson (1990, 136); Griffith (1999 ad 797–99). On *erôs* and justice in the ode, see Santirocco (1980, 191) and Oudemans and Lardinois (1987, 143).

42. Cf. 74: lying in mutual *philia* with her brother, Antigone says, she will "commit a pious crime" (*hosia panourgêsas'*). The oxymoron expresses not only the clash of the two laws, civic (*panourgêsas'*) and religious (*hosia*), but also the way in which love confounds questions of legality.

43. Irigaray (1993) is an attempt to formulate an ethics from the destabilizing effect of sexual difference on the law; see also Irigaray (1985, 214–26), Chanter (1995), and Ziarek (1997, 133).

44. Derrida (1992), especially pp. 21–29.

45. Hence Derrida's polemical claim that "deconstruction is justice" (1992, 15, cf. 20–21).

46. The attitude of the Chorus is hard to determine in this *kommos*. First they try to cheer Antigone with the promise of glory (817–22, 834–38), then they condemn her criminality (853–56); their final words (872–75) are frustratingly vague. If they form a belated jury for her crimes, they are hung. See further Hester (1971, 34–38).

47. The tragic motto "wisdom through suffering" (*pathei mathos*; Aes. *Ag.* 177) may then be reread not as a teleological progression (with *pathei* as an instrumental dative) but as a localization (with *pathei* as a locative) of wisdom in the very mire, the aporia, of suffering.

48. 179, 1026, 1050, 1098, 1242, 1265, 1269. For divergent opinions on this quality in the play, see Nussbaum (1986) and Knox (1964). In his *First Alcibiades*, Plato defines *euboulia* as the knowledge that pertains to participation in the governance of the city (*politeias koinônountôn epistêmên*) and that allows the city to be preserved and better run (*eis to ameinon tên polin dioikein kai sôizesthai*; 125e4–126a4).

49. Benardete (1975 § 37.4); Oudemans and Lardinois (1987, 137–38). The text and meaning of these lines are unsure: see Griffith (1999 ad loc).

50. Note, too, the belated entrance of Eurydike ("Wide-justice") for whom *dikê* will necessarily come (if at all) too late; see Segal (1981, 194–96). Derrida speaks of the aporia created by the urgency of decision that obstructs the horizon of knowledge; he quotes Kierkegaard: "The instant of decision is a madness" (1992, 26), a good gloss on *atê*.

51. Cf. Benardete (1975 § 10.10): "The city would stand between the human that defies the impossible in one sense and the divine that demands the impossible in another. The city would owe both its existence and the precariousness of its existence to the impossible demanded by the gods and the impossible defied by man as man." Cf. Euben (1997, 177–78), who posits a synthesis of the play's conflicts at the level of the democratic audience.

52. The Chorus alludes to Dionysus as god of theater at lines 1146–47 and 1151–52; see Segal (1981, 200–207). For tragic aporia as a site of justice, see Stavrakakis (2003, 126).

53. I would like to thank Erik Gunderson, Mark Griffith, and Paul Allen Miller for their valuable comments on this chapter. Thanks are due, too, to the students of my Athenian Law seminar at Ohio State University in autumn 2003, for talking through the "mystical foundation of authority" with me. Finally, I am grateful to Denise McCoskey and Emily Zakin for organizing both the conference and the collection.

REFERENCES

Benardete, Seth. 1975. A reading of Sophocles' *Antigone*: I, II, III. *Interpretation* 4: 148–96; 5: 1–55, 148–84.

Butler, Judith. 2000. *Antigone's claim: Kinship between life and death.* New York: Columbia University Press.

Butler, Judith, Ernesto Laclau, and Slavoj Žižek. 2000. *Contingency, hegemony, universality.* London: Verso.

Carey, C. 1996. *Nomos* in Attic rhetoric and oratory. *Journal of Hellenic Studies* 116: 33–46.

Chanter, Tina. 1995. *Ethics of eros: Irigaray's rewriting of the philosophers.* New York: Routledge.

Conklin, William E. 1997. Hegel, the author and authority in Sophocles' *Antigone*. In *Justice v. law in Greek political thought*, ed.
Leslie G. Rubin, 129–51. Lanham: Rowman and Littlefield.

Copjec, Joan. 2002. *Imagine there's no woman: Ethics and sublimation*. Cambridge, MA: MIT Press.

Cover, Robert M. 1986. Violence and the word. *Yale Law Journal* 95:
1601–29.

Derrida, Jacques. 1992. Force of law: The "Mystical Foundation of
Authority." In *Deconstruction and the possibility of justice*, eds.
Drucilla Cornell, Michel Rosenfeld, and David Gray Carlson, 3–67.
London: Routledge.

Douzinas, Costas and Ronnie Warrington. 1994. Antigone's law: A
genealogy of jurisprudence. In *Politics, postmodernity and critical
legal studies: The legality of the contingent*, ed. Peter Goodrich, Costas
Douzinas, and Yifat Hachamovitch, 187–225. London: Routledge.

Euben, J. Peter. 1997. *Antigone* and the languages of politics. In *Cor-
rupting youth: Political education, democratic culture, and political
theory*, 139–78. Princeton, NJ: Princeton University Press.

Fish, Stanley. 1989. *Doing what comes naturally: Change, rhetoric,
and the practice of theory in literary and legal studies*. Durham:
Duke University Press.

Foley, Helene P. 1982. The "female intruder" reconsidered: Women in
Aristophanes' *Lysistrata* and *Ecclesiazusae*. *Classical Philology* 77:
1–21.

Foley, Helene P. 2001. *Female acts in Greek tragedy*. Princeton, NJ:
Princeton University Press.

Freud, Sigmund. [1930] 1961. *Civilization and its discontents*. Trans.
James Strachey. New York: W. W. Norton.

Gellrich, Michelle. 1988. *Tragedy and theory: The problem of conflict
since Aristotle*. Princeton, NJ: Princeton University Press.

Goldhill, Simon. 1986. *Reading Greek tragedy*. Cambridge: Cambridge University Press.

———. 1994. Representing democracy: Women at the Great Dionysia.
In *Ritual, finance, politics: Athenian democratic accounts pre-
sented to David Lewis*, ed. Robin Osborne and Simon Hornblower.
Oxford: Clarendon.

Griffith, Mark, ed. 1999. *Sophocles Antigone*. Cambridge: Cambridge
University Press.

———. 2005. The subject of desire in Sophocles' *Antigone*. In *The soul
of tragedy: Essays on Athenian drama*, ed. Victoria Pedrick and Steven M. Oberhelman, 91–135. Chicago: University of Chicago Press.

Guthrie, W. K. C. 1971. *The Sophists, Part I*. Vol. 3 of *A history of Greek philosophy*. Cambridge: Cambridge University Press.

Hamilton, John D. B. 1991. Antigone, kinship, justice, and the polis. In *Myth and the polis*, ed. Dora C. Pozzi and John M. Wickersham, 86–98. Ithaca, NY: Cornell University Press.

Harris, Edward M. 2004. Antigone the lawyer, or the ambiguities of nomos. In *The law and the courts in ancient Greece*, ed. Edward M. Harris and Lene Rubinstein, 19–56. London: Duckworth.

Hegel, G. W. F. [1807] 1977. *Phenomenology of spirit*. Trans. A. V. Miller. Oxford: Oxford University Press.

Henderson, Jeffrey. 1991. Women and the Athenian dramatic festivals. *Transactions of the American Philological Association* 121: 133–48.

Hester, D. A. 1971. Sophocles the unphilosophical: A study in the *Antigone*. *Mnemosyne* 24: 11–59.

Irigaray, Luce. 1985. *Speculum of the other woman*. Trans. Gillian C. Gill. Ithaca, NY: Cornell University Press.

———. 1993. *An ethics of sexual difference*. Trans. Carolyn Burke and Gillian C. Gill. Ithaca, NY: Cornell University Press.

Jebb, Richard C., ed. 1902. *Sophocles Antigone*. Cambridge: Cambridge University Press.

Johnson, Patricia J. 1997. Woman's third face: A psycho/social reconsideration of Sophocles' *Antigone*. *Arethusa* 30: 369–98.

Just, Roger. 1989. *Women in Athenian law and life*. London: Routledge.

Knox, Bernard M. W. 1964. *The heroic temper: Studies in Sophoclean tragedy*. Berkeley: University of California Press.

Lacan, Jacques. 1989. Kant with Sade. *October* 51: 55–104.

———. 1992. *The ethics of psychoanalysis. The seminar of Jacques Lacan, Book VII*. Trans. Dennis Porter, ed. Jacques-Alain Miller. New York: W. W. Norton.

Lane, Warren J. and Ann M. Lane, 1986. The politics of *Antigone*. In *Greek tragedy and political theory*, ed. J. Peter Euben, 162–82. Berkeley: University of California Press.

Leonard, Miriam. 2003. Antigone, the political and the ethics of psychoanalysis. *Proceedings of the Cambridge Philological Society* 49: 130–54.

Lloyd-Jones, H., and N. G. Wilson. 1990. *Sophoclea*. Oxford: Clarendon.

Loraux, Nicole. 1986. La Main d'Antigone. *Mêtis* 1: 165–96.

————. 1987. *Tragic ways of killing a woman*. Trans. Anthony Forster. Cambridge: Harvard University Press.

Miller, Paul Allen. 2007. *Postmodern spiritual practices*. Columbus: Ohio State University Press.

Murnaghan, Sheila. 1986. *Antigone* 904–920 and the institution of marriage. *American Journal of Philology* 107: 192–207.

Neuburg, Matt. 1990. How like a woman: Antigone's "inconsistency." *Classical Quarterly* 40: 54–76.

Nussbaum, Martha. 1986. Sophocles' *Antigone*: Conflict, vision, and simplification. In *Fragility of goodness*, 51–88. Cambridge: Cambridge University Press.

Ormand, Kirk. 1999. *Exchange and the maiden: Marriage in Sophoclean drama*. Austin: University of Texas Press.

Ostwald, Martin. 1973. Was there a concept of *agraphos nomos* in classical Greece? In *Exegesis and argument: Studies in Greek philosophy presented to Gregory Vlastos*, ed. E. N. Lee, A. P. D. Mourelatos, and R. M. Rorty, 70–104. New York: Humanities Press.

Oudemans, T. C. W., and A. P. M. H. Lardinois. 1987. *Tragic ambiguity: Anthropology, philosophy and Sophocles' Antigone*. Leiden: Brill.

Paolucci, Anne, and Henry Paolucci, eds. 1962. *Hegel on tragedy*. Garden City: Doubleday.

Podlecki, A. J. 1966. Creon and Herodotus. *Transactions of the American Philological Association* 97: 359–71.

Rehm, Rush. 1994. *Marriage to death*. Princeton, NJ: Princeton University Press.

de Romilly, Jacqueline. 1971. *La loi dans la pensée Grecque des origins à Aristote*. Paris: les Belles Lettres.

Rosivach, Vincent J. 1979. The two worlds of the *Antigone*. *Illinois Classical Studies* 4: 16–26.

Santirocco, Matthew S. 1980. Justice in Sophocles' *Antigone*. *Philosophy and Literature* 2: 180–98.

Seaford, Richard. 1987. The tragic wedding. *Journal of Hellenic Studies* 107: 106–30.

Sealey, Raphael. 1990. *Women and law in classical Greece*. Chapel Hill: University of North Carolina Press.

Segal, Charles. 1981. *Tragedy and civilization: An interpretation of Sophocles*. Cambridge: Harvard University Press.

————. 1986. Sophocles' praise of man and the conflicts of *Antigone*. In *Interpreting Greek tragedy: Myth, poetry, text*, 137–61. Ithaca, NY: Cornell University Press.

Stavrakakis, Yannis. 2003. The lure of Antigone: Aporias of an ethics of the political. In A. L. Jones, ed. "Ignorance of the law," Special Issue, *Umbra*, 117–29.

Svenbro, Jasper. 1993. *Phrasikleia: An anthropology of reading in ancient Greece*. Trans. Janet Lloyd. Ithaca, NY: Cornell University Press.

Thomas, Rosalind. 1996. Written in stone? Liberty, equality, orality and the codification of law. In *Greek law in its political setting: Justifications not justice*, ed. Lin Foxhall and A. D. E. Lewis, 9–31. Oxford: Clarendon.

Vernant, Jean-Pierre. 1988. Tensions and ambiguities in Greek tragedy. In *Myth and tragedy in ancient Greece*, trans. Janet Lloyd, ed. Jean-Pierre Vernant and Pierre Vidal-Naquet, 29–48. New York: Zone Books.

Zeitlin, Froma I. 1990. Thebes: Theater of self and society in Athenian drama. In *Nothing to do with Dionysos?*, ed. John J. Winkler and Froma I. Zeitlin, 130–67. Princeton, NJ: Princeton University Press.

————. 1996. Playing the Other: Theater, theatricality, and the feminine in Greek drama. In *Playing the Other: Gender and society in classical Greek literature*, 341–74. Chicago: University of Chicago Press.

Ziarek, Ewa Plonowska. 1997. From euthanasia to the Other of reason: Performativity and the deconstruction of sexual difference. In *Derrida and feminism*, ed. Ellen K. Feder, Mary C. Rawlinson, Emily Zakin, 115–40. New York: Routledge.

6

Tragedy, Natural Law, and Sexual Difference in Hegel

ELAINE P. MILLER

As the different sexes constitute the sex-drive as differentials,
there must be a difference in their formation; their mutual
determinateness must exist as posited through the Notion.
The implicitness of both sides is not merely neutral, as it is in
chemism however, for on account of the original identity of
their formation, the same type underlies both the male and
female genitals. The difference is, however, that in one or the
other of these genitals, one or the other part is essential; in the
female this is necessarily the undifferentiated element, while in
the male it is the sundered element of opposition.

—G. W. F. Hegel, *Philosophy of Nature*

INTRODUCTION

Aeschylus' *Oresteia*, and, in particular, the final tragedy, the *Eumenides*, has been read as a celebration and legitimization of the instantiation of central institutions of democratic patriarchy (Zelenak 1998) and as a "myth of matriarchy" that affirms male social dominance by imagining that women once held power but rightly lost it by abusing that authority (Zeitlin 1996). This chapter will attempt to complicate these analyses through an examination of the ways in which sexual difference moves, in the *Eumenides*, from a merely biological or sociocultural concept to an articulation not just of specific roles or of a particular form of rule, but of the most fundamental ways in which power is articulated—that is, in the instantiation of natural law. I

149

will use G. W. F. Hegel's early work on "Natural Law," which reads the *Oresteia* as a performance and unveiling of the dialectical logic that grounds natural law as the basis for a rational state, as the starting point of my reading, and then consider why Hegel shifted his focus from the *Eumenides* to Sophocles' *Antigone* in his later discussions of natural law. I choose to read the confluence of sexual difference and law through Hegel because his analysis of natural law explicitly navigates between and seeks to overcome the shortcomings of both empirical and purely formal explanations of the instantiation of natural law.

Through a reading of Hegel's often overlooked text on natural law, I will revisit the *Oresteia* as a site of contestation of the very meaning of law, statehood, and ethical life. I will go beyond a strictly textual reading of Hegel, however, by considering these sites of meaning with reference to the emergence of articulated sexual difference at the end of the trilogy, a role that Hegel seemingly ignores, but which, I will argue, plays a significant role in his shift of focus to *Antigone* when discussing law in his later *Phenomenology of Spirit* and *Philosophy of Right*. An important part of my argument is that sexual difference (taken in a very specific sense, which I will elucidate) and natural law are equiprimordial in both Aeschylus' play and Hegel's account; it is a mistake to read the emergence of law at the end of the *Eumenides* as simply a justification, legitimization, or celebration of an already existing articulated difference. I will explicate this claim in what follows, especially since it reflects a critique by Hegel of so-called empirical accounts of natural law that illegitimately abstract from contingent features of social structures and then predicate them essentially of collective human life, deriving what was meant to be *a priori* from the *a posteriori*.

My subsequent argument is twofold, although the two points are necessarily intertwined: First, I claim that Hegel shifts from using the *Eumenides* to *Antigone* because he believes the latter provides a better illustration of the struggles inherent in the first emergence of true ethical life, in part because sexual difference and law emerge only at the end of the *Oresteia*, while *Antigone* presupposes this constituted difference. Second, I argue that *Antigone* is useful for Hegel because it represents the errors of two opposing and unidimensional conceptions of natural law that Hegel criticizes. Creon's position provides an illustration of the shortcomings of what Hegel calls an empirical understanding of natural law, whereas Antigone's position shows the one-sidedness of a purely formal understanding of natural law. Only in an overcoming of the abstraction of both positions can a full-fledged account of natural law emerge. My argument also draws on the psychoanalytic articulation of sexual difference, which I will elucidate with reference to Luce Iri-garay's reading of Hegel's discussion of Greek tragedy—in particular, his most well-known discussion of *Antigone* in the *Phenomenology of Spirit*—although ultimately I argue that she has misread Hegel when she addresses the relationship between tragedy and natural law.

HEGEL'S CONCEPTION OF NATURAL LAW

Hegel reads the formation of natural law as the "self-sacrifice" of the Absolute, which must separate off the inorganic (private right) from the organic (ethical life) in order to sacrifice the former, a part of itself, in the name of regeneration and rebirth, as "the performance...of the tragedy which the Absolute eternally enacts with itself" (Hegel 1975, 104). This inorganic is in fact aligned with the feminine, as Hegel makes explicit in his later *Phenomenology of Spirit* and *Philosophy of Right*. Hegel shifts his focus, as I have already noted, from the *Eumenides* to *Antigone* in the later works. The *Phenomenology* contains only a veiled reference to the Furies and primarily concentrates on *Antigone*, while the *Philosophy of Right* makes no mention of the *Eumenides* at all. Both tragedies arguably perform an erasure of sexual difference in channeling its productive power into the sexual neutrality of the state. Yet I argue that Hegel chooses *Antigone* not only because of its stronger portrayal of woman and, in particular, of the figure of the sister but also, even more so, because there is no fully fleshed-out conception of sexual difference—that is, a conception that would go beyond bare biological or natural difference—throughout most of the *Oresteia*. This reading is supported by the fact that Hegel famously aligns the opposing positions taken by Creon and Antigone with those of "man and woman" in general, something he does not do in his reading of the central conflict of the *Eumenides*.

In this opposition both of sexual difference and of law, the *Antigone* also rather nicely illustrates, to a greater extent than does the *Eumenides*, the two flawed conceptions of natural law that Hegel criti-cizes in the early work. Rather than resting content with the conception of natural law as tragic, as he initially argues, Hegel ultimately wants to think of natural law as progressing through an impasse caused by a con-flict between two equally valid yet—because one-sided—incompatible ethical claims. Sexual difference only emerges at the very conclusion of the *Eumenides*, in the articulation of human law, and thus cannot play a role in the articulation of natural law. For Hegel, true human law will be natural law, an equation that might surprise us until we recognize that Hegelian nature is never reducible to biology or physics, which, like the one-sided articulations of natural law, would reduce sexual difference to mere bodily differentiation, but rather could be thought of as a never completely adequate embodiment of the Absolute that nonetheless informs its development.

We might begin with the simple definition of natural law theory as a theory that gives priority to the conception of justice over that of law by appealing to a natural grounding for all law that is broader and more enduring than any code based merely on practical exigency. Legal positivism, by contrast, would give priority to the law over justice. Another way of putting this would be to say that a legal positivist or formalist defines justice as what the law (which would differ according to ruling structures) orders us to do; against this, one who believes in the logical priority of the idea of justice over that of law maintains that the notion of justice can be defined independently of that of any particular law or set of laws (Burns 1996, 12, citing Crocker 1963, 189–206). When such a higher ethical criterion for judging the adequacy or inadequacy of the positive law is referred to as "natural," or, in other words, as in some way inherent to the natural rights and constitution of the human being, it is traditionally referred to as natural law. This is to say that natural law might be equally referred to as ideal or ethical law, grounding that ideal or ethic in the highest nature of the human being. Hegel consistently contrasts "positive" or conventional law with genuinely ethical, or natural law, although he believes that the two should (and will) ultimately coincide. In premodern conceptions, natural law is equated with the natural order of being, or the rational structure of the cosmos, and often with teleological conceptions of nature and/or the will of god.[1] However, modern conceptions of natural law attempt to ground the "naturalness" of the law in human reason and in structures immanent to human institutions rather than in any external, natural order. This grounding of law in human reason—a grounding that is not, of course, unique to natural law—would be justified on the basis that human nature can be equated with reason and that therefore natural law can be discovered through the proper use of reason.

Hegel's essay "The Scientific Ways of Treating Natural Law, Its Place in Moral Philosophy, and Its Relation to the Positive Sciences of Law" considers two competing historical strains in modern natural law theory. The first strain, which Hegel characterizes as "empirical," manifests itself in the distinction between the state of nature and civil societies in the social contract theories of Thomas Hobbes and John Locke, among others, as well as in the natural sciences. Such empiricism, according to Hegel, illegitimately conjectures determinate natural characteristics of human beings by abstracting from contingent features of actual human beings, civil societies, or states of law, and then claiming that they are independent of or prior to any particular empirical state of affairs. Hegel compares the theory of a state of nature from which civil society emerges to a scientific theory that posits the emergence of the organized physical world from a state of chaos (Hegel 1975, 63). This is an attempt to derive what was intended to be *a priori* or "natural" from what is actually *a posteriori*, resulting in stories of the coming into being of civil society from a state of nature that remain mere conjecture. It thus remains what Hegel calls "content without form," and therefore arbitrary.

The second form of natural law theory, called "formalism" by Hegel, concerns the ideal of natural secular right, possibly traceable to the idea of Christian right, which manifested itself in the eighteenth century in Germany in the philosophical individualism of the ethical and legal theories of Immanuel Kant and Johann Gottleib Fichte, and in France as the political individualism of the French Revolution. The natural right of a person, according to this view, is the *a priori* absolute right from which every theory of right or law should be constituted, and to which any modification of existing laws should be oriented. Only the coexistence of persons necessitates any constraint on the guarantee of individual freedoms to all. Hegel criticizes this conception of natural law as excessively contentless, as "form without content." It does not seek to show how the purely formal principle of natural right relates to specific rights, duties, and obligations, much less the laws and institutions of a state. In addition, Hegel criticizes Kant in particular for reducing practical reason to logical consistency. The rationality of ethical life, according to Hegel, is not manifested merely in the logical consistency of one's practical maxims of action, but in the unity of one's life. Moreover, and importantly, ethical life cannot be examined merely at the level of the individual, but must take as its point of departure the ethical community.

In his mature work, the *Philosophy of Right*, Hegel demonstrates that theories of society that prioritize the abstract, autonomous, self-interested individual as existing prior to the community, completely overlook the historical, social, and ethical conditions that make the emergence of modern subjectivity possible in the first place. Natural law, far from preceding conceptions of community or society, can only emerge as a concept at a particular historical stage that presupposes various permutations in the form of community. Rather than being a fixed or ahistorical position, natural law represents a specific stage in the dialectical progress toward freedom, yet although it emerges as a concept together with modern subjectivity, natural law, unlike the concept of the individual subject taken abstractly, is intertwined with the notion of community and the state.

Hegel thus proposes a third definition of natural law, one that has been characterized both as form plus content, and as "organic" (Burns 1996, 52; Hyppolite 1996, 38–39), reflecting its dynamic, generative nature. Unlike the other versions, this natural law theory is not grounded in the individual, although it does leave room for and value subjective freedom. This ideal is a living and organized community, traceable to Greek antiquity and perhaps most specifically to the philosophy of Aristotle, yet with the recognition that the rise of liberal individuality, too, was a necessary step in the historical development of ethical life.

Hegel strives to maintain a balance between the empirical and the formal by simultaneously refusing to consider a state that is merely theoretical or imaginary in nature and by insisting that his philosophy is not that of any particular state that has existed in nature. There is always a discrepancy between the spirit of a particular people and the absolute spirit that appears within it. The residue is also called "fate," or "the inorganic," the element of necessity with which the individual and the community must ultimately be reconciled. In anticipation of his later system, Hegel refers to the various shapes of world spirit that will ultimately be unified with the divine substance of the absolute, but which, within time, must struggle with physical nature, death, and necessity (objectivity), not always recognizing their ultimate unity with the whole. For this reason, Hegel characterizes the history of natural law as tragic:

> There is nothing else but the performance, on the ethical plane, of the tragedy which the Absolute eternally enacts with itself, by eternally giving birth to itself into objectivity, submitting in this objective form to suffering and death, and rising from its ashes into glory. The Divine in its form and objectivity is immediately double-natured, and its life is the absolute unity of these natures. (Hegel 1975, 104)

He goes on almost immediately to refer to the *Oresteia* as specifically illuminating or exemplifying this performance of birth, death, and rebirth, in particular in the final scene of the *Eumenides*:

The picture of this tragedy, defined more particularly for the ethical realm, is the issue of that litigation between the Eumenides
(as powers of the law in the sphere of difference) and Apollo (the
god of undifferentiated light) over Orestes, conducted before the
organized ethical order, the people of Athens. (Hegel 1975, 460)

Within this tragedy, the conflict is not presented as a diametrically
opposed binary antagonism, in Hegel's view, but involves three separate
protagonists: the Eumenides, who are at least implicitly aligned with
what Hegel will later call the divine law or the law of the family, the side
of Clytemnestra and perhaps Electra; Apollo, who represents the "new"
Olympian gods, and Orestes; and the people of Athens as a still legally
unarticulated ethical whole, what Hegel will call in his reading of the
Antigone the law of the state,[2] which has not yet come into being. Only
through the bringing together of these separate antagonistic groups will
natural law be established.

The inception of law is accomplished symbolically with a vote; the
people judge between Apollo and the Eumenides in deciding whether
Orestes is to be considered justified in having killed Clytemnestra, his
mother, or whether he is to be condemned as having committed the
unforgivable crime of matricide. When the result is a draw, however,
they cannot settle the conflict:

In the human mode, Athens, as the Areopagus, puts equal votes in
the urn for each litigant and recognizes their co-existence; though it
does not thereby compose the conflict or settle the relation between
the powers or their bearing on one another. (Hegel 1975, 460)

Thus, Athena, the patron goddess of Athens, must step in to break the
tie. Hegel completely identifies the goddess with the city:

But in the Divine mode, as Athene, Athens wholly restores to the
people the man [Orestes] who had been involved in difference by
the god [Apollo] himself; and through the separation of the powers
both of which had their interest in the criminal, it brings about a
reconciliation in such a way that the Eumenides would be revered
by this people as Divine powers, and would now have their place
in the city, so that their savage nature would enjoy (from the altar
erected to them in the city below) the sight of Athene enthroned on
high on the Acropolis, and thereby be pacified. (Hegel 1975, 460)

The important thing about this particular tragedy, on Hegel's view, is that it brings about a reconciliation between private and public, individual desire and ethical life. This would also be the function of natural law: natural law brings together human beings in both their natural and spiritual state as ethical—that is, intersubjective beings—rather than either expressing their original state in a mythical state of nature prior to conventional law or referring to a higher, intelligible noumenal self that can never be fully captured by conventional law.

Thus, for Hegel the *Oresteia* tells the story of the inception of natural law out of the conflict between three opposing forces: the retributive justice that demands punishment of one family member by another for crimes deemed most heinous and unnatural by the gods (the chain of such acts in the case of the house of Atreus has developed into a "family curse"); the prohibition against the violation and killing of family members, equally ancient and considered equally heinous (patricide, matricide, incest) by the gods; and the judgment and determination of the community to which the family belongs but who nevertheless are not part of the family (taken as one whole rather than an aggregate of diverse opinions) concerning these same crimes. Another way of thinking of this three-way antagonism might be as the conflict Hegel negotiates in his definition of natural law between (1) the passion-inspired killing of one person by another ungoverned by any law other than that of revenge (something like a Hobbesian state of nature); (2) the existence of certain laws that seem to remain constant over time and enact prohibitions almost according to a higher intuition of human nature, something like a noumenal self, against killing, incest, and so on; and (3) the existence of an organized body of human beings who recognize that the singular pursuit of private vendettas undermines the harmonious running of the community.

TRAGEDY AND SEXUAL DIFFERENCE

Within the context of the natural law essay, Hegel's general definition of tragedy on the plane of ethical life is the splitting off of private right (which Hegel also calls the inorganic) from ethical life (the organic), an operation that ethical life performs on itself, in an act of self-sacrifice. Private right includes the spheres of the family and of need and right, which, later in history, includes the bourgeois state for whom private interest is everything. It is inorganic precisely because private; it is not interested in the workings of the whole. Ethical life, or the organic, concerns those properly political elements that take the whole community as their point of departure. Hegel aligns the Furies and the mother they avenge with private right, and Apollo and Athena with ethical life considered in its human and divine nature. But it is only at the end of the trilogy that Orestes (and Apollo) comes to be aligned with the synthesizing power of Athens/Athena. First he must pass through the agonizing conflict between the ancient divinities' prohibition against matricide and his own conviction that in killing his mother he was carrying out a command in line with a higher god and a concomitant higher vision of human nature.

To understand how the alignment of the sexes with the two sides of law is not a merely contingent or sociological or cultural phenomenon, we can look both to the tragedy Hegel cites and to his own philosophy of nature. In a passage from the *Eumenides*, Apollo is arguing with the Chorus of Furies over Orestes' matricide. The Chorus first accuses Apollo of misconstruing the Zeus-given justification for the murder. If, they say, Zeus had higher regard for a father's destiny than that of a mother, why did he place his own father, Cronos, in chains? Apollo responds that chains can be broken, but death can never be reversed. The Furies ask again, then why is the murder of a mother more justifiable than that of a father? Apollo responds as follows:

> Then learn the truth, the one named mother
> Is not the child's true parent, but the nurturer
> Of the newly sown seed. Man mounts to create life,
>   whereas woman is a stranger fostering a stranger,
>   nourishing the young, unless a god blights the birth.
>   (654–60)

He then points to Athena as proof that there can be a father without a mother (664). This passage refers to a version of theory of generation that Hegel also espouses in his *Philosophy of Nature*, in which the female, undifferentiated element, merely provides the material for conception, while the male element contributes the active principle or "subjectivity" (Hegel 1970, 3:175). Male and female genitalia, on Hegel's account, are homologous, although formed to greater and lesser extents. The relative lack of differentiation in the female (attested to by her "shrunken scrota," or labia, the "unemerged testicle" enclosed within her ovary, and the fact that the effusion of blood to the genitals results not in productive tumescence but in menstruation) accounts for the relative passivity of the female principle in this theory, while the relative differentiation and externality of the male genitals account for the activity of the male principle.[3]

Hegel uses the same language of lack of differentiation and sundered opposition to characterize the spiritual nature of men and women in his discussion of ethical life in the *Philosophy of Right*:

> One sex is spirit in its self-diremption into explicit personal self-subsistence and the knowledge and volition of free universality, i.e. the self-consciousness of conceptual thought and the volition of the objective final end. The other sex is spirit maintaining itself in unity as knowledge and volition of the substantive, but knowledge and volition in the form of concrete individuality and feeling. (Hegel [1821] 1952, 166)

Thus "nature," and specifically sexual difference, is already something spiritual.[4] The point I am trying to make here is that in aligning sexual difference with the distinction between divine and state law, or private and public right, and in addition, by defining natural law as the self-sacrifice of the inorganic by the organic, Hegel is providing natural law with a grounding in nature—albeit a "nature" that only comes into being simultaneously with the law that articulates it—that cannot be found in either the empirical or the formal models. The former must imagine a state of nature that may never have existed (read: bare biological definition of sexual difference), while the latter appeals to a noumenal self—defined precisely in its distinction from nature—that cannot be directly experienced or even ever really known. But according to Hegel in the *Philosophy of Right*, as we have just seen, "the difference in the physical characteristics of the two sexes has a rational basis and consequently acquires an intellectual and ethical significance" ([1821] 1952, 165). This basis is attested to both physically (in the relative lack of differentiation in the female genitalia and the "sundered opposition" of the male genitalia) and spiritually (in the clear distinction of the roles of the sexes, divided into feminine undifferentiated "unity of feeling" and masculine dirempted "self-consciousness of conceptual thought").

In the *Oresteia* there is no initial clear cut conflict between divine and state law, between the allegiances of men and of women (sexual difference), or even, in the beginning, between the old and the young gods, as the chorus of Furies puts it in the *Eumenides*. Electra invokes both Zeus and the Earth, and Orestes invokes Apollo in the move to avenge their father's death, but both invoke retributive justice (death of the mother for death of the father), not an articulated law of the state.

Clytemnestra seizes power not in the name of a law of the divine or of the family, but, at least in the eyes of her children, for the love of power. When Apollo seeks to convince Orestes to kill his mother, he motivates him with the threat, not of Zeus' anger, but of the Furies who will spring from his father's spilled blood to torment him (280–90). Electra sides with her father against her mother and the memory of her sacrificed sister, yet she invokes both the Earth and retributive Justice, forces that seem aligned with the Furies rather than Zeus, in the desire to bring back Orestes to avenge their father (125–50). Electra's language reflects this inchoate status of law, this fundamental ambivalence, this lack of clarity as to where divine loyalties lie. She asks, "What is good? What is evil? Can we ever conquer Ruin?" (338) and cries, "I want Justice from injustice" (399). In addition, Pylades says to Orestes, when the latter hesitates to kill his own mother, that it is "better to be hated by every man on earth than hated by the gods" (900). Yet the final conflict is couched as one between the new pantheon of gods (Zeus, Apollo, and Athena) and the inception of a justice of the state, and the ancient spirits, the Furies and a Justice (Dikê) who is a vengeful goddess. The inception of human law comes only at the conclusion of the *Eumenides*. And it is also only at the end of the trilogy that paternity is deemed the true parental principle, both in reproduction and in law. Thus, "natural law" only comes into being through the establishment of human law, though natural law continues to be defined, as Hegel claims, in its relation to the absolute—that is, in relation to a justice that precedes law and to which formal law is held accountable.

Given Hegel's earlier text on natural law and the choice of the *Oresteia* to illustrate it, we see that nature or natural law, even in his later reading of *Antigone* in the *Phenomenology*, is not something that is simply excluded from the law of the state, as feminist scholarship on Hegel often asserts.[5] Even the *Eumenides*, for this reason, I would argue, contains more than a simple mythical justification for male social domination. Human law itself, prior to any particular content, is defined through sexual difference. And this is done not through an exclusion of the natural but precisely in its name—that is, in the service of a gradual synthesis of nature and spirit. The *Oresteia*, and, in particular, the *Eumenides*, is an overcoming equally of an old sense of justice as of an old sense of sexual difference, both entering into the realm of the symbolic.

One interpretation of natural law that Hegel does *not* discuss in this essay, and which might seem the most obvious way in which tragedy, natural law, and sexual difference might be linked, is the way in which Irigaray seems to define the term in several of her works. Her analysis includes an examination of Hegel's purported use of natural law, but she draws her conclusions primarily from his reading of *Antigone* in the *Phenomenology of Spirit*, where woman is aligned with divine law or the law of the family, and man with the law of the state, and natural law is not explicitly invoked. Irigaray seems to equate natural law, whether she is discussing Hegel or not, with those laws that either predate or are not covered by the laws of the state and which tend to remain constant over time rather than fluctuating according to who is in power. For her, natural law refers both to laws that are generated from supposed natural differences between the sexes, and to the private sphere as opposed to the public. She seems to generate this assumption from Hegel's reading of *Antigone* in the *Phenomenology of Spirit*,[6] even though she does not invoke Hegel every time she discusses natural law. The equation of *themis*, or divine law, in the name of which Antigone acts, with natural law, and *nomos*, the law of the state, on which Creon grounds his authority, with positive law, is commonplace in many commentaries on *Antigone*. However, when Irigaray is commenting specifically on Hegel's interpretation of *Antigone*, she errs in calling the law that Antigone follows natural law, since Hegel refers to *themis* only as the law of the family or divine law. Despite the common tendency of commentators to call *themis* natural law, in fact this presupposes a particularly narrow version of the premodern interpretation of natural law as reflecting the natural order of being (or the way of the gods), exemplified mainly through roles defined according to sexual difference. Although in other places that Irigaray discusses natural law, she is not explicitly commenting on Hegel, she nonetheless seems to take his reading of Antigone as her point of departure.

For example, in *Democracy Begins Between Two*, Irigaray writes,

> Natural law has, for the most part, been left to the custody of the family...[and] is supposed to produce and protect life. It is also meant to ensure coexistence between the individuals who make it up: natural or private coexistence, as it is referred to, in which the State has no powers of direct intervention. (2001, 55–56)

As we have seen, for Hegel private right is precisely what is sacrificed in the development of natural law. Indeed, the original title of the *Philosophy of Right* was a double one, with *Naturrecht und Staatswissenschaft im Grundrisse* (Natural Law and the Science of the State in Outline) appended to the more well-known title. Although Irigaray's critique rightly focuses on the sacrificial nature of the relationship of the feminine, the private, and the family to the emergence of civil society and law, she represents natural law neither in a correctly Hegelian manner nor in the manner of any of the previous versions of natural law theory, and this weakens her argument.[7] For Hegel, natural law is not separate from the state but is precisely the aim of the state in its organic development. For Aristotle and Thomas Aquinas, ideal or natural law would never be aligned with the feminine or the family.

Irigaray's embrace of natural law understood as either prior to the state or independent of it is problematic both for its misreading of Hegel and for the way in which it seems to bolster a kind of naturalism of which she has been accused and which even an appeal to her psychoanalytic background to temper what she means by "natural" seems insufficient to counter. I will argue that neither Hegel nor Irigaray has a bare concept of nature understood as a state of nature or biological bedrock. Interestingly, however, Irigaray seems more open to such a critique given her appeal to natural law understood in a sense very different from his.

SEXUAL DIFFERENCE AND LAW

At the same time that I am arguing that, for Hegel, the nature in natural law refers neither to pure biology (which, on Hegel's account, might be as mythical as the state of nature imagined by social contract theorists) nor to some noumenal character of humans, I want to avoid the misunderstanding that I am claiming that, for Hegel, nature in general and sexual difference in particular are simply determined by culture or convention and thus are subject to indefinite fluctuation— an account that would be as empirical as the biological one. On the contrary, just as natural law is called natural because it is fixed in a kind of spiritual particularity, sexual difference, which emerges with natural law, eventually acquires a definite and fixed status, albeit not one that is simply determined by natural functions, in generation or otherwise. Thus, it is not the case that just because sexual difference and human law emerge concurrent with each other that, with the deliberate alteration of specific laws, one could also bring about a concomitant change in sexual identity. This is why law, properly speaking, is "natural law" for Hegel; spirit emerges from nature, and although what it expresses is something very different from the fantasy of raw nature, and indeed opposed to it, its rooting in "nature" nevertheless provides a justification and demonstration of its rectitude.

To illuminate this "third state," which explains sexual difference neither through natural determination nor through social and cultural convention, I turn to elucidations of the psychoanalytic conception of sexual difference by Charles Shepherdson and Joan Copjec, as well as to Jacques Derrida's articulation of the relationship between justice and law in "Force of Law." I do so not to argue that Hegel otherwise has much in common with psychoanalysis or deconstruction, but to move from here to Irigaray's psychoanalytically and deconstructively informed conception of sexual difference and its relation to her reading of Hegel, particularly of his analysis of *Antigone* in the *Phenomenology of Spirit*.

Shepherdson begins his "*Adequatio Sexualis:* Is There a Measure of Sexual Difference?" with a reference to Freud's decisive move to separate the psychoanalytic conception of human illness from the model of organic medicine. Shepherdson calls this "the origin of psychoanalysis" (1995, 445). "The 'body,'" he writes, "is no longer a purely 'natural' phenomenon...but refers us to 'the existence of the subject,' which is in turn governed by the symbolic order" (ibid., 446). This is as true for sexual difference as it is for the symptoms of a so-called mental illness. I have argued above that something of this kind is true for Hegel as well, although, of course, Hegel is not discussing symptoms or illnesses, or even the body per se, in his analysis of Greek tragedy. As Irigaray has famously argued, and as I elaborate here, Hegel's philosophy of nature, in particular his discussion of animal sexuality, is imbricated with his discussion of sexual difference with reference to ethical life and to tragedy.

However, as Copjec clearly shows in her essay "Sex and the Euthanasia of Reason," although sex is never a simple, natural fact for psychoanalysis, "it is also never reducible to any discursive construction" (1995, 204). She goes on to clarify that this does not mean that sexual difference is prediscursive or that it is not a product of signification. Rather, the subject is, as Copjec puts it, "at the same level as the law" that articulates it. The subject neither dictates the law of her sexuality, nor is she at the mercy of its dictates, but she "can only be conceived as the failure of the law, of language" (ibid., 209). We should note the implied equation of law and language here, for it is important for both Hegel and Irigaray as well, as I will elaborate later. Copjec writes, "*In* language and yet *more than* language, the subject is a cause for which no signifier can account. Not because she transcends the signifier but because she inhabits it *as limit*" (ibid., 209). She refers to Etienne Balibar's articulation of the relation of the political subject to the law, in which he insists that it is the identity of "citizen subject" to be both the one who makes the law and the one who is subject to it (Balibar 1991, 48). This is not to say that the citizen *is* the law, but rather to express the idea that the citizen as an identity comes about simultaneously with the articulated law, neither before nor after. This notion of the equiprimordiality of identity and law echoes what we have been expressing with reference to the coemergence of sexual difference and law.

To examine how this idea of the intertwining of sexual identity and law relates specifically to the question of natural law, I will now briefly examine Derrida's articulation of the relationship between justice and law in "Force of Law." Arguably, there is less of a disjunction between Derrida's understanding of the relationship between justice and law and Hegel's reading of the same relationship than might usually be assumed.

Derrida has been accused of according certain fundamental philosophical concepts no uncontested, stable meaning. Yet Derrida writes of justice as a kind of possible, nondestructible outside that subjects the law to constant vigilance, that does not allow unjust conventions to become sedimented or complacent. Justice invokes "the sense of a responsibility without limits" to the other, and so enjoins us to recall "the history, the origin and the sense, thus the limits, of concepts of justice, law, and right, of values, norms, prescriptions that have been imposed and sedimented there, from then on remaining more or less readable or presupposed" (Derrida 2001, 247–48). From this definition we can call Derrida a natural law theorist in Hegel's highest sense, since Justice as a concept can neither be reduced to the empirical, nor can it be understood as an *a priori* absolute right from which all laws should derive. Derrida is clear that, for him, Justice does not operate as a regulative principle, and it is characterized as absence rather than presence. If it comes into being as a quasi transcendental at all, it is simultaneous—that is, co-constituted, with law itself.

In his famous and contentious statement "Deconstruction is Justice," Derrida argues that it is because law itself (which he distinguishes from Justice) *is* constructible and deconstructible, and because justice is undeconstructible, that deconstruction itself is made possible. In an eloquent defense of deconstruction against its critics, he describes its task as

> address[ing] itself to singularity, to the singularity of the other, despite or even because it pretends to universality. Consequently, never to yield on this point, constantly to maintain a questioning of the origin, grounds and limits of our conceptual, theoretical or normative apparatus surrounding justice—this is, from the point

of view of a rigorous deconstruction, anything but a neutraliza-
tion of the interest in justice, an insensitivity toward injustice.
On the contrary, it hyperbolically raises the stakes in the demand
for justice, the sensitivity to a kind of essential disproportion
that must inscribe excess and inadequation in itself. It compels
to denounce not only theoretical limits but also concrete injus-
tices, with the most palpable effects, in the good conscience that
dogmatically stops before any inherited determination of justice.
(Derrida 2001, 248)

This conception of Justice, not as the natural state preceding the
inception of Law or as an absolute that precedes and grounds law, but
rather as the outer limit of law, one that serves always to question its
claim to a secure origin that would grant it immunity from interrogation
and a grounding that could, in turn, dictate unwavering theoretical or
normative frameworks, is not so far from the co-constitution envisaged
by Hegel. Such a conception evokes Copjec's articulation of the subject
inhabiting the signifier as its limit (in language and yet more than
language), given the proximity of law and language. It also manifests
the same attempt that we can see in Hegel to ground knowledge in the
thing-in-itself without thereby taking identity, whether sexual or civil,
as a simple given.

For, as Derrida writes, there is no origin of authority without already
positing the law; the founding moment of law "exceeds the opposition
between founded and unfounded, or between any foundationalism or
anti-foundationalism" (2001, 242). The instituting moment of law implies
a "performative force," an interpretive violence that "no justice and no
earlier and previously founding law, no preexisting foundation, could, by
definition, guarantee or contradict or invalidate" (ibid., 241). The same
might be said for sexual difference as we are reading it. This is to say that
concepts of law and about sexual difference, as they evolve historically,
are not merely *about* reality or seeking to represent an external reality,
but rather are the in-itself of those things themselves—that is, they are
natural. That they evolve and can be transformed is due to the vigilance
of the idea of justice, which is both an other to thought and what constitutes it. This is what makes natural law both natural and lawlike.

At the same time, the insistence that deconstruction "addresses itself
to singularity" does seem to set it apart quite radically from Hegel's conception of natural law. Hegel has been held up as the prime example of
ethical theories that embrace the universal at the expense of the singular,
as critiques of Hegel from Søren Kierkegaard and Friedrich Nietzsche to
Emmanuel Levinas and Irigaray have pointed out. Hegel's conception of

law and ethical life, like his articulation of the necessary emergence of the universal in language in the section "Sense-Certainty" of the *Phenomenology of Spirit*, arises from the fundamental impossibility of "saying what we mean"—that is, of addressing the singular in the terms of the singular. Irigaray addresses a similar question when she tries to think of a duality of universals, or of sexed universals. For Irigaray, woman, as the nonuniversal, has been excluded from the sphere of law and rights by virtue of her historical alignment with the private. The couple, she writes, is interesting because it forms a special case, because it is located at the junction of private and public, of subjective and objective.

IRIGARAY AND NATURAL LAW

At the opening of "The Universal as Mediation" (in *Sexes and Genealogies*), Irigaray makes a reference to Hegel's conception of law:

> Hegel analyses how the law wavers between two poles:
> —the prevalence of a formalism that is largely arbitrary, needed to mark a decision or to set boundaries, yet always in search of some solid content to fill the forms out.
> —The existence of some laws that stand close to the content of action and that show little variation in their expression: thou shalt not kill, steal, etc. (1993, 128)

Irigaray goes on to identify the first of these poles as what is often redefined as the law of the state, and the second as deriving from an ethics that at least originally is of divine order (ibid.). Since Freud, however, she asserts, "we have been habitually forced to face the question of a law that could be applied to lovers or married couples and the way they are located at the junction of private and public, of subjective and objective, of *Moralität* and *Sittlichkeit*" (ibid.). This clear reference to Hegel reflects their common concern that individual morality and ethical life have been conflated,[8] that natural law as it is commonly conceived takes as its point of departure the atomistic individual rather than the community, or, in Irigaray's case, the couple. For Irigaray, additionally, Hegel's conception of the law of the state is fundamentally flawed because it requires a sacrifice of the private and the feminine, a sacrifice of what she calls "natural law." This sacrificial order appears to be complicit with the Oedipal theory of the move from the law of the mother to the law of the father.

For Irigaray, too, the dichotomy between nature and nurture is a false one when thinking about sexual difference. Her emphasis is on the civil identity of woman, precisely what Hegel seems to sacrifice in his account of coming to natural law:

> The question as to whether belonging to a gender is the effect of a biological destiny or of social conditioning fails to take into account the fact that being or becoming a woman means acquiring a civil dimension which is appropriate to "feminine identity", a culture which corresponds to one's own body and specific genealogy, one's own way of loving and of procreating, of desiring and of thinking. Feminism's blindest alley is to force women into a deconditioning which strips them of their feminine identity in order to attain an undifferentiated state of universality to be shared in a masculine or neutral world. (Irigaray 2001, 36)

Yet Irigaray continues to appeal, as we have seen, to the generative power of a kind of idyllic natural law independent of the state, even while she is criticizing the deep divide that Western philosophy, perhaps in particular social contract theory, has created between natural (understood in her own sense) and state law:

> Natural law has, for the most part, been left to the custody of the family. The latter…is supposed to produce and protect life. It is also meant to ensure coexistence between the individuals who make it up: natural or private coexistence, as it is referred to, in which the State has no powers of direct intervention. This natural coexistence is based, first and foremost, on the body of the woman, on her procreative properties, on her qualities as mother and, in a secondary manner as wife. This natural coexistence also involves children's bodies, and the feelings between mother and child. Only one part of man belongs to natural coexistence: the part of sexual desire, and of the marital and paternal authority linked to it. Another part of man moves between natural and civil coexistence and, as such, enjoys civil rights which are not, however, appropriate to women and children. (Irigaray 2001, 56)

This account of natural law seems very close to Irigaray's earlier critique of Hegel's analysis of Antigone in the *Phenomenology*. However, Irigaray's concern here is the current law of the state and how it might be transformed to include sexuate rights by looking back to what she calls natural law. For Irigaray, a transformed symbolic order, including a transformation of state laws and institutions, can only be properly accomplished if it emerges from a recognition of the sexual duality of nature or natural law.

As Margaret Whitford has noted, there is both a nod toward and a transformation of social contract theory implied in Irigaray's conception of nature and its relation to the symbolic order, one that we might compare to Hegel's critique and attempt to overcome both an essentialist and an empiricist definition of natural law, including sexual difference. Whitford argues that Irigaray posits sexual difference in "nature" as the female imaginary, while also putting it into the future as a horizon of thought and action that might transform the symbolic order, in the same way that Jean-Jacques Rousseau puts nature into both the primitive past (as the "state of nature" that has been corrupted by civilization) and in the future, as something to be created in order to criticize progress (Whitford 1991, 190). This would seem to align Irigaray's use of natural law with the "empirical" strain Hegel criticizes.

However, Irigaray also at times uses divine law as a term for Justice as a kind of corrective to law. She writes, for example, that divine law "takes up the slack" when formal laws are inadequate to meet each individual situation, especially in certain contexts: sexuality, love, and marriage (Irigaray 1993, 128). Finally, Irigaray also uses natural law as a term for natural order. She points out that Greek tragedy is full of examples of loss of respect for the natural order, in particular for the feminine:

> This drama is played out in the appropriation of woman's sex by man in the rape of Kore by the god of the underworld, the abduction and sacrifice of Iphigenia during the Trojan war, the legalized murder of Clytemnestra, the burial of the Furies beneath the city of Athens, the glory of Athena who proclaims herself daughter of the father alone and denies her maternal heritage, the incarceration of Antigone in the stone cave outside the city. (Irigaray 1993, 134)

Beyond the non-Hegelian use of "natural law" for "natural order," the examples are not as parallel as Irigaray implies. Antigone and Polyneices are a brother and sister united (he in death) in the observance of divine law against the law of the state. Electra and Orestes are a brother and sister united in their appeal to the gods to avenge what they see as the murder of their father by their mother in a base grasping for power (the sacrifice of Iphigenia, their sister, is not mentioned as they invoke divine Justice). There is no clear alignment of one sex with divine law,

the other with human, until the trial of Orestes at the very end of the
Eumenides. Because Antigone's role as protectress of the family and of
the requirements of the gods over and against the law of the state is, by
contrast, clearly defined, she does not waver or question the meaning of
good and evil, the line between justice and injustice.

In addition, Irigaray claims that there is no dialectical relationship
between the sexes in Hegel, and that this is why he treats the family as
a unit whose law can enter into a dialectical relationship with the law
of the state. She writes,

> If gender were to develop individually, collectively, and histori-
> cally, it could mark *the place where spirit entered human nature,*
> the point in time when the infinite passed into the finite, given
> that each individual of a gender is finite and potentially infinite
> in his or her relation to gender. In Hegel's view, the family con-
> stitutes a unit. It has to, since there is no dialectic between the
> sexes. This imposed unit upsets the whole of Hegel's construction.
> This is where spirit fails to penetrate into nature to spiritualize it.
> (1993, 139)

In Electra and Orestes' relationship, or even the conflict between Orestes
and Clytemnetra, as presented by Aeschylus, it is true that there is no
dialectical opposition. But in *Antigone* there *is* a dialectical relationship,
and this is precisely what Hegel is seeking out, even if he ultimately
sublates Antigone's contribution to it. In addition, in the *Oresteia,* what
is sacrificed is an older sense of retributive justice; in *Antigone*, it is
more explicitly the feminine.

DIVINE LAW, THE LAW OF THE STATE, AND NATURAL LAW

As we have seen, Irigaray conflates divine law, as Hegel describes it in
the *Phenomenology of Spirit* in his analysis of the tragedy *Antigone*,
with natural law. In the *Phenomenology*, divine law and state law are
conceptualized as in dialectical conflict with each other, and Hegel came
to think that this oppositional relationship is most clearly articulated in
Sophocles' *Antigone*. In addition, Hegel explicitly aligns divine law—or
the law of the family, as he also calls it—with woman (Antigone), and
the law of the state with man (Creon), although the two cannot really
be separated from each other insofar as each provides authentication
for the other:

We do indeed see [the ethical realm] divide itself into two essences and their reality; but their antithesis is rather the authentication of one through the other, and where they come into direct contact with each other as real opposites, their middle term and common element is their immediate interpenetration. The one extreme, the universal self-conscious Spirit, becomes, through the individuality of the man, united with its other extreme, its force and element, with *unconscious* Spirit. On the other hand, the divine law has its individualization—or the *unconscious* Spirit of the individual its real existence—in the woman, through whom, as the *middle term*, the unconscious Spirit rises out of its unreality into actual existence, out of a state in which it is unknowing and unconscious into the realm of conscious spirit. The union of man and woman constitutes the active middle term of the whole and the element which sunders itself into these extremes of divine and human law. (Hegel [1807] 1977, 278)

Without this explanation, it is easy to see why one might confuse the divine law with natural law, and the law of the state with the spiritual. For Hegel, *both* are both natural and spiritual, in fact, each performing the unifying middle term for the other in the identity of divine and human, natural and spiritual:

The universal ethical beings are...the substance *qua* universal, and the substance *qua* an individual consciousness. Their universal actuality is the nation and the Family; while they have their natural self and operative individuality in man and woman. (Hegel [1807] 1977, 276)

At the same time, both remain one-sided, abstract versions of natural law. Indeed, we might say that Creon represents the so-called empirical strain of natural law that Hegel criticizes in the "Natural Law" essay, while Antigone represents the formal strain. As such, the tragedy of *Antigone* provides a better vehicle for illustrating Hegel's theory of natural law than does the *Eumenides*.

The structure of *Antigone* and its position within the *Oedipus* trilogy at first glance seems to be both familiar ground and a new direction for Hegel. Like the *Oresteia*, this trilogy deals with a family curse and involves complex relations between children and parents that include the killing of a spouse, patricide, and matricide. Both the *Eumenides* and *Antigone* form the conclusion to their respective trilogies. However, the main protagonist of the earlier plays emerges quite early on as the son Orestes. Antigone, by contrast, is the heroine of only one of the plays, and her role as daughter and sister seems to overshadow her individual identity. Moreover, sexual difference seems to play a much more important role in *Antigone* than it does in the *Oresteia* or even in the two *Oedipus* tragedies. Orestes' sister Electra is a relatively passive, more typically feminine character, closer to Ismene than to Antigone. By contrast, Antigone's brothers, Polyneices and Eteocles, disappear as minor characters beside her, introduced only at their death and in memory.

The question naturally arises, why does Hegel situate his discussion of the *Oresteia* within his treatment of natural law, in the earlier essay, while, in the *Phenomenology of Spirit*, he divides his discussion of justice into divine and state law, without mention of natural law? From the perspective of law that Hegel focuses on when examining both tragedies, the conclusions of the two trilogies are nearly diametrically opposed. Whereas the *Oresteia* ends with the inception of natural law, the highest form of law, the *Antigone* story marks the move from natural law understood as the unified law of a living community to the splitting and opposition of law into divine and human (as well as "masculine" and "feminine") law, to the breakdown of community which leads—not within the trilogy itself but within Hegel's account of the development of Spirit—to the lifeless atomism of legal status in the *Phenomenology of Spirit*. Only with the emergence of the modern, liberal conception of subjectivity out of this atomism, can ethical life, and natural law in its complete Hegelian sense, be enriched and fully achieved.

I argue that, although Hegel does not use the term "natural law" here, he is in fact making a similar argument to that in the "Natural Law" essay, but using Creon and Antigone's diametrically opposed positions to illustrate the one-sidedness of either a purely "empirical" or a purely "formal" approach to law. Creon articulates a version of the "empirical" understanding of natural law, where nature is reconstructed retroactively and absolutely from the perspective of the already established state, and laws are to be unquestioningly followed simply because they are established and maintained by the authority that is now in power. He assumes that humans unchained from the laws of the state will fall into chaos, that the natural state of human beings without a ruling power is lawlessness, thereby projecting an essence onto human beings that is illegitimately derived *a posteriori*. For him, law is empirically derived and external, imposed by the ruler as the only means of avoiding anarchy:

> One must obey the man whom the city sets up in power in small things and in justice and in its opposite. This is the man whom

I would trust to be a good ruler and a good subject, and when assigned his post in the storm of battle to prove a true and noble comrade in the fight. But there is no worse evil than insubordination! This it is that ruins cities, this it is that destroys houses, this it is that shatters and puts to flight the warriors on its own side! But what saves the lives of most of those that go straight is obedience! In this way we have to protect discipline, and we must never allow a woman to vanquish us. (665–75)

Moreover, Creon makes the mistake of grounding the absolute freedom of the individual ruler (himself) on an irrational foundation—that is, on a set of self-interested needs. Completely caught up within the world as it has contingently come about, Creon does not realize the fatal error he has made until the very end. Since he has no conception of the law as timeless, he only learns when it is too late the shortcoming of his devotion to a one-sided principle. His regrets over the deaths of his son and wife are lamentations that also recognize his own finitude, his confinement within the web of temporality.

Antigone, by contrast, explicitly puts the relationship between divine law (Justice) and human law (law) into question, clearly privileging a kind of Kantian/Fichtean reading of natural law, where nature refers to a noumenal nature of the human being (here in its relationship to the gods) that precedes any conventional putting into practice of law, and that can provide an absolute corrective to laws that are in error. She makes an implicit appeal to the transcendental character of morality. In one of her most famous speeches, she addresses the question of justice in terms of its timelessness:

It was not Zeus who made this proclamation, nor was it Justice who lives with the gods below that established such laws among men, nor did I think your proclamations strong enough to have power to overrule, mortal as they were, the unwritten and unfailing ordinances of the gods. For these have life, not simply today and yesterday, but for ever, and no one knows how long ago they were revealed. (450–55)

Antigone is a character who always already knows how she will act, because for her the law is timeless and absolute. Because she does not work with laws that have been generated in time, she also does not learn anything in the tragedy, but dies with the same conviction with which she begins. As such, she is in touch with an origin of law and authority that does not unfold in time.

The fact that Creon accepts the precedence of the ancient laws at the end of the tragedy seems to indicate that this form of natural law has won out. For Hegel, however, Justice neither precedes law nor follows from it; rather, both co-constitute each other, although this relationship is not immediately historically apparent. The distinction between Justice and law emerges initially as a one-sided opposition or contradiction (as in the *Eumenides*), one that can only be reconciled in a properly ethical community. This does not happen in the ethical life of the Greeks. First, spirit must pass through the dry conventional impasse of an even more developed form of the "empirical" version of natural law—that is, through "Legal Status."

Hegel is often read to be privileging the ethical community of the Greeks, and clearly there is an element of nostalgia for classical times in his account. But as both the *Phenomenology of Spirit* and the *Philosophy of Right* make clear, the account of community in ancient Greek times remains only a preliminary, if exemplary, stage of ethical life. Interestingly, however, the *Phenomenology* moves from a description of Greek ethical life to a discussion of the atomism or abstract individual personhood of legal status, exemplified by citizenship under the Roman empire, whereas the later *Philosophy of Right* begins with the notion of personhood as its most rudimentary starting point, moving to something that resembles the Greek community only in the culminating stages of the account of the development of ethical life. Whereas the earlier work treats of the Greek "tragic" community in a roughly chronological way as somewhat primitive, the later work restores to it the important ethical status accorded to it in the "Natural Law" essay. Nevertheless, Hegel continues to reject the social contract notion of an atomistic, individualistic state of nature that precedes the emergence of a mutually cooperative community. If the *Philosophy of Right* begins with abstract personhood, it is because of its conceptual lack of sophistication rather than its precedence in chronology to the community. The new version of community that ultimately emerges in both the *Phenomenology* and the *Philosophy of Right* is enriched but not replaced by the modern concept of subjectivity, a development that occurs historically after the Greek concept of community to which it ultimately contributes.

CONCLUSION

I have argued that sexual difference functions as more than a biological or sociocultural concept in the *Eumenides* and *Antigone*, that it can be read as coming into being coterminously with law, and as essentially intertwined with the inception of natural law. Hegel's "Natural Law" essay, which reads the *Oresteia* as a performance of the inception and structure of natural law as the basis for a rational state, together with his analysis of *Antigone* in the *Phenomenology of Spirit*, in their careful attempt to overcome the shortcomings of both empirical and purely formal explanations of the instantiation of natural law, and, implicitly, of sexual difference, provides the impetus and structure for such a reading.

Hegel particularly harshly criticizes the empirical account of the emergence of natural law for its reliance on contingent particulars that it then reconstructs as essential. The argument that sexual difference is, to put it in Hegelian language, "spiritual" rather than biological or socially constructed seeks to overcome those explanations of the emergence of natural law in its relation to sexual difference that ground it in contingent historical events, whether the scheming of patriarchal authorities or the retroactive mythmaking of those in power to justify their position.

Nature itself, on this reading, gets articulated with the articulation of the law; sexual difference comes into being with the law. Nature does not precede law or provide its reason for being, but is coterminous with it. At the same time, *Antigone* provides a clearer illustration than the *Eumenides* of the shortcomings of the two historical theories of natural law that Hegel opposed in his early "Natural Law" essay. The analysis in the *Phenomenology* allows for an illustration of the one-sidedness of both a purely empirical (and thus contingent) and a purely *a priori*, formal, or timeless, conception of natural law. Natural law is not what gets excluded or sublated in the first section of "Ethical Life"; rather, natural law gains an essential condition for its possibility in the overcoming of the abstractions of both positions.

For Hegel, the dialectical conflict that gives rise to natural law only comes into being *subsequent* to the inauguration of the divide between human and divine law and their alignment with male and female understood as spiritual, not merely biological, opposites. Natural law ultimately emerges when we recognize the falsity (that is, mutual one-sidedness) of the opposition between divine and human law, but that opposition must first be clearly defined and intensified in order to be overcome. The intensification is accomplished in part by the alignment of the sides with sexual difference. If there remains what Derrida might call the "mystical foundation of authority" at the origin of the institutions of law and sexual difference, it can only be indicated retrospectively and negatively, as what exceeds the oppositional structure of male and female, human and divine.

NOTES

1. Such theories of natural law can be found in Aristotle and Thomas Aquinas most famously, but also in the Stoic conception of a rationally ordered universe.

2. See Hegel ([1807] 1977, 263–89).

3. In *Making Sex: Body and Gender from the Greeks to Freud* (1990), Thomas Laqueur traces this ancient theory, among whose most influential proponents were Aristotle and Galen, that persevered up until the eighteenth century and sometimes beyond. The difference in Hegel's account is that the counterpart to the male ejaculation of sperm in females is limited to menstrual fluid, which has nothing to do with orgasm or conception. The two-sex theory that replaced the one-sex model could be seen as allotting women a distinct and perhaps not merely passive or subservient sexual identity. The fact that Hegel does not espouse the two-sex theory, which was accepted by scientists in his time, provides further evidence that he believed sexual difference was not merely anatomical or biological, but was articulated spiritually and first truly came into existence through law.

4. It is beyond the scope of the chapter to support this claim adequately, but for an excellent and extremely thorough account of the "spirituality" of Hegel's conception of nature, see Alison Stone, *Petrified Intelligence: Nature in Hegel's Philosophy* (2005).

5. Simone de Beauvoir was perhaps one of the first to make this claim. She writes in *The Ethics of Ambiguity* that "Hegel tells us in the last part of the *Phenomenology of Spirit* that moral consciousness can exist only to the extent that there is disagreement between nature and morality. It [moral consciousness] would disappear if the ethical law became the natural law" (Beauvoir 1948, 10). Here, Beauvoir seems to equate Hegel's "divine law," which he aligns with woman and with unconscious duty, with natural law, or at least with nature. Tina Chanter, too, writes that "Hegel sees Antigone herself as no more than an instrument of nature, as the vessel through which Polyneices' death is transformed from something merely natural into something willed, deliberate, human. Antigone, in Hegel's account, as a mere woman, is relegated to the realm of the merely natural" (Chanter 2002, 34). Chanter does acknowledge that Antigone struggles against the power of nature. Hegel, however, is quite explicit in saying that the relations of the family (which presumably includes even such passive figures as Antigone's

sister, Ismene) are ethical only to the extent that they are *not* merely natural (i.e., contingent on simple need or appetite; Hegel ([1807] 1977, 268). He goes on to clarify the *natural* relationship of human beings as manifesting a connection that is "an *immediate* connection of separate, actual individuals" (ibid.) Insofar as divine law is ethical, it is spiritual, and thus binds together rather than separates. However, he does argue that the family as a spiritual entity is "more natural" than the community, and that the community, in taking a male member away from his family, must "subdue the natural aspect...of his existence" (ibid., 269).

6. See Luce Irigaray, "The Eternal Irony of the Community," in *Speculum: Of the Other Woman* (Irigaray 1985, 214–26).

7. Even if one could argue that Irigaray in this passage is referring to a premodern conception of natural law, that she does so in terms that seem to come directly from her critique of Hegel in "The Eternal Irony of the Community" (see n. 6) misrepresents that tradition as well as Hegel, for the Aristotelian and Thomistic conceptions of natural law do not place it solely on the side of the private/domestic, the religious, and the feminine.

8. The *Philosophy of Right* (Hegel [1821] 1952) addresses at length the distinction between morality and ethical life.

REFERENCES

Aeschylus. 1998. *Oresteia*. Trans. by Peter Meineck. Indianapolis: Hackett.

Balibar, Etienne. 1991. Citizen subject. Trans. James B. Swenson Jr. In *Who comes after the subject?*, ed. Eduardo Cadava, Peter Connor, and Jean-Luc Nancy. London and New York: Routledge.

Beauvoir, Simone de. 1948. *The ethics of ambiguity*. New York: Citadel Press.

Burns, Tony. 1996. *Natural law and political ideology in the philosophy of Hegel*. Brookfield, VT: Avebury.

Chanter, Tina. 2002. *Ethics of eros: Irigaray's rewriting of the philosophers*. New York: Routledge.

Copjec, Joan. 1994. Sex and the euthanasia of reason. In *Read my desire: Lacan against the historicists*. Cambridge, MA: MIT Press.

Crocker, L. G. 1963. *Nature and culture: Ethical thought in the French Enlightenment*. Baltimore: Johns Hopkins Press.

Derrida, Jacques. 2001. Force of law. In *Acts of religion*, ed. Gil Ani-
    djar. New York: Routledge.
Hegel, G. W. F. [1807] 1977. *Phenomenology of spirit*. Trans. A. V.
    Miller. Oxford: Oxford University Press.
———. [1821] 1952. *Philosophy of right*. Trans. T. M. Knox. Oxford:
    Oxford University Press.
———. 1970. *Philosophy of nature*. Trans. and ed. Michael John
    Petry. New York: Humanities.
———. 1975. *Natural law: The scientific ways of treating natural
    law, its place in moral philosophy, and its relation to the positive
    sciences of law*. Trans. T. M. Knox. Philadelphia: University of
    Pennsylvania Press.
Hyppolite, Jean. 1996. *Introduction to Hegel's philosophy of history*.
    Trans. Bond Harris and Jacqueline Bouchard Spurlock. Gainesville:
    University of Florida Press.
Irigaray, Luce. 1985. *Speculum of the other woman*. Trans. Gillian
    C. Gill. Ithaca, NY: Cornell University Press.
———. 1993. *Sexes and genealogies*. Trans. Gillian C. Gill. New
    York: Columbia University Press.
———. 2001. *Democracy begins between two*. Trans. Kirsteen Ander-
    son. London: Athlone.
Laqueur, Thomas. 1990. *Making sex: Body and gender from the
    Greeks to Freud*. Cambridge: Harvard University Press.
Lumsden, Simon. 2001. Tragedy and understanding in Hegel's dialec-
    tic. *Idealistic Studies* 31 (2/3): 125–34.
Shepherdson, Charles. 1995. *Adequatio Sexualis*: Is there a measure of
    sexual difference? In *From phenomenology to thought, errancy, and
    desire: Essays in honor of William J. Richardson, S.J.*, ed. Babette
    Babich, 445–72. Dordrecht: Kluwer Academic.
Sophocles. 1994. *Antigone. The women of Trachis. Philoctetes. Oedi-
    pus at Colonus*. Trans. and ed. Hugh Lloyd-Jones. Cambridge, MA:
    Harvard University Press.
Stone, Alison. 2005. *Petrified intelligence: Nature in Hegel's philosophy*.
    Albany: SUNY Press.
Whitford, Margaret. 1991. *Luce Irigaray: Philosophy in the feminine*.
    London and New York: Routledge.
Zeitlin, Froma I. 1996. *Playing the other: Gender and society in clas-
    sical Greek literature*. Chicago and London: University of Chicago
    Press.
Zelenak, Michael X. 1998. *Gender and politics in Greek tragedy*. New
    York: P. Lang.

7

————

MARRYING THE CITY

Intimate Strangers and the Fury of Democracy

EMILY ZAKIN

Fury, "the bloody needles that tear at young guts" and the world of animality must be reserved for war against foreigners.

——Pierre Vidal-Naquet,
"Hunting and Sacrifice in Aeschylus' *Oresteia*"

To some people the idea of being buried alive by mistake is the most uncanny thing of all...And yet psychoanalysis has taught us that this terrifying phantasy is only a transformation of another phantasy which had originally nothing terrifying about it at all, but was qualified by a certain lasciviousness—the phantasy, I mean, of intra-uterine existence.

—Sigmund Freud, "The Uncanny"

At the opening of *The Eumenides*,[1] Apollo's priestess Pythia honors the successive gods Earth, Themis, and Phoebe, who were the first to hold the gift of prophecy (1–5). These gods, related to one another through matrilineal descent (the latter two are characterized as "daughters of Earth" who each in turn assume their "mother's place" [3–6]), can be contrasted with, even while they foreshadow, Athena, the decisive figure of the play who has no maternal descent but is the daughter of Zeus. Whereas Earth and her daughters represent the natural order, including the order of sexual difference and kinship relations, Athena represents the law of her father[2] and, ultimately, also the order

177

of human law. Pythia's speech marks specifically the transition from nature to industry and civic order, noting that Phoebe "gave it [prophesy] as birthday gift" (8) to Phoebus (Apollo), who proceeded to Delphi, where the industrious sons of Hephaestus had built roads, transforming "the wilderness to a land that was no wilderness" (14). The advent of civilization is thus portrayed as predicated on a transference of power and authority from the female to the male. As Froma Zeitlin[3] has compellingly observed, the motif of a birthday gift alludes to a "second birth" (105), one determined by a paternal principle and proclaiming, even decreeing, a strictly masculine line of descent. The play thus opens with an apparent testament to maternal lineage, only to displace it almost immediately with one that promises that sons are born only from fathers,[4] a theme that is attested to and reiterated throughout the discourses of both Apollo and Athena.

In addition to the daughters of Earth (Themis and Phoebe) and the daughter of Zeus (Athena), the play presents a third genus of divine daughter, the "daughters of Night" (1034), the Erinyes: early in the play, they cry, "Mother, o my mother night, who gave me birth" (320), beckoning and calling forth ferocity with their invocation of maternity and darkness. While Athena ultimately sides with the paternal principle, and the earthly daughters willingly bestowed their gift on a brother, the Erinyes persevere and act on behalf of the value of the maternal line, brutally possessing and holding onto their power as they pursue their birthright "vengeance" (320).

And yet the last lines of the *Eumenides* promise "peace forever" (1045). As the Eumenides proceed on their journey toward "the primeval dark of earth-hollow" (1036), the newly formed Chorus pronounces that their reconciliation to the city shall portend silence, harmony, and tranquility. Pythia's honorific is thus mirrored and repeated at the end of the play by another peaceful transition of power; what had been threatening violence and disruption, the will to tear apart the city, is mutely absorbed into law. Just as we are told that the first gift had been made seamlessly and successfully, even lovingly, so the conclusion attests to another immaculate passage to harmonious political order.

This dramatic repetition of the passage to civilization bears analysis. Phoebe's initial gift to Apollo had already inaugurated the building of cities through the endeavors of sons, and Athena, moreover, had already awarded the victory to Orestes, thereby instantiating human law; the text's conclusion insists not only on establishing the source and locus of order and authority but also on the eradication of any lingering doubt as to the law's power to eradicate dissensus or division. It is not enough that the human order of *nomos* transforms *physis*, or that masculine lineage, represented by Athena, sublates maternal ancestry. The Erinyes, those enduring divine daughters, must additionally be engaged in and to the civic enterprise, assimilating their will to its purposes, surrendering to its ruling principle. In demanding a final abdication and submission, the ending of the *Eumenides* tragically entombs the fears and desires that sustain and threaten the order of the *polis*. Political stability is promised against the fear of inner strife and decomposition. The opening recall of Delphic history, this memory trace, does not then stave off but churns up and elaborates a fantasy of patrilineal descent and perfect peace, eliding the one with the other, and thus provides a sepulchral vision of the democratic imagination.

Reading Julia Kristeva's analysis of the uncanny together with the mythical transformation of the Erinyes into the Eumenides, and the constitution of a democratic body politic that their burial commemorates, this chapter will pursue a double hypothesis, allying exogamy with democracy and detecting in their entanglement a primordial drive toward totalization and repression of discord. In their transformation into Eumenides (the benevolent ones), the Erinyes become divine metics or resident aliens (Vernant and Vidal-Naquet 265) and are willingly confined to their new home; discord is not violently overpowered, but surrenders itself, the force of reason overtaking the forces of night. But the fury that the law inters and consumes, repressing and satisfying a desire for return to the darkness of the womb or the crypt, remains and returns outwardly, in ever more elaborate forms of aggression.

THE UNCANNY

Sigmund Freud's essay, "The Uncanny"[5] elaborates a fundamental tenet of psychoanalysis, namely that what appears as a terrifying fear might very often conceal a more fundamental desire. In the exemplary case alluded to in the epigraph at the beginning of this chapter, he detects the way in which a specific phantasy of death screens a desire to return to the first home, the womb. It is the desire for return that is feared; desire and fear are intertwined, as are birth and death, home and terror. A wish that is repressed or kept in darkness returns in horrifying form, grown grotesque when brought to light. But this terror also keeps secret the desire at its heart. Freud further demonstrates that this play of desire is not only an individual experience of everyday reality but also a textual phenomenon, one quite often manifested in aesthetic works.

Freud defines the uncanny as "that class of the frightening which leads back to what is known of old and long familiar" (*SE* 17:220). If *heimlich* refers to what is both familiar and secret, that which is secreted away in the home or "concealed...withheld from others" (ibid., 223), *unheimlich* indicates what, in a formula Freud borrows from F. W. J. von Schelling, "ought to have remained secret and hidden but has come to light" (ibid., 225). Far from being opposed, the words are implicated in one another: just as *heimlich* in its connotation of secrecy suggests something "dangerous" (ibid., 226) and powerful, *unheimlich* as a secret no longer kept in its secret place suggests the return of something familiar (ibid., 241), the return of the repressed. The ambivalence of both words, the meaning of each slipping into the other, itself points to the blurring of boundaries, the uncertainty of identity, the confusion of desire and revulsion, that is the mark of the uncanny.[6] As a secret out of place, no longer or perhaps too effectively repressed but thereby strange and estranging (ibid., 241), "secretly familiar" (ibid., 245), the uncanny carries a horrifying power [7] (ibid., 244), perturbing and agitating desire.

In *Strangers to Ourselves*, Kristeva takes up Freud's concept of the uncanny in order to elucidate the psychic underpinnings of our political experience of strangeness and its disturbing effect on the apparent security of rule by law. In developing the concept of the uncanny and following out its political trajectory, Kristeva argues that political community is also perturbed by what it represses and its return. What is apprehended as alien, a stranger to the city-state and thus terrifying, manifests or represents what already dwells within the heart of the city as its hidden secret force, the aggressive energy that drives it. The threat the foreigner poses to political cohesion, turning "'we' into a problem" (Kristeva 1991, 2), is thus fundamentally a threat not of the outsider but of the insider: "The foreigner lives within us: he is the hidden face of our identity, the space that wrecks our abode" (ibid., 2). It is the uncanny strangeness within ourselves that is "unamenable to bonds and communities" (ibid., 1). Kristeva thus postulates a fundamental disorder within both the psyche and the *polis*, an irreconcilable dehiscence, self-division, or residue that resists integration or social containment. Just as the psyche is alien to itself, so too is the *polis*.[8]

In a later text, *Intimate Revolt*, Kristeva situates "fantasy" within its Greek context, aligning it with "the Greek root—*fae, faos, fos*—[that] expresses the notion of light and thus the fact of coming to light, shining, appearing, presenting, presenting oneself, representing oneself... the intimate creation of representations," and she claims, "We all have fantasies, whether seductive or terrifying; this is inevitable" (2002, 63).

And fantasy, of course, always presents and represents the fulfillment of a wish. Primal fantasies[9] distinguish themselves in representing the origin of the subject and its relation to others (ibid., 66). These stories of origin are inventions, but ones that necessarily emerge with the conundrums of subjectivity and sociality (Who am I? Where did I come from?). Primal fantasies are, for Kristeva, as well as for Freud, "presubjective" (ibid.), having a kind of archaic structure that is "mysteriously encrypted in the psyche" (ibid.). There is an elemental or mythical element to such fantasies; while neither biologically imperative nor historically accurate, such schemas instantiate and carry hereditary truths and memories,[10] immortalizing in subjectivity what apparently resolves enigmas, and thereby giving shape to psychical reality. Kristeva also describes fantasies as "transitional organisms, hybrid constructions...that play with both repression and the return of the repressed" (ibid., 65). Fantasy itself is a "crossroads" (ibid., 66) of this play of repression and desire, a compromise between competing forces, and "the favored place for their formulation" would be in aesthetic forms (ibid., 66) that portray metamorphoses that respond to or placate psychical or political uncertainties.[11]

For Kristeva, strangeness emerges as a trauma that has not only individual but also political significance, and thus when the stranger (and his or her radical otherness) appears as a threat to bodily and social unity, it most fully personifies the menace that the unconscious itself poses to political order and psychic stability. While the limit to the political "we" might appear to emanate from without, it does so as a mechanism of pacification, an attempt to alleviate the *polis* of its inner precariousness by externalizing it, thereby burying the fundamental trauma of political invention and order, its abandonment of a maternal home and denial of violent origination. Enduring myths, then, might be read not merely as historical artifacts but as themselves tombs of desire and fear, conveying something endemic to psychical and political life.

Aeschylus' *Oresteia* trilogy, and, in particular, the final scenes of the *Eumenides*, presents an exemplary instance of this dynamic of pacification. As dramatized by Aeschylus, the conciliation of the Erinyes expresses something fundamental about the democratic drive, in its demand for an undivided body politic and community of citizens. An illusion that has had a long future, and the fantasies, threats, and hopes it embodies, presents a mythical stage for the experience of the uncanny and its supercession.

WEDDED BLISS

Athena addresses the Erinyes as strangers: "Who are you?" she asks of what she calls this "novel company" (405); neither human nor part of the Olympian order, the Erinyes are rather chthonic deities whose ancestry is more archaic than that of the new gods. As such, they are both familiar and unfamiliar (primal and secret, but unlike anything else). In Athena's confrontation with the Erinyes, we see law both in collision with another form of justice (*dikê*) and appropriating its own other by abjuring any principle of inassimilable alterity. Athena would have us believe that the collision of *dikê* against *dikê*[12] can be finally and fully resolved, that the law of the city can take in, welcome, and absorb the force of blood (digesting both maternity and death) without remainder or residue. But, as Kristeva reiterates, "Strangeness (or foreignness)— the political facet of violence—would underlie elementary civilization, be its necessary lining" (1991, 46) and cannot be harnessed. As the perpetual motor of democracy, this drive toward harmony is also its unceasing instability and self-loss. Kristeva reminds us that Freud's uncanny reveals "an immanence of the strange within the familiar" (ibid., 182–83), a familiar that is "tainted" by its "improper past" (ibid., 183). Athena articulates the conflation of the alien with the threatening when she appeals to the Erinyes not to turn the citizens' "battle fury inward on themselves" (863); the apprehension of internal discord, the concern that hostility and bloodshed will emerge from within, must be allayed, thereby ordaining that each assume a proper place within the city's limits.

Having deemed the vote to be either "our destruction or our high duties confirmed" (748), and sworn that they "shall let loose indiscriminate death" (502) and "anarchy" (525) or "confusion of goods" (554) in retaliation should Orestes be acquitted, the future they foresee is one of destruction, not the work of life. Following Athena's tie-breaking "final judgment" (735) to acquit Orestes, a judgment also predicated on Athena's claim that "there is no mother anywhere who gave me birth" (735), the Erinyes rail against their "disinheritance" (780) and the younger gods whose "treacheries have taken [their] rights away" (845), and they vow "to let loose on the land vindictive poison" (810). Athena, however, offers them "a place of [their] own" (805). Unlike Apollo, who had demanded that the Erinyes "leave this house" (180), Athena does not command but persuades; unlike Apollo, who had expelled them from his place of residence, Athena invites them in.[13]

The extension of this invitation, through which the Erinyes are integrated into the *polis*, can be viewed as analogous to the scenario of marriage. Beguiled by Athena's pledge that "no household shall be prosperous without [their] will" (895), the Erinyes finally acquiesce to "this home at Athene's side" (915) and vow that "civil war fastening on men's ruin shall not thunder in our city" (977–79) and that "passion for revenge and bloodshed for bloodshed" (982) shall be replaced with "grace" and "love" (985). Promised the role of guardians of childbirth and fertility, they join the city as their own, appropriated to it in a kind of wedding ceremony wherein they are granted their province: "You shall win first fruits in offerings for children and the marriage rite" (835), Athena proclaims in inducing them to "share our country" (869). She further expounds on this new power, declaring that "no household shall be prosperous without your will" (895) and that as benevolent rather than malevolent beings, the new Eumenides shall "make the human seed be kept alive" (908). Even more, "to them is given the handling entire of men's lives" (930). Athena propositions the Erinyes with household power, the sustenance, management, and caretaking of human lives. In accepting Athena's proposal, the Erinyes agree to "pronounce words of grace...let no barren deadly sickness creep and kill. Flocks fatten. Earth be kind to them, with double fold of fruit in time appointed for its yielding. Secret child of earth, her hidden wealth, bestow blessing and surprise of gods" (940–48). Human flourishing, the caretaking of corporeal life, becomes their domain.[14] In their journey to the city and below, the Erinyes suffer the opposite of exile, namely immigration, living in a foreign land that takes them in. The implacable ones are moved. In their acquiescence to the lawful rule of men, the Erinyes concede to becoming alien to themselves.[15]

Marriage and the reproduction of citizens is, of course, crucial to the stability and growth of the *polis*. But the Erinyes had represented relations of blood kin, not marriage, and they had intervened where there was a crime of blood, not one in the legal relationship of marriage. As Sarah Iles Johnston shows, the Erinyes feed on "*intra*familial strife... they care little about how a family reaches out to form links with others" (1999, 255). Their loyalty is to the natal family, not the conjugal one. While the *polis* subordinates kinship to exogamous marriage, demanding that "the mother abdicate her primacy to make way for the new connections, the new order, that marriage creates" (ibid., 261), the Erinyes instead support the priority of the "blood link between mother and child" (ibid.). This commitment to the protection of blood kinship is premised on an inner tension, however, since the continuance of kinship requires that girls abandon their natal family and that men accept a stranger as a wife (ibid., 263). Kristeva also iterates "the violence that underlies the marriage bond: a pact between strangers" (1993, 18) that is based both on aggression and its assimilation, since the bride is fundamentally a foreigner. Exogamy, in other words, provides a solution to the unfamiliar, creating unity where there had been difference. Because, as Johnston puts it, the family "is constantly required to renew itself by incorporating the very elements from outside that might threaten its integrity" (1999, 256), the home must grapple with foreignness by making it disappear into itself.

While the allegiance of the Erinyes is with the *genos* rather than the *oikos* (not with exogamy but with descent[16]), the allegiance of the Eumenides, as we have just seen, is to the future generations of the city and the well-being of its citizens. The Erinyes have as their purpose the preservation of the past, the Eumenides the production of a future. Whereas Apollo privileges "married love" (217) over either "kindred blood" (213) or the "right of nature" (218), the Erinyes had allied themselves with the "motherblood" that drives them (230), invoking not only kinship but also one transmitted through the maternal line (echoing the play's opening and its record of matrilineal descent).[17] The Eumenides thus not only switch their loyalties to the *oikos* and the *polis* over the *genos* but also to the future over the past. Their nonproductive, noneconomic (neither *oikos* nor *nomos*, neither law nor home) attachment to the past gives way to a working forward that is economic in every sense: They become part of the city's productive and fertile future, recuperated for the welfare of its citizens. They are chewed up and regurgitated, thrown up into the law so the past might be forgotten.

In the metamorphosis of the Erinyes into Eumenides, Aeschylus thus presents an isomorphism between democracy and exogamous marriage.[18] The repression of aggression in favor of law is also a conjugal relation, familiarizing the strange and procuring elemental force for generative and reproductive purposes. Portrayed as threatening outsiders that the *polis* must not only accept but contain and attach to its own principles, the Erinyes manifest a coincidence between wives and the secret force of law. They are invited, persuaded, and induced to give the blessings of fertility, to sanction in this way marriage and childbirth. Athena, as Johnston writes, "craftily incorporates the Erinyes in such a way as to turn their natural interests toward the creation of new citizens and social bonds" and thus also toward "the erasure of familial boundaries" (1999, 264), what had previously been their sole concern to preserve. Their relation to the *polis* in this way parallels or reiterates both the structure of exogamy and that of democracy: in being incorporated into the city, they are also like marriageable daughters who must take their place in a new home. In taking over the protection of the fertility of the city and enforcing the laws, they shift their identification from the maternal perspective of the "mother-child relationship" to the "marital relationship" (ibid., 261), accepting their permanent encryption. Thus seduced by Athena, the Erinyes marry the city, becoming, like wives, incorporated strangers (and no longer unmarried virgins on the side of avenging mothers), topologically akin to a woman of the *oikos*, secreted away in her proper place. Accorded and acceding to the status of welcomed guests (and no longer "polluted outcasts"), by relocating into this new domicile, they take their "proper place" in a home that is hidden and obscure, an underground cavern from which the fertility of the city is their primary concern. Entering an enclosed space, more similar to a woman's place in the interior of the house than a man's political space in the public sphere, the Erinyes become symbolically aligned with the tomb they enter.

The procession at the end of the tragedy might then further signify not only a wedding but also a funeral, the collapse of natality and mortality into one another.[19] With this blurring of boundaries (wedding as funeral, womb as crypt), we see another form of the uncanny—death, kinship, and maternity are not so much reconciled as repressed, hidden, wrested away, and incorporated, only to return in the guise of their ostensible contrary, enforcing its principles and priorities. Yet this mythical, self-authorizing, originary violence[20] of democracy is itself occluded by the celebratory conclusion that resolves fury into an historical memory that is fully past, which can be mourned and commemorated but no longer allowed to breathe, an economic support or livelihood but not a life.[21] In portraying the union of the Erinyes to the city as a triumphant event, the text not only sides with Apollo and his hypervaluation of paternity and reason, displacing origin into a wholly masculine order through the violent collusion of exogamy with the founding of democratic institutions, but it also contains (holds in, limits, but also keeps and retains) conflict. Moreover, where conflict becomes containment, there the city refuses to be alien to itself. Peace, law, and paternity do not so much take precedence over discord, affect, and maternity as expropriate their force for self-serving and self-preserving ends.

Athena embodies the idea that the city can take in productively what threatens the city, neutralizing its force. Along with this productivity, she also represents the fantasy of a nonmaternal birth, of self-creation and sovereignty.[22] Though articulated and displaced in the speech of a

god, the fantasy of absolute self-sovereignty entails sepulchral inclusion of its other, night. Motherless Athena is therefore the one to entice
the Erinyes, to bring them into the paternal line, facilitating patrimony
between male citizens. Reabsorbed into the good of the city, aggressivity is both buried and consumed, turned toward the fertile reparation of
division, a fantasy of a perfect dialectic, of sublation without remainder.
But the enclosure of the Erinyes and its promise of the city's self-possession is a futile dream.

DEADLY SELF-POSSESSION

Kriste va warns of the dangers of believing in psychic or political
wholeness and univocity, unity without limits; the alien, she surmises,
will return in monstrous form elsewhere, from the outside, as a barbarian,
devouring, irrational. The danger of consuming the other is that we will
find it devouring us instead, provoking fury against fury. What Kristeva
calls the "impossible alchemy" of loving the other (2002, 228) produces
its own foreigner by denying one's "irreconcilable conflictuality, the
dramatic splitting that constitutes [one] and that detaches [one] from
any will for control, power, or even unity" (ibid., 237). For Kristeva
then, an organism that both tolerates and represses difference (a
difference represented by particularity and corporeality) portends the
reemergence of an alien force that will always return. The "paradox" or
"vicious circle" (Kristeva 1991, 96) of political legislation is that "it is
precisely with respect to laws that foreigners *exist*" (ibid.). The *nomos*
that encloses, fortifies, or walls the city simultaneously insists on its
outside, bringing it into being. Self-preservation is self-defeating.

Kristeva expresses discomfort with the later Stoic idea of "absorb-
ing all men" into "human universality" "founded on the community
of reason" (1991, 57); in such a form of universal cosmopolitanism,
"the foreigner becomes 'he who exiles himself from the rules of the
City'" (ibid., 59). Just as she cautions that "any political commitment....
[that] settles the subject within a socially justified illusion—is a security
blanket" (1982, 136–37), she even attributes to "a law that would be
absolute, full, and reassuring," a law that is too self-satisfied and certain
of its completion and closure, the danger of fascism, terror, or totalitarianism.[23] In describing the dangers of an "absolute solution" (Kristeva
1991, 97) to foreigners who "have the fearsome privilege of causing a
State to confront an other," Kristeva cautions us to attend to a relationship that she claims always leads to "new exclusions or persecutions"

(ibid.). While "political jurisdiction might appear as a "safeguard," the pressures of identity will tend to proliferate "until its machinery jams" (ibid.). Aggressivity, like the repressed, always returns, if in ever more insidious ways.[24] The desire for order is mirrored by aggression against that order, just as aggressivity is mirrored by its binding in imaginary unity. The drama of the *Eumenides* presents a peaceful return home, and in this respect it inverts Freud's formula of the uncanny: it overtly celebrates a kind of homecoming while shielding itself from the terror of shattering and disintegration. But just as an experience of horror might obscure a secret desire, so too the dream of harmonious return might hide a fundamental aggression.

A last detour through Freud's theory of the drives is perhaps necessary, in order to clarify both his political energetics and his theories of time and memory. In *Beyond the Pleasure Principle*, Freud's agitated and animated speculations on the primitive, instinctual, and elementary characteristics of the death drive, he reiterates the arc of excitation and release that characterizes the motor and mental apparatus. While Eros is the force of binding, engendering greater and greater unities, offering structure and organization, Thanatos is the force of unbinding, disintegration, fragmentation, and deformation. This force, Freud tells us, is silent, mute, and singular, unable on its own to attain discharge. Thanatos is thus never isolated but always manifested in a fusion with Eros, on which it depends for the disposal of its own demands. On its own it is timeless, without logic or contradiction, nothing but a compelling propensity.

Envisaging a primitive organism, a "little fragment of living substance" (*SE* 18:27), Freud postulates a pure surface of exposure "on the border between outside and inside" (ibid., 24) whose task it is to deal with unbound energy insofar as it is merely a receptor for excitation. In receiving excitations, the organism is disturbed and a crust forms "as a result of the ceaseless impact of external stimuli" (ibid., 26), a kind of armor, "shield," or "protection," which is itself "inorganic," a deadness in the midst of life, a capacity to lessen the "original intensity" of stimuli (ibid., 27). "By its death," Freud writes, "the outer layer has saved all the deeper ones from a similar fate" (ibid.). This lifeless scab of productive mediation is consciousness that can only push energy outward, discharging it, or inward, facilitating pathways.

Since the "backward path" of return to the inorganic is "obstructed" (*SE* 18:42), the movement outward of unbound energy is a kind of originary fiction, a corridor of death only available to that postulated primitive organism whose drive ensures that its own extinction is immediate. The movement inward is the movement of life and growth, binding energy in the development and detours of organic vitality, laying down "permanent traces" (ibid., 26), which provide stable and contained routes for energetic transfer, a kind of constancy that will ultimately determine the dominance of the pleasure principle. Although the pure drive is before time, a kind of nonexistence in the nonspace between excitation and extinction, once bound it can move forward and backward in different variants of repetition, binding memories and foreseeing development.

With this account of binding, Freud has solved a central conundrum, elucidating the principle of *constancy* that governs pleasure, and thereby marking a distinction between the pleasure principle and the death drive that would otherwise be indistinguishable from one another. Though Freud concludes his text with the assertion that "the pleasure principle seems actually to serve the death instincts" (*SE* 18:63), at the same time, insofar as the pleasure principle governs bound energy, it is the principle of life, and life requires the *accumulation* of energy, a diversion from the perfect inertia or absolute reduction of energy demanded by the death drive. Whereas the death drive expresses "the *conservative* nature of living substance" (ibid., 36), the life instincts emerge with the advent of an animating tension that propels toward "change and development" (ibid.) and whose *still more conservative* energies endeavor to "preserve life" (ibid., 40). Though Eros is "perpetually attempting and achieving a renewal of life" (ibid., 46), "conjugating," "rejuvenating," and bringing together a variety of living substance, the life instincts are nonetheless "conservative to a higher degree" (ibid., 40) rather than liberated and liberating, because they are fundamentally repetitive in their work of binding and structuring.

The formation of a coherent psychical unity is first and foremost the constitution of an imaginary unity, a reflective surface, in response to the "exigencies of life," to the impossibility of de-animating oneself through the discharge of excitations, to the persistence of life and its permutations. Insofar as the ego, or its peripheral edge, is crusted and dead, it guards against the stimuli, both internal and external, that might impinge on the psyche, overwhelm it, traumatize it. The secondary processes are continuations of this crustiness, less dead than the perceptual crust, but also less alive than the propulsive force of the primary processes, and they aim to master and contain excitations, to follow the tendency toward constancy of the pleasure principle. By this logic, the economy of the ego, and of the tendency toward greater and greater unities, is deadly and deadening, and yet it provides a necessary fortress for the detour of life.[25] As this reading of *Beyond the Pleasure Principle* has shown, the very onset of excitation produces dissension between the phantasmatic element this intensity introduces and the binding force of the ego. Life productively incorporates the energy of death, binds aggression, deadens itself, and defends its borders, for the purpose of peace forever.

FURIOUS REPETITION

The Erinyes appear as an external threat, an emanation of something prepolitical, primal, and bound to blood, tearing dangerously at the burgeoning institution of democratic and rational law with the pressing image of excessive substance, a radical otherness that appears to menace social unity and political order. But they also represent, manifest, and embody the family curse of the house of Atreus, that which is both most strange and most familiar to its members, that element interior to their ancestry that drives their actions and binds them violently together. At the conclusion of the play, the organizing principle of democratic society is doubled, comprising not only a fantasy of absolute otherness, "like no seed ever begotten," (410) Athena says of them, but also one of reconciliation in which difference and drive are fully absorbed into the social fabric. The effect is a paradox in which exclusion is accomplished precisely by inclusion, such that, as Michael Naas puts it, "that which always exceeds the limits of the city and threatens its legitimacy will now inhabit its very interior" (1995, 4). Otherness has been given a place. Defusing the Erinyes' threat to instigate civil war (to be permanently disruptive forces in the *polis*) as vengeance for Orestes' aquittal of the crime of matricide, Athena has persuaded them instead to accept her invitation to be incorporated into the city as *Semnai Thea* (revered or feared ones), to stay on in Athens as protectors of the law and guardians of justice.

The city incorporates the force of the Erinyes, containing their threat and transmuting fury into benevolence—the Eumenides become the guardians of justice, ensuring, through fear and reverence, that the laws are obeyed by men, and keeping both anarchy (chaos, fragmentation, particularism) and tyranny (absolute authority) at bay.[26] An external threat of disorder is transformed (assimilated, domesticated[27]) into an internal protection of order:[28] "The ancient avengers of matricide will protect and preserve the city of Athens—the city that now judges offenses in a court of law and respects the bonds and codes of patriarchy and marriage" (Naas 1995, 2).

In staging a democratic fantasy of sovereign authority and civic isonomy secured by an uneasy reconciliation between gods and law, the *Oresteia* performs an imaginary metabolization of crisis (Kristeva 2002, 267). The absolution of difference into unity, or the dissolution of unrest into rational order, presages the democratic propensity to swallow the alien. The safe passage to civilization is figured repeatedly as an overcoming of discord in reason and a marriage of aggression to law. The city buries the threat of fragmentation and returns it to its home. The Eumenides nonetheless do remain as a testament to the founding violence of democracy, an entombed commemoration of and memorial to the fated nexus of blood and law that brings it into being.

The birth of the *polis* establishes the city as the site of order only at the expense of closing the gaps between piety and legality, *oikos* and *polis*, *nomos* and *physis*. In this reassuring script, the Erinyes do not impede but make possible, through their abdication, the self-constitution of *polis*; the law is born as the integration of the monstrous into a facilitating protector of the *polis*. It is not just the inhuman Erinyes who are the uncanny secret; the secret is in the very form of forgetting the familiar and familiarizing the strange, in the very form of memory and forgetting that gives way to life by displacing its own relation to violent origin. We might thus conclude that, in its desire to contain everything, democracy is condemned to live out the political impasse of the uncanny to which it is bound, the return of the repressed and the crises contained in the paradoxes of alienation.[29] Faced with some alterity excessive to order (whether psychical or political), some element that can be neither contained nor integrated, on the one hand, and neither exiled nor excluded, on the other, the city recoils. The borders we might wish for, which might protect against "the danger 'outside' which must not be let in, and the danger 'inside' which must not be let out" (Vernant and Vidal-Naquet 1988, 279) are impossible, just as it is the impossible yet enduring task of the Eumenides, as that of democracy whose principle they ironically represent, to keep at bay both particularism and absolute authority, those permanent dangers that lurk within (and not without) democratic order. In attempting to exteriorize something that reemerges on the interior (through exile), or interiorize something that reemerges on the exterior (through assimilation), political order attempts to grapple with a fundamental placelessness that ultimately cannot be sated or appeased and that is permanently unsettling. Unsettled, unreconciled, this strangeness resists any final closure and renders totality impossible but not the drive toward it.

The *Eumenides* mythologizes the advent of the citizen subject to law while both insisting on and suppressing a fate inherited through maternal blood. The Oresteian myth instantiates paternal lineage as the only true blood relation[30] and vividly displays, and conceals, its drives toward domestication and resolution, the refusal of residue or debris, in the paternity of peace. As a myth of origins of the juridical structures of democratic citizenship, "forevermore...the ground where justices deliberate,"[31] as Athena says (685), it contains and reveals the symbolic matrix (with all its paradoxes) of the body politic. Jacques Lacan has compared the memories of the hysteric to that of the dramas "in which the original myths of the City State are produced before its assembly of citizens" (2006, 212), claiming that in both discourses the relation to material history is symbolic, conveying a timeless temporality that gives birth to truth. We might still, 2500 years later, see in these "original myths of the City State" the staging of a drama that pulls inexorably on history and in which, as Lacan puts it, "a nation today learns to read the symbols of a destiny on the march" (ibid., 212). In the rubbles and ruin of history, no less than tragic drama, we witness the fissures of civic and psychic identity, the failures of self-possession that are repeatedly repressed and return in ghostly form.

NOTES

1. I rely here on the translation provided by Richard Lattimore in *Oresteia* (1953). All citations are to line number.
2. "I am always for the male with all my heart, and strongly on my father's side" (738). Athena, according to Apollo, is "proof" that "there can be a father without any mother" (663); moreover, he asserts, she "was never fostered in the dark of womb" (665).
3. Zeitlin's project is to read the *Oresteia* as "a gynecocentric document, an inquiry into the nature and limits of feminine power" (1996, 113), charting the transformation of "feminine power" from "*political* power" to "*ritual* power" (ibid., 113). While my argument in this chapter is indebted to the groundbreaking work and persuasive claims made by Zeitlin in "The Dynamics of Misogyny: Myth and Mythmaking in Aeschylus's *Oresteia*" (1996), my own contentions are less concerned with misogyny than with the features of the *Eumenides* that align the origins of democracy with marriage and unification.

4. Hephaestus himself, however, has no father; born only of a mother, he is reliant on *techne*, perhaps as prosthetic compensation for lack of a father.

5. All references are to the *Standard Edition* and will be cited as *SE* followed by volume and page number.

6. The uncanny is neither inside nor outside, but on the border, demonstrating the fragility of the boundaries between civil and wild, *nomos* and *physis*, *polis* and *oikos*, reason and violence, future and past, womb and tomb, masculine and feminine, mortal and divine, human and animal. The reversibility of horror and awe, the monstrous dissolution of familiar human order, invades all forms of identity and unity.

7. Abjection, with its precarious play between identity and dissolution, inside and outside, is a primary, even primordial, form of the uncanny (see Kristeva's *Powers of Horror*).

8. In describing a self unknown or unfamiliar to itself, Lacan invokes "the truth of 'I is an other'" (2006, 24), indicating a primary discord or "vital dehiscence" or "obscure foundation" of the rational will (ibid., 23), the most basic trait of unconscious life.

9. In their seminal essay, "Fantasy and the Origins of Sexuality" (1986), Jean Laplanche and Jean-Bertrand Pontalis make explicit the bond between the origins of fantasy and fantasies of origin.

10. Freud's great insight in developing the theory of infantile sexuality and thereby of the unconscious is the indistinction between memory and fantasy, the psychical reality of the latter.

11. Works of art, like dreams, do not simply conceal a latent meaning behind a manifest one, but are themselves workings (cf. Lyotard 1989).

12. This is not, however, to be understood as a simple conflict between blood justice and law, since Apollo himself appropriates the right of blood and the power of birth to the paternal principle. Though Apollo claims to have "cleaned [Orestes] of the stain of blood" (578), he also denies parentage to the mother: "The mother is no parent of that which is called her child, but only nurse of the new-planted seed that grows," he says in response to the Chorus of Erinyes' claim that Orestes has "spilled his mother's blood," and he goes on to call the mother "a stranger" (655–60).

13. The Erinyes' resolve is broken by Athena's "sweet beguilement" (885). Although, initially, Athena appeals to flattery and force, not guile: "You are goddesses" (823) and "I have Zeus behind me...I am the only god who know the keys to where his thunderbolts are locked" (825), even then she asks whether she need speak of that and turns

next to reason before inviting persuasion to her side. The *Peitho* or Persuasion that Athena calls on has been the subject of much scholarly work. See especially Naas, *Turning: From Persuasion to Philosophy.* "Athene turns not to a higher law but to seductive speech and magical spells—to powers of turning, subversion, and reversal. Thus, while Persuasion might seem to represent the power of 'reasoned' compromise and 'gentle discourse' between two consenting parties in a political debate, she is also, in the *Oresteia*, related to the usurpation of reason and the overcoming of discourse" (1995, 3). Naas here detects the violent element of rational law and its assimilation of otherness to it, the way in which reason deploys the very violence it suppresses, undermining itself in its very expression. Focusing on the theme of persuasion, Naas writes that "while the fundamental ambivalence of persuasion is and must be repressed in Aeschylus if the law court of the Areopagus is ever to gain legitimacy, this repression occupies the forefront of the dramatic scene...Aeschylus at once erases and inscribes the trace of an original turning, at once forgets and memorializes the ambivalence of Persuasion as the goddess of turning" (1995, 4–5). While this chapter also pursues the repression at the core of Aeschylus' vision of legitimacy, my concern is not specifically with the persuasion of law or reason, but with its tendency toward totalization. What is figured as drive (an archaic yet perennial element, a foreign, uncanny element) is overwhelmed by what is figured as law, and law forgets this moment of its own self-creation out of alien elements, even as it takes them up into its own authority.

14. As Naas astutely notes, "Their power is in no way undone—only repressed and displaced—since traces of the Furies' disappearance can now be found in every harvest, every newborn, and every speech in the law courts, where the spells of Persuasion are invoked and the guileful usurpation of reason and order is reenacted" (1995, 4). The disappearance of the Erinyes presents itself with both the flourishing of human life and the discourse of the law courts, leaving traces that not only mark the turn from disruption to productivity, from death to life or fertility, but also from reason to its intimate other, violence and aggression.

15. As Naas puts it, "Persuasion turns the Furies away from violence and disorder only by turning them away from themselves, only by turning them into the Semnai, the Venerable Ones" (1995, 3).

16. The Erinyes identify with the way in which "the family survives only by anchoring its identity firmly within the past" (Johnston

1999, 256). The Erinyes are provoked by violence within the family to further violence, and are even willing to destroy the family in the here and now, in their aim to preserve this past.

17. They also claim not to have pursued Clytemnestra because "the man she killed was not of blood congenital" (605) but pursued Orestes who was nursed through his "mother's intimate blood" (609). The dispute with Apollo concerns the priority of filial or conjugal relations (bonds of blood or bonds of law).

18. The Erinyes are figured as wives but not mothers: their domestication and transformation into Eumenides is isomorphic with the speeches denying maternity in the debate between the Erinyes and Apollo concerning the privilege of the marriage bond (a relation of law) or that of the filial bond (a relation of blood).

19. Johnston's reading leads up to but does not quite make explicit this point.

20. In "Critique of Violence" (1986), Walter Benjamin distinguishes between mythical violence, which establishes and maintains the law, and divine violence, which would suspend or dissolve the law.

21. A melancholic city that has swallowed its indigestible other, moved forward, and relegated violence to historical past, is also one in which the mute voices of night remain undead.

22. Athena presents this as a divine, not human, possibility, although Apollo's speech transfers this possibility to the human realm.

23. In *Intimate Revolt*, Kristeva claims that "totalitarianism is the result of a certain fixation of revolt in what is precisely its betrayal, namely, the suspension of retrospective return" (2002, 6); terror arises from within democracy as the fixity of its relation to its other, its alien. The law unifies the city only to find its enemies without and its borders threatened.

24. Athena appears as a mediating principle, favoring a fair trial (573); she respects both the "rights" of Orestes (475) and the "work" of the Erinyes (476), and her concern is to resolve the dilemma that Apollo's one-sidedness does not, in order to avoid the outcome in which "the venom of their [the Erinyes] resolution will return to infect the soil" (480). It is for this reason that she establishes "a court into all time to come" (483).

25. Given that, as Freud says, the "elementary living entity" has "no wish to change" (*SE* 18:38) and there is "no universal instinct toward higher development" (ibid., 41), toward "perfection" or "sublimation" (ibid., 42), both of which Freud calls "benevolent illusions," the emergence of instincts of life is remarkable. Indeed, it is only the disquieting effect of immersion in a "world of powerful energy"

(ibid., 27), the impact, imposition, and impingement of external exigencies, that leads the organism to develop. It is trauma, unpleasure, and intensity that generates life and keeps one alive. And life itself, Freud repeatedly reminds us, remains an attempt to return, along "circuitous paths" (ibid., 38), to an earlier state. It this attempt at circuitous return that creates the "vacillating rhythm" (ibid., 41) between life and death and the temporality of past, present, and future.

26. Athena advocates law, "no anarchy, no rule of a single master" (695; also 526). This statement is startlingly echoed, though with a strikingly different emphasis by Lacan in his depiction of modern society in the essay "Aggressiveness in Psychoanalysis": "Ours is an immense community, midway between a 'democratic' anarchy of the passions and their hopeless leveling out by the 'great winged hornet' of narcissistic tyranny" (2006, 99).

27. Zeitlin remarks that this "act of domestication will be presented in collective, social, nonheroic terms, with violence yielding to open persuasion, Peitho" (1996, 103).

28. This conversion is precisely the work of repression, expending energy to transform an internal danger into an external one, one less difficult to guard against.

29. While I am drawn to this conclusion, Kristeva's insight is different: that it is with regard to this impossible relation of internal and external, blood and law, nationalism and democracy, that we might pursue the political promise of the uncanny and the recognition that "only strangeness is universal" (Kristeva 1993, 21). For Kristeva, alienation provides an opportunity for the political relation to the foreigner to be resignified, an invitation to resist the mirror of identity and embrace finitude and alterity as internal rather than external limits, and to develop new forms of community that refract rather than obliterate (or stabilize) our differences.

30. "Like Athena, Orestes now belongs wholly to his father" (Zeitlin 1996, 113).

31. Because the ground of justice is mythical, democracy is born from the violent imposition of origin.

REFERENCES

Aeschylus. *Oresteia*. 1953. Trans. Richmond Lattimore. Chicago: University of Chicago Press.

Benjamin, Walter. 1986. Critique of violence. In *Reflections: Essays, Aphorism, Autobiographical Writings*, ed. Peter Demetz, 277-300. New York: Harcourt Brace Jovanovich.

Freud, Sigmund. 1955a. The uncanny. In *The standard edition of the complete psychoanalytic works*, ed. James Strachey, 17: 219–252. London: Hogarth.

———. 1955b. *Beyond the pleasure principle*. In *The standard edition of the complete psychoanalytic works*, ed. James Strachey, 18:7–64. London: Hogarth.

Johnston, Sarah Iles. 1999. *Restless dead: Encounters between the living and the dead in ancient Greece*. Berkeley: University of California Press.

Kristeva, Julia. *Powers of horror*. 1982. Trans. Leon S. Roudiez. New York: Columbia University Press.

———. 1991. *Strangers to ourselves*. Trans. Leon S. Roudiez. New York: Columbia University Press.

———. 1993. *Nations without nationalism*. Trans. Leon S. Roudiez. New York: Columbia University Press.

———. 2000. *Crisis of the European subject*. Trans. Susan Fairfield. New York: Other Press.

———. 2002. *Intimate revolt: The powers and limits of psychoanalysis*. Trans. Jeanine Herman. New York: Columbia University Press.

Lacan, Jacques. *Écrits*. 2006. Trans. and ed. Bruce Fink. New York: Norton.

Laplanche, Jean, and Jean-Bertrand Pontalis. 1986. Fantasy and the origins of sexuality. In *Formations of Fantasy*, ed. Victor Burgin, James Donald, and Cora Kaplan, 5–34. London: Methuen.

Lyotard, Jean-Francois. 1989. The dreamwork does not think. In *The Lyotard Reader*, ed. Andrew Benjamin, 19–55. Oxford: Blackwell.

Naas, Michael. 1995. *Turning: From persuasion to philosophy*. Atlantic Highlands: Humanities Press.

Segal, Charles. 1986. *Interpreting Greek tragedy*. Ithaca, NY: Cornell University Press.

Vernant, Jean-Pierre, and Pierre Vidal-Naquet. 1988. *Myth and tragedy in ancient Greece*. Trans. Janet Lloyd. New York: Zone Books.

Vidal-Naquet, Pierre. 1988. "Hunting and Sacrifice in Aeschylus' Oresteia." In *Myth and Tragedy in Ancient Greece*, ed. Jean-Pierre Vernant and Pierre Vidal-Naquet, trans. Janet Lloyd, 141–59. New York: Zone Books.

Zeitlin, Froma. 1996. The dynamics of misogyny: Myth and mythmaking in Aeschylus's Oresteia. In *Playing the Other: Gender and society in classical Greek literature*, 87–121. Chicago: University of Chicago Press.

8

Playing the Cassandra

Prophecies of the Feminine in the Polis and Beyond

PASCALE-ANNE BRAULT

> Silence gives grace to woman.
>
> —Sophocles, *Ajax*

> Hence we must hold that all of these persons have their
> appropriate virtues, as the poet said of woman: "Silence gives
> grace to woman," though that is not the case likewise with a man.
>
> —Aristotle, *Politics*

A young woman stands by the gates, striking all by her silence. She has come with the king as a war prisoner, an unwilling concubine. Her name is not given, and her presence remains unexplained, as the haughty king meets his deceitful wife and engages in a dialogue fraught with ambiguity. Silent, she witnesses the long exchange between the spouses and the subsequent persuasion of the king, who consents to enter the palace by treading on the red carpet laid down before him by his wife. Just before doing so, however, he introduces his silent companion as the "choicest flower of rich treasure," his most coveted gift. With these words, this introduction, the king walks into the palace, there to meet his gruesome fate.

But she remains outside, speechless, impervious to the queen's injunctions that she speak or make a sign with her hand. Left to be persuaded by an assembly of old men to enter the palace, she appears not to understand and makes no attempt to communicate. But then, just when it seems she will never speak, she breaks into a visionary monologue that evokes horrors of the past, present, and future. As we come to see, this consummate outsider to the *polis* knows not only the city's past and present but also the tragedy it is soon to undergo.

And yet, for some obscure reason, her speech remains utterly unpersuasive. The old men hear her words but do not understand them, interpreting her speech not as prophetic utterance but as the ravings of a madwoman. She is a prophetess, we come to understand, but one doomed never to be believed. She is described as a swan singing her saddest and most beautiful song just before her death, a song of both the king's death and her own, for she knows that she too is soon to die. Through this young babbling woman on the brink of death, the very future of the *polis* and the political intrigue in which it is caught are revealed, even if the *polis* itself will remain, for a time, deaf to this revelation.

AESCHYLUS' CASSANDRA

This tale is told in several places in classical literature, but nowhere more dramatically or more powerfully than in Aeschylus. While Cassandra appears in literature before Aeschylus, it is primarily from the *Agamemnon* that we have received the legend of Cassandra as a prophetess doomed never to be believed. Though she shares the gift of prophecy with Calchas and Tiresias, her words, unlike theirs, are systematically unheeded, misjudged, or misinterpreted. Like other prophets in fifth-century tragedy, Cassandra seems to have access to the future, but unlike her male counterparts, her voice is inarticulate and unheard by those around her, at the limits of the human reason. As a woman, her prophecy is "other" than that of male prophets; as a "barbarian," her language is "other" than that of the Greeks; as a captured concubine, her status is "other" than that of the wife, the daughter, or the sacrificed maiden. Cassandra is not heeded, it seems, because she is a woman, because in the public sphere credit is rarely given to the woman who does not speak with a male voice, who does not speak with reasoned appeals, arguments, or judgments to justify her claims. Because Cassandra speaks not simply with her mind but with her body, with shrieks and cries, her utterances are taken to be madness, even hysteria, by the old men who listen to her.

Yet, at the level of the narrative of the *Agamemnon*, the marginalized Cassandra becomes central to the development of tragic irony, her unheeded words providing a background for the reinterpretation of past events and the perception and representation of present and future ones. Cassandra is thus shown to be a figure at once subjugated to men and privileged in the expression and revelation of "truth"—that is, in the *mise en scène* of "truth" as revelation. Indeed, as my reading of Aeschylus will show, Cassandra is both the bearer of a prophetic truth or knowledge about the future whose curse is never to be believed and the sign of another—what I shall call—"tragic" sense of truth. The necessary impossibility of her being believed thus exemplifies and reflects, I claim, the tragic necessity inherent to Greek tragedy. It is through Cassandra that Aeschylus' spectator would have had access to the inarticulate, mute recognition of the inevitable, to the cry beyond words or reasons, to the transformation of the human and the civilized into the inhuman, the barbarian, and the animalistic, to the tension of a "truth" that is not essentially *about* the future but is an almost unbearable revelation *of* it. For in fifth-century tragedy, Cassandra is not simply the bearer of some concealed knowledge about the future but the bearer of time and tragedy, embodying all the characteristics that transform the heroic into the *tragic*.

By facilitating the transition from a relation of knowledge, or the lack thereof, within the narrative to one without, from the internal audience's misunderstanding of Cassandra's words to the external audience's understanding of them, Cassandra turns our attention away from the correspondence between speech and fact, away from a simple knowledge of the future, toward the revelation of that knowledge and that future—that is, toward "truth" as revelation.[1] Cassandra's relationship to the knowledge of past, present, and future events is thus rooted in the tension between a discourse that is suppressed, discredited, or disbelieved by those around her and a narrative present or future that reveals the "truth" of what she says. Her foreignness can thus be seen as indicative of a more fundamental otherness within prophetic discourse. What is revealed is not *simply* and perhaps not even *essentially* the truth about the future and about the *polis* but, always obscurely, *the truth of this revelation*.

Through Cassandra, we come to see that tragedy is essentially related to the feminine, to a certain feminine element that tragedy must suppress or deny but can never totally ignore. Though Cassandra was doomed never to be believed, her function was always to bring the future or the past into the present in a necessarily obscure and misunderstood way. By understanding "truth" not simply in terms of a correspondence between speech and event, but as an unveiling or disclosure, Cassandra's function in tragedy becomes more significant and, I think, more powerful for contemporary critique. Though she is the object of male domination, she is also, paradoxically, a privileged place of disclosure.

If Clytemnestra is the ultimate woman of state, so much so that it is difficult to distinguish her from a man, Cassandra reveals not simply some countertruth or countersovereignty to the state but a mode of revelation that precedes the state that is prepolitical, that bears on the state but can have no influence and exercise no persuasion on it. If Clytemnestra joins Agamemnon, Aegisthus, and others in the dialectic of power within the state, Cassandra reveals the consequences—perhaps even the ultimate tragedy—of that sovereignty.

This reading of tragic drama will allow us to see more clearly what possibilities more or less present in tragedies will later become emphasized, developed, or forgotten by the tradition. It is no doubt thanks to this powerful representation of her by Aeschylus that someone like Lycophron will devote an entire poem to her in the third century BCE or that an author like Christa Wolf (1984) will write a pseudoautobiography of her some twenty-two centuries later.[2] Only by going beyond the representation of Cassandra as a stereotype of female madness and hysteria, only by looking closely at her complex position in Greek tragedy, can Cassandra help us rethink our notions of truth and the future.

PROPHECY IN THE *AGAMEMNON*

Aeschylus' *Agamemnon* makes use of a whole network of prophetic terms and images to explain events that took place in the past as well as those that will take place in the future. The predictions of Cassandra, the intuitions and fears of the Chorus, and the references to the prophecies at the origin of the Trojan War are all used to create a series of relationships and tensions between past, present, and future. As Jacqueline de Romilly argues in her essay "L'Évocation du Passé dans l'*Agamemnon* d'Eschyle,"

> Aeschylus believes in divine justice. He believes that the gods, with time, punish the guilty ones. He thus believes that an old fault prepares, announces, and explains the dramas he describes. Hence, in order to make this relationship visible and to show how, in the end, a long chain of years and generations comes together to form a design full of meaning, he was led to place before a decisive act one or several recollections of the past always reaching as far back as possible and often combined with an anticipated view of the events to come. (1967, 93)

The opening speech of the Chorus fulfills this function of recalling to the spectator, and later, the reader, the auguries that framed the taking of Troy. Ten years earlier, the seer Calchas had deciphered through an omen of two eagles devouring a hare and its brood the triumph of Atreus' two sons over the Trojans.[3] Though the omen made it clear that the war against Troy would be won ("In time they that here issue forth shall seize Priam's town" [126–27]), doom was also foreshadowed in the death of Iphigenia (198–201) and in Artemis' wrath over this sacrifice, "a wrath that exacteth vengeance for a child" (155). The words of Calchas thus predicted the future, and time proved that "the art of Calchas failed not of fulfillment" (249).

The Chorus' recalling of past prophecies is immediately followed by fears and auguries in the present. The Chorus thus not only repeats and retells past prophecies concerning Troy but also actually itself performs them through prophetic intuitions that it cannot wholly master or understand, through words that give no indication of exactly what is to come but nonetheless express some impending doom: "Why ever thus persistently doth this terror hover at the portals of my prophetic [*mantipolei*] soul? Why doth my song, unbidden and unfed, chant strains of augury?" (975–79). These prophetic fears and presentiments serve to bridge past, present, and future, opening up, as it were, the field of present action, giving it depth by reaching out to its origins in the past and projecting its consequences into the future. These fears already precede the arrival of Cassandra, thereby infusing the play with a sense of impending doom.

At the level of the narrative, this process translates into a merging of the different dimensions of linear time. This can be seen in the evocation of the victory of Agamemnon, a victory that, according to the omen, is still to come, but that, at the time of the (re)enunciation of the past augury, has already taken place, though it is still unknown to the Chorus. The prophetic sequence thus produces an intersection of past, present, and future, reinforcing and remarking the opening words of the watchman: "All hail, thou blaze that showest forth in the night a light as it were of day, thou harbinger of many a choral dance in Argos in thanksgiving for this glad event!" (22–25). The recalling of the omen by the Chorus thus confirms the watchman's words announcing the long-awaited return of Agamemnon. This threefold evocation of the prophetic (the omen of Calchas in the past, the fears of the Chorus in the present, and the event prophesied by Calchas that are still to come in the future) is voiced not by Cassandra but by the Chorus. Hence it is the Chorus, a Chorus of male elders that, one could say, initially plays the role of Cassandra, or "plays the Cassandra," though its vision is blurred and its presentiments remain without clarity or definition.

Because the tragedians always used prophecy for some textual purpose or design, we must always ask what role prophecy plays or what function it performs within the development and logic of the narrative. In the *Agamemnon*, the introduction of the prophetic compresses past, present, and future into the narrative, thus creating tension between the three. Because of differences in knowledge and sequence in the play, the events of the play do not coincide exactly with their ordering in history. The watchman and the spectators have seen the torch-sign that announces the return of Agamemnon, while the Chorus, still unaware of the signal, recalls the past omen that predicted this return. When, later in the play, the Chorus is told of Agamemnon's return, the narrative history coincides with the events, thereby leading to the ultimate coincidence of prophecy and event, future prediction and present enactment—the visions and words of Cassandra in front of the Chorus as Agamemnon is slaughtered inside the palace.

THE FOREIGNER

Cassandra's ability to see into a future that is denied to the Chorus isolates her from her audience and prevents her from communicating meaningfully with them. This sense of estrangement and discursive isolation is paralleled by her status as a foreigner in Mycenae. Described by Agamemnon as a gift from his army (*stratou drēm'*; 955; cf. Benveniste 1973, 54–55), we soon understand that Cassandra is an enslaved captive, a foreigner, *tēn xenēn* (Aeschylus 1970, line 950). Emile Benveniste's definition of this important and essentially ambivalent word is significant in this regard and helps explain why Agamemnon requires Clytemnestra to treat Cassandra with kindness: "The free man, born into a group, is opposed to the stranger (Gr. *xenos*), that is to say the enemy (Lat. *hostis*), who is liable to become my guest (Gr. *xenos*, Lat. *hospes*) or my slave if I capture him in war...In ancient civilizations, the status of a slave puts him outside the community" (Benveniste 1973, 289).

The word *xenos*—here the feminine *xenē*—will be repeated by the Chorus (1062, 1093) and echoed by Clytemnestra herself who speaks of the foreignness of Cassandra's speech and hand gestures and thus supposes that she cannot understand Greek (1050, 1061). This supposition might seem rather natural, given Cassandra's foreign origins, but it is actually somewhat odd considering the conventions of Greek tragedy.

As Thomson remarks, "By a very simple and acceptable license, the tragedians, like the epic poets before them, and indeed like all poets, invariably assumed in their characters, Greek and barbarian alike, a knowledge of their native attic" (Thomson 1966, II, 87). Since it turns out that Cassandra does understand and speak Greek, the reason for these numerous references to Cassandra's apparent inability to understand or speak the language of the other protagonists and the audience would be designed, according to Thomson, to identify this entire scene with an initiation to the mysteries:

> In the fifth century B.C. the Eleusian Mysteries were open to all Greeks (Hdt. viii.65.4), provided that they were in a state of ritual purity, and barbarians were excluded with the formula that their speech was unintelligible...Thus, by insisting that Cassandra will yield to *persuasion*, and receive the words addressed to her *within her heart*, provided that she *speaks Greek*, Clytemnestra insinuates that the ceremony about to be enacted within the palace is a holy mystery, into which her new household slave is being initiated. (ibid., 86)

Thomson's hypothesis cannot be entirely discounted, especially since the text can itself be read as a process of initiation, but Clytemnestra's use of the term *barbaros* (1051)[4] in relation to Cassandra's native tongue goes beyond initiation and beyond expressing her enmity toward her husband's captive and her foreign language, for it will be not only Cassandra's language but also her *voice* that will prove to be foreign. Cassandra is a foreigner not only through her national identity but also through her prophetic utterances. Though we have no means of knowing whether Clytemnestra is aware of these powers at this point, she will later say that Cassandra is either mad or prophetic (*mainetai*; 1064).

Cassandra is a *xenē*—a captive, a slave, a foreigner. But it is the voicing of prophecy that ultimately alienates her; even among those who share her tongue, her speech remains incomprehensible. No longer in the presence of the Trojans, Cassandra's language becomes doubly foreign or, rather, more foreign than any foreign language. The ability to speak Greek implies the ability to be intelligible, and yet even when Cassandra does speak Greek, her narrative remains unintelligible to the Chorus.

Talked about by Agamemnon and then talked to by Clytemnestra, Cassandra strikes by her silence. So much so, in fact, that the Chorus thinks she needs an interpreter (1062). This need later undergoes an ironic reversal when the Chorus becomes perplexed at Cassandra's words. When she later utters her prophecies in Greek, it is the Chorus and not she who is perplexed and in need of an interpreter. Though the Chorus are able to grasp the fact that Cassandra is prophesying, they are unable to understand the meaning of her words. A tension or ambiguity is thus created between Cassandra's purely mantic speech and the Chorus' more rational language. Once again, Cassandra is isolated from the audience within the play, isolated in and through her silence. Silence is perhaps the mode of speech that threatens the *polis* most, not the female silence that, as Sophocles would say and Aristotle would cite, gives grace to a woman, that can be opposed in the *polis* to male speech, but the silence that brings ruin to the state and its reason.

Cassandra's initial silence is thus not without meaning or purpose, so that when she finally does speak, the passage from silence to speech is all the more forceful due to the duration of her silence and all the assumptions and speculations at play behind it. Later in the play, Cassandra will have no problem expressing herself and being understood in her apostrophe to the Chorus, explicitly acknowledging that she does indeed know the Greek language (1254). But even there, Cassandra's voice works on different registers—at the very limits of Greek and of any other human language. She starts with a cry invoking Apollo and then moves to lyrics. Though not unusual in the mouth of the Chorus, such lyrics are rarely uttered by protagonists. In fact, the Chorus and Cassandra actually seem to swap roles during this exchange, Cassandra using lyrics, and the Chorus, the trimeters expected of Cassandra. The cry and the lyrics reflect the intensity of Cassandra's emotions, setting her off from both the other protagonists and the Chorus. Since her warnings concerning the murders about to take place are not heeded, Cassandra will remain foreign to the others in both the form and content of her speech. Though her language is understood, her words are strange, indeed incomprehensible. As Bernard Knox has argued, Aeschylus' use of the prophetess Cassandra as the third actor is strange, and yet it is this very strangeness that justifies her presence in the play. When Cassandra finally "bursts out in a torrent of speech and song" (Knox 1979, 42) that will last for some 250 lines, everything changes. As Knox writes,

> the whole play has been moving with the slow sureness of some natural force towards the moment of Agamemnon's death, and now, when that moment seems at hand, the rhythm of the action is brusquely interrupted...Suddenly, just as we begin to think that she will never speak, she does. (ibid., 43)

THE NIGHTINGALE'S SONG

Because it is so foreign and unintelligible to human ears, Cassandra's prophetic "tongue"—not quite a language—is sometimes compared to an animal's cries or a bird's screech. Cassandra opens her lamentation with "a formulaic cry of grief and terror" (Knox 1979, 43), "not a real word consisting of syllables, but an utterance open to improvisation, and therefore belonging to a very primitive level of language" (Heirman 1975, 257). Breaking her silence, Cassandra utters a cry that is midway between the articulate and the inarticulate: *hotototoi potoi da* (1072). Her prophetic speech about the future remains outside the reach of the Chorus because it remains at the limits of the intelligible. L. J. Heirman recounts other instances of such cries in Greek tragedy and concludes that it is either women or foreigners who utter them, as if they were "regarded as unmanly, as un-Greek, or as both" (Heirman 1975, 259). In Mycenae, Cassandra is both unmanly and un-Greek.

But in addition to being a woman and a "foreigner," Cassandra is also a prophetess—a threefold reason, then, for being unintelligible. It is precisely this unintelligibility that Aeschylus wishes to draw our attention to, an unintelligibility that breaks into the public space and makes itself heard as such. At the limits of language, Cassandra utters a cry that marks the threshold between what can be understood by the Chorus and what cannot. It is no coincidence that the limit is marked by a woman, a prophetess, taken by force from a foreign land. Heirman writes,

> Cassandra utters these syllables, this fivefold call in a climax of both sound and accent, followed by the wide opening of the shattering *da*, not as pathetic expression of an emotional breakdown foreboding her violent death, but as a device that serves to change the quality and level of her own consciousness into clairvoyance, by forcefully expelling all her breath in one great scream. The exact monotonous repetition in line 1076 shows that these sounds are more than lament. It marks them as willful and ritualistic. (1975, 261)

This cry performs the passage from mere sound to lamentation and prophetic language. The repetition of the cry at 1076 and its echo at 1080 endow the whole passage with a rhythm in accordance with the ritualistic aspect of prophecy.

This inaugural utterance of Cassandra is matched first by Clytemnestra's characterization of Cassandra as a swallow (1051) and then by the Chorus' description of her as a nightingale (1140–45). In the first of these two descriptions, the foreignness of Cassandra's speech is explicitly emphasized: "Well, if her speech be not strange and outlandish, even as a swallow's, I must speak within the compass of her wits and move her to comply" (1050–53). Outside or at the limits of *logos*, the barbarian's language is at first compared to the obscure cries of a bird. The second instance similarly insists on the lack of clarity in Cassandra's words: "Frenzied in soul thou art, by some god possessed, and dost wail in wild strains [*nomon anomon*] thine own fate, like some brown nightingale that never ceases making lament (ah me!), and in the misery of her heart moans *Itys, Itys*, through all her days abounding in sorrow" (1140–45). Cassandra indeed expresses herself at the limits of meaning, but she ultimately rejects the Chorus' comparison of her to a nightingale because her fate will not, she says, be as sweet or kind as that of Procne.[5] She will not be so lucky as to be transformed, like Procne, into a nightingale, but will instead be slaughtered like a sacrificed animal.[6] "Ah, fate of the tuneful nightingale! The gods clothed her in winged form and gave her a sweet life without tears. But for me waiteth destruction by the two-edged sword" (1146–49).

The *nomon anomon* stresses perfectly the unintelligibility of Cassandra's song. Pietro Pucci calls this formula a "privative oxymoron," an "exemplary tear in language" that plays at different levels and can be interpreted as "a song not song," a "melody without melody," a "meaningless moan," or even, as Nicole Loraux suggests, "a song without rules," "a song without law," or, to keep the ambivalence, a "measure without measure." The border wavers between a confused, unclear song and one that is unruly, *déréglée*. As Pucci argues, "the comparison with the nightingale's song is a justification for the feminine moaning that defies the limits of meaning."[7]

After she has been slain by Clytemnestra, Cassandra is compared one last time to a bird. Clytemnestra says, "She, who like a swan, hath sung her last lament in death, lies here" (1444–46). In the *Historia Animalium*, Aristotle claims that the swan's song is triggered by the approach of death. Cassandra's speech, which opened as a bird's cry, now comes to its logical conclusion in this final comparison. The sweet song of the nightingale has been transformed into the swan's song of death and lamentation. Since the swan was, as Socrates tells us in the *Phaedo*,[8] the bird of Apollo, it was thought to be endowed with the special gift of prophecy before its death. Cassandra is indeed the prophetic swan to which Socrates will compare himself. But instead of accepting death, like Socrates, at the hands of the Athenians in the hopes of attaining a better lot in the afterlife, Cassandra is led off to be slaughtered by Aegisthus and Clytemnestra, her only hope for the future being to avenge herself against her slayers.

CASSANDRA AND THE FUTURISTIC PRESENT

As soon as Clytemnestra reenters the palace where the "sacrifice" is to take place, Cassandra begins to invoke Apollo (1072), the cry *hotototoi potoi da* punctuating the invocation of Apollo that follows (1073–77). Occasioned perhaps by Cassandra seeing a statue of Apollo at the entrance of the palace, this cry of woe and terror structures Cassandra's first outpouring of language. It is emphasized, moreover, by what appears to be the ambiguity of the expression *apollōn emos* (1081, 1086), which can mean either "my Apollo" or "my destroyer"—or, indeed, can be heard as both at once. Cassandra's cry is thus followed by an ambivalent phrase that combines past, present, and future; that is, she invokes her past relation to Apollo and Apollo's hand in causing her present misery and future demise (1082). The Chorus, for its part, does not understand how the name of Apollo could be associated with a cry of woe. This is the beginning of a misunderstanding that will continue intermittently throughout the exchange between Cassandra and the Chorus, which will acknowledge that Cassandra is indeed inhabited by the god (1084).

The first part of this dialogue between the Chorus and Cassandra concerns the fate of the house of Atreus, "a house of Heaven loathed, a house that knoweth many a horrible butchery of kin, a human shambles and a floor swimming with blood" (1090–92). The future of this particular *polis* is thus steeped in the past. Cassandra's description in the present tense of what seems to be an ongoing slaughter but is, in reality, the slaughter that is about to take place opens at line 1100 with Cassandra questioning Clytemnestra's design. As Eduard Fraenkel justly notes, the suspense and sinister effect of this whole passage are intensified by the fact that the Chorus does not discover the identity of the person mentioned by Cassandra until seven lines later (Fraenkel 1962, 498). Clytemnestra—whose wickedness (*kakon*) is amplified by the repetition of the word *mega*—is soon to be revealed to the Chorus through Cassandra's descriptive vision. For the moment, Cassandra is here simply describing what she perceives—that is, Clytemnestra attending to Agamemnon within the palace. Fraenkel comments,

The *telos* at which Clytemnestra's actions are aimed is not yet perceptible to Cassandra when she speaks these words, however

much she may fear the outcome of this action (1107 *tode*) which
she sees before her...In using the present tense [*proteinei*] Cassandra returns from the possibilities of the future to what her vision
shows her now. (ibid., 500, 501)

Cassandra describes the action step by step, presumably as it is occurring
or is just about to occur, from Clytemnestra stretching forth her hands
to Agamemnon being ensnared in her net. This vision seems to be lived
in the present by Cassandra, who cannot leap ahead as it were to the
ultimate outcome but must, much like the spectators of tragedy, know
and yet not know, anticipate and yet wait for the unfolding of events in
the present. Death is always just out of reach in her narrative, always
just at the end of the last word. The narrative moves toward it, not
like a *telos*, but like a limit, the limit of narrative itself, the end of the
representation of the future in the present. Cassandra does not have a
clear, detached vision or knowledge of what will happen but a much
more visceral, present vision of the events unfolding before her eyes. Her
function is thus less to know in advance than to see and reveal, in the
present, to the external audience, things that will remain unintelligible
to the ears of the *polis*.[9]

A kind of simultaneity, or at least the semblance thereof, is thus
evoked in the words of Cassandra, who seems to depict actions that are
actually happening as she speaks, moving between the future and the
present of the indicative mood. Following David Aune's classification,
her enunciations fall into the category of "prescriptive oracles"—that
is, those that use the "futuristic present" (Aune 1983, 56). This futuristic present reduces the distance between the prediction of the event and
its advent, propelling it, as it were, toward its realization. This simultaneity is itself announced or mediated by a Chorus that speaks and yet
does not really know what it is saying. Whether the simultaneity comes
from the reenunciation by the Chorus of a past oracle that has now
been fulfilled, or whether it occurs through the prophetic wording of
Cassandra in the present indicative, the essential point is that past, present, and future are fused and confused in a play of differing temporal
frames. Such confusion serves more than just dramatic effect; it is the
very expression of truth as *alētheia*, the expression of a "truth" that is
at once revealed and concealed, at once present and still to come.

This prophetic enunciation transforms the present into one that is
always yet to come, always just a word away. The future, then, is not
some present that simply has not yet arrived but a hollowness or rift
within the present itself. In Cassandra's speech the action is not narrated

in an eternal present but lived and experienced in a present that is always moving out of itself. Cassandra lives this tension between present and future and narrates in a time that can be understood in terms of neither the present nor the future. The "futuristic present" is thus a future that is already happening, that is already a present—that is, not a static event that is yet to come but a living future-present, a present always to come. The portion of Cassandra's vision that concerns Clytemnestra's murdering of Agamemnon (1100–29) is thus reported by the prophetess in the present as if she were living and experiencing the vision of events on the verge of taking place.

Cassandra's vision and vivid description of Clytemnestra catching Agamemnon in her snare (1114–18, 1125–29) continues this process of presencing the future (cf. Fraenkel 1962, 502–5): "Ha, ha, see there, see there! Keep the bull from its mate! She hath caught [*labousa*] him in the robe and gores him with the crafty device of her black horn! He falls in a vessel of water! It is of doom wrought by guile in a murderous bath that I am telling thee" (1125–29). As Fraenkel remarks, nothing indicates at first that Agamemnon is the object of this violence. In fact, "the audience familiar with country life must at first suppose that the cow is threatened" (Fraenkel 1962, 510)[10]. It is only with the feminine participle *labousa* that the reversal is made clear and that "the veil is torn asunder and the unheard-of horror revealed: in this case it is the female that is the unnatural aggressor" (ibid.), the woman who is goring the male. The tension has been building since line 1100 as Cassandra progresses from a general to a more and more detailed description of Clytemnestra's guile. The bath and the net finally take their place in a scene of murder, though we will later have confirmation of the deed in Agamemnon's actual death cry, "The desperate cry of the dying man cannot match the horror aroused by the vision of the seeress" (1343–45). As Fraenkel rightly observes, "What the Greek poet makes us see with our mind's eye is infinitely more forcible in its effect than anything actually shown on a stage could be" (1962, 516).

Cassandra's vision ends with this powerful presentation of Agamemnon's death. What follows has a more reflective tone to it. Cassandra returns to the past of Troy and Mycenae, and then leaps forward to her own future and the future of the house of Atreus—that is, to the future organization of the *polis*. But her words are by then deprived of the tone of the futuristic present. A temporal distance is reinstated within the prophetic discourse that transforms the future back into a present that simply has not yet taken place. Cassandra can now leap ahead into the future because it is a future that has been preordained, already written, as it were, though not yet fulfilled. The "truth" of the futuristic present, the "truth" that requires time in the present, that can be located neither in the present nor the future, is replaced by a truth where all things are present in their possibility, be they in the past, the present, or the future. "Truth" as the narrative disclosure of the future in the present has thus been eclipsed. The immediacy of Cassandra's vision is thus lost and what is regained is the temporal frame of most prophetic discourses and, along with it, the political—a tale of two powerful cities and of the most powerful families within them.

Ernesto Grassi (1980) characterizes this difference within the prophetic language as that between the semantic and the rational planes of discourse. According to him, the Chorus and Cassandra are at first unable to communicate because each moves in a space and a time of its own. The Chorus moves in the realm of expoundable rationality and in a time that makes the future appear simply as a *possibility*. It speaks, in the text, in the grammatical form used for reporting the past. Its language, therefore, is temporal, in the sense that it attempts to grasp and to reflect the unfolding of events and their relations. Cassandra's space, on the other hand, is determined by the simultaneous nature of the vision in which the movements of time are fused, becoming parts of an immovable, necessary, and no longer merely possible instant. In accordance with her "seer's" gifts, Cassandra speaks in a pictorial language that is distinguished from that of the Chorus by frequently falling back on participial phrases. Only in the second main passage (1136–1214), when the vision loses its quality of futuristic present, and when, according to Grassi, Cassandra's discourse responds to the demand for explanation, does a "dialogical relationship" develop between the Chorus and Cassandra.[11] The futuristic present, the pictorial, to use Grassi's term, opens up a tragic space within the political.

CASSANDRA IN AND BEYOND THE STATE

Having questioned the justice of the Trojan war, Cassandra shifts the terms of the debate and the focus of attention. As Knox argues, Cassandra has "no call to action or repentance, no moral judgment, nothing except the vision of reality, of what has been, is, and will be" (1979, 47). Hence, the Chorus requires of the third actor "precisely the knowledge of reality that Cassandra alone can give them" (ibid.). Two purposes or designs are thus simultaneously at work in the *Agamemnon*: Clytemnestra's murderous purpose and the plans of Zeus. The Chorus' task is to discover the nature of both: "not to act, but to understand, to understand what is happening, and what will happen and why, to pierce through the uncertainty to the moral law. They struggle to find some light in the darkness which throughout the play shrouds the will not only of Clytemnestra but also of Zeus" (ibid., 48). Cassandra presents the Chorus a concrete vision of things to come. But, this knowledge of reality is never coupled by the Chorus with their own intuition of a moral understanding. As persuasively stated by Simon Goldhill, with Cassandra "we have referential language, language that is not only true, but also capable of accurate prediction; but language that is incapable of being received" (1984, 82). Not until time catches up with Cassandra's vision, not until both her death and Agamemnon's prove her right, does the Chorus come to grips with the reality and achieve an understanding that translates into a call for action: "summon the townsfolk to bring rescue hither to the palace," "charge [Clytemnestra and Aegisthus] with the deed," "vote for action of some sort" (1348 and foll). Until then, "without the ability to say what has happened or to predict what will happen, they are unable to act" (Goldhill 1984, 88). Cassandra's prophecies now actually enable the Chorus to understand the meaning of the murderers' act: "a plan to set up a tyranny in the State" (1354–55). It is thanks to Cassandra's prophecies that they become the only ones in the play able to understand Zeus' edict that man learns through suffering. As pointed out by Knox, neither Agamemnon nor Clytemnestra nor Aegisthus learn anything. The Chorus alone is able to know that Clytemnestra too will pay for her deed—the laws of political intrigue having to yield to another, more divine law. In its final apostrophe of Clytemnestra, the Chorus even evokes the eventual vengeance of Orestes, already predicted by Cassandra. Thus, while Cassandra's words appear to have little effect before her death, they seem to echo within and transform the Chorus sometime after.[12] In that sense, what Anne Carson says about Electra, Niobe, and Procne can be applied to Cassandra as well though in her case the effect of her words is most potent after her death: "Each of these three women manages to say what she means from within an idiolect that is alien or unknown to other people. Each of them manages, although stuck in a form of like that cuts her off from the world of normal converse, to transect and trouble and change that world by her utterance" (2001, 44).

As Timothy Reiss writes, "The tragic...is the trace of the inevitable gap between the human known and knowable and all that escapes discourse" (1980, 20). Cassandra stands between the knowable and the unknowable and thus is, as such, essential to tragedy and to the

eventual understanding by the internal audience of the fragility of
political power. She is essential for revealing—and thus, in some sense,
making known—this gap between the knowable and the known, for,
according to Reiss, "what tragedy 'tells' us...is that man can know. The
protagonist may remain 'in the tragic' but not the spectator, not the one
who constructed the code" (ibid., 24).

Cassandra represents the possibility of knowledge and understanding
beyond the state, a notion of the right beyond political justice. Through
her, the Chorus of the *Agamemnon* gains an understanding of the
unavoidability of fate. Through her words, the spectator learns about
the future, or rather, relearns what was already known, namely, that
Agamemnon would be killed, that Orestes would avenge his father, and
so on. But at the same time as Cassandra reveals the future and makes
knowledge possible, she points to the necessary absence of significance
and to the necessary blindness of those who must learn through suffering. Revealing not simply some truth that will one day come to pass—
her own death, the revenge of Orestes, the reorganization of the house
of Atreus—but, more significantly, this very process of revelation, this
tension between revelation and concealment, Cassandra reveals another
conception of truth itself, a "truth" that no *polis* can accommodate.

CASSANDRA'S CURSE

In Aeschylus, the doomed prophetess, the prophetess undone by the
prophet Apollo (1275), is to some extent avenged by Apollo through the
hand of Orestes. A circle thus seems to close itself: Cassandra, originally
cursed by Apollo for breaking her vow to marry him, is avenged by
him in the end—or at least that is what she thinks. Richard Kuhns has
argued that the curse can be attributed to Cassandra's disregard for the
bond of marriage with Apollo, in other words, to her disregard for one
of the essential bonds of the *polis*, as the rest of the *Oresteia* is intent on
showing. For Kuhns, Cassandra's punishment is the result of a "violation
of the marriage vows and female duty," of "the covenant of marriage,"
a punishment meted out by a god who "argues for the rights of the male
and the sacredness of marriage" (Kuhns 1962, 40–41). Kuhns justifies
his argument by pointing to *The Libation Bearers*, where Apollo helps
Orestes punish Clytemnestra for precisely these reasons.

Having broken the sacred bond between herself and Apollo, Cassandra is also seen by Clytemnestra as having destroyed the union between
Agamemnon and her. "And here she lies, his captive, and auguress, and
concubine, his oracular faithful bedfellow, yet equally familiar with the

seamen's benches. The pair has met no undeserved fate" (1440–44). Clytemnestra thus uses this justification to kill the woman who broke the sacred bonds of marriage between herself and Agamemnon. But by doing so, Clytemnestra actually strengthens the bond between Cassandra and Agamemnon, granting them a sort of union in death. As Loraux points out, there is in tragedy an equation of death and marriage—a theme that Euripides will later develop in his presentation of Cassandra as Agamemnon's wife to be: "To die with...A tragic way for a woman to go to the extreme limit of marriage, by, it must be said, drastically reordering events, since it is in death that 'living with' her husband will be achieved" (Loraux 1987, 26). Though the death of Cassandra is not a suicide, and therefore cannot be seen as a desire to intensify or immortalize her relation with Agamemnon—as is the case, for example, of Dejaneira or Evadne—her death is nonetheless what seals her union with him. As Apollo's *parthenos*, Cassandra is sacrificed, just as Iphigenia had been; both, in a sense, are wedded through sacrifice (cf. *Iphigenia at Aulis*, lines 460–61).

Having broken her vows with Apollo, having been presented as a housebreaker by Clytemnestra, Cassandra's fate is to marry her captor in death. Cassandra thus dies not as a breaker of bonds but as a partaker in them, a partner in a covenant of marriage that will be sealed by death. Homer had already emphasized in the *Odyssey* (11.421) the creation of an unbreakable bond between these two, the accomplishment and apotheosis of the union between them, as Agamemnon recalls in Hades his concubine's death and her plaintive cry by his side.

THE TRAGIC "TRUTH" OF CASSANDRA

Though it might seem that she has the potential to warn others about death, and so prevent it, Cassandra's presumed betrayal of Apollo has the effect of making Cassandra unable to persuade—or else, those around her unable to be persuaded. Her curse thus has the effect of poisoning those around her, making them unable to be persuaded of the truth that would heal or help them: "Ever since that fault, I could persuade no one of aught" (1212). Moreover, when it comes to knowledge about her *own* future, Cassandra's vision is as incomplete and obscured as those around her.[13] She knows that she will die, but does not know the exact reasons why (though she thinks she does). She mistakes the tensions at play in Mycenae as a family feud when it is really more of a political struggle. It is the Trojan War that is on trial, its justifications and validity. Agamemnon is coming back after ten costly years of war, a victor returning empty-handed and alone—except for Cassandra. Yet, Cassandra does seem to know about Iphigenia, whose fate she is going to reenact and repeat, and whose death she might be said to avenge. But when she says that her death, the death of a woman, will be avenged by the death of another (i.e., Clytemnestra's), she is rather mistaken, for Clytemnestra's death will avenge Agamemnon's; it will be repayment for the crimes of a murderous wife and mother, not for the murder of a concubine. Though she is the mouthpiece of Apollo, she has no ability as an interpreter. She herself is affected by the part of the curse that prevents belief. Like her audience, she too is given the truth about the future but she too is fooled and does not understand it. She is fooled concerning both the nature of her curse and the reasons for her death. Finally, though Cassandra is able to *predict* what she thinks to be the future, she does not *experience* it as she was able to experience the death of Agamemnon at the hands of Clytemnestra. While other prophets' words also fall on deaf ears, while other prophets cannot influence or change for the better the future that they predict,[14] Cassandra appears uniquely afflicted, her prophecy not simply a way of motivating or explaining actions, but a means of staging the relationship between tragedy and truth, for the revelation of truth and the ignoring of it seem important not only for Cassandra but also for the development of a notion of fate, for a sense of the inevitable within tragedy. Hence, we must ask not only about the effect of Cassandra's inability to persuade those within the narrative or the play but also about her effect on an audience who reads or witnesses this inability.

What, then, is the relationship between Cassandra and her audience(s), between Cassandra and the Chorus who cannot understand her, or between Cassandra and an external audience that knows everything already in advance? Is it Cassandra's inability to persuade that is at issue, or rather, the audience's inability to be persuaded? Melanie Klein interprets the inability of the Chorus to understand Cassandra as a sort of denial of the truth, a protection against anxiety:

> The Elders, who are very sympathetic towards Cassandra, partly believe her; yet in spite of realizing the validity of the dangers she prophesies for Agamemnon, for herself and the people of Argos, they deny her prophesies. Their refusal to believe what at the same time they know expresses the universal tendency towards denial. (Klein 1975, 293)

Denial is a potent defense against the persecutory anxiety and guilt that result from destructive impulses never being completely under control. Such a psychoanalytic reading might help us to reinterpret the curse of Apollo in a rather startling way. From this perspective, it is not so much Cassandra who is diminished in her ability to persuade but her listeners, who, because of their denial, are unable to be persuaded. For what is to be rejected or denied is perhaps not, in the end, a couple of gruesome deaths and turmoil within the *polis*, but precisely the *revelation* of these events, the ambiguity of knowing and not knowing, of being free for a future that has already been ordained.

The foreign must remain foreign and thus denied, turned away from, and rejected, for the dramatic effect of the play depends both on the external audience understanding Cassandra's truthfulness and on her immediate audience not comprehending it. The foreign must *necessarily* remain foreign to the internal audience, since only in this way can the tragic tension be maintained. For the external audience, then, for us, it is this very event of revelation—and not so much the revelations themselves—that is put center stage.

If Cassandra's revelations concerning the future do indeed serve to emphasize the inevitability of human events, the inescapability of fate, then denial of these revelations or blindness to them helps to reveal not only a notion of fate or *Moira* that transcends human actions and decisions but also a tension between revelation and concealment, human knowledge and *Moira*. Such a tension cannot simply be overcome by understanding human knowledge as the imperfect approximation of *Moira*, of what is simply fated to happen, because humans must live this tension and live it as the "truth" of human existence. We asked earlier whether "truth" might be communicable only through the feminine. The question must now be reformulated to ask whether "truth" might be uncommunicable, whether it might first be "truth" and not Truth only through the feminine, whether "truth"—the "truth" of tragedy—has less to do with the prophetic utterance that finds authentication in the future as with the muted, female voice that expresses and performs its own incommunicability. "Truth" would thus not be understood as the correspondence between prediction and event, speech and fact, but as a tension between different planes of knowledge and revelation, different perspectives and interpretations—a "truth" that is always at the limits of the *polis*. The direct consequence of placing the incommunicability of "truth" at the core of the feminine is that it establishes a link between the feminine and the impossibility of any clear and simple revelation of "truth"; that is, it makes possible the revelation that "truth" is the very tension between revelation and concealment.

NOTES

1. In his translation of Heidegger's "*Alētheia*" essay, Capuzzi adds this note about *alētheia*: "Although Heidegger positively discourages us from doing so, we offer the following philological information: *alēthesia* is a substantive form constructed from *alēthēs* (*-es*), an adjectival form of *alētheia*....*Lēthō* is a collateral form of *lanthanō*, I escape notice, am hidden, unseen or forgotten by others. Gaisford describes *alēthes* as that which does not sink into *lēthē*, the source of oblivion. Liddell-Scott translates *alēthes* as 'unconcealed.' Hence *alēthesia* might be rendered as 'unconcealedment'" (Heidegger 1975, 103). Detienne (1999) in his investigation of the relationship between prophecy and truth refers to *Homeric Hymn to Hermes*, 561; Sophocles, *Oedipus the King*, 299; Euripides, *Iphigenia in Tauris*, 1256–67, 1276–79; Aeschylus, *Agamemnon*, 1241; Aeschylus, *Seven Against Thebes*, 710; and Pindar *Olympian Ode*. The temple of Apollo is also described by Pindar as the "seat of truthful oracles [*alathea mantiōn thōkon*]" (*Pythian XI*, Loeb, 6).

2. Were we to continue this analysis of Cassandra beyond the tragic playwrights of the fifth and fourth centuries, we would see how she was transformed by the later tradition, becoming little more than a stereotype by the time of Lycophron in the third century BCE. The Cassandra of Aeschylus, and to some extent Euripides, is not the one-sided, static figure we will later find in Lycophron; she is not the mere representative of female deception as opposed to male truth.

3. "The kingly birds, one black, one white of tail, hard by the palace, on the spear-hand, in a station full conspicuous, devouring a hare with brood unborn checked in the last effort to escape" (114–20).

4. Hugh Lloyd-Jones notes, with regards to this line, "the Greeks called foreigners, particularly Orientals, by the contemptuous name *barbaroi* (barbarians), originally descriptive of what they thought to be their incoherent speech, which was sometimes compared to the twittering of swallows" (1970, 73).

5. According to one legend, Tereus cut out the tongue of Philomena, his wife Procne's sister, after having raped her, so that she could not reveal what happened. But Philomena wove her story into a tapestry, and, as revenge, the two sisters killed Tereus' son, Itys, and served him as a dish for Tereus' dinner. To save them from Tereus' anger, the gods transformed them into birds, Procne becoming a nightingale and Philomena a swallow. Cassandra thus cannot accept the

comparison with Procne precisely because her fate will not be as fortunate as hers. Procne, unlike her, has no reason to cry.

6. In "Hunting and Sacrifice in Aeschylus's *Oresteia*," Vidal-Naquet draws illuminating connections between various images of hunt and sacrifice to show how Agamemnon and Orestes are presented as both the hunters and the hunted. The eagles that eat the hare "with brood unborn" (1990, 154) can be identified, as they are by Calchas, with the sons of Atreus who will ransack Troy, or with the attendants at the death of Iphigenia, at the "murder of Iphigenia," "this corrupt sacrifice" (ibid., 156). Agamemnon is not only a leader of a battle but an eagle or lion that leads a hunt. "We are about to pass from the world of battle to that of the animal hunt that is wild and impious" (ibid., 157). Finally, Cassandra is identified with a hound, Clytemnestra with a lioness, and Aegisthus with a wolf; "the hunt and the sacrifice—these meet each other at the precise point where man has become no more than an animal" (ibid., 157–58). The metaphors vary, however, for as Vidal-Naquet notices, the capturing is described with hunt metaphors, whereas the execution itself uses images borrowed from stock farming. Thus, the protagonists become the objects of either a "perverted hunt" or a "corrupt sacrifice," and any act that is sacrilegious—be it a hunt or a sacrifice—must meet with punishment and revenge.

Cassandra's death is exemplary in this regard; she is truly the "ideal" sacrificial victim. By going willingly to her death (1295–96), she turns her own murder into a sacrifice, which is precisely what Clytemnestra hopes she will do. This explains why no one drags her into the palace, why Clytemnestra makes sure not to compel her, not to force her into a death that would turn sacrifice into murder.

7. Pietro Pucci develops this argument very convincingly in "La tragédie et le rituel," a lecture given at the Ecole des Hautes Etudes in Paris on March 14, 1989. Among the respondents were Detienne, Loraux, and Vincent Delacombes.

I will show that this seeming lack of meaning partakes of the nature of prophetic signs, just as Cassandra's silence at the beginning of the play is already the bearer of prophetic discourse. Lyotard examines the nature of this silence in *The Differend*.

> Back from Troy, Agamemnon has just entered the palace of Atreus, leaving Cassandra, his captive, motionless in the chariot. Clytemnestra entreats her to come in, too. Frozen by her vision of the impeding crime, Cassandra neither hears nor answers: "She bears herself like a wild creature newly captured" (1063). The queen grows impatient: "but

if failing to understand our language, you do not catch my meaning, then instead of speech, make sign with thy barbarian hand."
—Silence as a phrase. The expectant wait of the *Is it happening?* as
silence. Feelings as a phrase for what cannot now be phrased. The
immediate incommunicability of desire, or the immediate incommunicability of murder. The phrase of love, the phrase of death. "Femininity" or "bestiality" as a blank in the argument (*logos, phônè*).
The suspense of the linking. (Lyotard 1988, 70)

    This pause in Cassandra's speech, this silence preceding her
speech, is open to all the interpretations proposed by Lyotard. It is
open not only to suspense but also to the impossibility of putting
into words the horror to come.

8. In the *Phaedo*, Socrates claims that the swan's last song is one of
celebration; because the swan is Apollo's prophetic bird, it must
know about the immortality of the soul and so must be rejoicing in
its song (84e–85b).

9. As Blanchot writes, the role of prophecy, and perhaps the same is
true of tragedy, is the revelation not of a future that will one day
be present but of a future that can never be present, a future that is
always to come, like death.

To foresee and announce some future is no great feat if this future
takes place in the ordinary course of events and finds expression in
the regularity of language. But prophetic speech announces something impossible....When speech becomes prophetic, it is not the
future that is given, but the present that is withdrawn and, along
with it, all possibility of a firm, stable and lasting presence. (Blanchot 1959, 117–118)

10. See Fraenkel (1962) on the Greek convention of representing man
and woman as bull and cow.

11. The passage from the plane of the semantic to that of the rational
takes place, claims Grassi, through the metaphor of the nightingale,
which the Chorus uses to describe Cassandra (1146; see Grassi
1980, 23).

12. Though Reiss applies the following to Renaissance tragedy, it seems
equally relevant to Greek tragedy, and specifically to the *Agamemnon*, where Cassandra is the one who articulates the tensions
between meaning and unmeaning: "This absence of significance,
this impossibility of attaining to meaning in discourse, is...what we
call the tragic. Tragedy is the discourse that at once produces and
absorbs that absence called the tragic" (Reiss 1980, 3).

13. Cassandra will not discuss her own fate until line 1137, when she links what is going to happen to her to Agamemnon and his kindred.
14. While the Greeks are warned by Calchas of Athena's anger at Ajax's sacrilegious deed (Apollodorus' *Epitome V*), they are unable to take any measures to make atonement for Ajax's transgression.

REFERENCES

Aeschylus. 1933. *Agamemnon, Libation bearers*. Trans. H. W. Smyth. Cambridge: Harvard University Press.

———. 1970. *Agamemnon*. Trans. Hugh Lloyd-Jones. Englewood Cliffs, NJ: Prentice Hall.

Apollodorus. 1921. *The library*. Trans. Sir James George Frazer. Loeb Classical Library. London: William Heinemann.

Aune, David. 1983. *Prophecy in early Christianity and the ancient Mediterranean world*. Grand Rapids, MI: William B. Eerdmans.

Carson, Anne. 2001. Screaming in translation: The *Electra* of Sophocles. In *Sophocles. Electra*, trans. A. Carson, 41–48. Oxford: Oxford University Press.

Benveniste, Emile. 1973. *Indo-European language and society*. Trans. Elizabeth Palmer. Coral Gables, FL: University of Miami Press.

Blanchot, Maurice. 1959. *Le livre à venir*. Paris: Gallimard.

Detienne, Marcel. 1999. *Masters of Truth in Archaic Greece*. Trans. J. Lloyd. New York: Zone Books.

Fraenkel, Eduard, ed. 1962. *Agamemnon*. Oxford: Clarendon.

Goldhill, Simon. 1984. *Language, sexuality, narrative: The Oresteia*. Cambridge: Cambridge University Press.

Grassi, Ernesto. 1980. *Rhetoric as philosophy: The humanist tradition*. University Park: Pennsylvania State University Press.

Heidegger, Martin. 1975. *Early Greek thinking*. Trans. D. Krell and F. Capuzzi. New York: Harper & Row.

Heirman, L. J. 1975. Kassandra's Glossolalia. *Mnemosyne* 28: 257–67.

Homer. 1938. *The odyssey*. Trans. A. T. Murray. Cambridge: Harvard University Press.

Klein, Melanie. 1975. *Envy and gratitude*. New York: Free Press.

Knox, Bernard. 1979. *Word and action: Essays on the ancient theater*. Baltimore: John Hopkins University Press.

Kuhns, Richard. 1962. *The house, the city and the judge: The growth of moral awareness in the Oresteia*. Indianapolis & New York: Bobbs-Merrill.

Loraux, Nicole. 1987. *Tragic ways of killing a woman*. Trans. A. Forster. Cambridge: Harvard University Press.

Lycophron. 1921. *Alexandra*. Trans. G. Mooney. London: G. Bell and Sons.

Lyotard, Jean-François. 1988. *The differend: Phrases in dispute*. Trans. G. Van Den Abbeele. Minneapolis: University of Minnesota Press.

Pindar. 1937. *The odes*. Trans. Sir John Sandys. Cambridge: Harvard University Press.

Plato. 1932. *Phaedo, Phaedrus*. Trans. H. N. Fowler. Cambridge: Harvard University Press.

Reiss, Timothy. 1980. *Tragedy and truth*. New Haven, CT: Yale University Press.

de Romilly, Jacqueline. 1967. L'évocation du passé dans l'*Agamemnon* d'Eschyle. *Revue des Etudes Grecques* 30: 93–99.

Thomson, George, ed. 1966. *The Oresteia of Aeschylus*. 2 vols. Prague: Academia.

Vidal-Naquet, Pierre. 1990. Hunting and sacrifice in Aeschylus's *Oresteia*. In *Myth and tragedy in ancient Greece*, trans. J. Lloyd, ed. J.-P. Vernant and P. Vidal-Naquet, 150–74. New York: Zone Books.

Way, A, trans. 1912. *Euripides*. London: William Heinemann, New York: The Macmillan Co.

Wolf, Christa. 1984. *Cassandra: A novel and four essays*. Trans. I. Van Heurck. New York: Farrar, Straus and Giroux.

9

THE LOSS OF ABANDONMENT IN SOPHOCLES' *ELECTRA*

DENISE EILEEN MCCOSKEY

In the spring of 1926, American playwright Eugene O'Neill settled on the idea of writing, in his own words, a "modern psychological drama using one of the old legend plots of Greek tragedy" (1947, 530). Of the various myths offered by Greek tragedy, O'Neill quickly decided that the house of Atreus was "psychologically most interesting," and from the beginning he placed special emphasis on the character of Electra, for O'Neill found Electra's ancient renditions distinctly unsatisfying, scornfully proclaiming, "in [the] Greek story she peters out into undramatic married banality. Such a character contained too much tragic fate within her soul to permit this—why should (the) Furies have let Electra escape unpunished? Why did the chain of fated crime and retribution ignore her mother's murderess?" O'Neill vowed, in contrast, to give his Electra a "tragic ending worthy of (her) character" (530). And, indeed, the ultimate fate of the Electra character provides the dramatic culmination of O'Neill's own trilogy, *Mourning Becomes Electra*, a trilogy that otherwise takes Aeschylus' *Oresteia* as its structural model.[1]

I would like to take O'Neill's frustration with Electra's descent into so-called "undramatic married banality" as a starting point for this chapter. I begin with O'Neill's passionate disappointment in Electra's ancient form because I find in his reaction the essence of an important question, which, it has to be said, is nonetheless slightly gruesome— does Electra deserve more tragedy in her life? Or, to phrase it somewhat differently, does Electra merit a greater share in the ideologies and activities that are being contested around her in Greek tragedy, and in which she at times participates, a status that would also require she share the consequences of those deliberations? If Orestes is stained by matricide, should she, too, not get her portion rather than simply fade away as she does in Aeschylus' *Libation Bearers*? In opening with

221

the terms of O'Neill's indignant characterization of Electra's fortunes, I must admit that I am less interested in the workings of marriage, an institution Kirk Ormand has elucidated skillfully with regard to Electra in his important study *Exchange and the Maiden: Marriage in Sophoclean Tragedy* (1999), documenting in particular the ways in which Electra's decline in Sophocles can be linked structurally to her ultimate containment within the Greek institution of marriage and the paradoxical positions it assigns women.[2] Rather, in this chapter, I would like to examine closely the process of Electra's diminishment in Sophocles' play by exposing the playwright's depiction of the young woman's changing emotional state, a dimension of Electra's character that gives insight into the desires that both animate and ultimately betray her.

Significantly, although Sophocles' *Electra* follows roughly the same plot as Aeschylus' *Libation Bearers* (dramatizing the return of Orestes and the subsequent murders of Aegisthus and Clytemnestra), Sophocles' version, like that of Euripides, focuses its attention throughout on the predicament of Electra, who has long been waiting for her brother, Orestes, to return from his exile so that they can exact vengeance on their father's murderers.[3] In this way, although Sophocles' play begins with Orestes' secret arrival home, the young man exits soon after and does not reappear for some one thousand lines. It is Electra instead who dominates the first part of the play, filling the stage with her deep sorrow and perpetual mourning. In fact, Electra's affiliation with her dead father is so central to her own self-definition and purpose that it seems only natural when she is falsely told that her brother, Orestes, too, is dead and unable to return and help restore their family. Distraught at first by this news, Electra soon dreams of fulfilling the revenge herself, a fantasy that is cut short in the play when she turns her attention instead to an urn containing what she believes are her brother's remains. Although reluctant at first to give up her attachment to this urn, Electra eventually succumbs to the recognition of Orestes and a reunion with her living brother. Orestes then silences his sister's exuberant outburst and assumes full control of events, bringing the play to its close by first killing Clytemnestra and then drawing Aegisthus into the house to meet his identical fate.

As this brief summary suggests, in the course of Sophocles' play, Electra keenly experiences two forms of abandonment—the first, an abandonment by her male kin, and the second, an abandonment in the sense of a giving over to excess, as she first engages in extreme mourning and anger for her father, then a surfeit of pleasure at the reemergence of her brother.[4] Notably, Electra's own dreams of power and glory reach their climax when she hears the contrived story of her brother's death; it is in this space that Electra is able to fantasize openly of committing the revenge crime herself, or as she imagines it, fulfilling the role of tyrannicide. Orestes' sudden reappearance, however, derails such fantasy, and it is the "loss of abandonment" in both senses, both in the return of her brother and his subsequent suppression of her role in the murder and her excessive pleasure, that I interpret as initiating Electra's final descent into what O'Neill calls her "undramatic banality." In this chapter, then, I want to chart the specific ways Electra's own discursive strategies and political desires lead her to this disappointing end, most especially her willing passage from a state of anger, *orgê* (ὀργή), to one of pleasure, *hedonê* (ἡδονή), a drastic transformation sanctioned by Orestes that serves both to trivialize Electra's once tragic status in the plot and to herald her final subordination to her brother's empty reign.

MOURNING AS ABANDONMENT

Sophocles' play provocatively opens by displaying two very different versions of the inheritance left by Agamemnon's death. Returning home after a long exile, Orestes arrives onstage first and is immediately addressed by his companion, an elderly slave, as the "child of Agamemnon" (1–2). The slave then establishes the city as a world of exclusively paternal prerogatives and claims, seeking to reintegrate the young man wholly into his father's household. Orestes, in turn, invokes his father and paternal protection throughout his own speech that follows (33, 51, 67, 69), pointedly avoiding mention of his mother. Anne Pippin Burnett perceptively calls Orestes' initial desire in this scene a "masculine revenge impulse," noting specifically its articulation in terms of the god Apollo's will (1998, 120); we might go even further in suggesting that Orestes evinces not just a "masculine impulse," but one that is exclusively reverent to the paternal line. The play is far from clear at this point, however, about the virtues of such affiliation; there is, after all, a manifest emptiness in Orestes throughout this opening scene (Burnett 1998, 121).[5] Twice in the first five lines the old slave refers to Orestes' great longing for his city while in exile, yet Orestes himself seems so cut off from the object of his desires that the slave is forced to identify the city even as it stands physically before them. So, too, as many critics point out, there is a certain ambiguity inherent in Apollo's ostensible instruction that Orestes gain entry to the city with a trick, a *dolos*—that is, the lie that he has died competing in the god's games (35ff.).[6]

When Orestes departs to make an offering at his father's grave, Electra enters and is promptly identified by the Chorus of women solely through the maternal line—that is, as the child of a "most wretched mother" (121–22). Although Electra, like her brother, declares her primary allegiance to their dead father, her mode of expression nonetheless presents a marked contrast to Orestes' (Kitzinger 1991, 301–5).[7] For one, where her brother seems manifestly detached from his emotions, Electra holds steadfastly to her passions, proclaiming her overwhelming despair and her strict adherence to perpetual mourning in highly emotional terms. So central is this public mourning to Electra's position and purpose that she declares in her opening speech that she will never cease such lamentations (104), and only after that prays for vengeance and Orestes' return (115–120).

Pledged into perpetuity, Electra's sorrow remains central to her self-definition and her bid for meaning among the violent events that threaten to overwhelm her.[8] Thanking the women of the Chorus for their attempts to comfort her, for example, Electra begs that they allow her this release, this abandon (ἐᾶτέ μ' ὧδ' ἀλύειν, 135). As a number of scholars have noted, there is a recurrent verbal play between "release" (λυτήριον) and "libation" (λουτρόν), between unloosing and ritual observance, throughout the play (e.g., Kitzinger 1991, 311; Segal 1981, 276). In fact, "release" (λυτήριον) is the very last word Electra utters, although by that point it will have acquired very different connotations. Charging her with being forgetful of all moderation, the Chorus begins advocating the idea of release as an absence of trouble rather than an embrace of, or fulfillment by, ritualized emotion early in the play. Sternly chiding Electra for destroying herself with such mourning, they propose that by doing so, she forbids herself any release from her troubles (ἐν οἷς ἀνάλυσίς ἐστιν οὐδεμία κακῶν, 140–42). And once such a strategy has been initiated, the play persistently undermines the young woman's attempt to fashion abandonment as a site of self-expression rather than as a marker of loss.

For her own part, Electra reveals a keen ability at self-analysis when she admits that she, too, perceives her excessive anger, her orgê (222), giving a concrete name to a more intimate source of her actions and fantasies than simply her father's death. Indeed, Electra recognizes that it is precisely this passion or anger that opens the depth of possibilities for her character (emboldens the "tragic nature" that O'Neill so admired).[9] In part, the term orgê helps establish Electra's similarity to a number of other complex, albeit not unproblematic, figures in Greek tragedy.[10] That the centrality of this emotion to Electra cannot be explained solely through Agamemnon's death is underlined by the women of the Chorus, who note wryly that none of Electra's siblings have responded to their father's death in the same way (153). Moreover, both Electra and those around her perceive her *orgê* as having its own distinct, and at times dangerous, generative powers. Disapproving Electra's harsh words for her sister, for example, the Chorus chides her "by the gods, say nothing from anger" (μηδὲν πρὸς ὀργὴν, 369).

Given Electra's own reliance on her "anger," it is surely significant that she perceives identical emotion in her mother, accusing Clytemnestra during their vicious argument of being carried away by it (πρὸς ὀργὴν ἐκφέρῃ, 628). Although the play highlights certain structural differences between mother and daughter, not least the hypersexuality of the adulterous mother versus the enforced chastity of the unmarried daughter, there is therefore a significant and persistent mirroring of the two via their emotions and motivations. Indeed, Electra longs to inhabit the role of mother, even as she claims to be repulsed by her own. Despite her own complex attitudes towards maternity, Electra nonetheless adopts harsh (and ultimately self-destructive) discursive methods in order to detach from her mother and so prepare for the impending matricide by trying to unravel its taboo.[11]

MATRICIDE AS TYRANNICIDE

Like Aeschylus' earlier trilogy, Sophocles' play recognizes well the thematic doubling of house and kingdom that is so central to the crisis engendered by the murders in the house of Atreus. Given the void created by Agamemnon's death and Orestes' initial masquerade as a stranger, in fact, the crisis in Mycenae seems to revolve entirely around the royal women as Sophocles' play opens. Electra's own motives and desires are drawn out almost exclusively via other women: the sympathetic Chorus, the reluctant Chrysothemis, and the enraged Clytemnestra. Indeed, Electra's lengthy verbal confrontation with her mother comprises the play's central *agôn*.[12] In contrast, Clytemnestra's lover Aegisthus remains absent until the play's final scene and Orestes seems little better when departing from the stage shortly after his clandestine arrival.

Such male hesitation and avoidance, moreover, are precisely what the women seem to expect. Having been told scornfully by Electra that Orestes is always "*intending* to do something" (305–6), the Chorus asks her if she knows whether her brother is "actually coming or only intending" this time (319) then reminds her that "a man likes to hesitate when doing great things" (320), to which Electra simply and emphatically responds, "And yet I myself, saving him, did not hesitate at all" (321).[13] The reference to Electra's conduct of this earlier deed (i.e., the sending of Orestes into exile as a baby, a feat praised already in the first scene by the old slave) ostensibly sets two female actions in regard to male kin powerfully against one another: the saving of a brother versus the killing of a husband (and king).[14] Clytemnestra herself recognizes the continuing rupture of her daughter's long-ago action, this "stealing" of her son, when she calls the very threat of his return "Electra's doing" (296). She later accuses Electra of raising her executioner (603–4), casting Electra as a kind of pseudo-mother to the entire revenge plot.

As her actions with the infant Orestes suggest, Electra attempts to replace Clytemnestra as Orestes' mother throughout the play; more fundamentally, Electra also vies to negate the maternal bond itself, depriving Clytemnestra's status as mother of any discursive significance. When Clytemnestra defends the killing of Agamemnon to Electra, she alludes to her rights as mother but focuses her main energy on outlining Agamemnon's failures as a father (516–51).[15] Electra, however, vigorously defends her father and turns the attack back toward Clytemnestra and her relationship with Aegisthus, expressing disgust that Clytemnestra is literally "making children" (παιδοποιεῖς) with the usurper, while casting her legitimate ones aside (585–90).

Many passages in the play suggest similar ambivalence about the procreative impulses of women in the play. In quite violent imagery, the Chorus describes Agamemnon's murder itself as the "birthing of a monstrous shape" (198–99). The Chorus likewise calls attention to Electra's dangerously misplaced maternal desires, admonishing her at one point "not to give birth to further troubles" (235) with her grieving. Later, they accuse her of "giving birth to wars" (218–19). For both women, then, the prospect of maternity seems bound up with the capacity for violence and destruction. It is little wonder that, professing love for her children despite their hatred of her, Clytemnestra calls giving birth a "terrible" or "strange" thing (δεινὸν τὸ τίκτειν ἐστίν, 770).

Although she herself is caught up within the speculations about violence and illegitimacy that attend mothering in the play, Electra, despite her desires to mother Orestes, nonetheless seeks to destabilize the meanings of maternity when she tries to mitigate the pollution of the impending matricide. In effect, by denying her mother's maternity, Electra undertakes the death of her mother in language before the children commit the deed itself. Calling it the "ultimate outrage" that Aegisthus sleeps in her father's bed alongside her mother, for example, Electra wonders openly whether "mother" is indeed the word to use of Clytemnestra (272–74).[16] Toward the end of the play, Electra more explicitly negates the status of Clytemnestra as mother, calling her in one devastating turn of phrase an "unmotherly mother" (μήτηρ ἀμήτωρ; 1154), and, still later, professes she is called a mother but is nothing like one (1194).

Part of this stratagem for displacing Clytemnestra's maternity entails Electra's persistent attempt to frame her relationship with her mother as one of political hierarchy rather than blood tie, of ruler and subject rather than mother and daughter. Electra thus seeks to present herself as politically marginalized in regard to the city and its female ruler rather than displaced from bonds of kinship, asserting early in the play that she exists in a state of political servitude to her father's murderers (264). Noting this linguistic shift, Clytemnestra later accuses Electra of complaining to everyone that she boldly and unjustly rules her daughter (520-22). Persistently calling attention to her marginal status in the city, Electra refuses, as Chrysothemis begs her, to yield to those in power (396). In perhaps the most direct attack on her mother, Electra proclaims that she considers Clytemnestra more a tyrant, a δεσπότης, than a mother (597–98). As Molly Ierulli argues, then, "the tension between mother and daughter owes some of its intensity to its similarity to, and questioning of, the tension between the ruler and the subject" (1993, 220). Electra is not the only one to observe the political aura of Clytemnestra; seeing Clytemnestra, Orestes' slave derisively remarks that she has the look of a tyrant, τύραννος (664).

Electra's strained attempt to recast her mother as ruler and herself as political subject rather than daughter is never quite absolute, however, for when Clytemnestra recognizes the capacity for rebellion in her subject-daughter, she pointedly attributes the threat to their dangerous intimacy. Recounting Orestes' persistent vows to kill her, Clytemnestra remarks that it was Electra's unremitting proximity in the house (ξύνοικος) that made her the greater danger, accusing her daughter of drinking out her very life's blood (785–86).[17] Using a term explicitly related to the household, Clytemnestra's placement of her conflict with Electra within the bounds and bindings of the *oikos* underlines the precarious nature of women's power within the city, as well as the confusing boundaries between city and household that trail the house of Atreus and its violent acts.

Even more, Clytemnestra's own claims to political authority stand in stark contrast to the imagery of a dream that haunts her. As reported by Chrysothemis, Clytemnestra's dream depicts Agamemnon's return from the dead and his planting of the royal scepter, taken back from

Aegisthus, into the hearth, from which emerges a branch that shades all of Mycenae (417–23). Placing Agamemnon at its center, the message of the dream seems clear—that the restoration of family and kingdom entails Agamemnon assuming the dominant procreative role (putting the scepter in the hearth), with Aegisthus acting as his primary antagonist. Foretelling a complete circumvention (or passivity) of motherhood, the dream, in short, anticipates a political succession ordained solely by the father (Bowman 1997, 141–43; Ormand 1999, 70–72).[18] In this way, the symbolic structures at work in the dream suggest that power and succession in the city are irrevocably aligned with the masculine, even though the city in the present seems to offer the illusion of female action and power. Notably, in response to the dream, the nervous Clytemnestra sends Chrysothemis to place offerings on Agamemnon's grave, while she herself prays to Apollo for assistance—that is, she turns to the tomb of her mortal husband (however unlikely his sympathy given her role in his murder) and the masculine god Apollo in trying to maintain her control over both "the house of Atreus and the scepter" (651).

Despite attempts to distance herself from her mother, Electra has her own political yearnings and they, too, take shape in the absence of men. Acted in public, outside the house, Electra's mourning serves in part as an act of political resistance, inviting the city to remember the familial violation that displaced their king, while drawing attention to her own disruptive role in the ensuing political struggle. That Clytemnestra and Aegisthus, in turn, recognize the danger of such expression is clear from Chrysothemis' warning that if her sister does not cease her mourning, the two are planning to imprison her in a dungeon outside the country's borders (378–84).

When she hears of Orestes' alleged death, Electra seizes on the additional loss to imagine for herself not a place at the margins but an emphatic entry into the city and its symbolic power structures, casting herself and her sister in the glorious role of tyrannicides.[19] In her blissful articulation of this fantasy, Electra's passions and ambitions intersect fully, the one form of abandonment (by male kin) yielding to self-expression and fulfillment through the other (action and excess). Significantly, Chryosthemis identifies her sister's *orgê* as the precise source of such a sweeping vision, begging her sister to check such passion before it destroys them (1009–11). But Electra's moment of supreme ecstasy cruelly turns out also to be the beginning of her own displacement, as the radical nature of her fantasy, like Clytemnestra's dream, paradoxically contains within itself the seeds of its own dissolution and, ultimately, the foundations for the reemergence of male political authority.

When Electra first describes her plan of vengeance to Chyrsothemis, she paints a splendid picture of what they could accomplish. This is surely the moment when Sophocles permits his heroine to claim for herself the possibility of a future containing much more than "undramatic married banality." Electra enthuses,

> Then don't you see what a glorious reputation you will
> certainly win for yourself and for me, by listening to what
> I say? Who when he sees us, citizen and foreigner alike,
> will not hail us with words of praise: "Look, my friends,
> at these two sisters, who saved their father's house;
> who took no thought for their own lives, but came forward
> to kill enemies who then were firmly established. Everyone
> should love them both, everyone should revere them,
> and at festivals and city gatherings everyone should
> honour their courage." Everybody will certainly
> say such things about us, so that in life and death
> our fame will never die.
> (973–85, trans. J. March)

The very formulation of Electra's fantasy reveals her awareness of the public nature of the murderous act and her efforts to establish its intrinsic meanings for the *polis*. Not only does she evoke terms related to public honor, like good reputation (973), but she also quotes the delighted reaction of public onlookers, including both citizens and foreigners. These putative observers demand not only love but also worship of the sisters, as well as public festivals for the whole city in their honor (982). In eliminating any reference to the private nature of the act, Electra completes her logic of casting Clytemnestra in solely political terms by portraying the revenge solely as an act of tyrannicide,[20] while the potential consequences of matricide remain unspoken. With a daughter's dream of undertaking political assassination alongside her sister on behalf of their father, we are a long way, at least momentarily, from the intentions of Aeschylus' Electra or even Sophocles' own Antigone.[21]

Still, the precise terms of the praise Electra envisions jar with the city and its customary association of such honors with the male citizen body. After all, the word "courage" itself (*andreia*), with which the sisters, according to Electra, will be credited, reveals deeply gendered connotations in its linguistic connection to "man" (ἀνήρ).[22] So, too, Electra's expansive claim that the deed will bring them "undying glory" evokes a hallmark of the fifth-century Greek aristocratic male ideal. The glorious image of sister-avengers is further punctured by Chrysothemis (992ff.), who refuses to help and, like Ismene in *Antigone*, seeks to persuade her sister that it is precisely because they are women that they are not as strong as their enemies (997–98). Having heard the sisters' argument, the Chorus itself does not directly repudiate the deed Electra proposes; in fact, they initially praise her subsequent resolve to act alone (Burnett 1998, 125–26).[23] In affirming her desire, however, they attempt to alter drastically the terms of such fantasy. For one, they disregard the union of sisters proposed by Electra's vision, an alliance that not only stands in contrast to her own earlier adamant identifications with her male kin but also to the standard pairings across sexual difference generally demanded by the myth, beginning with the erotic union of Clytemnestra and Aegisthus and continuing in the sister-brother team of avengers.[24] Adhering to the necessity of sexual difference, then, the Chorus subtly undermines Electra's proposed pairing of like to like by professing that Electra seems willing to die, if only she can first "kill the double Fury" of Aegisthus and Clytemnestra (1080).[25] Such a rich phrase serves to inscribe the lovers as the prospective victims of her plot; it also, by evoking the stain of matricide in the image of the Furies, skillfully seeks to bind Electra once again within the roles and obligations of the *oikos* rather than *polis*. Indeed, just as they recognize the imperative of sexual difference, the Chorus will continue to insist on the conceptual significance of the *oikos*, and thus the crisis of matricide, until the very end.[26]

In response to Electra's attempts to claim her position as a political subject, even tyrant killer, the Chorus thus strains overall to hold Electra within other conceptual and gendered frameworks. Such contrasting visions get to the heart of how female power in the house of Atreus should (or can) be conceptualized and expressed in the wake of the father's death and whether, for example, Electra's *orgê* can serve as a site of political resistance and as fuel for political fantasy. Yet such deliberation is cut short, for having opened this possibility of Electra's dramatic political action, Sophocles soon abolishes her fantasy by returning Orestes to the plot, an act that requires that the siblings confront one another face-to-face for the first time. It is the moment that Electra has dreamt about for years, yet their recognition ultimately pivots around Orestes' desire for domination and his concomitant fear of pleasure, two drives to which Electra, although initially resistant, eventually capitulates.

IF IT MAKES YOU HAPPY

When Orestes returns to the stage, still concealing his identity, he claims to be seeking Aegisthus (1007, 1101), an announcement that renews his own attempt to define both the city's power structures and the upcoming conflict exclusively in masculine terms. In doing so, Orestes likewise resumes his almost willful blindness to the impending matricide. Orestes' persistent refusal to engage emotionally with his mother or with the upcoming violence might not be so noteworthy if we were not told twice that, while in exile, Orestes had frequently expressed open hatred for Clytemnestra, as well as a desire to kill her. Hearing of his death, Clytemnestra, for example, notes that although she never saw Orestes again, he accused her of killing his father and "threatened to do terrible things" (779–80). Electra says even more explicitly that Orestes used to send her secret messages about their mother, pledging to return as an avenger against her (1154–56).[27]

There is little evidence of such passion in the young man when he actually returns home, and the language of emotion, especially pleasure, increasingly suggests danger and corruption in the play. Clytemnestra, for example, is shown laughing inappropriately as she "celebrates" the anniversary of her husband's death (277). Once Orestes has revealed his identity to his sister, he later professes that they will soon put an end to their "enemies' laughing" (1295). Electra earlier addresses her brother's pseudofunerary urn and similarly underlines her desolation by noting that their enemies are now laughing at them and that Clytemnestra herself is "mad with pleasure" at her son's supposed death (μαίνεται δ' ὑφ' ἡδονῆς; 1153).[28] Electra's use of the term *hedonê* is critical here, as is her equation of mother's pleasure with deviation; first associated with her mother as a subversive emotion that requires repression and punishment, *hedonê* will evoke a similar response from Orestes when Electra, too, ultimately becomes defined by it.

When Orestes finally reveals his true identity to his sister, Electra at first refuses such a revelation; instead, she desperately clings to the notion of her brother's death and his ostensible abandonment of her as symbolized by the urn, an item she calls her most intimate possession (1208).[29] In fact, Electra only recognizes Orestes as her brother when he shows her their father's ring, "a stage symbol of paternal authority" (Dunn 1998, 441). The language of her recognition highlights the importance of pleasure, a theme already attached to his return in an earlier exchange between Electra and Chrysothemis. In that scene the language of pleasure (ἡδονή) abounds, as Chrysothemis joyfully rushes onstage to tell her sister that she has seen locks of hair on their father's grave, locks that can only have come from their brother. When Electra obstinately denies that Orestes could be alive, Chrysothemis, astonished, wonders that her words have not given her sister pleasure (921). Still Electra does not relent; pointedly refusing her sister's offer of pleasure and a living Orestes, she turns instead to the fantasy made possible only by his absence.

When she later accepts the reunion with Orestes at his insistence, Electra thus receives the pleasure offered by a brother where she had refused it previously from her sister. At this point, Electra gives in completely to the joy such recognition offers. In fact, Orestes soon worries that she is "too won over by pleasure" (τὰ δὲ δέδοικα λίαν ἡδονῇ νικωμένην, 1271–72). Pointedly naming her new emotion "pleasure" (ἡδονή), Orestes conspicuously marks the shift of Electra's emotional excess from "anger" to something far different, nor is such realignment inconsequential. As we have already seen, going "mad with pleasure" is the precise (and disturbing) reaction credited to Clytemnestra when she hears of Orestes' death. So, too, as pleasure and its suppression become increasingly implicated in Orestes' own rise to power, this change irreversibly situates Electra as an object capable of causing Orestes discomfort and so demanding his control.

While Electra had at first resisted the recognition of her brother and its consequences, she now proclaims her own eagerness to enter this new system. Begging that Orestes not stop her, that he not deprive her of the pleasure in seeing his face (1278), Electra even advances an astonishing claim that she, when hearing of his death, purposely silenced her own anger, her *orgê*—that is, that she literally held her passion "voiceless" (ὀργὰν ἄναυδον; 1283).[30] While this statement initially seems little more than specious (after all, Electra was anything but quiet when hearing of Orestes' ostensible death), it dramatically documents Electra's own collaboration with the play's shifting logic by eagerly curbing, and thus silencing, the very passion (*orgê*) she earlier recognized as so central to her purpose, while embracing the emergent (and clearly dubious) language of pleasure instead. Electra then makes her submission to her brother complete by proclaiming him both the arbiter of her pleasure (noting that what pleases him pleases her) and its true owner (since he is the one who has bestowed it upon her) (1302-03). In essence, having repudiated her anger, Electra now willingly gives up all claims to emotional possession, and so relinquishes the expressive mode by which she previously and so adamantly defined herself.

The consequences of Electra's capitulation—including her own fervent suppression and surrender of her *orgê*—are immediately apparent. For one, she suddenly seems to lose grip on the idea of her dead father, her primary source of identification at the play's outset, asserting that she would now even be able to believe it if she saw her father come back to life (1316–17).[31] The clearest indication of Electra's change in status occurs when she orders Orestes to assume mastery over her and reminds him (and the audience) where she would have been without him: "Rule me now, as you wish; for I, on my own, would have had one of two results; either I would have saved myself gloriously or I would have destroyed myself gloriously" (1319–21). With such a formulation, Electra confirms her permanent status as humble subject (emphatically granting Orestes the type of control she found so reprehensible when exercised over her by Clytemnestra and Aegistheus), her own dreams of tyrannicide and public acclaim long dissipated. Even more, Electra's own speech highlights her repudiation of any possibility of self-expression through what we might call the dramatic or heroic, as she explicitly associates καλῶς with both options now denied. Indeed, in calling attention to the glorious, if violent, outcomes that have been made obsolete by her submission to Orestes' rule, Electra seems for the last time to admit what might have been possible before her final loss of abandonment and simultaneous embrace of obedience and "banality."[32] Later Electra acknowledges Orestes' new prominence in the city and her own departure from its margins, declaring firmly that she at last has been wise enough to side with those in power (1464–65).

Following this critical negotiation of power between the siblings, Orestes takes charge of the murder plot. Having been ordered by the old slave to go inside and kill Clytemnestra, the siblings enter together (along with silent character Pylades, Orestes' friend and Electra's future husband), but Electra returns almost immediately to assure the Chorus that "the men inside are completing the act" (1398–99)—that is, that the revenge is now an entirely masculine project.[33] Female action has thus been converted to inaction, and Electra's own distance from the deed is further underlined when she begs Orestes to strike Clytemnestra a second time, as if for her (1416). The Chorus' reaction to Clytemnestra's killing, in which they connect public and private, signals the ways in which the deed remains, in their eyes, a particular concern for both the city and the family, crying out "o city, o unhappy child" (1413), but the children themselves seem eerily unmoved. Only the Chorus and Clytemnestra herself interpret the murder in broader terms, with the former framing it as a rightful exchange of blood for blood (1417–23).[34] When

Clytemnestra begs her son to pity "the one who bore him" (1410–11), she, too, points in vain to the prohibition of matricide (Segal 1981, 261), albeit in a transparently self-serving manner. Orestes, on the other hand, silent throughout the murder, emerges simply to tell Electra that her mother will no longer dishonor her (1426–27).[35]

Given Orestes' relentless suppression of his own emotions within the course of the play, it follows that his final bid for control in his father's city remains premised on his ability to both limit and deny the emotions of others as well. The expression of pleasure in particular seems to cause the young man great anxiety and to demand his singular control. When Electra begs that he not silence her pleasure, for example, Orestes remarks suggestively that he would be angry if he saw anyone else doing it (1279).[36] Such hostility and fear become played out even more explicitly in Orestes' final encounter with Aegisthus, who is associated with pleasure from the very moment of his return from the "outskirts of the city," "rejoicing," as Electra describes it (1432).

Language of pleasure reverberates throughout this final scene. Believing that there is visible evidence of Orestes' death inside the house (1455), Aegisthus declares that Electra's words bring him more pleasure than usual (1456), to which she ominously retorts that he should rejoice, if it makes him happy (1457). Orestes then reemerges from the house and reveals Clytemnestra's dead body to her lover. Now fully aware of the death that awaits him, Aegisthus dares the young man to kill him outside, in public view, taunting him that an honorable act should not require concealment (1493–94). In what Michael Ewans calls Orestes' "complacent little lecture on the desirability of summary execution" (2000, 124), however, Orestes hotly proclaims that Aegisthus will not die "according to his pleasure" (καθ' ἡδονὴν, 1503), but assures that his death will be "bitter," as is right for anyone who acts against the law (1505–7).[37] Orestes then leads Aegisthus inside, demonstrating that just as he has taken possession of Electra's pleasure, he will assume similar mastery over Aegisthus. It is this loaded reference to the denial of Aegisthus' pleasure rather than revenge for his father that finally clinches Orestes' ascent to the throne.

SO HAPPY TOGETHER?

Electra remains onstage after the men have gone inside, but she no longer speaks. Her final words point to the depth of her transformation in the play, for in urging Orestes to kill Aegisthus, Electra proclaimed that only then would she get a release from her sufferings (1489–90). With the word "release" (λυτήριον) now reinterpreted by the young woman as a lack of feeling, and thus drained of any connotations of her previous ritual self-expression and *orgê*, the young princess then becomes silent for good. The play itself is left to conclude only with the Chorus' quiet assurance to the silent Electra, whom they call the "seed of Atreus," that she has indeed achieved a kind of freedom from her suffering, but they dare not admit its exorbitant cost. After all, what could Orestes' new regime possibly promise such a loyal subject?

I began this chapter by suggesting, in agreement with O'Neill, that Electra "peters out into undramatic married banality" by the end of Sophocles' play, as she does in many ancient versions of the myth; some critics have even called her final condition madness.[38] One way to address Electra's ultimate embrace of "banality," however, is to suggest that if she is indeed diminished in the course of the play, the whole world around her also follows suit—that is, the entire tragedy itself becomes submerged in the banal, reduced to a world where matricide is meaningless and the prevailing masculine hero does little more than advocate capital punishment as a deterrent to crime.[39] In this view, we might perceive Electra, who proposes a kind of public glory in both victory and defeat, not as marginalized by her femininity, but rather representative of an entire aristocratic political order in decline, a tragic position akin to what Peter Rose has argued for Ajax in another play by Sophocles (1995, 69ff.).[40] We might thus argue that Sophocles seeks in this play not to affirm the kind of patriarchal order that emerges in Aeschylus' earlier trilogy, but instead to call attention to its fundamental emptiness.

My own route to Electra, however, began not with O'Neill's provocative writings, but rather long before when reading an essay by Virginia Woolf, who movingly used the young princess and her mournful speech as the paradigmatic example of what Woolf considered the enduring resonance of the Greeks. Noting Electra's own complicity in the emotional suppressions within the play, Woolf highlights both Electra's mystifying status in the play and her continuing resonance, writing, "As she silences her own complaint, [Electra] perplexes us again with the insoluble question of poetry and its nature, and why, as she speaks thus, her words put on the assurance of immortality" (1966, 124). More recently, I was struck by Edith Hall's study of the history of *Electra*'s staging in Britain, for although Hall shows that the play itself was adapted to promote a variety of political positions beginning in the seventeenth century in England, she asserts, "It was only as women began to study the play in earnest that the character of Electra and her conflicts with her mother and sister began to strike chords of recognition" (1999, 288).[41]

What, then, might be the traces of Electra as recuperated by such a genealogy of women's or, as I prefer, feminist readings and productions? What, to borrow Woolf's phrasing, might Electra reveal as insoluble, not only about poetry and its nature, but also about sexual difference and civic life? Such questions seem critical to me, in no small part, because Electra has so often been obscured by figures like Antigone when charting Greek tragedy's convoluted treatment of sexual difference and the workings of the Greek city. Hall suggests, "Female authors have been attracted to the emotional (rather than the political) potential" of the *Electra* (290), but that proposition seems to me to evade the very central claim of Sophocles' play, namely that the emotional is intrinsic to political foundation and order, whether prefaced on its tortured expressions from the margins (as Electra) or on the repressions that lead to power and control (as Orestes).

Moreover, unlike Antigone, Electra remains alive at the end, mutely haunting the city and its means of establishing order. But we are also left to confront the grounds for Electra's submission to her own containment, to her brother's authority as king—her simultaneous mothering of Orestes and unmothering of Clytemnestra and her abandonment of a fantasy of tyrannicide, a possibility she deems glorious even in defeat. Finally, I have not had time to consider here what Electra's willingness to relinquish her abandonment means when set against the drives of her mother, who not only killed a king but also retained her *orgê* and *hedonê*, however threatening and uncanny, until the very end.[42]

NOTES

1. Floyd (1981, 185–209) presents a lengthy account of O'Neill's work on his trilogy. Nugent, however, challenges Electra's "gains" in O'Neill's reworking, arguing, "Despite O'Neill's explicit *claim* to investigate the Electra figure, in practice he has rigorously repressed feminine sexuality, initiation, and satisfaction" (1993, 259). I am grateful to Nugent for calling my attention to O'Neill's own suggestive writings about the myth.
2. Ormand concludes, "By championing the endogamous view of the *oikos*...[Electra] has enabled Orestes' return and, on some level, the return of order to the house. She fails to realize (within the

bounds of the play) that once so enabled, Orestes will coopt both house and drama from her...The paradox of the woman's role in the (re)generation of that *oikos* becomes Electra's tragedy, just as it was her mother's nightmare" (1999, 78).

3. The relative dates of Sophocles' and Euripides' *Electra*s have long been a topic of some scholarly controversy, although Harder suggests, "most scholars are now more or less agreed that, for metrical reasons Euripides' play must be dated between 421 and 418 and Sophocles' play somewhat later, perhaps around 410" (1995, 15). See also Ormand n. 2 in this volume for discussion of the relative dating of the two plays; Ormand wisely refuses to take a stand on the issue.

4. The primacy of father and brother to Electra's position is due in large part to her status as an unmarried woman when the play opens. In fact, the very name Electra seems to derive from the term *alektros*, meaning, "without a bed" (see the discussion of Kamerbeek's views in Ormand 1999, 62–63 and 178 n.8). Ormand argues, moreover, that Sophocles disturbingly presents Electra as symbolically married to her dead father in a number of passages (1999, 65).

5. Jean-Paul Sartre utilizes this same opening in his stage adaptation of the myth, *Les Mouches*, a work based primarily on Sophocles' version. Sartre places even greater emphasis on Orestes' initial hollowness as he returns from exile, but the young man eventually becomes a paradigm of the existentialist hero, accepting fully the burdens of his past and freedom.

6. Segal argues, for example, that "(t)he lie about the Delphic festival at the exact center of the play is a paradigm for the corrupted ritual and civic order" (1981, 282). The Orestes in flesh offered by the play also pales next to the Orestes of the elaborate *dolos*, who earns a glorious demise. Segal discusses some of the symbolism involved in the story, recounted at great length later in the play (267–68, 281–83).

7. Kitzinger writes of "Elektra's ability to articulate the need for the integrity of words, deed, and feeling" (1991, 308), an integrity that clashes with Orestes' initial recourse to lies and deception. Kitzinger takes the use of language as key to tracing the changing role of both characters, arguing that, by the end of the play, speech itself (especially that of Electra's) has become so devalued that the final murders are achieved without *logos*—that is, "without a linguistic system of value and comprehension" (301). While Kitzinger's analysis has been invaluable to me, I want to interpret their

respective emotional states rather than connection to language as a manifestation of the broader impulses that construct the siblings' relationship. On the importance of language, see also Segal (1981, 283–87).

8. Seaford, focusing on the rituals attached to Greek mourning, notes that Electra's refusal to cease her mourning makes her reintegration into the world of the living impossible, just as it prevents Agamemnon's full incorporation into the world of the dead (1985, 316). Clytemnestra similarly perpetuates the suspended status of her daughter and dead husband when she initiates monthly festivals on the anniversary of Agamemnon's death (317). In this way, Seaford argues, "the ritual of mourning has been perverted by both sides into a weapon in a conflict within the kinship group, a conflict which is uncontained by any temporal, moral, or ritual limit, and which is intensified by the perversion of the natural relationship between mother and daughter" (1985, 320).

9. Stanford reviews the meanings of the term in writers like Aristotle, noting that it has a cognate with a Greek verb for "swelling" (1983, 30–33). Konstan discusses the meaning of the term *orgê* in Aristotle's *Rhetoric* (2005, 23).

10. In Sophocles alone, the term *orgê* is attributed to, or claimed by, characters like Antigone, Ajax, Jocasta, and Oedipus.

11. Electra, at one point, marks such similarity openly, noting that if she carries out the behavior Clytemnestra accuses her of, she "does not dishonor her mother's nature by much" (609). See also Segal (1981, 261–62) for their many similarities.

12. For lengthier analysis of Electra and Clytemnestra's *agôn*, which she calls "the moral center of the play," see Kitzinger (1991, 312–17). In particular, Kitzinger helpfully unravels Electra's puzzling reference to the law that those who kill must be killed in turn (lines 582–83), a stance that seems on the surface to predict her own downfall, as well as Orestes', if they complete the revenge. Electra's overall logic revolves around her primary loyalty to Agamemnon's household, even though she adamantly refuses to contemplate her father's violation of it in regard to her own sister. Thus, Electra denounces the crisis Clytemnestra invites by aligning herself sexually with forces outside the house (i.e., a form of exogamy), while she herself strives to embody the virtues of internal marriage and endogamy, albeit not without serious strain (Ormand 1999, 66–67 and 69). Contrary to general practice, then, it is not the daughters of the house of Atreus who threaten to weaken the household by

marrying outside, but the wife who has herself been brought in by marriage. See also Burnett (1998, 137–38) and Segal (1981, 251).

13. Sommerstein points out that even as Electra longs for Orestes' return, she does not necessarily conceive of him as undertaking the act of vengeance (1997, 199–200). At one point, she notes bitterly that although Orestes professes a desire to come, he "does not think it worth appearing" (172).

14. Electra's removal of the baby Orestes from the royal house can be compared to the actions of Jocasta and the slave in saving the baby Oedipus. See Buchan in this volume for discussion of the many consequences of that latter event in Sophocles' *Oedipus Tyrannus*. Sommerstein outlines the play's often ambiguous treatment of who bears primary responsibility for Agamemnon's murder, concluding that it initially places greater emphasis on Clytemnestra (1997, 200–203).

15. When Clytemnestra labors to devalue the status of Agamemnon as father, she reminds Electra that Agamemnon murdered his own daughter, Iphigenia; Clytemnestra further declares that Agamemnon's role in "sowing" (533) holds nothing like the pain of actually giving birth (533).

16. A few lines earlier, she describes her relationship with her mother, the woman who bore her, as "all hatred" (261–62).

17. Despite my emphasis on its potential political resonance, such an image also casts Electra herself as a kind of Fury—that is, in terms of a more primeval and familial revenge (Winnington-Ingram 1983, 216). Burnett notes Sophocles' linguistic linking of Electra with the Furies through the play's punning use of "*alektra*" at lines 489–94 (1998, 140–41; see also Ierulli 1993, 227).

18. Bowman links Clytemnestra's dream to Apollo's oracles, arguing both collaborate in establishing the patriarchal political order demanded by the play (1997, 131).

19. Kitzinger considers the lie about Orestes' death, the *dolos*, the major turning point in the play, writing that it "changes everything, not as a direct cause but mysteriously and pervasively" (1991, 322). Its effect on Electra, according to Kitzinger, is irreversible, for after hearing that Orestes is dead, Electra, previously truthful to the extreme, becomes submerged in the pattern of lies that surrounds her (301). On the significance of Orestes' *dolos*, see also MacLeod (2005). Ormand links the change in Electra following the announcement of Orestes' death to her presumed new status as an *epikleros*, a very specific figure in Greek law often translated

loosely as "heiress" (1999, 73). Her elevation to this status, Ormand continues, disrupts Electra's view of the world, given that "(s)he has spent the play arguing that the bloodline is paternal, and passes through the male line," yet is now "caught in the recognition that it can pass through the female" (74).

20. Emphasizing the political stakes of Electra's fantasy, Juffras argues that it intentionally evokes the contemporary Athenian cult of the Tyrannicides (1991, 99). She goes even further in suggesting that the fantasy imparts a vision of "a public statue commemorating Electra and Chrysothemis, on a parallel with the paired statues of Harmodius and Aristogeiton that stood in the Agora from the fifth century on" (103). In short, "(w)hat Electra imagines is not a reception fitting for men or for women *per se*, but more specifically, the appropriate response to tyrant slaying" (103). For another interpretation of the fantasy, see Burnett (1998, 124–26).

21. Although, Lane and Lane (1986) propose a more expansive "politics" in Antigone's words and deeds than is generally recognized, noting, for example, the ways in which she claims to represent the views of the city's residents and not just the obligations to her family.

22. Bassi notes that this is the only occurrence of the term *andreia* in Sophocles (2003, 41), and that by applying the term to a woman's putative deed, it "points to the absence of masculinity in its traditional or normative form and the emergence of a manliness that is no longer *aner* specific" (42). My own reading of it suggests instead that the term references an emergent masculine symbolic apparatus in the play that Electra herself fails to recognize.

23. Ierulli traces the broader relationship between Electra and the Chorus in the play, arguing that over time "the chorus is converted to Electra's view of the righteousness and necessity of what she does" (1993, 219, also 221–25)—that is, by the end "Electra has persuaded the chorus that her praxis of lament and memory, seen by them as excessive at first, is right and natural" (229). In doing so, Ierulli disputes the presumption by many scholars that Sophocles' use of a female Chorus waters down the play's political dimensions, calling attention to Electra's striking address of them as *politides* near the end of the play (1993, 219). See also Ormand in this volume for a discussion of Electra's address and the particular significance of the word in this context.

24. This pattern has encouraged many writers to hint at incestuous undertones in Electra and Orestes' bond.

25. Juffras discusses the use of dual forms throughout the speech to refer to the sisters (1991, 101). References to the myth's reliance on duality or "twoness" recur throughout Sophocles' play. Clytemnestra's dream brings Agamemnon to his wife for a "second coupling," for example, and Electra ultimately demands that her brother strike Clytemnestra a second time (1416). My interest in this idea here was greatly influenced by Zeitlin's demonstration of the importance of numbers (and their confusion) in Oedipus' myth, what she calls the "arithmetic of self" (1986, 111ff.)

26. Against this *oikos*-centered view of the Chorus, Burnett makes the critical observation that when Orestes and Pylades finally undertake the murder without Electra, they act as "a fraternal instead of a copulating pair" (1998, 134), insinuating that, unlike the pairing of female like-to-like posed by Electra's fantasy, a pairing deemed impossible by both Chrysothemis and the Chorus, the fraternal bond is capable of trumping other types of union in Orestes' burgeoning political order.

27. I am indebted to Sommerstein for drawing my attention to these passages (1997, 206).

28. Similarly, when the slave returns from the house, Orestes pointedly does not ask how his mother received the news of his ostensible death, but instead only whether "they" were pleased inside (1343–44).

29. Not surprisingly, many scholars have offered extensive readings of the urn's symbolic function. See, for example, Segal (1981, 278–80, 287–89), who argues that "the urn symbolizes the ambiguity of language, its power to distort and manipulate" (282). Burnett, on the other hand, proposes that it serves both as a substitute for the baby Orestes and thus as a kind of womb (1998, 128–29). Burnett (131) and Segal (1981, 288) both make the important observation that Clytemnestra is touching the urn as she is killed. Although the urn is only visible in this later scene, Dunn (1998, 438) reexamines the dense language of Orestes' initial description of it in the opening scene (54–55) in order "to cast new light" on its many subsequent meanings in the play. Ringer makes the urn and its meanings central to his reading of the play's structure (1998, 185–212).

30. The suppression of speech plays a significant role in marking the transfer of power throughout the play. For example, in a dense exchange following the announcement of Orestes' death, Clytemnestra and Electra tangle over speech and its forced stoppage, with Clytemnestra at one point turning jubilantly to the old slave who

has conveyed the false report and telling him he deserves great reward "for stopping Electra's many-tongued cry" (798; cf. 641). There is an ominous correlation between Iphigenia's voicelessness in death (548) and Electra's own self-silencing.

31. In fact, the category of father has become so destabilized to her that she addresses the old slave himself as "father" (1361).

32. While my reading emphasizes the sinister consequence of Orestes' awakening (i.e., suggesting that it leads to the displacement of Electra), Burnett sees the scene in more positive terms, arguing that the siblings' embrace brings about a necessary synthesis of the play's two main trajectories "of freedom and duty, emotion and reason, clean impulse and dutiful criminality, in a word, of sister and brother" (1998, 131).

33. Sommerstein usefully traces the way the play builds and confuses expectations about who will actually carry out the murders, noting that it is not consistent throughout the tragedies (1997, 198). Electra's entrance into the house (as if she is going to participate) followed by her almost immediate return has therefore invited a range of interpretations, with some focusing on Electra's own outlook (does she still think she is going to take part?) and others on Sophocles' interest in playing with the audience's expectations (Sommerstein 1997, 212–13).

34. Sommerstein argues that the Chorus ultimately approves the deed, although he points out that they, unlike Electra and Orestes, avoid the word "mother" (1997, 207–8).

35. This silencing can also be credited to the delicious irony that, according to the limited number of actors allowed by Greek staging conventions, both Orestes and Clytemnestra would have been played by the same actor.

36. He openly calls for the repression of memory until the right time in lines 1251–52.

37. Segal notes that the terms of Orestes' brief justification suggest an embrace of "the harsh *lex talionis*" (1981, 251), implying that "the avengers run the risk of coming to the same level as the criminals" (252).

38. Burnett calls Electra "a reification of paradox and disorder" (1998, 141), then later adds that she is also "(a)bsurd, monstrous, uncanny, useless, defined by what she is not, and manipulated by divine falsehood" (141). In terms of the "married" portion, if the larger myth holds, Electra stands poised to be given away in marriage to Orestes' friend Pylades, and given that Pylades occupies an entirely

nonspeaking role in Sophocles' play, it would be difficult to find a more convincing personification of the banality that awaits her.

39. Segal writes, "(t)he inversions of life and death and of *logos* and *ergon* in the play...generalize the tragedy from the personal suffering of Electra to the tragedy of a whole city, a whole civilization" (1981, 289). He later adds, "The human figures are left to themselves, but in this highly concentrated and barren world they seem to have little scope for regeneration" (290). Burnett, in contrast argues, "(t)he Sophoclean *Electra* ends in success, a fact distressing to those who think that revenge tragedy must always condemn its own violence" (1998, 138). Readers of the play have therefore been notoriously divided over whether the abrupt ending, what Burnett calls an "unrestful ending" (1998, 132), provides a "positive" or "negative" closure to the entire drama and they often point, in particular, to the surprising absence of the Furies at the play's end.

40. Arguing that Sophocles' play provides harsh criticism of a "new amorality" emerging in Greek society in the late fifth century, one in which expediency displaces moral responsibility, Ewans (2000, 123–24) points out that "(c)apital punishment without trial was regarded as characteristic of anti-democratic tyrannies and oligarchies" (125). Segal also attempts to place the values of the play in the context of the late fifth century (1981, 290–91).

41. The first unadapted staging of Sophocles' play in Britain was performed at Girton in 1883, with Janet Case, who later served as Woolf's Greek tutor, playing the lead role (Hall 1999, 291).

42. For recent reevaluations of Clytemnestra, see especially Komar (2003).

REFERENCES

Bassi, Karen. 2003. The semantics of manliness in ancient Greece. In *Andreia: Studies in manliness and courage in classical antiquity*, ed. R. M. Rosen and I. Sluiter, 25–58. Leiden: Brill.

Bowman, Laurel. 1997. Klytaimnestra's dream: Prophecy in Sophokles' *Elektra*. *Phoenix* 51: 131–51.

Burnett, Anne Pippin. 1998. *Revenge in Attic and later tragedy.* Berkeley: University of California Press.

Dunn, Francis M. 1998. Orestes and the urn (Sophocles, *Electra* 54–55). *Mnemosyne* 51: 438–43.

Ewans, Michael. 2000. Dominance and submission, rhetoric and sincerity: Insights from a production of Sophocles' *Electra*. *Helios* 27: 123–36.

Floyd, Virginia, ed. 1981. *Eugene O'Neill at work: Newly released ideas for plays*. New York: Frederick Ungar.

Hall, Edith. 1999. Sophocles' *Electra* in Britain. In *Sophocles revisited: Essays presented to Sir Hugh Lloyd-Jones*, ed. J. Griffin, 261–306. Oxford: Oxford University Press.

Harder, M. A. 1995. "Right" and "wrong" in the Electra's. *Hermathena* 159: 15–31.

Ierulli, Molly. 1993. A community of women? The protagonist and the chorus in Sophocles' *Electra*. *Metis* 8: 217–29.

Juffras, Diane M. 1991. Sophocles' *Electra* 973–85 and tyrannicide. *Transactions of the American Philological Association* 121: 99–108.

Kamerbeek, J. C., ed. 1974. *The plays of Sophocles, Part V: The Electra*. Leiden: E. J. Brill.

Kitzinger, Rachel. 1991. Why mourning becomes Elektra. *Classical Antiquity* 10: 298–327.

Komar, Kathleen L., ed. 2003. *Reclaiming Klytemnestra: Revenge or reconciliation*. Urbana: University of Illinois Press.

Konstan, David. 2005. Aristotle on the tragic emotions. In *The soul of tragedy: Essays on Athenian drama*, ed. V. Pedrick and S. M. Oberhelman, 13–25. Chicago: University of Chicago Press.

Lane, Warren J., and Ann M. Lane. 1986. The politics of *Antigone*. In *Greek tragedy and political theory*, ed. J. P. Euben, 162–82. Berkeley: University of California Press.

MacLeod, Leona. 2001. *Dolos and Dike in Sophokles' Elektra*. Leiden: Brill.

March, Jenny, ed. 2001. *Sophocles Electra*. Warminster: Aris and Phillips.

Nugent, S. Georgia. 1993. Masking becomes Electra: O'Neill, Freud, and the feminine. Repr. in Clifford Davidson, Rand Johnson, and John H. Stroupe, ed., *Drama and the classical heritage: Comparative and critical essays*, 254–72. New York: AMS Press. (Orig. pub. 1988).

O'Neill, Eugene. 1947. Working notes and extracts from a fragmentary work diary. In *European theories of the drama with a supplement on American drama*, ed. B. H. Clark, 530–36. New York: Crown. (Orig. pub. 1931.)

Ormand, Kirk. 1999. *Exchange and the maiden: Marriage in Sophoclean tragedy*. Austin: University of Texas Press.

Ringer, Mark. 1998. *Electra and the empty urn: Metatheater and role playing in Sophocles*. Chapel Hill: University of North Carolina Press.

Rose, Peter. 1995. Historicizing Sophocles' *Ajax*. In *History, tragedy, theory: Dialogues in Athenian drama*, ed. Barbara Goff, 59–90. Austin: University of Texas Press.

Seaford, Richard. 1985. The destruction of limits in Sophokles' *Elektra*. *Classical Quarterly* 35: 315–23.

Segal, Charles. 1981. *Tragedy and civilization: An interpretation of Sophocles*. Cambridge: Harvard University Press.

Sommerstein, Alan H. 1997. Alternative scenarios in Sophocles' *Electra*. *Prometheus* 23: 193–214.

Stanford, W. B. 1983. *Greek tragedy and the emotions: An introductory study*. London: Routledge and Kegan Paul.

Winnington-Ingram, R. P. 1983. The *Electra* of Sophocles: Prolegomena to an interpretation. In *Oxford readings in Greek tragedy*, ed. E. Segal, 210–16. Oxford: Oxford University Press.

Woolf, Virginia. 1966. On Sophocles' *Electra*. In *Sophocles: A collection of critical essays*, ed. T. Woodward, 122–24. Englewood Cliffs: Prentice-Hall. (Orig. pub. 1925.)

Zeitlin, Froma I. 1986. Thebes: Theater of self and society in Athenian drama. In *Greek tragedy and political theory*, ed. J. P. Euben, 101–41. Berkeley: University of California Press.

10

ELECTRA IN EXILE

KIRK ORMAND

INTRODUCTION: CITIZEN WOMEN?

In Sophocles' *Electra*, a quickening of dialogue marks Electra's recognition of her brother Orestes. Having alternated lines of dialogue for some forty-five lines, at line 1220 brother and sister begin to speak to each other in half-line bursts: Electra expresses her disbelief at Orestes' arrival, and Orestes, each time, assures her that he is alive and standing before her. Finally convinced, Electra turns and addresses the Chorus (1227–29):

ὦ φίλταται γυναῖκες, ὦ πολίτιδες,
ὁρᾶτ' Ὀρέστην τόνδε, μηχαναῖσι μὲν
θανόντα, νῦν δὲ μηχαναῖς σεσωμένον.

[Beloved women, citizen women,
you see Orestes here, dead by a trick,
and now saved by a trick.][1]

The scene is fraught with pent-up emotion. Electra, who until now had been cruelly led to believe that Orestes was dead, recognizes her brother with an immediate public proclamation of his presence. She seems to need the women of the Chorus as witnesses to verify what she has not previously dared believe.

The passage is important for another reason as well. It is generally taken to be the earliest known use of the specifically female form of the common word for citizen, *politês*—that is, *politis* (Patterson 1987, 55).[2] Electra turns to a Chorus of "citizen women" to announce her brother's return; but what does the term "citizen woman" mean in this

247

context? It has long been recognized that women in Classical Athens did not share in full citizenship rights: they could not vote or speak in the Assembly, could not hold political office, typically lived their entire lives under the guardianship of a man (whether father, husband, or brother), could not speak or be referred to by name in the Athenian courts, and were restricted in the size of economic transactions that they could make on their own behalf.[3] Even further, the question has been raised whether women were thought of *as citizens* at all. As Nicole Loraux argues, Athenian citizenship depends ultimately on a fantasy of male lineage deriving from Erechtheus, a quasi-autochthonous early king of Athens (Loraux 1993, 116–23). Linguistically, women citizens live under a curious ellipsis: there is literally no feminine form for the word "Athenians" in Greek (*Athenaioi*). Even the word *politis* appears quite late in the development of Athenian citizenship.

Cynthia Patterson argued in an important article twenty years ago, however, that though there is no female equivalent for the masculine term *Athenaioi*, citizen women are frequently referred to as *astai* and *Attikai*. These surely are citizens, in the sense that they can be distinguished from women who are not. The linguistic asymmetry, however, is significant. The term *astê* (related to *astu*, which refers to the city in its geographical aspect) denotes citizenship in its communal sense, and is "suggestive of physical relationship to the native land" (Patterson 1987, 56). Athenian women—that is, *astai*—belong to Athens in both a geographic and deeply social sense: they are seen as indigenous, and entrusted with a variety of ritual and familial functions.[4] Moreover, such women are eventually defined as the only women who can legitimately produce more citizens.

In significant ways, *astu* and *polis* describe the same thing. Either can be used to refer simply to the physical place that is the Athenian city. Nor should we imagine that the *astu* is somehow devoid of politics. But when we look at the nouns that denote a person from the *astu* or from the *polis*, (*astos/astê* and *politês/politis*, respectively) the two words function as a pair of marked and unmarked terms. While *astos/astê* can be used to denote citizenship in a geographical, social, or specifically political context, *politês/politis* is a term that nearly always refers to participation in political life.[5] *Astu* and *polis*, then, are not different entities, but the terms express a different relation between person and state, especially for women, whose sense of belonging to the *polis* is, at least initially and perhaps always, indirect.

The terms of Athenian citizenship underwent a significant change in the middle fifth century, and with that change women's participation

in the *polis* specifically became codified. In 451/450, the famous leader
and general Pericles introduced legislation into the Athenian Assembly
that excluded from having "a share in the *polis*" those who were not
"born from two *astoi*" (Aristotle, *Athenaiôn Politeia* 26.4).[6] In effect,
Pericles' law excluded those women who were not *astai* (and, necessarily, all of their sons and daughters) from the closed community of the
Athenian polity. Whatever effect this law had on the Athenian community—and I believe that it must have been devastating, at least for
some households—it also, as Patterson points out, implies a kind of
citizenship for women, in the ability to produce citizen sons.[7] The physical aspect of the word *astê* is still important here: for just as the Athenian soil is imagined to have produced the first Athenian kings, so too
these *astai*, who belong to the Athenian soil, produce all future citizens.
It is in the wake of this shift in the social and political definition of
citizenship that a surprising new word shows up: suddenly, sometime
after 451/450, we see *political* citizen women (*politides*). The coinage
of the word *politis* (plural *politides*), which I have translated "citizen
women," in the passage of Sophocles above, thus marks an important
shift in the status of women in the Athenian *polis*. Specifically, the feminine form presents women as a marked term within the political entity
of Athens, and recognizes certain women as belonging directly to the
civic body—not through their children, and not only to the social and
geographical entity of the city.

Electra's outburst in Sophocles' play, then, is a significant first use:
why *politides*? Why does she not address these young women as simply
"women," or "friends," or commonly enough, as *astai*? I suggest that it
is, in part, because Orestes' return is a political act: he comes not only
to retake his household from Aegisthus and Clytemnestra but also to
reclaim the throne of Mycenae. As we will see in the discussion that
follows, Athenian tragedy often engages in a curious mapping in which
it translates the stories of archaic dynasties into terms more appropriate
to the democracy of fifth-century Athens. So here, Orestes returns as
the legitimate heir in order to rule not just the royal household but also
the city—by implication, peopled by citizens. Since the onstage Chorus
is made up of women, Sophocles uses a word that means, emphatically,
citizen women.

If Orestes has been an exile in Sophocles' play, in Euripides' version
of the same story that exile is doubled: both Orestes and Electra are
in exile throughout the action of the drama, and both are returned to
exile at its close. In the remainder of this chapter, I intend to explore the
gendered qualities of that political exclusion. Euripides, as it turns out,

is quite careful in his use of terminology, and especially of his deployment of terms derived from the *poli-* and *ast-* stems. His play becomes,
in part, a meditation on what it means to exile a woman, a person who
even when occupying the seat of "citizen" has none of the participatory
rights of citizen men. More importantly, in the course of his *Electra*,
Euripides uses the ideological distance between the archaic systems of
social identification that underlie all Greek tragedies on the one hand,
and the contemporary system of "citizenship" on the other, to represent
and intensify Electra's isolation from family, community, and city.

EURIPIDES' *ELECTRA*, OR HOW TO EXILE A WOMAN

From the very first lines of Euripides' play, the characters are displaced.
We find ourselves, surprisingly, neither in nor near the royal house of
Agamemnon that we know Orestes must come home to reclaim. The
plot elements are disturbingly familiar (certainly from Aeschylus and
possibly from Sophocles): Electra lives in a state of degradation while
waiting for her brother to return from exile. Once Orestes does return,
he is reunited with his sister in a stylized recognition scene. Together,
they manage the murder of their mother and stepfather, and then deal—
or, here, fail to deal—with the consequences. But in this version, all of
this critical action takes place not by the walls of Mycenae, but near the
squalid hut in the Argive countryside where Electra lives with her nobly
born but impoverished husband. As a result, crucial elements of the plot
as we know it seem disjointed and out of place: when, for example, the
Messenger speaks of signs left at the tomb of Agamemnon, the tomb is
not onstage (as it probably was in Aeschylus' version) but imagined in
one of many offstage locales referred to some miles away.[8] Euripides has
exiled the myth itself from its proper place.[9]

Within this context, Electra experiences the denigration of social status
that is her lot in all three extant tragic versions of her story as a form of
exile. She even uses the standard word for exile, *phugas*, of herself at line
209 (Zeitlin 1970, 650n23). But her exile is not the same as that of Orestes.
Orestes' arrival at the borderline of Argive territory marks his reentry into
his birthright. For Electra, that borderline is the location of her current
home, and the setting of the play serves as a place of static limbo away
from both city and paternal hearth, away, in fact, from all social identity.
As is citizenship, exile, too, is a gendered experience: for Orestes, it is
both a familial and a political state, mutable within the bounds of political

action. For Electra, as we will see, it is a familial state but not a political one, and more, a personal state divesting her of subjectivity.

In the section that follows, I explore various aspects of Electra's exile in the first part of the play, particularly in relation to the notion of citizenship that one might presume to precede such an experience. To make my point most clearly, let us consider a passage briefly that occurs at the end of the play. At this juncture, Orestes has killed both Aegisthus and Clytemnestra. He and Electra experience what various scholars have seen, acutely enough, as a form of psychic breakdown.[10] But their sense of confusion is bluntly divided on gender lines (1194–200):

> Ορ. ἰὼ Φοῖβ᾽, ἀνύμνησας δίκαι᾽
> ἄφαντα, φανερὰ δ᾽ ἐξέπρα-
> ξας ἄχεα, φόνια δ᾽ ὤπασας
> λάχε᾽ ἀπὸ γᾶς Ἑλλανίδος.
> τίνα δ᾽ ἑτέραν μόλω πόλιν;
> τίς ξένος, τίς εὐσεβὴς
> ἐμὸν κάρα προσόψεται
> ματέρα κτανόντος;
> Ηλ. ἰὼ ἰώ μοι. ποῖ δ᾽ ἐγώ, τίν᾽ ἐς χορόν,
> τίνα γάμον εἶμι; τίς πόσις με δέξεται
> νυμφικὰς ἐς εὐνάς;

[Or: Alas, Phoibos, you hymned obscure justice, but you practiced clear pains. You have bestowed a murderer's lot away from the land of Greece. To what other *polis* will I go? What pious host will look on my face, now that I have killed my mother?

El: Alas, alas for me. Where will I go? To what dance, to what marriage? What husband will receive me into his marriage bed?]

I will return to these lines in greater detail toward the end of my argument. For now, I simply note the shock of the two characters' different responses to their upcoming exile. For Orestes, exile is a question of social relations ("what host?") and also of political ones, in the root meaning of the word: "to what *polis* can I go?" For Electra, exile is to be understood in terms of marriage and dances. Taken out of context (as I have here) the lines are indeed stark. I hope to show, however, that they are consistent with a gendered structure of exile that Euripides builds throughout the play, one in which Electra—whose name in antiquity was etymologized as *a-lektros*, "the unmarried one"[11]—experiences exile as a function of marital status and of religious festival rather than of city and political identity.

Electra's sense of isolation is partly a function of the play's unusual setting in the plains of Argos, at some remove from any city center. But early in the drama, familial relations come to the fore. In all three of the *Electra* plays, the title character deeply resents the way that Clytemnestra has diverted the family inheritance away from Electra and Orestes—Agamemnon's patrilineal heirs—to the family of Aegisthus (Ormand 1999, 68–72). In this play that notion is taken to its logical extreme: Electra suggests that her mother and Aegisthus have had new children who will then be the familial heirs (60–63)[12]:

ἡ γὰρ πανώλης Τυνδαρίς, μήτηρ ἐμή,
ἐξέβαλέ μ᾽ οἴκων, χάριτα τιθεμένη πόσει·
τεκοῦσα δ᾽ ἄλλους παῖδας Αἰγίσθῳ πάρα
πάρεργ᾽ Ὀρέστην κἀμὲ ποιεῖται δόμων.

[For the all-destroying daughter of Tyndareus, my mother, threw me out of the house, as a favor to her husband. And having borne other children for Aegisthus, she makes Orestes and me irrelevant (*parerga*) to the house.]

The same verb that will be used shortly to describe the old nurse's separation from the city—"throw out" (*ekballo*; cf. 412)—is here used of Electra's removal from her home (*oikos*). Even more interesting, however, is the phrase in line 63: Electra describes her brother and herself as *parerga domôn*. The phrase is not a common one and, taken literally, means something like "deeds standing beside the house." My translation above ("irrelevant") does not quite capture the physical aspect of Electra's removal, a removal that here is both literal and metaphorical. Because of her marriage to the farmer, she lives on the far borders, away from her father's home; at the same time, she and Orestes are in danger of being left behind by the new marriage and new bloodline that Aegisthus and Clytemnestra have brought into being.

This brief speech is typical of Electra's complaint in this play; when she speaks of her isolation, it is generally not from the city at all, but from home, house, family. Her language, however, reminds us of the political situation: at line 209, toward the end of her lyric complaint, she describes herself as "an exile from her paternal home" (*dômatôn patriôn phugas*; 209), and the word *phugas* is the standard term used of political exiles. Later on, when she is trying to inflict her mother with shame for the way that she has been treated, she goes a step further (1008–10):

Ηλ. τί δ'; αἰχμάλωτόν τοί μ' ἀπῴκισας δόμων,
ἠρημένων δὲ δωμάτων ἠρήμεθα,
ὡς αἵδε, πατρὸς ὀρφαναὶ λελειμμέναι.

[What then? You displaced me, a war prize, from my home, and I have been captured from a captured house. Like these (slaves), I am an orphan, bereft of my father.]

Electra's debasement here operates on multiple social levels: she is kicked out of home, she is made into a war prize and slave, and she has been orphaned. Her isolation, at least as she presents it, is complete. It is worth noting, however, that here, as always, Electra emphasizes home and father; these are the terms through which she understands her social identity and her current state.

Many critics have seen Electra's unceasing complaint in this play as not fully justified at best, and seriously unattractive at worst (Arnott 1981, 182, 186; Michelini 1987, 187n23). As both Michael Lloyd and Froma Zeitlin have pointed out, however, her complaint is appropriate for a person in her state of mourning, and is, moreover, indicative of her complete isolation from society (Lloyd 1986, 2–3,7; Zeitlin 1970, 648–50). It is not simply that she has been removed from the *astu* or from her family: Electra's anomalous marriage in which she has no sexual relations deprives her, as Zeitlin comments, "of her proper social status and of her normal role in the family and community. It has made her virtually an exile" (Zeitlin 1970, 650; cf. Michelini 1987, 192). We see this emphatically when the Chorus of young unmarried women invites Electra to join in a festival of Hera, we presume at the site of the Argive Heraion (171–80):

Χο. ἀγγέλλει δ' ὅτι νῦν τριταί-
αν καρύσσουσιν θυσίαν
'Αργεῖοι, πᾶσαι δὲ παρ' 'Η-
ραν μέλλουσιν παρθενικαὶ στείχειν.
Ηλ. οὐκ ἐπ' ἀγλαΐαις, φίλαι,
θυμὸν οὐδ' ἐπὶ χρυσέοις
ὅρμοις ἐκπεπόταμαι
τάλαιν', οὐδ' ἱστᾶσα χοροὺς
'Αργείαις ἅμα νύμφαις
εἱλικτὸν κρούσω πόδ' ἐμόν.

[Ch. He said that the Argives announce a sacrifice in three
days, and all the *parthenikai* ("maidens") will process to
Hera.
El. Not with fineries, nor with golden necklaces, friends,
does my heart fly, wretched; nor setting up dances with
the Argive brides will I pound my whirling step.]

Few critics have found this a sympathetic moment, especially when, in the
following lines, the Chorus offers to lend Electra the necessary fine clothes
and she rejects their offer. But to read Electra as needlessly wallowing in
self-pity misses the point: the festival at the Heraion is almost certainly a
celebration of the wedding rites between Hera and Zeus (Zeitlin 1970,
661–66), and it is specifically open to *parthenikai*, young unmarried
women. Electra cannot participate as a married woman.

Just a few lines later, however, we see the other side of Electra's
ambiguous social status (310–14). Electra speaks:

ἀνέορτος ἱερῶν καὶ χορῶν τητωμένη
ἀναίνομαι γυναῖκας οὖσα παρθένος,
αἰσχύνομαι δὲ Κάστορ᾽, ὃς πρὶν ἐς θεοὺς
ἐλθεῖν ἔμ᾽ ἐμνήστευεν, οὖσαν ἐγγενῆ.

[Deprived of festivals and sacred dances, I avoid the women
(wives?), since I am a *parthenos*. And I am ashamed of Castor
who, before going to the gods, wooed me, since I am his kin.]

Although married and eligible to claim the status of *gunê*, Electra
cannot do that either, since she has not had sex. As a direct result of this
ambiguity of status, she bars herself from the regular social activities
that should be available to her in the form of dances and festivals. At the
same time, there is a sense of familial disgrace as well: in lines 313–14
we learn that Electra must avoid her kinsman and former suitor, Castor.
Everything piles up into a beautifully overdetermined sense of isolation:
Electra is banned from her father's house, a marriage to Castor, her legal
inheritance, her *astu*, and the religious festivals of the Argives. She quite
literally has no secure social role; and this social, sexual, and religious
indeterminacy is the full expression of her exile.

All of these forms of isolation stem from Electra's unorthodox marriage. It is worth noting, then, that the marriage itself does not conform
to Athenian marriage law. When Orestes questions Electra as to why
she and her husband have not had sexual intercourse—he takes it at

first as an insult—Electra responds that the farmer's reasons are fully honorable (258–59):

Ορ. καὶ πῶς γάμον τοιοῦτον οὐχ ἥσθη λαβών;
Ηλ. οὐ κύριον τὸν δόντα μ' ἡγεῖται, ξένε.

[Or. And how is he not pleased, obtaining such a marriage?
El. He does not think that the one who gave me was my
    guardian (*kurios*).]

These lines point specifically to fifth-century Athenian marriage law in which a woman's legal guardian—in Electra's case, her father or, after his death, her brother Orestes—is empowered to arrange a woman's marriage (Harrison [1968] 1998, 12, 30–32; Demosthenes 46.18).[13] Although her husband is evidently a Mycenaean, and well born (though poor; 248–53), Electra's marriage is not a legal one; that, in part, is why it has never been consummated, and why it constitutes an act of exile from Electra's citizen status.

The Athenian audience watching this play, furthermore, would have understood Electra's complaint about being banned from civic religious festivals as a function of citizenship.[14] Participation in such festivals was one of the many ways that Athenians—and citizens of other city-states, though our evidence is best for Athens—defined and solidified the citizen body. To take only one well-known example, the fourth-century legal speech against Neaira (Ps.-Demosthenes 59) presents a situation in which the defendant has endangered the citizenship by passing off her daughter as an *astê*.[15] The larger argument, which need not detain us here, is that a man named Stephanus has been living with Neaira as if she were his wife (and not a courtesan), and has tried to pass off her children (whether with him or otherwise) as legal citizens. One of Neaira's daughters is married off as a citizen woman, thus producing the possibility of yet more illegitimate citizens. This same daughter, moreover, has illegally participated in Athenian cult (Ps.-Demosthenes 59.73):

καὶ αὕτη ἡ γυνὴ ὑμῖν ἔθυε τὰ ἄρρητα ἱερὰ ὑπὲρ τῆς πόλεως,
καὶ εἶδεν ἃ οὐ προσῆκεν αὐτὴν ὁρᾶν ξένην οὖσαν, καὶ τοιαύτη
οὖσα εἰσῆλθεν οἷ οὐδεὶς ἄλλος Ἀθηναίων τοσούτων ὄντων
εἰσέρχεται ἀλλ' ἢ ἡ τοῦ βασιλέως γυνή, ἐξώρκωσέν τε
τὰς γεραρὰς τὰς ὑπηρετούσας τοῖς ἱεροῖς, ἐξεδόθη δὲ τῷ
Διονύσῳ γυνή, ἔπραξε δὲ ὑπὲρ τῆς πόλεως τὰ πάτρια τὰ

πρὸς τοὺς θεούς, πολλὰ καὶ ἄγια καὶ ἀπόρρητα. ἃ δὲ μηδ'
ἀκοῦσαι πᾶσιν οἷόν τ' ἐστίν, πῶς ποιῆσαί γε τῇ ἐπιτυχούσῃ
εὐσεβῶς ἔχει, ἄλλως τε καὶ τοιαύτῃ γυναικὶ καὶ τοιαῦτα ἔργα
διαπεπραγμένῃ.

[And this woman (Neaira's daughter) sacrificed the unnamed sacrifices on behalf of the *polis*, and she saw what it was not proper
for her to see, since she is a foreigner, and being such she went in
to where no one else from all of the Athenians go, other than the
wife of the *basileus*. And she swore in the sacred priestesses to the
sacrifices, and she was given as wife to Dionysus, and she practiced the paternal rites to the gods on behalf of the *polis*, many,
and holy, and not to be named. Which, since it is not allowed to
anyone to hear them, how can it be pious for some random person
to perform them, especially this sort of a woman, and a woman
who has done the sorts of things she has?]

The language of secrecy and exclusion is quite normal for Greek cult
practice. The function of such religious ceremony is, in part, to define
those citizens who are part of the *polis* and can participate, and those
who are not and cannot. When, therefore, Electra says that she is barred
from dances and festivals, it is a serious statement about her exclusion
from a woman's role in the city.[16]

In fact, Barbara Goff has recently argued that the latter half of the fifth
century in Athens saw a shift in a number of traditional cult practices
in order to bring them more in line with the principles of the democracy.[17] The most important example is that of the selection of the priestess
of Athena Nike: an inscription that dates to the mid-fifth century (IG i³
35) declares that the priestess will be selected "from all the Athenians"
(Goff 2004, 183; Patterson 1987, 53). Women must, then, be thought of
as included in the collective noun "Athenians" at this point. If, as Goff
argues, this inscription marks a change in practice, then that change and
others like it are significant: "What seems to me utterly crucial, however, and yet is largely overlooked in the secondary literature, is that this
reorganization of ritual practice also aligns women, specifically, with the
democratic procedures of their city. The politically self-conscious city
rearranges an element of women's ritual practice so that it deliberately
models the political practice available to male citizens" (Goff 2004, 184).

Given this emerging practice in the mid-fifth century, it is little wonder that Electra expresses her exile in terms of exclusion from ritual
practice. Like the citizenship law of 451/450, these changes in cult

practice were specifically redefining female citizenship in democratic terms, and Electra's exclusion would resonate with those changes.

To exile a woman from the city, then, one does so by exiling her from proper marital relations, and thus from civic involvement in official cult. Even in exile, furthermore, we find that the relation to the city that Electra has been denied is not a direct, political relation. In this regard, Euripides' diction is surprisingly careful, and he observes the distinction that Patterson infers between *astai*—that is, citizens in their communal, social sense—and *Athenaioi* (or *politai*), citizens in their masculine, political sense. When Orestes first lays eyes on his sister and wonders about her diminished physical status, he asks specifically about her life away from the city (246–51):

> Ορ. ἐκ τοῦ δὲ ναίεις ἐνθάδ' ἄστεως ἑκάς;
> Ηλ. ἐγημάμεσθ', ὦ ξεῖνε, θανάσιμον γάμον.
> Ορ. ᾤμωξ' ἀδελφὸν σόν. Μυκηναίων τίνι;
> Ηλ. οὐχ ᾧ πατήρ μ' ἤλπιζεν ἐκδώσειν ποτέ.
> Ορ. εἴφ', ὡς ἀκούσας σῷ κασιγνήτῳ λέγω.
> Ηλ. ἐν τοῖσδ' ἐκείνου τηλορὸς ναίω δόμοις.

[Or: Why do you live here so far from the *astu*?
El: I married, stranger, into a deathly marriage.
Or: I groan for your brother. To someone of the
   Mycenaeans?
El. Not to whom my father hoped to give me once.
Or: Tell me, so that hearing, I can tell your brother.
El. I live in his house, on the far borders.]

Again, her marriage is the direct cause of Electra's living situation; even her house on the border is not hers, but emphatically her pseudohusband's (*ekeinou*, 251). In specifying Electra's physical isolation from the city, moreover, note that Orestes asks not why she lives so far from the *polis*—that is, the political city—but from the *astu*, the geographic city. As a woman, that is the "city" to which she should ideally belong.

Similarly, the Chorus of young women in this play, who seem doomed to isolation primarily because they have been dramaturgically linked to Electra, complain that they do not know what is going on (298–300):

> Χο. κἀγὼ τὸν αὐτὸν τῷδ' ἔρον ψυχῆς ἔχω.
> πρόσω γὰρ ἄστεως οὖσα τὰν πόλει κακὰ
> οὐκ οἶδα, νῦν δὲ βούλομαι κἀγὼ μαθεῖν.

> [Ch: And I also have desire in my mind for this. For,
> living far from the *astu*, I do not know the bad things
> going on in the *polis*, but now I also wish to learn
> (about them).]

Note here that we see a double relation expressed. In terms of geography, these young women live far from the *astu*; the bad things going on (of which they profess ignorance) take place in the *polis*. This is not to say that if these women lived in the city, they would take an active part in politics. Rather, it suggests that physical dislocation has exaggerated their usual state of being in which they could at least hear about political events (in this case, the mistreatment of Agamemnon's corpse after death). Similarly, at lines 118–19, Electra suggests that the *politai* (citizens, again) call her "wretched" (*athlia*). Women can *hear* the *polis*, even if they cannot participate in it. Women, as *astai*, are not political citizens; but the women of the Chorus are removed even from the *astu* that gives them an indirect standing in that polity.

Now, that might seem to be stretching the point. There are only so many ways to say "city" in ancient Greek, and it is within the bounds of possibility that Euripides is simply exercising poetic variation in the two examples above. If so, however, he does so with remarkable consistency. When Electra sends for the old male nurse to help her entertain her (still unrecognized) guests at line 408 and following, she describes him as "exiled from the *polis*" (*poleos ekbeblêmenos*, 412). Men, even relatively minor characters, are exiled from the *polis*; women from the *astu*.

ORESTES, OR HOW TO EXILE A MAN

Where the language of Electra's exile is consistently that of marriage and home, Orestes' exile is repeatedly both a familial and political state, and styled so that those two institutions blur into one another. Early on in the play, before he has revealed his identity, Electra asks Orestes if her brother is enduring exile (*phugê*, 233). He responds (234), "He is destroyed, not respecting one custom of the *polis*." More directly, when the old nurse (himself an exile from the *polis*, as we have seen) is encouraging Orestes, he refers to both paternal lineage and city (610–11):

ἐν χειρὶ τῇ σῇ πάντ᾽ ἔχεις καὶ τῇ τύχῃ
πατρῷον οἶκον καὶ πόλιν λαβεῖν σέθεν.

[You hold in your hand and in your fortune
the ability to take both paternal home and your *polis*.]

For Orestes, as we might expect, the "paternal home"—here his birth-right as the son of King Agamemnon, but to an Athenian audience also his legitimate right to inheritance—is identical to his city. Orestes is a citizen in terms that any Athenian would understand: he is the son of a citizen, the ruler of an *oikos*.

Orestes will, indeed, take back both home and *polis*, and again, Euripides' care in the use of diction calls out the ambiguity of the situation. Aegisthus, necessarily, is an interloper in both the line of Agamemnon and therefore also in the city of Argos. It is significant, therefore, that he will die outside the city walls, while taking part in a festival of the nymphs in a nearby grove. His lack of legitimate status is signaled to the reader through a careful manipulation in the status of his attendants. When Orestes is first contemplating confronting Aegisthus at his sacrifice to the nymphs, he asks how many men are with him (628). The old nurse responds that there is nobody there who is an *Argeios*—that is, an Argive citizen, just as an Athenian citizen is an *Athenaios*—but only house slaves (629). A little later, when Orestes approaches the sacrifice and is invited to join in, however, he addresses those present as *astoi* (793–96):

ἀλλ' εἶπ' Ὀρέστης· Ἀρτίως ἡγνίσμεθα
λουτροῖσι καθαροῖς ποταμίων ῥείθρων ἄπο.
εἰ δὲ ξένους ἀστοῖσι συνθύειν χρεών,
Αἴγισθ', ἕτοιμοι κοὐκ ἀπαρνούμεσθ', ἄναξ.

[But Orestes said, "We just now have purified ourselves,
in the clean bathing-water of the flowing stream.
And if the citizens (*astoi*) need strangers to sacrifice with
  them,
Aegisthus, we are ready and will not refuse, King.]

Here, the followers are addressed as citizens, but citizens in the same sense, perhaps, that women are: their participation in cult indicates that they belong to the town but may not have full adult political privileges. Indeed, it would be surprising if these "house slaves" did have such privileges.

The word *astoi*, however, allows Euripides a certain and necessary ambiguity; for once Orestes kills Aegisthus, these same people must become Orestes' subjects and proper citizens of Argos. That is exactly what happens in the event: as the Messenger retells the killing, Orestes and Pylades immediately address Aegisthus' followers (847–49):

Αγ. εἶπε δ'· Οὐχὶ δυσμενὴς
ἥκω πόλει τῇδ' οὐδ' ἐμοῖς ὀπάοσιν,
φονέα δὲ πατρὸς ἀντετιμωρησάμην
τλήμων Ὀρέστης· ἀλλὰ μή με καίνετε,
πατρὸς παλαιοὶ δμῶες.

[Messenger: And he said: "Not with ill-will do I come to this *polis*, nor to my companions, but I, daring Orestes, have avenged the death of my father. But do not kill me, household slaves of my father from the old days."]

Two things happen here. First, we must note that for Orestes, the familial issue of avenging his father's death is again simultaneous with his recovery of the *polis*. It is necessarily a political event. Second, there is a careful mapping of the notion of the fifth-century *polis* onto legitimate rule. As the rightful heir to his father's kingdom, Orestes not only regains his birthright—and incidentally, asserts his authority as head of the household over his father's former slaves, no longer calling them *astoi*—but he also invokes in that moment a *polis* with which his and their interests are aligned.[18] He is Mycenaean king and fifth-century citizen all at once.

If we return, then, to the quotation with which this investigation began, we can see that Orestes' and Electra's responses to the proclamation of exile are neither inappropriate nor shocking. Electra thinks of exile in terms of family and, especially, marriage (Mossman 2001, 382; Zeitlin 1970, 666) while for Orestes it is a question of what city (*polis*) he can go to. Within this dichotomy, however, there is some space in which to move, and both Electra and Euripides explore that space. We will now turn to that most political of women, Clytemnestra, before examining in more detail the arresting ending of the play.

THE WOMAN IN THE *POLIS*: CLYTEMNESTRA

Since Aeschylus' portrayal of her in the *Oresteia*, Clytemnestra has always represented that most dangerous of women, the woman who acts in the place of the male. To some extent this role is inevitable in the myth, since she literally diverts Agamemnon's line of inheritance to Aegisthus and his heirs. In Euripides' version, she is perhaps less overtly masculine than the woman of "man-counseling heart" in Aeschylus (*Agamemnon*, 11). In Electra's eyes, however, she plays an inappropriate familial role in the *polis*.

Though I have argued that Electra has no direct political relation to the city, that does not mean she is unaware of the city or its workings. After Aegisthus is dead, she makes an incredible and troubling speech over his corpse that reads much like one-half of a tragic *agôn* (Michelini 1987, 215). Before doing so, however, she hesitates, concerned about what the *polis* might say (900–904):

> ΗΛ. αἰσχύνομαι μέν, βούλομαι δ᾽ εἰπεῖν ὅμως.
> Ορ. τί χρῆμα; λέξον· ὡς φόβου γ᾽ ἔξωθεν εἶ.
> ΗΛ. νεκροὺς ὑβρίζειν, μή μέ τις φθόνῳ βάλῃ.
> Ορ. οὐκ ἔστιν οὐδεὶς ὅστις ἂν μέμψαιτό σε.
> ΗΛ. δυσάρεστος ἡμῶν καὶ φιλόψογος πόλις.

> [El: I am ashamed, but I want to say something.
> Or: What is it? Speak. Thus you will escape your fear.
> El: (I am ashamed) to abuse the corpse, lest someone strike
>   me with ill-will.
> Or: There is no one who would blame you.
> El: Our *polis* is peevish and loves to find fault.]

Earlier, Electra has commented that the *poliêtai* (citizens) called her "wretched" (118–19); line 904 is the only other time so far that Electra has suggested a relation between herself and the city using a *polis* word. Her caution is consistent with her gendered position on the stage; as Mossman points out in a recent analysis, Electra speaks in much more careful, general terms when there are male characters onstage (as here) than she does in a private *agôn* with Clytemnestra a little later, when only "women" occupy the acting space (Mossman 2001). Her relation with the *polis*, then, is a largely negative one: she must be wary of the criticism of men.

In the event, Electra's speech over the head of Aegisthus—for which, we should recall, her brother is the immediate onstage audience—neatly expresses fifth-century Athenian concerns about women usurping control of the household and especially the production of heirs. Most striking are her lines concerning Aegisthus and Clytemnestra's marriage (931–35):

> πᾶσιν δ᾽ ἐν Ἀργείοισιν ἤκουες τάδε·
> Ὁ τῆς γυναικός, οὐχὶ τἀνδρὸς ἡ γυνή.
> καίτοι τόδ᾽ αἰσχρόν, προστατεῖν γε δωμάτων
> γυναῖκα, μὴ τὸν ἄνδρα· κἀκείνους στυγῶ
> τοὺς παῖδας, ὅστις τοῦ μὲν ἄρσενος πατρὸς
> οὐκ ὠνόμασται, τῆς δὲ μητρὸς ἐν πόλει.

[In all of Argos you used to hear this: "The husband is the wife's, and the wife is not the husband's." Though this is shameful, for a wife to run the household, not the husband; and I hate those children who are not called by the name of their male father, but by that of their mother in the *polis*.]

Electra, who feared what the *polis* might say about her, now reports that rumor about Clytemnestra has been rampant in the city. We should note the use here, again, of *Argeioi*, the linguistic parallel of *Athenaioi* to designate male citizens of the city of Argos. Even more pointed is Electra's concern about children who are known by their mother's name in the *polis*, an inversion of the norm that suggests a direct political identity for some women. As it turns out, this situation has historical parallels in the period of the classical *polis*.

Turning once again to Ps.-Demosthenes *Against Neaira*, we find that there are children known by their mother's name in fourth-century Athens (Ps.-Demosthenes 59.50–51):

τὴν γὰρ θυγατέρα τὴν ταυτησὶ Νεαίρας, ἣν ἦλθεν ἔχουσα ὡς τουτονὶ παιδάριον μικρόν, ἣν τότε μὲν Στρυβήλην ἐκάλουν, νυνὶ δὲ Φανώ, ἐκδίδωσι Στέφανος οὑτοσὶ ὡς οὖσαν αὑτοῦ θυγατέρα ἀνδρὶ Ἀθηναίῳ Φράστορι Αἰγιλιεῖ, καὶ προῖκα ἐπ᾽ αὐτῇ δίδωσι τριάκοντα μνᾶς...

ὁρῶν δὲ Φράστωρ αὐτὴν οὔτε κοσμίαν οὖσαν οὔτ᾽ ἐθέλουσαν αὑτοῦ ἀκροᾶσθαι, ἅμα δὲ καὶ πεπυσμένος σαφῶς ἤδη ὅτι Στεφάνου μὲν οὐκ εἴη θυγάτηρ, Νεαίρας δέ, τὸ δὲ πρῶτον ἐξηπατήθη, ὅτ᾽ ἠγγυᾶτο ὡς Στεφάνου θυγατέρα λαμβάνων καὶ οὐ Νεαίρας, ἀλλὰ τούτῳ ἐξ ἀστῆς αὐτὴν γυν- αικὸς οὖσαν πρότερον πρὶν ταύτῃ συνοικῆσαι.

[For the daughter of this Neaira, whom she brought with her as a small child, whom then they called Strybele, but now they call Phano, Stephanus himself gave her in marriage, as being his own daughter to an Athenian man, Phrastor of Aigilia, and he gave a dowry with her of thirty minas....

And Phrastor, seeing that she was not well-mannered, nor did she wish to listen to him, and having learned clearly at the same time that she was not the daughter of Stephanus, but of Neaira, and that he had been deceived at first, when he received her in betrothal as the daughter of Stephanus and not of Neaira, but on the understanding that she was the daughter of Stephanus with a citizen (*astê*) woman, to whom Stephanus had been married before this Neaira.]

The implicit logic of Apollodorus' speech is irrefutable: if Phano is not the daughter of Stephanus, as Phrastor initially thought, then she is not, in Athenian law, the daughter of another man, but is the daughter (only) of Neaira. In other words, she is not a citizen. Now, in Neaira's case, this problem of attribution comes about because the prosecution is arguing that Neaira is a courtesan and not a citizen. Under the circumstances, it is impossible to tell who the father might be; and in any case, it does not matter, since Neaira cannot produce citizen daughters unless she is herself an *astê*. Clytemnestra's case appears different at first—after all, everyone knows who the father is—but is not so different in effect. Clytemnestra's children are known by her name because she is the more powerful partner in her alliance with Aegisthus, and this puts the identity of her children under *her* control. Like Neaira, she has become a sexual subject. This, I would argue, is the specific specter that Electra's speech calls up: a loss of men's control over the citizen body when women control the household and thereby create a backdoor into civic identity and legitimate citizenship (Ormand 1999, 32–33).

What of Clytemnestra herself? Early on in the play, there is an indication that she, too, fears the wagging tongues of the *polis*. When Orestes asks the old nurse why Clytemnestra has not accompanied Aegisthus to the sacrifice, he responds that she fears the gossip of her demesmen (642–45); again we cannot miss the relation to fifth-century citizenship, which depended largely on acceptance by one's deme (Harrison [1968] 1998, 74, 90). Indeed, Orestes comments that "she knows she is being watched by the *polis*." Though these words are spoken out of Clytemnestra's presence, they seem to be confirmed by her own speech later; she speaks of the bad reputation that women obtain (1013–15) and complains of the reproach that women (unfairly) receive for infidelity (1039–40):

> κἄπειτ' ἐν ἡμῖν ὁ ψόγος λαμπρύνεται,
> οἱ δ' αἴτιοι τῶνδ' οὐ κλύουσ' ἄνδρες κακῶς.

> [And when gossip shines on us,
> those responsible—men—never are never criticized for
>   these things.]

Her relationship to the *polis*, then, is also defined by family and by the ability of the *polis* to regulate familial ties.

When, therefore, Clytemnestra and Electra finally argue onstage—after Electra has lured her mother to her house with a lie about having given birth to a male child—we should note that Clytemnestra's defense for having exiled her two children centers around Agamemnon's failure

as a political leader. Bitter, as always in myth, about Agamemnon's sacrifice of Iphigenia, Clytemnestra suggests that his motives were wrong
(1024–28):

κεἰ μὲν πόλεως ἄλωσιν ἐξιώμενος
ἢ δῶμ' ὀνήσων τἄλλα τ' ἐκσῴζων τέκνα
ἔκτεινε πολλῶν μίαν ὕπερ, συγγνῶστ' ἂν ἦν.
νῦν δ' οὕνεχ' Ἑλένη μάργος ἦν ὅ τ' αὖ λαβὼν
ἄλοχον κολάζειν προδότιν οὐκ ἠπίστατο,
τούτων ἕκατι παῖδ' ἐμὴν διώλεσεν.

[And if he, removing destruction from the *polis*,
or helping his home, and saving the other children
killed the one on behalf of many, it would have been
    forgivable.
But now, because Helen was lustful, and the man who took
    her as a wife
was not able to punish her,
On account of this he killed my child.]

The problem, it seems, is twofold. Agamemnon acted neither as a good
father, nor as a good leader of the *polis*. (This is the only time that
Clytemnestra mentions the *polis* in the play.) In the process, Clytemnestra
claims, he allowed the personal actions of two individuals to outweigh
his duty to two parallel collectives: home and state.

Electra answers Clytemnestra's speech in kind. She argues, in effect,
that because of her blind lust for Aegisthus, Clytemnestra responded
inappropriately to the political situation. Clytemnestra, she claims,
was the only woman of all the Greek women who was happy to hear
of Troy's successes, and dismayed at their failures (1076–79). In the
typical manner of Euripidean *agones*, rhetorical point matches rhetorical point. If Agamemnon was unduly influenced by private matters,
Clytemnestra's personal affair put her on the wrong side of the war.
This, in effect, encapsulates the difficulty of female citizens for the Athenians: women's private lives—notoriously difficult to control—are also
a public concern, and their potential disloyalty to husbands becomes a
threat to the state.

BANISHED, ONCE MORE

Once Orestes has killed both Aegisthus and Clytemnestra, the play teeters on the verge of losing the plot altogether. Unlike the fairly heroic Orestes of Aeschylus and Sophocles, this one seems near a breakdown, retelling and dwelling on the act of killing his mother (1190–1230). It is in this section, as we have already seen, that the reality of their upcoming exile begins to dawn on both Orestes and Electra (1190–1200). If the previous discussion has now made the two characters' gendered understanding of exile less surprising, it does not resolve the crisis that brother and sister—and the drama itself—now face. That crisis is resolved, as often in Euripides, through a *deus ex machina*, in this case in the person of Castor, Electra's maternal uncle and former suitor.

As we recall, Orestes wonders out loud what city he can go to, while Electra asks who will marry her. Immediately, Castor answers both questions: Electra, we are told first, will marry Pylades (1249). In the next line, we learn that Orestes must leave Argos. Once again, the dichotomy of signification that we saw before holds true here. Orestes will enter political exile, and this is primarily a civic matter. As Castor says, quite explicitly, "You are not allowed to walk in this *polis*, / since you killed your mother" (οὐ γὰρ ἔστι σοὶ πόλιν / τήνδ᾽ ἐμβατεύειν, μητέρα κτείναντα σήν; 1250–51). Even as an exile, however, this play emphasizes that Orestes will remain a thoroughly political animal. We learn at line 1273–75 that he will found a *polis* that will be named after him. Finally, of course, he must go to the *polis* of Athena for purification (1319). Orestes is banished from his own city, but not from political life.

Electra's experience is different. Electra is not exiled, as Castor will insist, but rather given to Pylades in marriage. Now, this declaration is surprising for a number of reasons. It is an innovation to the myth (though see Euripides' *Iphigenia Among the Taurians* 695–96, 915). It also masks two important silences in the text. The first, and most obvious, is that of Pylades; Electra's question at 1199–1200 ("What husband will receive me into his marriage bed?") is a legitimate one, if she shares, as she has claimed, in Orestes' pollution. But Pylades, silent as often, is not asked for an opinion, and we are left to assume that he will do what is necessary. The second, more telling silence, is that of the text on the existence of the farmer; that is, Electra is already married—though, we might note, has not been received into the marriage bed. Still, where is the farmer, and how is it that Electra's previous marriage simply disappears?

The farmer's disappearance is intriguing, if we care to think about the dramaturgy of the play. For it turns out that, observing the three-actor rule of Greek tragedy, the actor who played the farmer is now onstage playing the part of Castor (Marshall 1999–2000, 337–39). It is tempting to read the farmer's noble birth into the divine power that Castor wields. In a real sense, it is the farmer's previous actions that enable the god's proclamation here. Metatheatrics aside, however, it is important to note the exact order given by Electra's deified uncle (1249–50): Πυλάδῃ μὲν Ἠλέκτραν δὸς ἄλοχον ἐς δόμους,/ σὺ δ᾽ Ἄργος ἔκλιπ᾽· (Give Electra to Pylades as a wife in the home, / but you leave Argos). Orestes, as we noted earlier, is Electra's proper *kurios*, and the person who should contract her marriage. If Electra's earlier marriage to the farmer was understood as a form of exile because it was not legitimate, this marriage is fully within the familial and civic structure; it is an exile only in the sense that Pylades will take her with him to wherever he must now go.

Nonetheless, Electra finds this an insufficient resolution. She responds as if she has been exiled, just as her brother, which leads to some of the most brutal dialogue of the play (1308–15):

Ορ. ὦ σύγγονέ μοι, χρονίαν σ᾽ ἐσιδὼν
    τῶν σῶν εὐθὺς φίλτρων στέρομαι
    καὶ σ᾽ ἀπολείψω σοῦ λειπόμενος.
Κα. πόσις ἔστ᾽ αὐτῇ καὶ δόμος· οὐχ ἥδ᾽
    οἰκτρὰ πέπονθεν, πλὴν ὅτι λείπει
    πόλιν Ἀργείων.
Ηλ. καὶ τίνες ἄλλαι στοναχαὶ μείζους
    ἢ γῆς πατρίας ὅρον ἐκλείπειν;

[Or: Oh, my sister, having seen you at last, I am deprived of
    your affections immediately, and I leave you, as I am left
    by you.
Ca: She has a husband and a home. She has suffered
    nothing pitiful, except that she leaves the *polis* of Argos.
El: And what griefs are greater than to leave the border of
    my fatherland?]

Castor's response to Orestes' emotional farewell can only be felt as shocking; he has redefined Electra's existence as if family and home were her *only* set of relations, as if her existence as an Argive woman were of no consequence. Electra's immediate response, we note, echoes that notion of citizenship that we have seen as standard for women: as an *astê*, Electra belongs physically to the land of her city. And so here she cries out the grief of leaving the border of the land (*gê*) itself.[19]

Euripides, however, always has one more trick up his sleeve. If this marriage, like her previous one, is the defining term of Electra's new form of exile, it also becomes the means by which she—suddenly, and without precedent—comes to recognize her *political* status. For as Electra and Orestes say their final farewells, the word with which this study began—*politis* (i.e., "female citizen")—is uttered for the first time in the drama (1331–35):

⟨Ορ.⟩ οὐκέτι σ᾽ ὄψομαι.
Ηλ. οὐδ᾽ ἐγὼ ἐς σὸν βλέφαρον πελάσω.
Ορ. τάδε λοίσθιά μοι προσφθέγματά σου.
Ηλ. ὦ χαῖρε, πόλις·
χαίρετε δ᾽ ὑμεῖς πολλά, πολίτιδες.

[Or: I will no longer see you.
El: Nor will I come into your sight.
Or: These are my last words to you.
El: Farewell city (*polis*)! And farewell to you especially,
    citizen women (*politides*).]

For the first time, Electra addresses the *polis* itself, and in the same breath she addresses her companions in their capacity as citizens. The relative rarity of the word aside, I think Electra's address to the Chorus as *politides* strikes like a hammer blow. Electra's character has carefully avoided *polis* words throughout this play, except to express the idea that women should avoid being noticed by the *polis*. Every relationship that she has expressed concern for has been with family, father, and home. On the rare occasions that she has spoken of the city, or her situation has been spoken of, it has been the physical, geographic *astu*, not the *polis*. But now, as she is about to lose her brother forever, she breaks from her farewell to the only remaining member of her family to mourn the loss of these fellow *citizen* women.[20]

In brief, women's citizenship as enacted by this play can only be recognized at the moment of its loss. That construction is no accident. I submit, rather, that it is a Euripidean comment on the structure of women's citizenship in Athens. In fact, the Periclean citizenship legislation of 451/450 mirrors this structure exactly. Women in Athens became, properly, citizens when certain of them were recognized as *astai*, capable of producing, through legally recognized familial structures, further *astoi*. That crucial historical moment both produced citizen women and excluded large numbers of women from citizenship forever. More to the point, it rendered even those citizens who were recognized as *astai* as citizens only through the structures of family and marriage. This was, as Patterson, Goff, and others have shown, a position of considerable status; but it is also a position marked by an uncrossable rift, by an exile within the *polis* from the workings of the political city. This, I suggest, is the meaning of Electra's final declaration of exile: her recognition of female citizenship is concurrently a moment of profound separation from the city itself.

I will close by suggesting that the particular festival that Euripides makes the background for this play further serves to emphasize Electra's ambiguous state, and to underline women's ambivalent relation to the *polis*. Zeitlin argued persuasively twenty-five years ago that most of the events of the play can be read as an ironic and perverted version of the celebration of the *Hieros Gamos* at the Argive Heraion (Zeitlin 1970, 659–69). To this important reading, I want to add a few thematic points.

First, we should note that Hera, while the goddess who oversees the rite of marriage, is not herself a goddess of childbirth (Burkert 1985, 133) and that the myths that surround the figure of Hera in Argos all involve young women who, having angered Hera, are isolated from humanity and prevented from having sexual intercourse. The most familiar of these is Io (a granddaughter of Argos), who is pursued by Zeus, turned into a cow, and then given to Hera. Hera sets the all-seeing figure Argos (not the same as Io's grandfather) over her as a guard. Hermes kills Argos so that Zeus can resume his attentions, at which point Hera sends a gadfly to chase Io over the known world. Io is finally returned to human form in the distant land of Egypt by the touch of Zeus, and shortly thereafter she gives birth to Epaphos, the ancestor of Aigyptos and Danaos; the latter will eventually return to Argos with his fifty daughters.[21]

The myth is far from simple, not least in the disconcerting multiplication of people and places named "Argos." Thematically, it is deeply concerned with the anomalous position of young unmarried women, emphasized in part by Io's literal dehumanization. Ken Dowden has seen in the story of Io a mythic prototype for priestesses of Hera at Argos who would have remained unmarried throughout their service (Dowden 1989, 132–33).[22] Electra begins to look rather like Io, and rather like such a priestess: *parthenos* and wife at the same time, belonging nowhere, living outside the city until she is "cured" by marriage and sent off in exile with Pylades. I suggest here that the associations of the cult of Hera at

Argos make, then, a perfect backdrop for the tale of Electra: like Io, she is a *parthenos* who cannot make the transition to married life, and is in fact prevented from doing so by a jealous mother-figure.[23]

Let me turn, in closing, to the unusual setting of the play once more. The role of various cities around the Argive plain in relation to the Argive Heraion during the archaic period is a matter of considerable dispute.[24] It appears that after military triumphs of the 460s, the city of Argos engaged in some myth making to invent an Argive past for the cult of Hera above the Argive plain (Hall 1995, 611–13). Regardless of the historical relationship between city and temple, however, the temple's distance from the city center in this play is both ideological and geographical. The setting at the Argive Heraion points to cult practice that predates the classical *polis* of Argos and represents the distance that women experience from civic identity. Women have a place in the *polis*, just as the cult of Argive Hera was undeniably important to fifth-century Argos, but it is a place defined by the archaic, prepolitical institutions of family and marriage. These institutions place women, even successfully married ones, on the imaginary borders of citizenship, just as the cult center of Hera occupies a space on the border between the *poleis* of Argos and Mycenae, where *parthenoi* celebrate the transitional rite of marriage. At the end of the play, Orestes is sent off to ritual purification and then to the civic space of Athens and the court of the Areopagos. Electra, like the cult of Hera itself, is finally located outside of *political* life; ironically, it is only that moment of exile that constructs a political identity—"*politides*," she calls out—that she has now lost.[25]

NOTES

1. All translations from Greek texts are my own and are as literal as possible.
2. We have no secure date for either Sophocles' *Electra* or Euripides'. Most scholars put Sophocles' play (and so the coining of this word) in the 430s or 420s, and many believe that Euripides' play was produced around 413, shortly after the Sicilian expedition (Denniston 1939, xxxiii–xxxix). I refuse to have an opinion on the vexed question of whether Sophocles' or Euripides' version came first; the fact that both authors use the rare feminine form of *politis*, however, suggests that they are writing in similar political contexts.
3. The bibliography on this issue is immense; a good summary can be found in Pomeroy (1975, 57–78). Schaps (1998) provides a good

discussion of what distinguished citizen women from noncitizen women in practical terms.

4. It is an easy mistake to underestimate the importance of this relationship in the Athenian imaginary. Despite the limitations mentioned briefly above, the role of *astai* was both important and valued, as Patterson (1987) argues. See also Goff (2004, 160–74).

5. Patterson (1987, 54) lists several political uses of *astos*, including Aeschylus' *Eumenides* 437.

6. Patterson (1987, 54–57) provides a useful discussion. The definitive work remains Patterson (1981); for an acute reading of the ideological implications, however, see Loraux (1993, 116–23). Loraux and Patterson disagree on the question of whether women were thought to be "citizens."

7. In Aristophanes' *Lysistrata*, the magistrate upbraids Lysistrata for complaining about the war, when he says, women "have no share in the war." Lysistrata replies, "We bear the war more than double; for first we give birth to children, and then we send them to battle as hoplites" (Aristophanes, *Lysistrata* 588–89).

8. Luschnig (1992) is particularly good on the ways that the setting creates a sense of displacement for characters and audience alike. See especially pp. 11 and 15 on the distant tomb, and 21 on the sense of insecurity that this fosters in the audience. Halporn (1983, 102, 111–12) also notes the distance of Agamemnon's tomb in this version.

9. Most scholars interpret the setting as evidence for Euripides' interest in "realism": Denniston (1939, xii), Michelini (1987, 182–85, 227), King (1980, 195, 209n25), Halporn (1983, 101), Arnott (1981, 181), Lloyd (1986). Goff (1999–2000) argues that this "realism" should be recognized as a literary mode rather than a transparent reproduction of real life.

10. Vermeule's brief introduction ([1958] 1992, 392–93) relies on a psychological reading, particularly of this point: "With the confused thinking of obsessive neurotics, they believe that killing their mother will somehow make her love them again, so that they can settle down and be happy. Their surprise at the results is more disturbing than their pain."

11. The earliest reference seems to be the lyric poet Xanthus (now lost), whose comments are summarized for us by Alienus. See Ormand (1999, 62–63) for a brief reference and discussion.

12. It is possible that the sacrifice to the nymphs that Aegisthus plans to make (625–26, 784–86) is for the well-being of expected children

with Clytemnestra. On this point, see Michelini (1987, 213–14). In any case, the question of heirs certainly motivates Electra's plot to lure her mother to her house, in which she pretends to have given birth to a male child (651–61). In the discussion of marriage that follows, I am indebted throughout to Zeitlin (1970, 647–51).

13. Lloyd (1986, 14) notes rightly that Orestes is Electra's *kurios*.

14. For a thorough analysis of women's participation in festivals as an expression of citizenship, see Goff (2004, 160–226). Zeitlin (1970, 648–49) also provides a brief useful discussion.

15. This passage has been frequently discussed. For a good summary, see Goff (2004, 171–174); Patterson (1994).

16. Of course, different cults in different cities held different require-ments for their participants. For a brief overview, see Goff (2004, 174–78). In general, as Goff says, "The various attributes that qual-ified a woman for participation in ritual activity were often similar to those for men in the political context" (Goff 2004, 174).

17. In the interests of space, I simplify Goff's elegant argument here considerably.

18. We may note in this context that the Chorus hails Orestes as a "firebrand for the *polis*" (*polei purson*) at line 587.

19. *Pace* Michelini (1987, 225), who argues that "Electra seems to have got off scot-free, in mythic terms, since she does not have to be involved in the process of trial and purification." It is true that Electra is not held as responsible for the crime in the same way Orestes is, but she appears to feel her exile just as keenly.

20. If we care to speculate that Euripides' version of this play is later than Sophocles' (and this can only be speculation), then this line becomes a subtle comment on Sophocles' heroine. Sophocles' Elec-tra recognizes her Chorus as citizen women in order to call atten-tion to the identity of Orestes. Here, Electra recognizes the *polities* as she loses her brother forever.

21. The myth is retold many places, most famously in Ps.-Aeschylus' *Prometheus Bound*. A useful summary can be found in Apollodo-rus, 2.3–4.

22. Hera herself forcefully reinforces this sense of never quite belong-ing, through the cyclical wonder of cult: we learn from Pausanias that the cult statue of Hera was bathed every year in the spring of Kanathos and thus returned to her unmarried state (Burkert 1985, 133; Pausanias 2.38.2).

23. Zeitlin (1970, 661) argues that Clytemnestra is presented in such a way as to suggest that she is the "priestess-goddess figure of Hera."
24. For a recent and thorough discussion, see Hall (1995). Hall argues that the Argive Heraion was probably primarily under the control of cities on the eastern side of the plain until the conquest of Mycenae by Argos in the 460s.
25. Burkert (1985, 134): "Whenever we learn any details about Hera's festivals we discover that it is never simply a joyful wedding feast, but a deep crisis in which the established order breaks down and the goddess herself threatens to disappear."

REFERENCES

Arnott, W. Geoffrey. 1981. Double the vision. A reading of Euripides' *Electra*. *Greece & Rome* 28: 179–92.

Burkert, Walter. 1985. *Greek religion*. Cambridge, MA: Harvard University Press.

Denniston, J. D., ed. 1939. *Euripides Electra*. London: Oxford University Press.

Dowden, Ken. 1989. *Death and the maiden*. London: Routledge.

Goff, Barbara. 1999–2000. Try to make it real compared to what? *Illinois Classical Studies* 24–25: 93–105.

———. 2004. *Citizen Bacchae: Women's ritual practice in ancient Greece*. Berkeley: University of Los Angeles Press.

Hall, Jonathan. 1995. How Argive was the "Argive" Heraion? The political and cultic geography of the Argive Plain, 900–400 B.C. *American Journal of Archaeology* 99: 577–613.

Halporn, James W. 1983. The skeptical Electra. *Harvard Studies in Classical Philology* 87: 101–18.

Harrison, A. R. W. [1968] 1998. *The law of Athens, Vol. I: The family and property*. Indianapolis: Hackett. Original edition published by Oxford University Press.

King, Katherine C. 1980. The force of tradition. The Achilles ode in Euripides' *Electra*. *Transactions of the American Philological Association* 110: 195–212.

Loraux, Nicole. 1993. *Children of Athena: Athenian ideas about citizenship and the division between the sexes*. Princeton, NJ: Princeton University Press.

Lloyd, Michael. 1986. Realism and character in Euripides' *Electra*. *Phoenix* 40: 1–19.

Luschnig, C. A. E. 1992. Electra's pot and the displacement of the settings in Euripides' *Electra*. *Dioniso* 62: 7–27.

Marshall, C. W. 1999–2000. Theatrical reference in Euripides' *Electra*. *Illinois Classical Studies* 24–25: 325–41.

Michelini, Ann Norris. 1987. *Euripides and the tragic tradition*. Madison: University of Wisconsin Press.

Mossman, Judith M. 2001. Women's speech in Greek tragedy: The case of Electra and Clytemnestra in Euripides' *Electra*. *Classical Quarterly* 51: 374–84.

Ormand, Kirk. 1999. *Exchange and the maiden: Marriage in Sophoclean tragedy*. Austin: University of Texas Press.

Patterson, Cynthia. 1981. *Pericles' citizenship law of 451–50 B.C.* Salem, NH: Ayer.

———. 1987. Hai Attikai: The other Athenians. *Helios* 13: 49–67.

———. 1994. The case against Neaira and the public ideology of the Athenian family. In *Athenian identity and civic ideology*, ed. A. L. Boegehold and A. C. Scafuro, 199–216. Baltimore: Johns Hopkins University Press.

Pomeroy, Sarah. 1975. *Goddesses, whores, wives, and slaves: Women in classical antiquity*. New York: Dorset.

Schaps, David. 1998. What was free about a free Athenian woman. *Transactions of the American Philological Association* 128: 161–88.

Vermeule, Emily. [1958] 1992. Introduction to *Electra*. In *The complete Greek tragedies, Vol. 4*, ed. David Grene and Richmond Lattimore, 390–94. Chicago: University of Chicago Press.

Zeitlin, Froma I. 1970. The Argive festival of Hera and Euripides' *Electra*. *Transactions of the American Philological Association* 101: 645–69.

11

ORESTES AND THE IN-LAWS

MARK GRIFFITH

INTRODUCTION:
THE STORY OF ORESTES AND ATHENIAN THEATER

Greek tragedy, as Aristotle observed, represents human "action, activity" (*praxis*), or, to be more precise, a "sequence/combination/ arrangement of actions" (*sustasis pragmatôn*),[1] and certain kinds of "activity" involving terrible sufferings inflicted on and by close family members—or narrowly averted—are especially well suited to the tragic effect. Particular mythological stories that encapsulated such actions most vividly therefore tended to be employed over and over in the Theater of Dionysus. Among the most frequently revisited of all was the story of Orestes and his family;[2] and Aeschylus' *Oresteia* and Euripides' *Orestes* both established themselves quickly and permanently as exceptionally popular and influential versions. Both of these dramas derive much of their theatrical and moral power from the simple premise that, in killing his mother, Orestes has committed an act that is both fully justified, because it avenged his father's (the king's) murder and obeyed the command of Apollo, and yet also supremely horrible and unjustifiable, because it violated the most precious and natural bonds of family affection, reinforced by age-old prohibitions against kin murder as represented by the Furies.

In Aeschylus' *Oresteia* (458 BCE), "right" is repeatedly said to collide with "right," "force" with "force," and we are reminded incessantly both of the impossibility of resolving the moral issues and of the disastrous consequences of failing to do so. In the third play, the split verdict of the Areopagus court confirms the impossibility of judging the act simply "right" or "wrong"; but Athena's brilliant and enlightened negotiations—typical (we are made to feel) of Athenian democratic principles and Greek patriarchal institutions in general—bring about an acceptable acquittal along with the restoration of Orestes to his (father's) household and kingdom. This outcome, even though it obviously flies in the face of actual Athenian law, is shown during the course of the final scenes to be welcome to almost everyone—Athenians, Argives, Greeks at large, Olympian gods, even the Erinyes themselves,[3] and thus "justice" (the "right" verdict) prevails, thanks to a far-ranging and effective collaboration of divine, aristocratic, and democratic interests united under the aegis of Athena, her father, and her city. Orestes' sister, Electra, and his comrade, Pylades, although they play important roles in assisting him in preparing and executing his vengeance, have no part to play in the final settlement,[4] which emphasizes instead the entirely positive and unifying consequences for both Argos and Athens of his recovery of home, entitlements, and authority.

In *Orestes* (performed in 408 BCE), Euripides returns to this archetypical scenario of conflicted familial motivations and their inescapably political implications. In this version, Orestes' and Electra's killing of Clytemnestra has already taken place, just six days previous to the opening of the play (39–40, 422). But the citizens have not rallied in their support: on the contrary, the two of them are being held under house arrest, pending a meeting of the Argive assembly at which their deed and its penalty will be assessed by popular vote. Orestes is himself in a state of collapse and subject to periodic bouts of hallucination in which he sees his mother's Furies coming at him. Electra is doing her best to look after him. Their hopes are pinned on Menelaus, who they hope will come back from Troy in time to rescue them by persuading the Argives to acquit them of any crime. But Menelaus, under pressure from Tyndareus (father of Helen and Clytemnestra), fails to speak up for them in the assembly, and the vote is for condemnation: they are ordered to commit suicide (as a form of judicial execution). At this point, Pylades arrives. (We are told that he had assisted the siblings in the killing of Aegisthus and Clytemnestra, but then had returned home for a few days in Phocis, only to find that his own family have now disowned him for his role in the matricide.) The three debate what to do, and suddenly come up with a bold plan to avenge themselves on Menelaus for his betrayal of them, and perhaps even to procure an escape for themselves: they will kill Helen and kidnap Hermione, the young daughter of Menelaus and Helen. It is soon reported by a Messenger that they have indeed killed Helen, and Orestes appears standing on the roof of the palace, holding a sword at Hermione's throat and yelling instructions to Pylades and Electra to set fire to the whole palace, while

Menelaus, in rage and frustration, yells back at him from below. Then Apollo suddenly arrives on high: he informs them that Helen was not in fact killed, but taken up unharmed into heaven; that Orestes shall marry Hermione, travel abroad (to Athens and elsewhere) to obtain purification and formal acquittal from his crime, and return to become king of Argos; that Electra and Pylades shall marry and go and live happily in Phocis; and that Menelaus can return to Sparta to be king there. So the play ends.

Many surprising twists, then—yet a familiar outcome. Once again, the act of vengeful matricide is presented as morally, even legally, problematic—neither completely right nor completely wrong, or perhaps both at once. And as long as Orestes' own community cannot decide whether or not the killing was justified, several issues remain up for grabs, including not only justice, purity, honor, and the very survival and mental health of the killer(s), but also political authority, family inheritance, and property ownership. To whom will (should) the palace of Agamemnon (the famous house of Atreus) now belong? Who will be ruler(s) of Argos? What will be the future status of these tyrant-slayers in a city that may or may not wish to be rid of tyrants? (Were Clytemnestra and Aegisthus in fact usurping and unpopular "tyrants"—as in the *Oresteia*—or merely the leaders of one temporarily dominant elite faction among many competing for preeminence in this city?) These issues are presented as being very much in flux as the play opens: different factions are jockeying for power, and various family members and friends, both from within the city and from outside, are bringing their influence and interest to bear on Orestes. And even as this play contrives (unlike, e.g., Euripides' *Electra*, and against all expectations and superficial plot clues) to end "happily"—that is, with the reconciliation of enemies, salvation of all four young heroes and heroines (if we include Hermione), and a round of marriages between them—nevertheless, the question of the tone of this ending, and the degree or quality of closure that it is felt to provide, has troubled modern critics immeasurably.[5]

In what follows, I propose to analyze the complex network of family obligations, age and gender dynamics, and reciprocal claims and counterclaims, within which Orestes, Electra, and Pylades find themselves caught. This network extends widely, from the royal/noble (and even partly divine) dynastic families headed by Agamemnon and Menelaus, sons of Atreus (then all the way back to Pelops and Tantalus, e.g., 4–14, 982–1012),[6] to the family and associates of Aegisthus (cousin of Agamemnon and Menelaus, and second husband of Clytemnestra—thus, Orestes' stepfather), some of whom are still resident and powerful in Argos (e.g., 893–95)—and further afield, intersecting with the family of Tyndareus of Sparta (father of Helen and Clytemnestra, and hence father-in-law of both Menelaus and Agamemnon), as well as with the Phocian family of Strophius and Pylades.[7] Zeus too is closely connected with Orestes' family, since (as everyone seems to be aware) he is the natural father of Helen, who herself, as Menelaus' wife, is Orestes' and Electra's aunt; so Zeus' son Apollo is therefore another relative, a distant but attentive cousin of Orestes and Electra.[8] In geopolitical terms, these relationships involve most immediately the cities (and also the wealth and palaces) of Argos and Sparta; and they extend before the play is over to involve also Phocis/Delphi, Arcadia, Mount Olympus, and even Athens.

It has been a truism of late twentieth-century criticism to argue that the plots of Greek tragedy normally involve collisions between the interests of *oikos* and *polis*, and between the old family-based power and morality structures of "Homeric" or "Archaic" Greek society and the civic concerns of democratic Athens. Whereas previous generations of scholars tended to emphasize issues of individual morality and character, or to analyze the religious and cosmological dimensions of each playwright's "world view," much recent scholarship has been driven instead by an interest in the social structures revealed by—and reinforced by—the emotion-packed adaptations of traditional myth that were presented each year in the Theater of Dionysus. In particular, distinctions of gender and ethnicity, tensions between civic duty and family loyalty, and patterns of ritual behavior and cult aetiology acted in the theater have all been shown to contribute powerfully to forming and modifying Athenian collective/civic consciousness.[9] In some tragedies (a minority, however), the clash between domestic and political interests is found to be reconcilable, to their mutual benefit. Thus, in the *Oresteia*, after the initial tangle of perversions and violations of family norms, we see political order restored and the sanctity of marriage and patriarchal rule reaffirmed, all through the enlightened judicial procedures of Athens and the collaborative networking of Olympian gods, elite human families, and democratic masses, a process that amounts to an in-depth, up-and-down restatement of the audience's own civic (as well as aesthetic-moral) values and pride. More often, the conclusion of a tragedy is less straightforwardly reassuring; but the exploration of these kinds of issues seems, in any case, to be typical of the Athenian theatrical experience of the fifth century BCE.[10]

In Euripides' *Electra* (dating probably from ca. 420 BCE), the integrity of the family of the Atreids is represented as being completely shattered, and the sense of collective solidarity or civic identity is almost entirely lacking. By setting the play at the Farmer's cottage, distant from the royal palace,[11] and providing an ending in which Orestes is required to leave the region of Argos completely and settle in remote Arcadia, Euripides has presented a version of the myth in which neither political nor familial order or benefit of any kind has apparently been achieved through the act of matricidal vengeance, though at the same time his focus on the character of Electra and her matrimonial assignment at the end to Pylades does perhaps remind an audience of dimensions of Aeschylus' trilogic plot that were left inappropriately silent and unaccounted for.[12] But in Euripides' later *Orestes* (408 BCE), the themes of (extended) family, inheritance, the house, gender roles, and marriage are brought much more emphatically (and literally) back to center stage, and the interface between these themes and the political workings of the city of "Argos" is, in its own way, I shall argue, as complicated and dramatically interesting as that of its illustrious Aeschylean predecessor. So even though this play nowadays is usually read either as an unrelenting (even absurdist) indictment of all aspects of late fifth-century Athenian society, or as an example of (merely) virtuoso escapist and/or melodramatic fantasy, I think it is instructive to explore the ways in which more traditional issues are redeployed and demystified within this brilliantly contrived and engaging masterpiece. For, as we shall see, the play presents a complicated and, in some respects, highly realistic, portrayal of a superelite extended family locked in a bitter and manipulative struggle both among its own members and against rival power blocks within the *polis*, and its outcome depends finally on the ways in which familial interests (above all, those of marriage and inheritance) and the political processes of "Argos" are able to find a mutually acceptable accommodation.

SOME PRACTICAL (DOMESTIC) GREEK REALITIES

Before we proceed to analysis of the play itself, however, a word must be said about families, both "nuclear" and "extended," in the ancient Greek—and specifically Athenian—context. The economic, legal, and psychosocial structures of the Classical Athenian family have, of course, been intensively studied over the last forty years or so from many different perspectives and drawing on a wide range of material, including documentary, literary, and visual evidence. In discussing a play like *Orestes* (or even the *Oresteia*, for that matter), we need to avail ourselves of all this evidence, while also bearing in mind that the society depicted in the Theater of Dionysus is far from a realistic or accurate portrayal of actual Athenian (or any other) social and familial relations.

In real-life Athens of the fourth and fifth centuries (and presumably in several other Greek cities, too, with fairly minor variations, though for these we have far less evidence), every family, every household (*oikos*, i.e., ideally or normally a physical and social unit comprising husband, wife, children and other dependents, servants, and possessions), was under constant pressure to maintain its wealth, integrity, reputation, and power, not only through assiduous labor and acquisition, but also through careful and judicious marriages, selective child raising and adoption, and alliances both local and further afield—in short, the vigorous pursuit of all its collective interests, both within and outside the law. And while it was the nuclear family that was usually the primary focus of day-to-day activities, interactions, and loyalties (often involving a small farm or business, though in the case of elites a broad range of estates and enterprises might be available), this was but one piece of the larger jigsaw puzzle of extended kin-group connections.[13]

A key factor both in the consolidation of individual family interests within Attica and in the inter*polis* networking of elite Greek families was always the arrangement of marriages and the accompanying "exchange" of women between families (in neolocal marriages) or retention of them (in endogamous marriages).[14] The decision by a father (or uncle, or whoever was *kurios* of the young woman concerned) as to who should marry a property-owner's daughter (who might also be the sister of a promising young citizen or two), as well as the choice of bride made by a son, was a matter of crucial importance for the prestige, security, and economic prosperity of the whole family unit. The "in-law" relationships that were thus established through marriage (Greek *kêdos*, a versatile term that we shall be considering in more detail below) not only could provide bases for long-range and local political-military alliances and interventions, but also served as symbols and guarantees of future favor, obligation, and entitlement. The disposition of brides was of course entrusted to men; but the looks, behavior, and reputation of the potential bride and/or the bride's mother might sometimes be factors, too—though the more this happened, the greater the strain placed on the whole process. (Having a supremely beautiful daughter is both a plus and a minus, as Tyndareus in our play has come to realize).[15] After the wedding, too, the behavior of the wife—and in due course, young mother—in her new home was likewise a crucial matter both for the relations between these two sets of in-laws and for the public reputation of (especially) the bride's family.

Although inheritance and marriage patterns in Classical Athens can be quite complicated to unravel (especially given the prevalence of adoption, premature death, divorce, remarriage, and uncertain status of *nothoi*), the basic principles governing choice of bride (or, from the other perspective, disposition of daughter in marriage) and selection of heir(s) were simple enough. As Cheryl Ann Cox has demonstrated, the aim above all was to maintain or increase the family's property while at the same time keeping it secure and under the control of the agnate (father's male) line:

> Essentially we have a balancing act of kinship endogamy with exogamy as families tried to extend ties and consolidate them. Kinship and local endogamy [i.e., marriage to a family member within the same deme] and adoption were closely linked together, as adoption could secure an alliance with a non-kinsman or a demesman or neighbor. Endogamy reinforced by adoption kept a balance of interests on both sides of the *ankhisteia*, or extended kin group...On the one hand, [the Athenian] marriage practices [represented in the surviving orations] often reveal a strong patrilineal orientation; on the other, whenever property is transmitted, it is common for concerns outside the patriline to surface. In the cases of some...families and kin groups...a sibling followed a sibling or a woman followed a kinswoman into a particular deme at marriage in order to secure affinal ties or to reinforce a claim to a kinsman's property. For other families and kin groups, kinship endogamy was resorted to when an estate came into crisis, or when...a kinsman faced political disgrace, or when a patriline lost a member through adoption.[16]

This tended to mean that, in good times, a more expansive policy was pursued, bringing in a bride from a distant deme (or even occasionally, among elites, from a foreign royal or noble family), whereas in leaner times, or at moments of crisis, an "endogamous" marriage was preferred, frequently giving a daughter to her cousin or uncle, or to an influential male member of her mother's family, in order to consolidate the kin group's resources and connections. In particular, Cox has observed that after especially disastrous setbacks to a family (e.g., exile, conviction for a crime, disreputable death on the part of the father or some other prominent male, or a financial catastrophe of some kind), the turn inward, to endogamy, was almost universal, as a means of "regrouping," both economically and perhaps psychologically: "Political disgrace, or threat of disgrace...may well have been the force behind the endogamous unions of [several] powerful families of the fifth century."[17]

How specific to Athens are these tendencies, and how variable? Did significant changes occur after 451 BCE as a result of Pericles' citizenship law? It is impossible to be sure of the answer to these questions, but it seems on the whole that Athenian late fifth-century marriage practices and attitudes were not very different from those of other Greek cities.[18] That is to say, while it may generally be true that post-451 patterns of marriage among the Athenian elite were brought into closer alignment with those of nonelites, and possibilities for intermarriage between illustrious superelites of different cities were now more or less unavailable to Athenians,[19] the large size of Attica overall, with its peculiar arrangement of widely separated rural and urban demes into "trittyes," certainly provided opportunities for variable patterns of "endogamy" and "exogamy" such as were not possible, for example, on a small island or remote Peloponnesian village—that is to say, "exogamy" for an Athenian might entail marrying someone from a distant deme rather than another *polis* altogether. (For metics, of course—not an inconsiderable portion of the "Athenian" theater audience—the law of Pericles made no difference at all.) Overall, we may conclude that the basic motivations and principles of marital selection operating in each and every Greek environment during this period seem to have been very similar.[20]

There existed both a strong centripetal pull[21] drawing the members of any family (to the degree of first cousins, i.e., those included in the kin-group's legal *ankhisteia*) into recognizing and preserving their common interests and needs, and also a tendency for fierce and divisive conflicts to arise between individual family members, or larger-scale struggles between different branches of an extended family—to say nothing about attempts, legal or illegal, by neighbors or other interested parties to take over, dominate, sabotage, or annex the property (and daughters) of a suddenly depleted or disadvantaged family for their own economic and/or political reasons. The bonds holding brothers and sisters together, or mothers and their children, were material and practical as well as emotional: they often formed the life-support system for otherwise vulnerable family members, protecting them (or at least buffering them) against the vicissitudes and plots of the outside world or of other unscrupulous family members.[22] This is certainly true of what we find in Athenian tragedy and comedy; and it appears to be true to a considerable degree of the world recorded in the documents and other texts (oratorical, biographical, historiographical) available to modern historians. These conflicting pressures and expectations were particularly intense among those families whose property holdings were most substantial and whose range of connections was most geographically and politically extended—that is, the elite, since they tended to maintain both rural and urban residences and land holdings, which greatly increased their ability to make and maintain contacts with other Athenian elites and foreigners, while it also exposed them to a wider range of opportunistic assaults on their property and interests.[23]

This meant that a boy or girl growing up within such a family needed to be constantly aware of whom his or her true "friends" were: Which *philoi* could be trusted? Which were out instead to dispossess or disgrace him or her? What plans might the family's bosses have in store for the household's future well-being? This is even more true, perhaps, for a girl than for a boy—though the youthful careers of, for example, Demosthenes or Lysias, or of the male friends of Neaera, provide vivid enough scenarios of domestic squabbling and chicanery, neighborly betrayal, and strategic endogamy galore, to leave no doubt at all that a young man might be quite unsure whether or not he would ever receive the inheritance that was his due, what pieces of real estate he might ever be able to call "home," and what political rights and roles might eventually be available to him, depending on the outcome of this lawsuit or that political coup.

In *Orestes*, certainly, the crucially significant positions occupied by daughters and wives (Electra and Hermione; Helen and Clytemnestra) form the nexus of an intricate series of power struggles and conflicts of obligation, and these female characters themselves initiate and execute some of the most critical actions, as we shall see. Lin Foxhall has shown persuasively that the restrictions on female "ownership" of "property" (whatever these terms mean in the Athenian context) and on political activity on the part of women by no means excluded women from taking a prominent part in the making of decisions and practical running of the *oikos*.[24] And even while our play is named after its domestically and politically challenged young male hero, and, for the most part, places him in the spotlight, we are never able to forget that his mother, his sister, his aunt, and his female cousin are intimately involved in almost every twist and turn of the action—and are the key to its eventual peaceful resolution.

In some respects, Euripides' focus in this play on property, marriage, and inheritance, as well as his depiction of pragmatic Argive politics (all of which I shall be examining in some detail below), might be regarded as a kind of "realism." Indeed, it is not inappropriate, I suggest, to see

Orestes as a kind of "domestic" or "social" drama, a step on the road to the New Comedy of the fourth century—even while it also, quite obviously, contains some of the most fantastic and extravagant elements of older-style, over-the-top tragedy (romance?) imaginable.[25] Perhaps the modern critical coinage "magical realism" might fit our play, with its peculiar combination (alternation) of practical, mundane, soap opera realities with flamboyant scenes of miracles, divine interventions, and bizarre plot twists.[26] For those "magical" or fantastic elements in no way, I think, cancel out or undercut the realism—though many critics have proposed this.[27] Rather, the combination of crude pragmatism and wild fantasy serves to denaturalize and demystify assumptions and patterns of behavior that otherwise are taken for granted. The "realism" of the economic, familial, and political relations that are shown working themselves out during the course of this play is designed not so much to contradict or deconstruct the world of Aeschylus and traditional Athenian tragedy as to reveal its fundamental structures (both aesthetic and moral) with greater clarity (blatancy) and less glamour. Kings, miracles, and gods are still integral to the story. But now the economic and practical realities of property ownership, travel, and political procedure have been allowed to intrude more nakedly into the decision making and the action; consequently, the sense of a natural and inevitable working out of a cosmic plan, integrating the Justice of Zeus, the Wisdom of Athena, and the Manifest Destiny of Athens in a seamless web of mutual benefit, is largely dissipated. This "Argive" world is made of the same components as that of the *Oresteia*; but they are arranged differently and less harmoniously.

The large and important questions—how different *was* Athenian society in 408 BCE as compared with the Athens of 458, how much had changed in the audience's material, political, and psychological circumstances as a result of Pericles' citizenship law, the ups and (increasingly) downs of the Peloponnesian War, the growing disillusionment about empire, and the bitter divisions, massacres, and lawsuits surrounding the oligarchic coup of 411—cannot be properly confronted and explored here. Nor is this the place to discuss at length the degree to which Aeschylus' or Euripides' audience did or did not think of "Argos" and the events of a tragedy in the Theater of Dionysus as resembling and speaking to their own contemporary *Athenian* situation.[28] But at least we should bear in mind that the physical Theater of Dionysus was almost certainly smaller in Aeschylus' day than it was in 408; and consequently, Euripides' audience was probably both less Athenian (there was room for more metics and out-of-town visitors) and also proportionately less elitist in its composition.[29] Furthermore, most Athenians would be aware that Argos (a community only seventy-five kilometers away from the edge of Attica, and a close ally of Athens for much of the fifth century) was in fact a democracy not unlike their own. So it was not a big mental stretch to imagine the events and relationships occurring in a fictional Argos as corresponding quite closely to those of a fictional (but imaginable) Athens.[30] By the late years of the fifth century, too, Euripides was composing plays with an eye to performance not only in Athens, but also abroad (Macedonia, Sicily, South Italy), and his target audience accordingly may by now have been more generally "Greek" than "Athenian." So, for example, the possibility of intermarriage between kin-members belonging to two different cities (Sparta and Argos, or Phocis and Argos) would not strike many members of this theater audience as being at all abnormal or unfamiliar—they were quite well aware that Argos never had any citizenship law like that introduced by Pericles, so its citizens, like Homer's heroes, were, and always had been, free to marry whom they wanted, near or far.

To sum up this introductory survey of the material "realities" amid which, or out of which, Euripides' latest plays were composed and presented: within the "domestic" and "real" Athenian world, the challenges facing a teenage male (especially one without a father) were not confined to military service, registration as a citizen, and civic-religious ceremonies—that is, his role within the civic community. There were many additional (prior) hazards that could, and often did, intrude between young men and the plot(s) of land, buildings, and other property that they might regard as rightfully, or potentially, theirs, and that might make it hard or impossible for them to rise to the position of prestige and authority to which their citizen birth might entitle them.[31] Likewise, there were always, for a young woman, the uncertain prospects of marriage to this or that distant (unknown?) suitor or close relative (cousin, uncle), prospects that might be known for years beforehand or suddenly concocted by the men of her family to meet some unexpected crisis.[32] In either case, these hazards might sometimes call into question their very identity, parentage, and social status. Who(se) am I, really? What shall (or can) I grow up to be? What is (or will be) mine, out of all the possibilities—and restrictions, and counterclaims—that my parents, uncles and aunts, siblings, half-siblings, cousins, and other family connections are placing on me? Which of my *philoi* can I truly trust, and which will turn out to have the power really to help me? For a boy (e.g., Orestes and Pylades), this means seeking to determine whom he should look to for support, for self-definition, and for collaboration in the public

world of the *polis*, as well as the maintenance and expansion of his family interests. For a girl (e.g., Electra and Hermione), these uncertainties
and anxieties mean, above all, waiting to find out who one's husband
will be—and in the meantime, perhaps lending support, intentionally
or not, to the claims of this or that male member of one's family in his
actions and negotiations with others.

Is all this too petty and mundane a "domestication" of the wild and
fierce (mythical, heroic, religious) impulses of tragedy? Is my emphasis
on Euripidean "realism" misguided?[33] We shall see. Of course, Athenian stage tragedies are not expected to present ordinary people facing
everyday problems and their various possible solutions (or failures). But
at the same time, it is hardly controversial to assert that family concerns
of the sort I have been describing can be detected in most of the surviving tragedies, though they are usually more deeply buried beneath the
surface than they are in *Orestes*.

LEAN ON ME:
YOUNG ORESTES' PERSONAL SUPPORT SYSTEM

Euripides' *Orestes* is the feeblest and most physically dependent of all
the young men to appear in extant Greek tragedy (with the exception
of the mangled and near-dead Hippolytus in the closing scene of that
play). When we first see him, he is lying in bed, asleep and covered in
blankets, while his sister stands by his head and tends to him;[34] indeed,
he is "stretched so extremely slack" (*lian pareimenôi*; 210) that the tip-
toeing Chorus of young Argive women fear he may be dead. When
he awakens, and we get to see and hear him speak (lamenting the
departure of sleep, which he regards as his "enchantment" and "aid
against sickness," *thelgêtron, epikouron nosou*, 211), he asks his sister
to wipe the foam from his lips and eyes (219–20), and to brush the
unkempt hair from his eyes (223–24); his limbs are unable to support
him (*anarthros eimi*, 228), and he needs her help to turn over or to raise
himself up—though he does agree to let her put his feet on the ground
for him (233–34) and "stand [him] up straight" (231), so as at least
to "give the appearance of health" (*doxan...hugieias*, 235). Nor is the
state of his mind any more robust than that of his body—the disease
that afflicts him is as much mental and spiritual as physical.

The theme of a young man's temporary weakness and insecurity, and
consequent need for the support and guidance of others, is not unique to
this play, of course. Indeed, some have seen the very essence of Athenian

tragedy as residing in its depiction of the process of ephebic crisis and successful or unsuccessful maturation.[35] But Orestes may be said to represent the paradigmatic case. If the two sons of Oedipus constitute the archetype of the irresoluble problem presented by a divided inheritance (Which son should get what, and how can the property not be depleted by the division?), then Orestes, only son of a wealthy and powerful king, embodies the opposite and less intransigent problem: how to ensure that this male heir actually survives to inherit the property and is not robbed of it by usurpers and/or an aggressive female (maternal) intervention.

The childhood and upbringing of Orestes are described variously in different sources. In almost all, however, he is said to have been removed from the palace as an infant and brought up elsewhere for the duration of the Trojan War, and for some years after his father's murder, by a family loyal to his father (and therefore, likely to harbor mixed feelings, at best, about his mother). Often it is the family Nurse who is specifically mentioned as having saved him from the clutches of Aegisthus and Clytemnestra; sometimes his sister Electra has directly helped, too.[36]

In the surviving dramas, descriptions of Orestes' helplessness as a baby (*Libation Bearers* 748–62, from the Nurse), or the accident he suffered while playing with his sister while they were both small children (Euripides, *Electra* 572–76), are emblematic of his inability yet to fend for himself and his reliance on close and loyal (female) family members to nurture him to manhood.[37] In Sophocles' *Electra*, Orestes' childish (preadolescent) ties are concretized through the presence of the Tutor whose topographical, tactical, and moral guidance is crucial to his successful return; and the Old Man of Euripides' *Electra* presents several similar characteristics. The famous recognition scenes of all three of these plays serve, among other dramatic functions, to enact Orestes' coming-of-age, as the young man begins to move beyond the status of dependency, even inferiority, in relation to his older sister and the support system required for an infant,[38] and prepare him to act, in collaboration with his sworn (male) comrade Pylades, like a man, in the name of, and in emulation of, his father.[39] This process of maturation is neither easy nor instantaneous; and it usually seems to take the partnership of a male comrade (Pylades) to see Orestes through the intermediate adolescent stage.[40] Even after the recognition, before (or while) Orestes kills his mother, in these plays he is regularly shown hesitating, turning to either Pylades or Electra for reassurance and encouragement, and recoiling in momentary dismay at the intimate prospect of—or direct contact with—his mother's (vulnerable, naked, maternal, or sexual) body.[41] After the matricide, too, there are moments when

Orestes is reduced to a cowering object of the Furies' pursuit, a suppli-
cant at Apollo's or Athena's shrine, a "rabbit" or "fawn" at the mercy
of the avenging "hounds" of his mother. Even his madness itself in several of these texts may be said to involve a regression to an incontinent
and incompetent state, one in which he is once again "like a child."[42]
Thus, the tradition of Orestes' "infancy" and immaturity enjoyed a
fairly long literary-dramatic tradition, even before Euripides' Orestes,
a tradition in which the young man's coming-of-age as a man of action
first requires his passing through several stages of extreme vulnerability
and dependency.[43]

This tradition is clearly traceable in the visual arts as well, even before
the production of Euripides' Orestes. Orestes is frequently shown in
postures of dependency, whether fearfully clutching the omphalos of
Apollo, or leaning on Electra or Pylades, or sitting or kneeling while
they stand above him. He is usually shown either younger than Pylades
or of equal age; and, of course, he is necessarily younger—and sometimes smaller—than his sister Electra.[44] This is a young man, then, who
is imagined as needing the support and loyalty of a trustworthy family
network in order to claim his proper place as king and avenger of his
father; characteristically, his role is that of a partner—often a junior
partner—rather than a leader. Deprived of his father as a baby, and
unable—to put it mildly—to count on his mother's love and nurture,[45]
he is represented as growing up to heroic stature through a combination of his own natural talents and the timely interventions of a nurse,
a sister(s), and an adoptive family (or "foster family") of guest-friends.
To them he owes his survival, upbringing, and education—and from
them he receives also armed and/or tactical assistance in his return from
exile, as he seeks vengeance and the recovery of his property and titles.[46]
Before Euripides, however, no version in the surviving traditions, poetic
or visual, seems to raise doubts about Orestes' ability at the crucial
moment to muster the manly (filial) qualities that will enable him to kill
Aegisthus and assume his father's place on the throne and in the city.
Like Hamlet, to whom he is so often compared, Orestes is intrinsically
one who is coming-of-age; and like Hamlet, he is expected to prove
himself, however tormented his soul, to be more than the equal, both
morally and physically, of his enemies.

In Euripides' Orestes, the dependent aspects of the young hero are
exaggerated, almost grotesquely so, and exploited to a new degree.[47]
Indeed, we might say that in this play Orestes' debility and "infantilization" have become almost his defining characteristics, and his progression into manhood appears to be in real jeopardy—a dynamic that

perhaps lends an even more extreme sense of the miraculous and otherworldly to his eventual "salvation" and divinely bequeathed recovery of wits, inheritance, and reputation.[48] Not only is he encountered in the opening scene lying helplessly in bed and being taken care of by his sister, but also, as the play proceeds, we learn that he was raised as a baby by Leda and Tyndareus (i.e., in Sparta), who "treated [him] just like their own two sons, the Dioscuri" (462–65). Tyndareus, as well as Leda, is said to have "smothered [him] in affection" (*polla de philêmat' exeplêse*, 462-63) and carried him around in his arms (*ankalaisi peripherôn*, 464), an image that Orestes finds impossible to drive from his mind when he has to confront his angry grandfather onstage (*aidôs m' echei es ommat' elthein*, 459–69, especially 460–61, "I am too embarrassed to look at him face-to-face"—a distorted echo of Aeschylus' Orestes, face-to-face with his mother's breast, *Libation Bearers* 896–904).

As the play proceeds, we see Orestes, in his efforts to stand up for himself in the world, entwine himself "flank to flank" first with Electra (*hupobale pleurois pleura*, 223), then with Pylades (*peribalôn pleurois emoisi pleura*, 800). He hangs from each of them in turn, as he is carried around the orchestra and on- and offstage (*ochêsô*, 802; cf. 878–83, 1015–17). This infantilization extends to other contexts as well. When Menelaus arrives (356) and asks the Chorus where he might find Orestes (remarking that he was "only a little baby in Clytemnestra's arms" when he last saw him, *brephos*, 377–78), Orestes is lying bundled up, alone onstage (since Electra has gone inside to rest); he then immediately throws himself on the ground to clasp his uncle by the knees in supplication (382), remaining in this posture for much of the scene that follows. Like the Chorus, Menelaus wonders if he is looking at a corpse (*tina dedorka nerterôn?*, 385). When old Tyndareus arrives, Orestes is initially too terrified and ashamed to face him (462–65), and apparently he spends the first half of the scene still cowering on the ground (456–543). A little later, Orestes' journey into town to face the Argive assembly (792–806) is only possible because Pylades is able to act as the "rudder for [his] foot" (*oiax podos moi*, 795) and virtually "carry [him] through the city" (*di' asteôs se...ochêsô*, 801–2); he returns in similarly helpless mode with Pylades still "directing his sickly limbs" (*ithunôn noseron kôlon*, 1015–16). His first reaction upon his return is to plan suicide with his sister, after an embrace (1044) that will "melt [him] up completely...breast to breast" (*ek toi me têxeis. kai s' ameipsasthai thelô philotêti cheirôn...ô stern' adelphês, ô philon prosptugm' emon ktl*, 1047–48).[49]

Orestes' dependency on others is thus a defining feature of his appearance throughout most of the play; and this dependency is both physical and mental/spiritual. At first it is his sister who provides the needed care and support (following a common pattern within fatherless families, as we noted above); but once Pylades arrives, this role is largely taken over by him instead—though the similarity and complementarity of Electra's and Pylades' roles comprise one of the more striking features of this play. That is to say, the degree of "sexual difference" between these two devoted supporters of the feeble Orestes is not as marked as we might have expected: either or both can serve as a precious source of "support" for a youthful and still highly vulnerable (even incapable) potential heir and citizen. On the other hand, it seems as if the debilitating effect of his mother's Furies, which Electra is more or less powerless to mitigate or dispel (indeed, there are moments when it appears as if she or the female Chorus are themselves part of the origin of Orestes' hallucinations), is most effectively and completely countered and neutralized only by Pylades' presence.[50] In any case, it is only when the revenge plot is hatched that Orestes begins to summon up the independent strength and energy to stand, run, and fight for himself—and even then he and Electra resort to the false (but believable) report that he has "fallen at Helen's knees as a suppliant" (*hiketês gonasi prospesôn*, 1332). In these later scenes, Orestes' manliness does prove sufficient at least (with Pylades' help) to overpower the unarmed attendants and women in the palace, to intimidate the Phrygian slave, and to capture Hermione and hold her hostage; and in the final confrontation with Menelaus, he cries out to Electra and Pylades simultaneously to set light to the palace, bottom and top (1618–20), while he himself stands poised to slit their hostage's throat. But his prowess is never really put to the test. For just as it begins to appear that the three of them may possibly be able to escape alive, the situation is suddenly defused by Apollo's arrival. Thus, we never find out exactly what (how much new harm) Orestes is now capable of inflicting with his own hand.

Overall, this visual and verbal representation of Orestes as an invalid or virtual child for most of the play is, as we have seen, an arresting innovation (or exaggeration of one strand of the previously existing tradition). It is as if he has reverted to the status of a baby[51]—or of someone over whom the Furies have successfully cast their "binding spell." It is especially striking that Euripides presents him initially lying on a bed—a stage prop that not only is usually associated with the female, interior space hidden behind the doors of the *skene* (and only visible when the *ekkuklêma* is used to bring out an interior tableau of some kind), but that also is likely to recall the stool or easy chair on which Aegisthus is so often shown in vase paintings leaning backward (toppling off it, in some cases) as Orestes advances to stab him. The staging of this scene, with Electra devotedly tending to her infantilized, helpless brother like a mother or nurse, was a matter of great interest and controversy in antiquity, it appears[52]—and it is the subject of perhaps the most remarkable surviving wall painting that depicts ancient Greek actors actually performing a scene from a known tragedy.[53]

IN-LAWS, SUPPORT SYSTEMS, AND OTHER "CONCERNS"

By presenting Orestes in this dependent posture, ever in need of protection and support from others—from his sister (Electra), from his uncle (Menelaus), from his friend and cousin (Pylades), from his grandfather and former guardian (Tyndareus), and even in the end, indirectly from his aunt and female cousin (Helen and Hermione), and directly from another cousin (Apollo-on-high)—Euripides has focused the audience's attention on the young man's inescapable involvement in a number of alternative, or complementary, "support systems." Someone always has to be there to take care of him; but the care can come from quite disparate sources.

The natural place for anyone to look for such care, of course, is one's *philoi*—the standard Greek term for a person's "nearest-and-dearest" (whether family or friends and associates); and Orestes in this play is no exception. He does indeed expect support and loyalty from his *philoi*. But the term's very broadness (as often) results in much confusion and disappointment when one set of *philoi* proves much more trusty and loving than another.[54] We do find a more specific Greek term, however, that is used several times with reference to the special claims for "concern" and "care" that surround this young hero's predicament: *kêdos, kêdomai*, ktl., a root that covers both "care, concern, distress," and, more specifically, "marriage-relation, in-law."[55] As we look at Orestes' primary "caregivers," both these sets of meanings tend to overlap. Obviously, the closest to him by blood and upbringing, and the most constantly supportive, is his sister, Electra, who has collaborated with him in the matricide (at least, to some degree),[56] has experienced the same misfortunes and uncertainties (except in not being subject to the onslaught of the Furies), and is condemned by the same vote of the Argives to die with him. As in Aeschylus' *Oresteia*, the two of them are thus united in everything,[57] except the degree to which they can each participate in public life—she cannot accompany him to plead their case in front of the Argive assembly. When the news of their condemnation is brought back, she first asks him to kill her himself with his sword (1037–40), before agreeing instead that they will embrace (1042–50) and then each commit suicide with the same sword and be buried next to one another (1052–53). Then, as Pylades' suggestion of a vengeance plot gains momentum, she again participates eagerly with the two young men in the action (more like her namesake in the two *Electra* plays than in the *Oresteia*), herself waiting "in front of the palace" (1216–17) and luring Hermione into Orestes' trap. In the final tableau, it is not certain whether Electra is visible on the roof with the other two—probably not, as she is ordered to "set light to the lower parts of the palace" (*huphapte dômata*, 1618);[58] but her presence is still strongly felt, and her supporting role is as indispensable to her brother as ever.

Almost as close to Orestes as Electra—indeed, in some respects even closer—is the beloved Pylades. The two of them, as so often in Greek tradition,[59] constitute a paradigm of homosocial companionship and blood brotherhood: Pylades is "a trusty man" (*pistos anêr*, 727), "dearest of all age-mates and friends and relatives to me [*philtath' hêlikôn emoi kai philôn kai suggeneias*, 732–33], indeed, you are all of these things to me" (*panta gar tad' ei su moi*, 733);[60] he is a true "comrade" (*hetairous*, 804), "like a brother" (*hôst' adelphon*, 882), "a friend-from-outside, yet better than ten-thousand blood-relatives" (*thuraios ôn, muriôn kreissôn homaimôn philos*, 805–6), the "most trusted virtual-brother...the trace-horse [sc. of their 'team']" (*pistotatos pantôn isadelphos*, 1014–15; *paraseiros*, 1017). Even more explicitly and unequivocally than Electra, Pylades is said to have "shared the bloodshed" with Orestes (*sundrôn haima*, 406; cf. *haim' epraxamen*, 1139, though *epebouleusa* ["I plotted with you," or "advised you too"], 1236, sounds less definite);[61] and increasingly it is to him that Orestes turns for physical and spiritual support as he struggles to defend himself and then to exact vengeance from his opponents. In the Greek *polis*, as a man comes of age and prepares to take action in the public sphere, it is properly his male friends, not his sister, who should be providing him with support; and these two male buddies (*hetairoi*) are drawn closer, it seems, by their decision not to inform Electra of their plan to appear before the Argives—on the grounds that she is likely to weep too much. Yet soon after they return, Orestes finds himself weeping as copiously as she (787–98, 1018–32, etc.), apparently another indication of the intense closeness, almost interchangeability, of the two siblings and of the "femininity" (at least, lack of distinctive masculinity) of Orestes' physical and ethical character.

The relationship of mutual trust, support, and self-sacrifice—and also of extreme daring and bloodthirstiness—shared by the two young men amounts to a brotherhood closer than one of mere blood (805–6). The two cousins behave as virtual twins, matching and exceeding the closeness of the two actual siblings' relationship. The terms of "comradeship" and "trust" exchanged by Orestes and Pylades tap directly into a deep cultural wellspring of elite homosocial "age-mate" groups and political "clubs/factions."[62] But their relationship in this play draws additional strength and resonance from two further facts: first, that Pylades, even though he is described as an "outsider" (*thuraios*, 805), is nonetheless related to Orestes and Electra[63] and is thus involved in the preservation of the same "noble stock" (*eugeneia*) that he insists is so unique to Orestes (e.g., 784, 870, 1155–57), and second, that Pylades and Electra are already engaged to be married. We learn this for sure only at 1078–1100—but we probably already anticipate it, both from the mythological tradition (e.g., Euripides, *Electra* 1249, 1284–87) and from the dynamics of the Pylades–Orestes relationship itself, as well as the common patterns of Greek marriage that we noted earlier—for a brother's best friend, and/or a father's guest-friend's son, constitute an ideal marriage partner for a girl—especially if he is also a cousin, from the father's side. Thus, the trio of young conspirators (like the famous Athenian "tyrant-slayers") are fused by the closest possible bonds of blood relationship, shared experience, age grouping, and anticipated marriage kinship.[64] And it is to the larger workings of this kinship and marriage tie that we now must turn our attention.

As we noted above, *kêdos* and its derivatives are often used in the specific sense of "relationship by marriage."[65] In our play, *kêd-* words are found no fewer than eight times: three times referring to Tyndareus' relationship to Menelaus as his father-in-law (*kêdeum' emon*, 477; *toumon echthos...kêdos t' emon*, 623; *to toude kêdos mallon heilet' ê patros*, 752) and the other five times to Pylades' "special care" for Orestes (*kêdeusô s' egô*, 791; *phila g' echôn kêdeumata*, 795; *ton d' nosêma kêdeuonta paidagôgiai*, 882–83; *podi kêdosunôi*, 1017; *kêdos de toumon kai son*, 1081), though in the last of these occurrences the sense of "marriage connection" is also present. It is as if these two systems of mutual support and obligation come into direct competition with one another, and Pylades' figurative "concern" for his beloved blood brother is felt at first to trump the practical constraints imposed on Menelaus by his heavy-handed father-in-law. Yet, as the occurrence of the phrase at 1081 shows, it would be a mistake to see this simply as a privileging of personal affection and devotion over legal, pragmatic obligation, as if pure comradely "love" conquers the imperatives of mere expediency and social-legal convention. For Pylades, even as this emotional language of "concern" is being employed to describe his tender relationship to Orestes, is in the same breath being reaffirmed as Orestes' intended brother-in-law.

> [Or.] As for marriage—you have lost out on this
>   unfortunate girl here [i.e., Electra]
> Whom I betrothed to you [katêgguêsa] in honor of our
>   comradeship [hetairian].
> Take another wife [allo lektron] and have children with
>   her!
> The relationship between you and me [kêdos de toumon
>   kai son] is over....⁶⁶
> [Pyl.] You are completely misguided about my thinking....
> I co-killed [sunkatektanon] with you, I don't deny it,
> And I planned [or "commanded"]⁶⁷ everything that you are
>   now being punished for.
> So I should also die with you and with her—
> For, since I agreed to marry her [lechos epêinesa],
> I regard her as mine, my wife [emên damarta].
>   (1078–81, 1085, 1089–93)

The "bonds, concerns" (kêdos, 1081) of blood-relationship, marriage, and conspiracy (hetairian, 1079; sunkatektanon, pant' ebouleus', 1089–90; cf. bouleumatôn, 1085) thus draw the three together in a mutually reinforcing knot that proves tighter and stronger than any other family or political ties that can be invoked against it. And it will be these bonds, in the end, that succeed (with some Olympian reinforcement)—despite all expectations—in restoring the fortunes of the house of Atreus and achieving an acceptable outcome for all.

The relationship that is depicted between these three youngsters, two men and one woman, strikingly blends and blurs their identities. Almost identical expressions are used to describe the physical and psychosocial "merging" of first Electra, then Pylades, with the emaciated and demoralized Orestes (223/800 and 284–5/1090 respectively); and all three characters participate in the ritual invocation to the dead Agamemnon (1204–49), a parody, or recapitulation, of the celebrated kommos of Aeschylus' Libation Bearers.⁶⁸ Even the erotic undercurrents commonly present in Greek male homosocial pairings seem to spill over into Orestes' and Electra's expressions of "melting together," "embracing," and dying together (1044–48).[69] Thus, as Orestes speaks of his intention of marrying off his beloved sister to his beloved comrade, the dynamics of three-way devotion are as intimate as could be imagined.

Then, as the news of the Argive death-verdict is brought home, once the immediate response (tears, suicide pact) is over, an interesting sequence ensues, one that both reinforces the solidarity of this interdependent trio and also injects a new note of "difference" among them. For whereas it is the male Pylades who initiates the idea of retaliation—not to let Menelaus get away scot-free, but to exact some measure of vengeance by killing Helen before they die (1105ff.)—Electra then proceeds to develop the plot in a new, and ultimately more creative, direction by proposing the capture of Hermione and use of her as a hostage to force Menelaus' cooperation (1177ff.), a plan that in the end (and in a manner that Electra herself obviously could not have anticipated) does indeed bring about "salvation" for them all, specifically through the potential for Hermione's (re)adoption into the extended family's marriage arrangements. Thus, it is female agents and female objects of exchange that bring about the successful resolution of the apparently hopeless impasse. Just as it was to his wife and niece, Clytemnestra and Electra, that Menelaus "led...and gave his maiden daughter" some fifteen years ago for safe tutelage (62–66), now once again it is Electra who insistently claims credit (*egô*, 1177–79) for the proposal that, she says, can bring "salvation...for all three of us, for you, for him, and for me" (*sôtêrian soi tôide t' ek tritôn t' emoi*)—that is, the proposal that her brother take that same maiden into his hands, fresh from her successful "propitiation" of Clytemnestra's spirit through libation and offerings of hair (cf. *preumenê*, 119) so that he can negotiate with her father about her future prospects.

As Orestes remarks, this proposal is a "stroke of divine forethought!" (*theou legeis pronoian*, 1179). It would be a mistake, certainly, to suggest that Electra's creative invention (the idea of taking Hermione hostage), as compared with Pylades' (the idea of murdering Helen), is meant to be understood as displaying her warmer or more sensitive (feminine?) character—for it is clear that Electra is perfectly willing to see Hermione killed (1199) if Menelaus will not capitulate, just as she relishes the prospect of the killing of Helen (1191). But it is probably significant that it should be the female ally (*philos*) of Orestes who is the one to articulate a plot that leads—through negotiation over a daughter/cousin—to the house's ultimate regeneration.[70] It was she, along with Helen, who began the process of neutralizing Clytemnestra's wrath through sending Hermione to the tomb in the first place, and now it is she who prepares the ground for her brother's marriage and establishment of his new in-law relationship (*kêdos*) with his uncle. And we are given a direct verbal clue to this switch of polarities, for whereas Orestes observed earlier that it was his own "understanding" (*sunesis*, 396) [sc. of the ghastly thing he had done] that was haunting him in the form of the Erinyes, now he can state that it is the special "understanding present in [his sister's] heart" (*to suneton...sêi psuchêi paron*, 1180) that will provide them with collective "salvation" (1178, *sôtêrian*).

In the climactic final scene, the reconciliation between the warring parties that is pronounced by Apollo is framed entirely in terms of arranged marriages. First, Menelaus, whose existing marriage has now been finally and mercifully annulled, since it is "required" (*chreôn*, 1635) and "commanded by father Zeus" (*keleustheis...ek Dios patros*, 1634) that Helen become immortal and dwell in the heavens (1633–37): he can now pick "another bride" (*allên numphên*, 1638) to bring home with him.[71] No less important (and inseparable from that remarriage-deal) is the stipulation that Menelaus will also receive the rule of Sparta "as a dowry from his wife," or "keeping [this] dowry of his wife" (*phernas echôn damartos*, 1661–63), the implication being that the divorce settlement arranged for the troublesome Helen, contrary to usual procedure (by which the wife keeps her dowry in returning to her father's house),[72] will allow Menelaus to gain possession of the throne that was the "dowry" for Helen's husband—which seems to entail that Tyndareus, Helen's official (i.e., human) father, is being required to step down in favor of the man who is Zeus' true son-in-law. Second, Menelaus must now "give" his daughter, Hermione, to Orestes in marriage (1653–57), so that the current of hostility that has been flowing between uncle and nephew—and between Sparta and Argos— throughout most of the play can now be neutralized (*neikous...dialuesthe*, 1679) and replaced by the in-law bond of betrothal, exchange, and mutual elite benefit (*soi de paid'egô kategguô...eugenês d' ap' eugenous gêmas onaio kai su kai chho didous egô*, 1675; cf. 1671–72).[73] Third, Pylades and Electra are instructed to marry, with Orestes reaffirming this "gift" of his sister to his best friend (*Puladêi d' adelphês lektron...dos*, 1658–59), and are assured that they will "live happily ever after" (*ho d' epiôn nin biotos eudaimôn menei*, 1659). These commands from Apollo seem all, at one level, arbitrary and at variance with the personal dynamics that we have witnessed onstage over the previous few scenes;[74] yet at another level they are entirely consistent with the pattern of "in-law" priorities that has pervaded the action of the play from start to finish. As an immensely powerful if distant[75] cousin of Orestes, Electra, and Hermione—and half-brother of Helen—Apollo is entitled to call these shots, and Zeus in the end is recognized as asserting claims as a father-in-law that are more powerful even than Tyndareus'.

The previous betrothal of Hermione to Neoptolemus will be cancelled by Apollo's violent intervention: "He will never marry her" (*hos d' oietai...gamein nin, ou gamei pote*, 1654–55), for "death is the deal for him" (*thanein gar autôi moira*). So the young northerner (outsider), unsupported by dynastic ties, will be eliminated through "Delphian assassination" (*Delphikôi xiphei*, 1656). The prosperous future of all branches of the Atreid family, and of Sparta and Argos, is thereby (it appears) assured. Whether Orestes and Hermione will also "live happily ever after" is not explicitly stipulated (as it is for Pylades and Electra, who are, after all, long-time fiancés of one another), but Orestes accepts it as a "fine and perfect conclusion" (*eu teleitai*, 1670). Their feelings for one another hardly come into consideration as yet; that is not usually the chief point of marriage. But there is no particular indication to suggest that this marriage will not do (and be) what it needs to do (and be). Greek mythology is after all (notoriously, by modern standards) full of brides who adapt quickly to the change of fortune whereby their captor (not infrequently the sacker of their city, and sometimes even the killer of their first husband) becomes their new husband and protector. The knife held so recently by Orestes at Hermione's throat (1653) presents—by such standards—no reason for us to doubt the likely success of this divinely sanctioned new marriage, even though the starkness and abruptness of this *volte-face* sharply accentuates the arbitrariness, even crudity, of such demystified marital power brokering.[76] The arranged marriages manage, in fact, at a single stroke to solve the urgent problems of inheritance and property ownership that have underlain the whole action of the play—problems that have tended often to loom larger than the mere guilt or innocence of Orestes.

Issues of inheritance and control over the house of Atreus are central, to be sure, in Aeschylus' *Oresteia*; but there the prospect of marriage between Pylades and Electra, or between Orestes and anyone, is never raised. In Euripides' *Orestes*, questions concerning family property and inheritance are no less frequently posed, as dynastic violence and divine interventions once again destabilize everything in Argos (and this time in Sparta, too), yet eventually succeed in combining to restore the house to the rightful heir(s)—that is, Agamemnon's son (and daughter)—against the attempts made by other claimants. Concern for property—and

especially, loss of land, home, and patrimony—is expressed constantly
in our play, not only by Orestes and Electra, but also by Menelaus and
Helen, and even by Pylades.[77] Menelaus and Helen seem to have lost
their home as well as their power base in Sparta; and Pylades' father
has just disinherited him and banished him from Phocis completely. As
for Orestes and Electra, they face the most uncertain future of all, and
their "inheritance" (both material and symbolic) is the most acutely
jeopardized. The pervasive sense of uncertainty as to whether they will
personally be exonerated, exiled, or executed, is thus compounded by
the additional anxiety as to whether their Argive house (if it is indeed
still "theirs") and its inherited possessions will be taken over by these
"Spartans," all of which adds further tension and mistrust to the intra-
family negotiations.[78] The eventually happy outcome promised by
Apollo to both the children of Agamemnon and Clytemnestra—in each
case involving marriage into an illustrious branch of their own extended
family—provides the unexpected yet logical denouement of the play.
In particular, Orestes' taking of Hermione from Menelaus (under
Apollo's guidance) to be his bride not only is supposed to mend the
rift between uncle and nephew, but also solves all the residency issues
at a stroke, since both Orestes and Hermione will henceforth be "at
home" in Argos as well as Sparta. The marriage may even perhaps mitigate the feud between Orestes and Tyndareus and return them to the
earlier state of intimacy and mutual devotion.[79]Such a dynastic "solution" to political crisis appears to be quite characteristic of the power
politics of the Archaic age of *turannoi* and aristocratic oligarchies, and
such intercity elite relationships and networks of marriage and guest-
friendship were far from obsolete in Greece—even in Athens—during
the late fifth century and beyond.[80] And on a less grand scale, as we
observed in the discussion of Greek social and familial relations, the
phenomenon of different branches of an extended family, owning—and
squabbling about—property in several different communities inside or
outside Attica, and attempting to enforce their claims, or consolidate
their strength, by any means possible, was quite widespread: smear
campaigns (including accusations of impurity and impiety), lawsuits on
criminal or civil issues (aided by *proxenos*-representation, if necessary),
confiscations, marriages, political canvassing, and so on—no holds
were barred, with families bitterly divided in loyalties and interests.[81]
Euripides' Athenian (and non-Athenian) audience would recognize,
even amid the bizarre excesses of matricide and Phrygian-slave arias, an
economic (or "domestic") struggle of an all-too-familiar kind.

The theater audience would also have recognized, in the discussions
that lead up to the Argive assembly and in the debate and vote that

are narrated as taking place there, a distorted version of the kind of legal-political maneuverings and democratic procedures (accusations and intimidation, foreign interventions and intercessions, ferocious debates and more or less popular votes) that tended to arise when Athenian (and other Greek *polis*-based) elite families were accused of high crimes.[82] The vote that is to be taken to decide the fate of Orestes and Electra is described as being that of the whole city of Argos (*ekklêton Argeiôn ochlon polin*, 612–13; cf. *edoxe d' Argei*, 46). It is before a democratic assembly that Orestes pleads their case (857–956), with speeches being delivered by (at least) four other Argives, leading up to a final vote from the citizens at large (*psêphôi edoxe*, 857–58; *en plêthei cherôn*, 944). Mention is also made by Tyndareus of a possible jury trial that Orestes could have initiated against his mother (*haimatos dikên diôkonta*, 500–501; *nomou*, 503) instead of killing her with his own hands. But at the same time, it is obvious to all that Spartan interests are continuing to play a major role; and in the end, the resolution of the crisis is engineered not only by the political institutions of democratic Argos, but also by powerful external agents deriving from Phocis, Delphi, and Olympus itself.

Euripides has set the action of this play in a sociopolitical context that resembles in several respects current Athenian (and Argive) practice—more so perhaps than is usual for tragedy.[83] Of course, both mythical "Argos" and also "Athens" itself under Theseus are not infrequently presented in tragedy as being governed at least partly in democratic fashion.[84] But perhaps no surviving tragedy gives us such an immediate and "realistic" picture as *Orestes* of the interactions between the different kinds of individual, local, and familial interests that fuelled discussions of policy in the assembly and prompted lawsuits between citizens, about which we hear so much in Aristophanes, Thucydides, and the orators. So the play is often read as a critique of late fifth-century Athenian democratic politics—a reading that entails focusing primarily on the male (citizen) participants and downplaying the prominence given to Electra, Helen, and Hermione, figures who would, of course, have no role to play in a contemporary Athenian "political" context. Indeed, it is true that the Argive assembly meeting that is narrated by the Messenger (852–956) is all-male, and the chief agents of Orestes' and Electra's fate appear on the face of it to be male, too (Menelaus, Tyndareus, Pylades, Apollo). But gender politics, alongside the workings of the democratic and militaristic homosocial institutions of the *polis*, turn out to be both indispensable and salutary, and the voices—and actions—of women in this play are by no means marginalized. The Chorus, who appear to be wives of the Argive elites (*philtatai gunaikes*, 136), are on the whole sympathetic to Orestes' and Electra's situation and appear to wish them to escape the death penalty, though they do express some horror at their deed. More particularly, nobody in Argos—or anywhere in Greece, for that matter—seems to be unaware of the degree to which Tyndareus' daughters are responsible for all of this. And as the play proceeds, Electra, Helen, and Hermione all make key interventions that bring to the surface the significance of the roles played by daughters and sisters of elites. Much of the public and private discussion by the men centers on the issue of controlling women and the need to punish breaches of proper marital behavior. As we have noted, it is the chain of decisions and actions taken by Helen and Electra, and centering on Hermione, that brings the human action to the point where Apollo's intervention can be successful.

Hermione is thus the key to the outcome of the play. She is in fact the one character whose conduct and person are both beyond reproach and entirely efficacious. She says little, it is true. As a (very) young woman,[85] she has little apparent authority or power to wield. Yet as a young elite female, she possesses (or embodies) immense social value, both as an object of potential exchange and as a representative performer of ritual acts on behalf of the family and community as a whole.[86] Even on first mention, she is described as being "a kind of comfort, relief" (*tina parapsuchên*, 62) for her mother's troubles and pains:[87] it is "in her that [Helen] rejoices and forgets about troubles" (*tautêi gegêthe kai epilêthetai kakôn*, 65). And this medical-ritual power of restoration turns out to be strangely successful. For when Hermione does perform an act of her own, on the instructions of her mother and cousin, it is in the furtherance of attempted reconciliation and propitiation of Clytemnestra's angry spirit (112–25, especially *preumenê*, 119) by means of libations and offerings of hair; and when she later reappears and speaks, toward the end of the play, it is to reassure Electra that she has indeed successfully "obtained the good will" of the murder victim (*labousa preumeneian*, 1323). This is, of course, an inversion of the usual motif in other Orestes/Electra-plays, in which it is at Agamemnon's tomb that such ritual offerings are made (unsuccessfully by Clytemnestra, impiously by Aegisthus, and vengefully by Orestes and Electra).[88] Here, Hermione acts simultaneously on behalf of both Helen and Electra— just as her final words in the play, as she departs indoors into the trap that has been laid for her by Orestes and Electra, cheerfully assert her readiness and ability to save the day for everyone: "Be saved—as far as depends on me!" (*sôthêth' hoson ge toup' eme*, 1345). The "salvation" that she provides will in fact extend to include everyone, just as Electra had intimated earlier (*sôtêrian*, 1178), as Hermione is converted, in a reversal of the process suffered by Iphigeneia and so many other sacrificial "victims" in tragedy, from animal prey into bride and object of unproblematic and nonviolent exchange.[89]

CONCLUSION:
THEY ALL LIVE HAPPILY EVER AFTER—THANK GOD!

In purely human-political terms, what follows after Orestes and Pylades return from the assembly meeting consists of an attempt at crude personal vengeance amounting almost to a *coup d'état*, conducted by three members of two closely related elite families and directed against two rival (and again, closely related) family members who they feel have betrayed and humiliated them. In Orestes' eyes, his bosom companion (*hetairos*) and virtual brother (*isadelphos*, 1015) has proven himself truer and nobler than any of his more immediate family, and their joint plan to kill Menelaus' wife and daughter, set fire to the palace, and go down fighting, originally designed as an act of desperate revenge and disgust, morphs into a sensational bid for escape—and for a shocking end to the glorious house of Atreus itself. But before the final decision can be made (Will Orestes actually kill his hostage? Will the palace go up in flames? Or will Menelaus grant the three of them safe passage out of danger?), another foreign, dynastic element intrudes from on high—overdue, sensational, yet not entirely unexpected. The interests of Delphi and Olympus—and even, indirectly, of Athens—at last, assert themselves, in the superhuman form of Orestes' and Electra's cousin, and Pylades' neighbor, Apollo.

As divinities, Apollo and his father, Zeus, have no direct, day-to-day involvement in (human) Argive politics, of course. But Zeus' close relationship to both Tyndareus and Menelaus (and his even closer relationship to Leda and Helen) is clearly an important factor in Apollo's intervention to save Menelaus and Helen's daughter (1633–37, 1673); and already, Zeus' interest in all the "blessed" Tantalids is affirmed from the opening lines (4–10, with 4–5, *makarios…Tantalos*).[90] Another factor is Zeus' support of the Greek war effort against Troy, for which Agamemnon and his descendants need to be rewarded and their opponents correspondingly punished (1639–42). As a Phocian, Pylades is felt perhaps also to embody some of Apollo's interest in Orestes' wellbeing (as in the *Oresteia*); but he, too, in any case, is descended from Zeus (*Zeu progone*, 1242–43),[91] and his perfectly timed arrival at the midpoint of the play thus has served almost as a rehearsal for Apollo's at the end. It is these two brilliant young ephebes, Pylades and Apollo, who therefore between them "save" the ailing Orestes and restore him and his household to a new and better life—through the grace of well-designed marriages. As often happens in Greek tragedy, this "salvation" is presented as being simultaneously an act of divine generosity and a mark of specifically Athenian political virtue, for Orestes is told (1648–52), "After you go to the city of the Athenians...the gods as judges of your case...will pass a most pious verdict (*eusebestatên psêphon dio-isousin*), from which you are to win [the case]." Only the courts of Athens, we may infer, are capable of representing properly the interests and wishes of the Olympian royal family. The citizens of Argos have shown that they cannot do it; and the greedy elites of Sparta will not either. But with the help of Delphian Apollo and the Phocians,[92] this elite network of families has managed (in the nick of time) to negotiate for itself a successful escape from its disastrous dynastic and internecine entanglements, and has found a means of recouping and consolidating its resources and power bases for the future, a process of "regrouping" that, as we saw, will be sealed by the most familiar and effective method possible—a double marriage.

The Phocian royal family (itself originally descended from Zeus) will henceforth include among its in-laws Tyndareus' granddaughter (Electra), herself also an in-law of Zeus and Apollo. The leading Argive family likewise will include not only an in-law of Zeus (Orestes), but also one of Zeus' direct descendants (Hermione)—and she will also cement an alliance with the two most powerful Spartan families, those of Menelaus and Tyndareus. The Phocian and Argive elites will continue to be linked with one another in renewed kin- and guest-friend alliances, both through the comradeship of Pylades and Orestes, and through the marriage of Electra to Pylades. Orestes' position—and likewise, the retrospective "justice" (legitimacy) of his matricidal act of vengeance—now emerges as unassailable. His new father-in-law blesses him: "Noble-born, [by] marrying [one] from noble-born, may you benefit!" (*eugenês ap' eugenous gêmas onaio*, 1676–77); and Orestes confirms this blessing by metaphorically "pouring a libation" to celebrate this reconciliation and betrothal (*spendomai*, 1680).

The ending (*exodos*) of *Orestes* has provoked sharply differing interpretations from modern critics. Many have found it absurd and disruptive, and have seen it as evidence of Euripides' (intentional or unintentional) surrender to decadent and/or sensationalist theatrical tastes, or else as a bitterly ironic and alienated refusal to offer any kind

of credible or satisfying resolution to the chaotic violence that has pre-
ceded.[93] Others have been less troubled by these moral dissonances and
have focused instead on the sheer theatricality of the denouement, with its
elements of surprise, scenic composition, and structural ingenuity.[94]But
almost all these critics agree, it seems, that the hastily arranged marriages that are proposed by Apollo and immediately accepted by the
human characters comprise a sudden new twist to the already complicated plot and have little to do, thematically or structurally, with what
has come before. Whether Apollo and his fellow Olympians are taken
to represent serious objects of religious belief and veneration[95] or an
ironic and conventional theatrical device introduced as a way of short-
circuiting the impasse produced by the moral and logical bankruptcy
of this play's characters and/or of contemporary Athenian society as
a whole,[96] the solution ("salvation") that they provide and the human
relations that they establish here are seen by almost all critics as arbitrary, capricious, and patently contrived—not as arising naturally or
consistently out of the preceding action.

I have suggested in this chapter, however, that the nexus of marriages
and in-law relationships that is (re)affirmed in Apollo's dispensation
is quite closely connected to, and almost a necessary continuation of,
themes that have been repeatedly touched on and intermittently emphasized in the earlier scenes. The Olympian dimension does not preempt
or disrupt, or even transcend, the human relationships and political-
economic motivations that have driven the preceding action, but rather
confirms and endorses them, for the Olympians are part of the same
nexus of "interests" as the Argive, Spartan, and Phocian elites with
whom they interact in this closing scene.

Why have critics not noticed these connections? As we have seen, they
are really quite prominent. This is not the place to attempt (yet another)
full-scale analysis of the role(s) of religion in Athenian theater, nor of
modern (nineteenth or twentieth century) currents of interpretation of
"the gods in Greek tragedy." I will confine myself to a few brief truisms.
Religion and the divine obviously fulfill a very broad range of functions
and satisfy a number of different needs in any society. By any definition,
however, "God" or "(the) gods" stand (among other things) as imaginative projections of, and mystified systems of reinforcement for, social,
familial, and political structures on the human plane. This was as true
for the Greeks of the fifth century BCE as it is for Americans, Europe-
ans, and other world citizens of the modern era.[97]The interface between
god(s) and humans may often (indeed, usually does) require emphatic
reminders at various stages and in various contexts of the huge gulf

that separates the two, and of the mysterious and mighty power that divinity exercises in ways that are not (and should not be expected to be) transparently clear to humankind. As Orestes remarks, when things are looking extremely bleak for him and his family, "We are slaves to (the) gods—whatever the gods are!" (418); and he continues, resignedly or indignantly, "[Apollo] is biding his time (*mellei*); that's the way gods are!" (*to theion d' esti toiouton physei*, 420, in David Kovacs' translation). Generally, however, one can see that, at bottom, god(s) behave(s) in very human ways and (usually) with very human motives.[98]

In the Tantalid–Pelopid–Atreid saga, the Olympian gods represent a superpowerful "aristocratic" family that, though it is not permanently resident as a group in any one Greek *polis*, has strong personal connections to particular locations, communities, and families. These connections are reinforced by both mythological narratives and cult practices ("traditions"). So, for example, as the *Oresteia* most brilliantly demonstrates, among Athenians, Athena was felt to be virtually a resident on the Acropolis, an invaluable "soldier" (*promachos*), guarantor of "victory" (*Nikê*), almost a fellow citizen or "co-ruler" (*archôn*) of the community.[99] Likewise, Apollo's devotion to his favorite places and communities (above all, Delos and Delphi) is celebrated not only in the Homeric *Hymn to Apollo*, but also in countless cult offerings, oracular consultations, Paeans, and religious/political embassies of all kinds that we find mentioned in the texts of Homer, Herodotus, Thucydides, and the tragedians. In many other cases, a god(dess) was said to "dwell in" or "visit' a favored place on a more or less regular basis, as a kind of *metoikos* or *xenos*.[100] The god's "interests"[101] in a particular community (*polis*, *chôra*, or *oikos*) would generally include land (often a specific "sanctuary, enclosure," *temenos*), expensive and gaudy buildings and display objects (temples, statues, votives, etc., *agalmata*), livestock and material supplies (meat, grain, fancy cloth), a treasury (containing bullion and coins), and immeasurable cultural capital in the form of verbal and ritual honors, commemorative titles, aetiologies, and stories. All of these forms of "wealth, blessedness" (*olbos*) could also be owned and advertised—in lesser degree—by elite human families, though restrictions on the ostentation and style of the ornamentation of privately owned buildings and types of *agalmata* were carefully maintained, lest any human should be tempted to "think more-than-mortal thoughts." Often one or more local noble and/or priestly families would trace their ancestry to the local divinity through a "marriage" (rape, or casual liaison) between a divinity and a local nymph or human "bride" (*numphê*). Such stories might provide explanations and justifications (aetiologies) for colonies, conquests, and the traditional domination by one particular family over the other residents of a community. Although many of these stories (*muthoi*) were set in the heroic or archaic past, new stories could always be generated or adapted and new connections built between leading families and dominant local (or more distant) divinities.[102]

When Apollo appears "on high" at the end of *Orestes*—perhaps hand-in-hand with Helen (*Helenên...hêd' estin*, 1629–32),[103] or gesturing upward toward her (1631–34) as she takes her imagined place in the heavens alongside her noble brothers, the Heavenly Twins, the "Zeus-Boys" (*Dioscuri*), patrons *par excellence* of Spartan elite male homosociality,[104] but also friends and saviors to all sailors, Athenian as well as others (cf. *nautilois sôtêrios*, 1636–37)—he speaks in the name of his "Father Zeus" (1634). But he also speaks as one who is unusually "close" to both Orestes and Menelaus (*hod' eggus ôn kalô*, 1626), in both literal and symbolic terms. By his personal intervention and immediate physical contact (for he personally "snatched up" Helen [1634 *hêrpasa*] and transported her into the heavens, just as he personally was imagined as giving Orestes a bow to ward off his mother's Furies [268–70]), he reaffirms the power of a superelite family (the Olympians) to reapportion wealth, property, prestige, and legitimacy, both on the domestic and on the interpolitical (international) fronts, when this suits their interests. And this reapportionment[105] is brought about, as we have seen, primarily through the disposition of brides. Orestes "put his trust" in the Lord Apollo (e.g., 29–31, 268–72, and 1670); and although this trust has been sorely tested and shaken during the course of the play (26–31, 276, 412–26, and 1666–70) as Tyndareus' personal political power machine extended itself over more and more of the Argive political landscape and over Orestes' crumbling support system, in the end Apollo and his father do not fail their long-favored in-law dependents. Indeed, Zeus would never let his own daughter Helen suffer too many indignities—let alone murder—and Apollo would not wish his own prestige to be tarnished by the conspicuous demise of his two promising young protegés, Pylades and Orestes.[106]

The solidarity of the trio of desperate and long-suffering young codependents is in the end rewarded, not so much because of their moral integrity (despite their repeated affirmations of "nobility," *eugeneia*, and "devotion," *philia*), as because of the built-in efficacy of the social system itself. After a disastrous period of familial misbehavior and collapse, this next generation (including, crucially, Hermione) will be able, it appears, to reestablish the kin-group's power, wealth, prestige, and line of inheritance over a string of locations and communities: Argos,

Arcadia (1647, Oresteion), Sparta, Delphi-Phocis, even the "city of the Athenians" (1648–52).[107] The key to this revival of family fortunes has been not so much the political institutions of democratic Argos (though these have not entirely failed), but rather the continuity and efficacy of marriage-kin loyalty and devotion (*kêdos*), and in particular the fact that Zeus himself is a more powerful and responsive father and father-in-law even than Tyndareus. (From an Athenian perspective, it is perhaps reassuring that the Spartan interests thus find themselves eclipsed by other less threatening and even more authoritative dynastic-religious pressures.) In the final tableau, the focus is on Hermione—as it so often is, in other plays, on Iphigeneia, her aunt, as she is grasped in the hands of her sacrificial butchers and the sword is raised to her throat while men and gods are attempting to decide how, and on what terms, the Trojan War shall take place;[108] Hermione alone embodies the family's potential for "healing" (*parapsuchê*) and regeneration, as all the other characters come to recognize. Tyndareus' daughters, despite their glorious parentage and brilliant opportunities, have failed signally to maintain the dignity and prosperity of their respective husbands' estates. One has been punished by death and eternal ignominy; the other is now returning to her (natural) father and leaving the scene of her disgrace forever.[109] A new start is needed. Whether or not the marriage of Orestes and Hermione is guaranteed to provide lasting prosperity, security, a good name, and happiness for both branches of the family, the prospects at the end of *Orestes* look brighter than they have for many generations preceding. That is as much of a "happy ending" (*eu teleitai*, 1670) as we are entitled to expect.

On an optimistic (or sentimental, or religious) reading,[110] this sudden (but, if my arguments are correct, not entirely unanticipated) conversion, through Apollo's guidance, of negative, vindictive, and (self-)destructive energies on the part of the young trio into reconciliation, intermarriage, and salvation for all their respective houses, is a vindication of the power of god(s), of youthful loyalty and love, and of marriage in the face of a corrupt and ineffectual political system. Instead of burning the Argive palace, bottom and top, or losing it to the rapacious attempts of Menelaus and Helen, Orestes and his supporters will reclaim and replenish it as their ancestral home,[111] while restoring its long-standing good relations with the royal houses of Sparta and Phocis as well. As for Apollo (and less directly, Zeus), his blessing is finally delivered to those who trusted in him, and despite the puzzling slowness of his arrival and the unsettling violence provoked by his decree to commit matricide, he has been shown not to be as foolish and uncaring or irresponsible as was asserted earlier in the play.

On a more cynical (or nihilistic, or ironic) assessment,[112] this play's representation of power politics conducted through competing family alliances, local factions, comrade conspiracies, and vested interests, with passionate loyalties matched by calculated betrayals, merely reaches its most absurd extreme with the instantaneous reversal of the trio's vengeance plan into a cheerful acceptance of marriage and goodwill for the future. "Apollo" (*deus ex machina*), on this reading, is simply Euripides' theatrical shorthand for the complete breakdown of moral order and social coherence and decency—a picture that many critics find to be consistent with the late fifth-century Greek world described by Thucydides (especially his analysis of *stasis* in Corcyra and elsewhere) and implied, too, by Plato's many disapproving references to the excesses and selfish follies of the Athenian democracy.[113]

A more pragmatic-materialist reading (a combination, it might be said, of these two contrasting views) might pick up on the ancient scholiast's comment that this ending is "rather like a comedy" (*kômikôteran*), and insist that the "political" and "domestic" aspects of the final flurry of reconciliations and marriages are neither inconsistent with the rest of the play nor destructive of the social fabric of contemporary Athenian life. Indeed, in many respects, the ending of this play—like almost everything else in it—merely exaggerates and thereby demystifies the mechanisms of dynastic politics that also drive the familial and inter-city negotiations played out in the *Oresteia* fifty years before. Athenian politics were perhaps not so very much changed after all: the local homosocial "clubs" (*hetaireiai*), out-of-town guest-friendships (*xeniai*), and, above all, interfamily alliances and marriage deals that had earlier fuelled the rise of the Peisistratids, of Cleisthenes and the Alcmaeonids (including Pericles), or of Miltiades and the Cimonids, were not of an entirely different kind and did not follow radically different rules from those that produced the oligarchic coup of 411 or the pro-Spartan junta lead by Critias in 404 (though such ultraconservatives as Thucydides and Plato liked to pretend that they did). This is, after all, how "politics" (and myth) tend to work in all ages; the rule of law and the authority and interests of the majority, even in a democracy, are always liable to be manipulated and undercut by the determined machinations of those who are wealthiest and best connected. And in presenting a distorted but recognizable picture of that world in the theater, the Athenian tragedians provided plenty for ambitious young men and women to learn—and to fantasize about.

The ending of *Orestes*—like the rest of the play—is neither morally reassuring, nor is it religiously inspiring (nor, for that matter, are the endings of Menander's plays). It contains little of the redemptive aura of late Shakespearian romance plays. Rather, the "arrangement of affairs" (*sustasis pragmatôn*: see p. 275 and n. 1) presents, in typically exaggerated tragic mode, the working out of a set of social oppositions and power relations that is very familiar (to the Athenians, and to other Greeks, too),[114] staging a provocative—yet far from novel— "resolution" to those old problems: Was Orestes right or wrong? What (would, should, or must have) happened after he and Electra killed their mother? What was (is) the final "verdict" on Apollo's (in)famous oracle? Aeschylus chose a resolution in which the structures of the Athenian *polis* (jury trial) and of aristocratic networking at the highest levels—including two Olympian divinities appearing in person—all converged efficiently and reassuringly to provide acquittal and "salvation" for Orestes and his family and the promise of Argive and (especially) Athenian successes for years to come. Fifty years and countless *Oresteia*s later, Euripides' play gives the Athenians a messier and more domesticated version of events, one in which the popular assembly's verdict is effectively overturned through the intervention of external superpowers (Phocis, Sparta, Delphi, Olympus), and the key negotiations are eventually brokered in terms of family interests and marriage arrangements, not political and legal institutions. Whereas in the *Eumenides* the salvation of Orestes and his "house"—and thus the justice of his act of matricide—hinged on the issue of paternity and Athena's lack of a mother, in *Orestes* it hinges on the person of Hermione (as daughter of Helen) and her capacity (passively but innocently) to reconcile the demands of all interested parties. In both cases, a female voice and presence are decisive, and sexual difference (via marriage) ends up being the key to the outcome. But Euripides' play highlights to an uncomfortable degree the human costs and personal fluctuations to which dynastic power politics are always subject, even as it also appears to show that any alternatives (democratic politics? a reliable legal system? individual codes of personal morality? opportunistic coups aimed at revenge and "regime change"?) will usually fall short, often chaotically so, of providing a more workable or just solution. Not a comfortable conclusion: certainly not as reassuring as that of the *Oresteia*, or as neat and tidy as the conventional "tragic" endings of loss and suffering preferred by most twentieth-century critics, but a familiar one.

We began with Aristotle, and we may end with Aristotle. The "arrangement of events/affairs" (*sustasis pragmatôn*) in Euripides'

Orestes, and the "salvation" that is thereby brought about, has certainly not solved the moral problems exposed during the earlier scenes of the play. We cannot really say that the values of family, or of God, have been shown to be superior in any serious ethical sense to those of the (obviously corrupt and fragmented) *polis*. Nonetheless, "unexpectedly, yet coherently/logically" (*para doxan, di' allêla*: Ar. *Poet.* 9.1452a2) we have watched a well-known elite family, one to which every theater audience can relate, find a way—a very typical and mundane way, for all its miraculous and bizarre twists—to resolve its seemingly impossible differences through the mechanisms most familiar to every member of a Greek household. This is a very "universal" plot ("the kind of thing that tends to happen," *hoia an genoito*: Ar. *Poet.* 9.1451a36), and the most traditional of happy endings. No wonder this was the most popular Greek tragedy of all time.[115]

NOTES

1. For example, see Aristotle *Poetics* 6.1449b24, 14.1453b2, and 1454a14.
2. From the three major surviving tragedians, we have Aeschylus' *Oresteïa*; Sophocles' *Electra*; Euripides' *Iphigenia at Aulis, Electra, Orestes, Iphigenia in Tauris* and *Helen*; and many other fifth-century (and later) playwrights handled the topic as well.
3. Modern adapters of the *Oresteia* sometimes suggest that Clytemnestra herself might not be entirely satisfied with the outcome (e.g., Martha Graham, Suzuki Tadashi, Ariane Mnouchkine). But they have usually had to change quite a lot from Aeschylus' text and staging to make this point.
4. Neither is mentioned in the later scenes of *Libation Bearers* or anywhere in *Eum.*; cf. Tarkow (1979).
5. Modern critics have generally recognized this moral confusion: but most have seen the first half of the play as being much more serious and morally engaging than the second, which strikes many as being whimsical, inconsistent, cruel, or sensationalist (or all of these). See Assaël (1996), Biehl (1968), Fuqua (1976, 1978), and esp. Porter (1994) for a survey of critical opinions, and pp. 275, 301–308 in the present article.
6. For discussion of Tantalus' significance and pedigree within this play, see Willink (1986) and Kyriakou (1998).

7. See below for discussion of the *suggeneia* between Pylades and Orestes mentioned at *Orestes* 732–33, 1232–33.

8. For Apollo's (and Hermes') close relationship to Strophius and Pylades in the *Oresteia*, see Garvie (1970), Griffith (1995, 90–95), and below.

9. The trend owes much to the (orthodox Marxist) work of George Thomson, first published in 1946, then in an expanded edition in 1966, and more recently to the (structuralist) analyses of Jean-Pierre Vernant and his collaborators at the Centre Gernet; for characteristic and influential Anglo-American specimens, see especially Winkler and Zeitlin (1990) and Seaford (1990). For an expression of dissatisfaction with this critical trend, see Griffin (1998).

10. For a thoughtful assessment of these issues, see Allan (2008).

11. Most tragedies, of course, place the action in front of a palace or temple, and the interplay between interior (domestic, feminine) and exterior (public, political, male) space is an oft-observed source of dramatic tension and meaning: see, for example, Padel (1990) and Wiles (1997). The marginality of the Farmer's residence in *Electra* thus underlines the ineffectiveness and lack of political relevance in this version of the tyrannicide and matricide. Orestes in fact never enters the palace or city-center of Argos at all in that play. As for the staging of Euripides' *Orestes*, with the young male hero represented center stage lying on a bed—this is as complete an inversion of the gender and status norms of tragic theater as could be imagined: see further below.

12. In the *Oresteia*, no mention at all of Electra is made after the revenge plot gets under way in the middle of the second play. Nor is Pylades involved once the matricide is completed.

13. On the Classical Greek (especially Athenian) family, in its various economic and sociological dimensions, see especially Wolff (1944), Just (1989), Foxhall (1989), Sealey (1990), Cox (1998), Patterson (1998), and Foley (2001).

14. For what follows, I am particularly indebted to Foxhall (1989), Cox (1998), and Foley (2001): further references can be found there. See further Griffith (2009b).

15. The frequency in Greek mythology (including tragedy) with which royal daughters are raped, seduced, or otherwise impregnated by extremely eminent heroes or gods (or else captured and enslaved as concubines), while obviously exaggerated, may not be entirely unrepresentative of real life, especially among the elite; that is

to say, the norms of courtship, betrothal, and "marriage" (and Greek *gamos, gamein,* and *gameisthai* covered a much broader range of interactions than English "marriage") were not always observed. (The numerous plots in New Comedy involving pre-marital and extramarital pregnancies reveal a similar slippage.) See further Patterson (1998), Sommerstein (2006), and Pedrick (2008). This is a topic to which I shall return elsewhere.

16. Cox (1998, 10, 30–31). Her evidence is drawn primarily from Attic gravestones (which routinely record a husband's and wife's respective deme of origin as well as those of their father and grandfather), along with the inheritance claims that can be recovered from the convoluted arguments of surviving orations by Lysias, Demosthenes, Isaeus, and others.

17. See Cox (1998, 34), and also her appendix (216–29), which focuses in detail on this connection between endogamous elite marriage and the need to consolidate a weakened estate or recover from a major public disgrace. As Cox warns, the evidence available for this appendix is necessarily drawn for the most part from later literary sources (Plutarch, Nepos, etc.), and therefore is less reliable and useful, in economic and geographical terms at least, than the gravestones and courtroom speeches on which the rest of her study is largely based. I return to this topic below, in relation to the marriages and property relations of *Orestes.*

18. On these issues (including also rape, illegitimacy, adoption, and further discussion of metics), see further Griffith (2009b).

19. For occasional exceptions, see Cox (1998); for ambiguities and de facto imprecisions, see Sealey (1990). Pericles' partnership/marriage with Aspasia of Miletus is of course the most celebrated example.

20. It also appears to be the case that Classical Greek marriage and inheritance patterns were, broadly speaking, similar to those of many other rural Mediterranean peoples, ancient and modern: see, for example, the studies by Laslett and Wall (1972), Goody, and others cited by Cox (1998).

21. This is what Glotz termed the "solidarity of the family" (1904); cf. Foxhall (1989) and Patterson (1998).

22. Cox (1998) has good discussions of "the father/daughter relationship" (92–94), "mothers and sons" (99–103), and "mothers and daughters" (103–4); and she devotes a whole chapter to "sibling relationships (105–29). See too Golden (1990).

23. See, for example, Davies (1971), Osborne (1985), Foxhall (1989), Cox (1998), and Jones (2004).

24. Foxhall (1989); cf. Foley (2001, 7–12, 61–79).

25. For useful, though purposely inconclusive, discussion of "romance," "melodrama," "tragi-comedy," and other terms often applied to Euripides' *Orestes* by modern critics, see Wright (2005) and further below.

26. The hypothesis and scholia suggest that *Orestes* is *kômikôteron* ("rather like a comedy"); cf. Wright (2005) and below.

27. See below, for discussion of the final scene in particular, with a brief survey of critical views.

28. We might add also the possible long-term effects of enforced evacuation of the countryside (exacerbated since 413 by the presence of a Spartan garrison in Decelea).

29. See Csapo and Slater (1995), Csapo (2002), Revermann (2006), and Roselli (2007). It is not known at what date the "theoric fund" was created to provide a subsidy for less well-off citizens who wanted to attend the theater but could not afford the fee.

30. See too, on the "heroic vagueness" of tragic settings, floating between "then" (the heroic age of Bronze Age monarchies) and "now" (the contemporary world of Athenian democracy), Easterling (1985) and Griffith (1998, 21–30).

31. Both as a matter of Athenian psychosocial fact, and as a recurrent pattern of tragic conflict and resolution, the anxious dilemma of a youth faced by such challenges to his safety and prospects of success, whether in the absence of his still-living father, or in the face of his father's opposition, or under the shadow of his dead father's posthumous reputation, provided rich material for mythic treatment, including in the Theater of Dionysus. For the theme of son-father rivalry in general, see Strauss (1993) and Cox (1998); for tragedy, see Griffith (1998, 30–35).

32. Even if already married, upon the death of her father or only brother, an *epiklêros* woman might be required to divorce her husband in order to marry a male member of the agnate line, and thus keep the property "within the family."

33. A different kind of political "realism" was seen by some of the ancient scholiasts as motivating Euripides' representation of the political arena of Argos in this play, and some modern scholars have followed them: thus, for example, Talthybius is interpreted as an allegorical version of the Athenian politician Theramenes (see Willink [1986] on *Orestes* 887–97, with further references).

34. See the hypothesis and scholia on this scene; also the Ephesian wall painting of actors in performance, discussed below.

35. Vidal-Naquet (1968), Winkler (1990), Lada-Richards (1999), and Seaford (1990); and on this theme in Euripides' *Orestes*, see especially Falkner (1983) and Porter (2003). Obvious examples of tragic "ephebes" include Neoptolemus, Hippolytus, Hyllus, Haemon, and Xerxes; but the model seems not really to fit the mature Oedipus, Jason, or Ajax. For critique of this "rite-of-passage" model for Greek ephebeia, see Dodd and Faraone (2003; especially the chapters by F. Graf and S. I. Johnston).

36. Stesichorus *PMG* 218; Pindar *Pyth.* 11. 15–18; Aeschylus, *Agamemnon* 877–87 and *Libation Bearers* passim; Euripides, *Electra* 15–18; and Sophocles, *Electra* 11–16. See further Gantz (1993).

37. In Stesichorus' sixth-century choral lyric *Oresteia*, of which small fragments survive (*PMG* 210–19), Clytemnestra's dream of giving birth to a snake (*PMG* 219) seems to focus less on the snake as baby (i.e., Orestes) and more on its resemblance to Agamemnon himself, in contrast to the dream of Aeschylus' *Libation Bearers*.

38. In the *Oresteia*, it is emphasized that the hair and feet of Orestes and Electra are of similar, almost identical, texture and size (*Libation Bearers* 174–76, 228–30; 205–10), a matter to which Electra in Euripides' *Electra* alludes with great sarcasm: see further Davies (1999). The piece of cloth that provides the final proof of Orestes' identity was woven for him as a baby by Electra (*Libation Bearers* 230–31). For the childhood origin and thematic significance of Orestes' scar in Euripides' *Electra*, see Goff (1991).

39. The lion cub "in time reveals the nature from its parents," as the Chorus of Elders puts it, *Agamemnon* 727–29.

40. On the crucial significance of the homosocial male bond of "sworn comradeship" (*sunômosia, hetaireia*) in the *Oresteia*, see Griffith (1995, 94–95).

41. See Loraux (1986). In *Libation Bearers* (896–909), Clytemnestra bares her breast to him, and he appeals to Pylades for reassurance or guidance. (Electra takes no part in these later scenes of *Libation Bearers*.) In Euripides' *Electra* 1206–26, it is Electra who urges him on as he shudders at seeing and touching his mother's neck, breasts, and genitals (the text for "genitals" is uncertain here). In Sophocles' *Electra*, he is more resolute, and takes the initiative in both killings with Pylades' help, while Electra merely

stands to the side, though she has previously been seen, in one of the most famous scenes from all of tragedy, carrying her brother's supposed ashes around the stage for minutes on end in a reprise of her former nurturing and quasi-maternal role.

42. On the madness of Orestes and its debilitating effects, see Pigeau (1981), Schlesier (1985), Hartigan (1987), and Bosman (1993), Theodorou (1993); cf. too the Pythia in Aeschylus' *Eumenides*, and the childish qualities of the Furies in the same text.

43. In the *Odyssey*, the close parallelism that is frequently suggested between Orestes and Telemachus reminds us further of this immaturity, as we are shown clearly the latter's growing confidence and independence from his mother as the poem progresses; cf. Falkner (1983). But Homer's Orestes himself is not described as being particularly immature.

44. There are numerous representations of Orestes as a vigorous young warrior lunging forward vigorously to dispatch the seated Aegisthus with a sword thrust through the chest: for example, *Lexicon Iconographicum Mythologiae Classicae* (*LIMC*) "Orestes" no. 71, and also several illustrations among *LIMC* "Aigisthos" nos. 4–27; Orestes is sometimes aided in the vengeance by a bearded (i.e., older), sword-wielding Talthybius. But examples of the other types of representation, with a less assertive Orestes, are common from the late fifth century on, e.g., the well-known fourth-century South Italian (Paestan) bell-krater by Python, surely influenced by Aeschylus' *Oresteia*: see Prag (1985, 48–51), with Plates 6–21, 30–33; also *LIMC s.vv.* "Orestes" by H. Sarian and V. Machaira (vol. VII.1, pp. 68-76; vol. VII.2, pp. 50-55), "Pylades" by V. Machaira (vol. VII.1, pp. 601-604; vol. VII.2, pp. 486-87), "Elektra" by I. McPhee (vol. III.1, pp. 709-19; vol. III.2, pp. 543-49); also Porter (2003).

45. In Aeschylus' *Libation Bearers*, there are intriguing moments that suggest his mother's role in suckling and nurturing him, but these are quickly countered by the Nurse's scornful commentary and Orestes' own accusations.

46. In the case of the Dokimasia Painter's famous depiction of the scene (Boston 63.1246), see Csapo and Slater (1995, plate 2B) and Prag (1985, fig. C21); mirroring the killing of Agamemnon on the other side of the krater (Csapo and Slater 1995, plate 2A), Electra (to the right, extending her arm), shows her warm support of her brother's action and (though, unlike her mother, she does not carry a weapon) she implicitly neutralizes her mother's

belated arrival on the scene (from the left). The identification of the female figures on the two scenes is debated: I follow Prag in seeing the axe-wielding woman in each case as being Clytemnestra. Other Attic vase paintings (see n. 44 above) show Talthybius or Pylades with a sword accompanying Orestes, sometimes holding Aegisthus or Clytemnestra prisoner as Orestes prepares to kill Aegisthus.

47. Falkner (1983) analyzes several of these features well, pointing out their similarity to aspects of Neoptolemus in Sophocles' recently produced *Philoctetes* (411) and arguing that Euripides' portrayal amounts to a virtual parody of that play and its theme of the young hero's "education" into the virtue that is naturally his (from his father): Orestes, he suggests, is shown being corrupted from his potentially noble *physis* by "the poisonous *philia* that bonds" him to Pylades and Electra (ibid., 291). Porter (2003) attributes the portrait of the debilitated hero in *Orestes* to a conventional notion of (every) ephebe's intrinsic femininity and vulnerability, a cultural notion manifested also in the adolescent male's conventional availability as an object of homoerotic desire; therefore, he sees this play as merely an extreme example of a more widespread Athenian phenomenon. Orestes' disease and disablement (disability?) in this view merely exaggerate a tendency toward neediness and timidity that is already discernable in some other male adolescents in Greek mythology. The additional detail of Orestes' "bow and arrows" lent to him by Apollo (in this play, perhaps merely imaginary: cf. 264–79, with the respective discussion in Willink's commentary), as several critics have pointed out, may confirm the ephebic associations, in contrast to an adult hoplite's sword and shield. This interpretation is not incompatible with my reading of the play.

48. This miraculous salvation, and the sense of a passing through and beyond worldly suffering into a better, new (divinely assisted) existence in the beyond, has been plausibly claimed by Giuliani (2001; with further references) as providing the impulse for the inclusion of these scenes of Orestes' sufferings and madness on so many South Italian funerary vases. Some of them are apparently inspired directly by Euripides' play. I shall return to this issue on pp. 306–307.

49. See Willink (1986) ad loc. for the oddly sexual (incestuous) overtones of these expressions; see also below.

50. See especially 790–91 (*alla kêdeusô s' egô*). Do Furies ever attack female victims? For the characteristics and appearance of Erinyes in fifth- and sixth-century art and poetry, with particular reference to the *Oresteia*, see especially *LIMC*, Parker (1983), and Prag (1985).

51. See Falkner (1983, 289).

52. See, for example, Bosman (1993) and Giuliani (2001) for discussion of the visual tradition, as well as the scholia to the play itself.

53. For the Ephesus wall painting (*Hanghaus* 2, late second century CE), see Strocka (1977), with good color illustrations. It is reproduced on the cover of the paperback edition of Willink (1986) and also in Easterling and Hall (2002, 357). Inexplicably, the painting itself is now, as of my visit in summer 2006 at least, inaccessible to visitors to the *Hanghaus* museum, although most of the other wall paintings there are nicely presented. If space permitted, it would also be worth discussing here the musical dimensions of the play, especially the use of lyrics set in the manner of the "New Music" and sung by Electra and the Chorus over Orestes' reclining body (also further lyrics later by the Phrygian), as a means of eliciting additional pathos. See West (1992, 201–2, 206–7, 284–85, and 351–55) and Csapo (2002).

54. Indeed, as Aristotle observes (*Poetics* 14.1453b, etc.), tragedies characteristically present cases of violence directed by *philoi* against one another—just as here, Orestes and Electra have killed their own mother, who previously had killed her husband, who had killed their daughter, etc. See further Blundell (1989) and Belfiore (2000).

55. See LSJ *s.vv.* "*kêdos,*" "*kêdô/omai,*" "*kêdeia,*" "*kêdemôn,*" "*kêdeuô,*" "*kêdeuma,*" "*kêdestês.*" The sense "relation by marriage" is most common in the forms *kêdos, kêdemôn, kêdestês, kêdeuô* (whereas other derivatives, especially *kêdomai*, usually mean "care for, grieve, be concerned, etc."; but n.b. *kêdeuô*, "carry out funeral rites"). The terms *suggeneia* (blood-relationship) and *hetairia* (comradeship) are also used in significant contexts in this play, as we shall see, but neither acquires quite the point that *kêdos* and its derivatives are given. On Euripides' terms for kinship and family, see Perdicoyianni-Paléologou (2002; though she does not discuss the *kêd*- terms).

56. The references are ambiguous, or contradictory: she herself "held the sword," it seems (*hêpsamên d' egô xiphous*, 1235); or did she just egg him on and abet him (284–85)?

57. See n. 38 above, on the recognition scene (identical footprints and hair); n.b. their almost indistinguishable voices in the *kommos* of Aeschylus' *Libation Bearers* (editors cannot decide which lyric lines to assign to which character).

58. See Porter's good discussion (1994).

59. See, for example, Euripides' *Iphigenia in Tauris* 708–10, *Electra* 82–83, and Golden (1990, 144), and n. 14 above, as well as Belfiore (2000); see also n. 8 above.

60. The language recalls that of Andromache to Hector at *Iliad* 6.429–32.

61. This is the reading preferred by Willink at 1236. Diggle, Kovacs, and others prefer the alternative *epekeleusa* ("I urged him on, gave him the command"); see now Robbins (2008) for discussion of Pylades' role in the murder (planner? adviser?).

62. See especially Burkert (1974), on the language and behavior associated with Athenian "comrades/political clubs" (*hetaireia*) in this play; see also Willink (1986) on 682–716 and his introduction, xxii–xxv (citing Gomme-Andrewes-Dover's commentary on Thucydides book 8, pp. 128–31). See too Griffith (1995, 70–72). Falkner (1983) focuses more on the "educational" aspects of Orestes' time spent with Pylades and Electra.

63. In some traditions (e.g., Pausanias 2.29.4, Euripides' *Iphigenia in Tauris* 918), Strophius was married to Agamemnon's sister, and Pylades was thus Orestes' cousin: see Willink (1986) on *Orestes* 1232–33. In the *Oresteia*, however, Strophius is instead a longstanding *xenos* ("guest-friend") of Agamemnon (*doryxenos* Ag. 880; cf. Griffith 1995, 69 –72, 87, 93–97). See above on 732–33 (*philtath' hêlikôn...kai suggeneias*). Even though he has been banished by his father (765), at 1075–76 Orestes mentions that Pylades can expect to be able to "return" home, for "[he] still has a city...and your father's house, and a great haven of wealth" (*soi men gar esti polis...kai dôma patros kai megas ploutou limên*), and at 1093–94 Pylades himself acknowledges that such a return is possible, though not appropriate. Thus, his domestic status, like Orestes' and Menelaus', is very much in flux.

64. The iconographic and literary parallels between Orestes and Pylades killing Aegisthus and Harmodius and Aristogeiton attacking the tyrant Hipparchus have often been noted (e.g.,

Prag [1985]). The further parallel between Electra and Harmodius' sister is not evident in the iconography, but seems relevant
nonetheless.

65. See n. 55 above.

66. Here the echo of 623 is almost exact.

67. See n. 61.

68. On the allusive, or parodic, elements of this invocation (and
other scenes in the play) in relation to the *Oresteia*, see especially Burnett (1971, 205–22), Rawson (1972, 155–57), Zeitlin
(1980), and Aélion (1983). But in Aeschylus' play, it is the female
Chorus that joins the siblings in the sung lamentation, a ritual in
which Pylades is in no way involved.

69. On the conventionally very close, and occasionally quasi-erotic
(or quasi-spousal), relations between brothers and sisters in
Greek culture, see Golden (1990), Cox (1998), Griffith (2005),
and below. Perhaps it would be most accurate to say that the
boundaries between "sibling affection," "romantic love," "sexual desire," and "homosocial, same-age friendship" were drawn
differently in Classical Greece from what is customary nowadays
in the United States or Western Europe. Terming such language
"erotic" may be anachronistic. But it is important to recognize
the full spectrum of these feelings and ties, and the areas of overlap between them.

70. Likewise in Euripides' *Helen*, *Iphigenia in Tauris*, and *Electra*
(and to some degree also in *Hecuba*, *Children of Heracleidae*,
Iphigenia at Aulis, and even *Medea*), it is a female's planning
(*mêchanêma*) that provides salvation (or at least escape) from an
apparently hopeless situation.

71. The line is excised by many editors. Whether Euripides or another
Greek dramatist wrote it, it seemed (and seems) quite appropriate to the theme and circumstances of this ending.

72. Likewise at 742 it is said that Helen "brought, led" her husband
to Argos (*ekeinê keinon êgagen*); he did not bring her (as a husband customarily "leads, takes" his wife—from the initial wedding ceremony onward).

73. The language of betrothal and marriage, whereby one man "gives"
(*dounai, ekdosis*) his daughter to another "for the plowing of
legitimate children," is, as many commentators have observed, a
form of "gift-exchange" or investment loan of reciprocal favors.
See Foxhall (1989) and Foley (2001) for further language of giving and goodwill between Menelaus and Orestes.

74. Almost all modern critics emphasize the disruptive effect of Apollo's arrival and of his mode of resolving things: see Greenberg (1962), Porter (1994, 251–89) with further references. Exceptions are Murray (1965), Burnett (1971), and Sourvinou-Inwood (2003), each of them (in quite different ways) emphasizing instead the "religious" aspects of the divine epiphany.

75. *Eggus ôn,* 1626; cf. *kategguô?* 1675. See pp. 281–82, 305.

76. I do not mean, of course, myself to endorse such a moral outlook. But as Sourvinou-Inwood (2003) insists, it is important to recognize the different assumptions that an ancient Greek audience brought to the issue of marriage (and of slavery, concubinage, and relations between the sexes in general), as compared with our own. See also Sommerstein (2006).

77. For a more extended discussion of this theme in the play, see Griffith (2009b).

78. For a useful discussion of the complicated and elusive nature of "possession" and "ownership" within the context of a Classical Greek household, see Foxhall (1989).

79. As we noted above, it was Tyndareus (presumably in his palace in Sparta) who "raised me when I was little, showered me with kisses and endearments, carrying 'Agamemnon's boy' around in his arms, he and Leda too, showing as much concern for me as for their own two sons, the Dioscuri" (642–5); cf. Will (1961). From these remarks of Orestes', it remains unclear how, when, and where Orestes and Pylades came to be such close "age-mates."

80. Anderson (2005); cf. Herman (1989), Maitland (1992), Griffith (2009b).

81. See especially Maitland (1992), Cox (1998), and p. 280–83 above.

82. See further Forsdyke (2006, 30–78, 240–77), and Griffith (2009b).

83. Argos, during the later fifth and early fourth century, was in fact a democracy with institutions and operations apparently very similar to those of Athens: see further Wörrle (1964), *Supplementum Epigraphicum Graecum* L (2000/2005) 410 (citing C. B. Kritzas), and Griffith (2009b).

84. See especially Aeschylus' *Suppliants, Agamemnon,* and *Eumenides;* Sophocles' *Oedipus at Colonus;* and Euripides' *Suppliants.* By contrast, Thebes, Thessaly, or Sparta in the Athenian theater are more often presented as being riddled with monarchical and oligarchical transgression: cf. Zeitlin (1993); and see *Or.*

126-31, 348-51, 1107-14, 1532, etc. for stereotypical "Spartan" behavior.

85. Presumably, Hermione is to be imagined as being about fourteen or fifteen years old. (West [1987] suggests seventeen to eighteen.) Orestes is perhaps seventeen, Electra nineteen or twenty. Pylades may be exactly the same age as Orestes, or (more likely) a couple of years older, since (a) his roles as "adviser," "rudder," and physical supporter—and especially the metaphorical reference to his "guidance, mentoring" (*paidagôgiai*, 883)—are much more appropriate if he is the older partner of the homosocial pair, and (b) he should not be younger than Electra if he is betrothed to marry her. In general, see Golden (1990).

86. For the prominent role of young maidens in the ritual activity of a Greek community, see especially Calame (1997). For virgin sacrifice in Greek tragedy in particular, see Foley (2001, 145–200) and Roselli (2007).

87. *Parapsuchê* is a rare word, found at Sophocles' *Ichn.* 317 and Euripides' *Hecuba* 280, but nowhere else before the fourth century. It appears to mean a "cooling draught" or "application" to relieve the heat and inflammation of a fever or wound. (The upsilon is short, so not related to *psûchê*, or "soul.")

88. For the pervasive elements of such parody and role reversal in the play, see especially Zeitlin (1980), Aélion (1983), and n. 5 above. On the theme of "salvation," see especially Parry (1969) and Falkner (1983, 291–92).

89. At 658–59, an allusion to this reversal is neatly made, as Menelaus is reassured by Orestes, "You don't have to kill Hermione [sc. as my father killed *his* daughter, Iphigenia]!" For the growing prominence of scenes of female sacrifice in later Euripidean tragedy, see Roselli (2007).

90. There is not space here to explore the difficult issues surrounding the significance of Tantalus in this play. See especially Willink (1986).

91. See also Garvie (1970) and Griffith (1995, 91), for discussion of the analogies between the pairs Pylades–Orestes and Hermes–Apollo, as well as of Phocis' connections with Delphi.

92. On the role of Delphi in elite Greek politics, both public and private, and the representation of oracles and prophets in tragedy, see Parker (1985), Bowden (2005), and Griffith (2009a).

93. See n. 112 below and Porter (1994, 1–44) for a survey of critical responses—to which may be added Dunn (1996, 158–79),

who finds "an extravagant medley...an exuberant and fertile chaos that stages a mad expansion of dramatic horizons" (179); also Holzhausen (2003) and Wright (2005), who provides useful remarks about "escape-tragedies" in general, but focuses largely on Euripides' *Helen*, *Andromeda*, and *Iphigenia in Tauris*, not specifically *Orestes*.

94. For example, Willink (1986) and West (1987).

95. A minority opinion among critics: for example, Murray (1965), Burnett (1971), and Sourvinou-Inwood (2003).

96. For example, Reinhardt (2003), Burkert (1974), Schein (1975), and many others: see Porter (1994, passim for references).

97. I do not need here to discuss whether this is also true of overt theocracies. Nor (obviously) is this the place for an extended discussion of the ideological nature and functions of "religion" in general. Religion of course does many different things, for many different kinds of people. My own assumptions about its general psychosocial dynamics and manifestations in culture owe much to the writings of Emile Durkheim, Mary Douglas, Eric Hobsbawm, Clifford Geertz, and Fredric Jameson: see, for example, Griffith (1995, 1998, 2005, 2009b).

98. A *New York Times*/CBS survey conducted in 2004 (in relation to the teaching of "Intelligent Design" and/or "Creationism" in schools) found that 55 percent of adult Americans believe that "God created humans in their current form," whereas only 27 percent opted for the idea that "Humans evolved from less advanced life forms, but God guided this process," and only 18 percent had no opinion or thought that God had nothing at all to do with the creation or evolution of the human race. In Archaic and Classical Greek, too, although the Olympians are not so explicitly credited with creating humans in their own image, Zeus is frequently described as the "Father of gods and men," as if his nature and "ours" are fundamentally the same; likewise, "Dê-Mother" (Demeter) and "Daughter" (Korê) were seen as models of universal human family types.

99. See Sommerstein (1989) on Aeschylus' *Eumenides* and Griffith (1995); cf. Sourvinou-Inwood (2003, 236–42) and Kennedy (2006).

100. Burkert (1985). For the Athenian context, see especially Parker (2005) and also references for *theoxenia*.

101. A common term to denote a god's "concern, interest" in a particular location or community is *melei* ("is dear to, is an object

of concern to"), in the formula "God X, to whom place Y is a concern, is dear"; cf. *Or.* 1689–90.

102. We may think, for example, of Peisistratus' importation of "Athena" (Phye), or the Alcmeonids' (or, e.g., Alyattids') extravagant cultivation and enhancement of Apollo's sanctuary at Delphi, as reported by Herodotus. Likewise, in the Judaeo-Christian tradition, the biological, symbolic, mythic, and territorial continuities between King David and his spiritual-political descendants (including, according to some, Jesus of Nazareth, through the "stem of Jesse," growing anew in Bethlehem), are supposed to guarantee various kinds of material and spiritual blessings, including control of Jerusalem—where the Prophet Mohammed in turn chose to stage his final departure from this world.

103. For discussion of the staging of this scene (Is Helen present with Apollo or not? And are lines 1631–32 authentic or not?), see Willink (1986) and West (1987).

104. Kennell (1995). See, too, the end of Euripides' *Electra*.

105. Terms for "portion, share, assignment, fate" are prominent in this scene, as a shorthand for what the Olympians assert "must" be accepted by all parties: *chreôn*, 1643, 1679; *chrê*, 1652; *peprôtai*, 1654; *moira*, 1656; etc. Each of these terms can also regularly signify material goods, finances, and property: for example, *chrêmata*, *poroi*, (*hektê*)*moroi*, ktl. Likewise, *daimôn* ("god, spirit")—like Latin-derived "fortune"—frequently occurs in words denoting "wealth" and "prosperity" (especially *eudaimonia*); so we find in *Orestes* that at first "the god is wealthy in evils towards me" (*ho daimôn d' es eme plousios kakôn*, 394; cf. 504), but later the "livelihood" for Pylades and Electra will be "happy and prosperous" (*biotos eudaimôn*, 1659).

106. Similar concerns in Aeschylus' *Oresteia* motivate Zeus and Apollo to protect the interests of Agamemnon and his son and heir, together with their sworn guest-friend allies (Strophius and Pylades), but in that treatment, Athena and Athens play a much larger role in negotiating the final settlement; see Griffith (1995, 94–107).

107. The Athenian trial is obviously not given nearly as large a role here as in Aeschylus' *Eumenides*; nor is comparable mention made of ties between the two cities of Argos and Athens as in *Eumenides*. But Euripides' audience will, to some degree, take this Aeschylean outcome for granted (once the Areopagus trial is mentioned); and the existence of the Athenian festival of the Anthesteria, with its prominent role assigned to the commemoration of Orestes'

solitary drinking as a visitor to Athens, will likewise assure the audience that they are positively affected too by this Apollonian dispensation. For such aetiologies, see further Dunn (1996, 46–63, 72–79, 93–97), Sourvinou-Inwood (2003), and Kowalzig (2007). For the possibility that Euripides may also have a wider non-Athenian audience in mind (some of whom may be accustomed to finding "salvation" from "sickness," or even from life itself, through divine intervention and entrance into a new and better world), see n. 114 below, and Giuliani (2001).

108. This was a favorite scene in fifth-century and later Greek visual art: for example, *LIMC s.vv.* "Iphigenia," "Polyxena." The tableau is described vividly by the Chorus of Aeschylus' *Agamemnon* (who themselves refer to "pictures," *en graphais,* 242). See Wohl (1998) and Roselli (2007), with further references.

109. Previous generations of distinguished brides have also contributed to the messy history of the Tantalid family (Aerope, etc.). But they cannot be discussed here.

110. See, for example, Spira (1960), Murray (1965, 80ff.), Ebener (1966), Steidle (1968), Burnett (1971), and Sourvinou-Inwood (2003, 386–402, 410–14); further discussion can be found in Porter (1994, 264–68).

111. Perhaps it is not fanciful to see Pylades' engagement with the "cornices, battlements" (*kataithe geisa,* 1620), and Electra's with the "underneath" of the palace (*huphapte,* 1618), as implying their potential roles for, on the one hand, supplementing the fame that rises to the skies, and, on the other, reconnecting the foundations of the house to the earth and generating new life within the bosom of the family.

112. Negative or ironic critical readings of the *exodos* are prevalent: for example, Reinhardt (2003), Von Fritz (1962), Arrowsmith (1963), Wolff (1968), Schein (1975), Falkner (1983), Willink (1986), Euben (1986), Dunn (1996), and Wright (2005); see further Porter (1994, 259–63).

113. On this "crisis of Athenian consciousness," see especially Reinhardt (2003), Murray (1965), and Burkert (1974).

114. On the likely composition of the theater audience(s) for a Euripidean play composed in 408 BCE, see Griffith (2009b). On the evidence for subsequent productions outside Athens, especially in the West, see, for example, Allan (2001), Easterling (1997), Dearden (2000), Giuliani (2001), and Revermann (2006).

115. I should like to thank William Allan, Donald Mastronarde, and the editors of this volume for their comments and advice on earlier versions of this chapter.

REFERENCES

Aélion, Rachel. 1983. *Euripide héritier d' Eschyle*. Paris: Société d'édition "Les Belles lettres."

Allan, William. 2001. Euripides in Megale Hellas: Some aspects of the early reception of tragedy. *Greece and Rome* 48: 67–86.

———,ed. 2008. *Euripides. Helen*. Cambridge: Cambridge University Press.

Anderson, Greg. 2005. Before *turannoi* were tyrants. *Classical Antiquity* 24: 173–222.

Arrowsmith, William. 1958. "Orestes. Translated and with an Introduction." In David Grene and Richmond Lattimore, eds. *Euripides IV*. Chicago: University of Chicago Press.

Assaël, Jacqueline. 1996. *Sunesis* dans *Oreste* d'Euripide. *L' Antiquité Classique* 65: 53–69.

Belfiore, Elizabeth. 2000. *Murder among friends: Violations of philia in Greek tragedy*. Oxford: Oxford University Press.

Biehl, W. 1968. Zur Darstellung des Menschen in Euripides *Orestes*: Ein Beitrag zur Interpretation. *Helikon* 8: 197–221.

Blundell, Mary Whitlock. 1989. *Helping friends and harming enemies. A study in Sophoclean ethics*. Cambridge: Cambridge University Press.

Bosman, P. R. 1993. Pathology of a guilty conscience: The legacy of Euripides' *Orestes*. *Acta Classica* 36: 11–25.

Bowden, Hugh. 2005. *Classical Athens and the Delphic oracle*. Cambridge: Cambridge University Press.

Burkert, Walter. 1974. Die Absurdität der Gewalt und das Ende der Tragödie: Euripides *Orestes*. *Antike und Abendland* 20: 97–109.

———. 1985. *Greek Religion*. trans, John Raffan. Cambridge, Mass: Harvard University Press.

Burnett, Anne Pippin. 1971. *Catastrophe survived: Euripides' plays of mixed reversal*. Oxford: Clarendon.

Calame, Claude. 1997. *Choruses of young women in ancient Greece*. Lanham: Rowman and Littlefield.

Cox, Cheryl Anne. 1998. *Household interests: Property, marriage strategies, and family dynamics in ancient Athens.* Princeton, NJ: Princeton University Press.

Cropp, Martin, Kevin Lee, and David Sansone, eds. 2000. *Euripides and tragic theatre in the late fifth century.* Champaign, IL: Stipes.

Csapo, Eric. 2002. Kallippides on the floor-sweepings: The limits of realism in classical acting and performance styles. In Easterling and Hall, 127–47.

Csapo, Eric, and William J. Slater. 1995. *The context of ancient drama.* Ann Arbor: University of Michigan Press.

Davies, John Kenyon. 1971. *Athenian propertied families, 600–300 B.C.* Oxford: Clarendon.

Davies, M. I. 1969. Thoughts on the *Oresteia* before Aischylos. *Bulletin de Correspondence Hellenique* 93: 214–60.

Diggle, James, ed. 1994. *Euripides Fabulae.* Vol. 3. Oxford: Clarendon Press.

Dodd, David B. and Christopher A. Faraone, eds. 2003. *Initiation in ancient Greek rituals and narratives: New critical perspectives.* New York: Routledge.

Dunn, Francis M. 1996. *Tragedy's end. Closure and innovation in Euripidean drama.* Oxford: Oxford University Press.

Easterling, P. E. 1985. Anachronism in Greek tragedy. *Journal of Hellenic Studies* 105: 1–10.

———. 1997. From repertoire to canon. In *The Cambridge companion. to Greek tragedy,* ed. P. Easterling, 211–27. Cambridge: Cambridge University Press.

Easterling, P. E., and Edith Hall, eds. 2002. *Greek and Roman actors.* Cambridge: Cambridge University Press.

Ebener, D. 1966. Zum Schluss des *Orestes. Eirene* 5: 43–49.

Falkner, Thomas M. 1983. Coming of age in Argos. *Physis* and *paideia* in Euripides' *Orestes. Classical Journal* 73: 289–300.

Foley, Helene P. 2001. *Female acts in Greek tragedy.* Princeton, NJ: Princeton University Press.

Foxhall, Lin H. 1989. Household, gender and property in Classical Athens. *Classical Quarterly* 39: 22–43.

Fritz, K. von 1962. Die Orestessage bei den drei grossen grischischen Tragikern. In *Antike und Moderne Tragödie,* 113–59. Berlin: W. de Gruyter.

Fuqua, C. 1976. Studies in the use of myth in Sophocles' *Philoctetes* and Euripides *Orestes. Traditio* 32: 29–95.

———. 1978. The world of myth in Euripides *Orestes*. *Traditio* 34: 1–28.

Gantz, Timothy. 1993. *Early Greek myth: A guide to literary and artistic sources*. Baltimore: Johns Hopkins University Press.

Garvie, A. F. 1970. The opening of the *Choephoroi Bulletin of the Institute of Classical Studies* 17: 79–91.

Giuliani, Luca. 2001. Sleeping Furies: Allegory, narration, and the impact of texts in Apulian vase-painting. *Scripta Classica Israelica* 20: 17–38.

Glotz, Gustave. 1904. *La solidarité de la famille dans le droit criminel en Grèce*. Paris: A. Fontemoing.

Goff, Barbara E. 1991. The sign of the fall: The scar of Orestes and Odysseus. *Classical Antiquity* 10: 259–68.

Golden, Mark. 1990. *Children and childhood in Classical Athens*. Baltimore: Johns Hopkins University Press.

Goody, Jack. 1983. *The Development of the Family and Marriage in Europe*. Cambridge: Cambridge University Press.

Greenberg, Nathan A. 1962. Euripides *Orestes*: An interpretation. *Harvard Studies in Classical Philology* 66: 157–92.

Griffin, Jasper. 1998. The social function of Attic tragedy. *Classical Quarterly* 48: 39–61.

Griffith, Mark. 1995. Brilliant dynasts. Power and politics in the *Oresteia*. *Classical Antiquity* 14: 62–129.

———. 1998. The king and eye: The rule of the father in Greek tragedy. *Proceedings of the Cambridge Philological Society* 44: 20–84.

———. 2005. The subject of desire in Sophocles' *Antigone*. In *The soul of tragedy: Essays on Athenian drama*, ed. V. Pedrick and S. Oberhelman, 91–135. Chicago: University of Chicago Press.

———. 2009a. Apollo, Teiresias and the politics of tragic prophecy. In *Apolline politics and poetics*, ed. V. Karasmanis, L. Athanassakis, R. P. Martin, J. F. Miller, 473–500. Athens: European Cultural Centre of Delphi.

———. 2009b. Extended families, marriage, and inter-city relations in (later) Greek Tragedy. In *Why Athens? A reappraisal of tragic politics*, ed. D. M. Carter.

Hartigan, Karelisa V. 1987. Euripidean madness: *Herakles* and *Orestes*. *Greece & Rome* 34: 126–35.

Holzhausen, Jens. 2003. *Euripides Politikos. Recht und Rache in "Orestes" and "Bakchen."* Munich: K. G. Saur.

Jones, Nicholas F. 2004. *Rural Athens under the democracy*. Philadelphia: University of Pennsylvania Press.

Just, Roger. 1989. *Women in Athenian law and life*. London: Routledge.

Kennedy, Rebecca Futo. 2006. Justice, geography and empire in Aeschylus' *Eumenides*. *Classical Antiquity* 25: 35–72.

Kennell, Nigel M. 1995. *The gymnasium of virtue: Education and culture in ancient Sparta*. Chapel Hill: University of North Carolina Press.

Kovacs, David, ed. and trans. 2002. *Helen; Phoenician women; Orestes / Euripides*. The Loeb Classical Library. Cambridge, MA: Harvard University Press.

Kowalzig, Barbara. 2007. *Singing for the gods: Performances of myth and ritual in archaic and classical Greece*. Oxford: Oxford University Press.

Kyriakou, Poulheria. 1998. Menelaus and Pelops in Euripides' *Orestes*. *Mnemosyne* 51: 282–301.

Lada-Richards, Ismene. 1999. *Initiating Dionysus. Ritual and theatre in Aristophanes' Frogs*. Oxford: Oxford University Press.

Laslett, Peter, and Richard Wall, eds. 1972. *Household and family in past time*. Cambridge: Cambridge University Press.

Loraux, Nicole. 1986. Matrem nudam: Quelques visions grecques. *L'écrit du temps* 11: 90–102.

Machaira, V. 1981. art. "Pylades". *Lexicon Iconographicum Mythologiae Classicae* VII.1.601–4; VII.2.486–87.

Maitland, Judith. 1992. Dynasty and family in the Greek city state. *Classical Quarterly* 42: 26–40.

McPhee, I. 1981. art. "Elektra," *Lexicon Iconographicum Mythologiae Classicae* III.1. 709–19, III.2. 542–49.

Medda, Enrico. 1999. La casa e la città: Spazio scenica e spazio drammatico nell' *Oreste* di Euripide. *Studi italiani di filologia classica*, 3rd ser., 17: 12–65.

Mossman, Judith, ed. 2003. *Euripides*. Oxford: Oxford University Press.

Murray, Gilbert. 1965. *Euripides and his age*. 3rd ed. London: Oxford University Press.

Osborne, Robin. 1985. *Demos. The discovery of Classical Attika*. Cambridge: Cambridge University Press.

Padel, Ruth. 1990. Making space speak. In Winkler and Zeitlin, 336–65.

Parker, Robert. 1983. *Miasma: Pollution and purification in early Greek religion*. Oxford: Clarendon.

———. 1985. Greek states and Greek oracles. In *Crux. Essays presented to G. E. M. de Ste Croix on his 75th birthday*, ed. P. Cartledge and F. D. Harvey, 298–325. London: Duckworth.

———. 2005. *Polytheism and society at Athens*. Oxford: Oxford University Press.

Parry, Hugh. 1969. Euripides' *Orestes*: The quest for salvation. *Transactions of the American Philological Association* 100: 337–53.

Patterson, Cynthia. 1998. *The family in Greek history*. Cambridge, MA: Harvard University Press.

Pedrick, Victoria. 2007. *Euripides, Freud, and the romance of belonging*. Baltimore: Johns Hopkins University Press.

Perdicoyianni-Paléologou, Helene. 2002. The vocabulary of kinship in Euripides. *Rivista di Cultura Classica e Medioevale* 2: 253–68.

Pigeaud, Jackie. 1981. *La maladie de l'âme: étude sur la relation de l'âme et du corps dans la tradition médico-philosophique antique*. Paris: Belles Lettres.

Porter, John R. 1994. *Studies in Euripides' Orestes*. Mnemosyne Supplement 128. Leiden: E. J. Brill.

———. 2003. Orestes the ephebe. In *Poetry, theory, praxis: The social life of myth, word and image in ancient Greece: Essays in honour of William J. Slater*, ed. E. Csapo and M. C. Miller, 146–77. Oxford: Oxbow.

Prag, A. J. N. W. 1985. *The Oresteia. Iconographic and narrative traditions*. Chicago: Bolchazy-Carducci.

Rawson, Elizabeth. 1972. Aspects of Euripides' *Orestes*. *Arethusa* 5: 155–67.

Reinhardt, Karl. 2003. The intellectual crisis in Euripides. In Mossman, 16–46.

Revermann, Martin. 2006. The competence of theatre audiences in fifth- and fourth-century Athens. *Journal of Hellenic Studies* 126: 99–124.

Robbins, Kristin. 2008. Innovations of character: The speaking role of Pylades in Euripides' *Orestes*. APA 139th Annual Meeting: Abstracts, 124.

Roselli, David Kawalko. 2007. Gender, class and ideology: The social function of virgin sacrifice in Euripides' *Children of Herakles*. *Classical Antiquity* 26: 81–169.

Sarian, H., and V. Machaira. 1981. art. "Orestes," *Lexicon Iconographicum Mythologiae Classicae* VII.1. 68–76, VII.2. 50–55.

Schein, Seth L. 1975. Mythical illusion and historical reality in Euripides' *Orestes*. *Wiener Studien* 88: 49–66.

Schlesier, Renate. 1985. *Der Stachel der Götter. Zum Problem des Wahnsinns in der euripideischen Tragödie. Poetica* 17: 1–45.

Seaford, Richard. 1990. The structural problems of marriage in Euripides. In *Euripides, women, and sexuality*, ed. A. Powell, 151–76. London: Routledge.

Sealey, Raphael. 1990. *Women and law in Classical Greece.* Chapel Hill: University of North Carolina Press.

Sommerstein, Alan H. 1989. *Aeschylus Eumenides.* Cambridge: Cambridge University Press.

———. 2006. Rape and consent in Athenian tragedy. In *Dionysalexandros*, ed. D. Cairns and V. Liapis, 233–51. Swansea: Classical Press of Wales.

Sourvinou-Inwood, Christiane. 2003. *Tragedy and Athenian religion.* Lanham: Lexington Books.

Spira, Andreas. 1960. *Untersuchungen zum Deus ex Machina bei Sophokles und Euripides.* Kallmünz: Opf. M. Lassleben.

Steidle, Wolf. 1968. *Studien zum antiken Drama.* Munich: W. Fink.

Strauss, Barry S. 1993. *Fathers and sons in Athens: Ideology and society in the era of the Peloponnesian War.* Princeton, NJ: Princeton University Press.

Strocka, Volker Michael. 1977. *Die Wandmalerei der Hanghaüser in Ephesos (Forschungen in Ephesos* VIII.1). Vienna: Österreichisches Archäologisches Institut.

Tarkow, Theodore A. 1979. Electra's role in the opening scene of *Choephoroi Eranos* 77: 11–21.

Theodorou, Z. 1993. Subject to emotion: Exploring madness in *Orestes. Classical Quarterly* 43: 32–46.

Thomson, George Derwent. 1946. *Aeschylus and Athens: A study in the social origins of drama.* London: Lawrence & Wishart.

Vidal-Naquet, Pierre. 1968. The black hunter and the origin of the Athenian ephebeia. *Proceedings of the Cambridge Philological Society* 14: 49–64.

West, M. L., ed. 1987. *Euripides. Orestes.* Warminster: Aris & Phillips.

Wiles, David. 1997. *Tragedy in Athens: Performance space and theatrical meaning.* Cambridge: Cambridge University Press.

Will, Frederic. 1961. Tyndareus in the *Orestes. Symbolae Osloenses* 37: 96–99.

Willink, C. W., ed. 1986. *Euripides. Orestes.* Oxford: Clarendon.

Winkler, John J. 1990. The ephebes' song: Tragoedia and polis. In Winkler and Zeitlin, 20–62.

Winkler, J. J., and Froma I. Zeitlin, eds. 1990. *Nothing to do with Dionysos? Athenian drama in its social context*. Princeton, NJ: Princeton University Press.

Wohl, Victoria. J. 1998. *Intimate commerce: Exchange, gender, and subjectivity in Greek tragedy*. Austin: University of Texas Press.

Wolff, Christian. 1968. Orestes. In *Euripides: A collection of critical essays*, ed. E. Segal, 132–49. Englewood Cliffs, NJ: Prentice-Hall.

Wolff, Hans J. 1944. Marriage law and family organization in ancient Athens. *Traditio* 2: 43–95.

Wörrle, Michael. 1964. *Untersuchungen zur Verfassungsgeschichte von Argos im 5. Jahrhundert vor Christus*. PhD diss. Erlangen Univ. Stuttgart.

Wright, Matthew. 2005. *Euripides' escape-tragedies: A study of Helen, Andromeda, and Iphigenia among the Taurians*. Oxford: Oxford University Press.

Zeitlin, Froma I. 1980. The closet of masks: Role-playing and myth-making in the *Orestes* of Euripides. *Ramus* 9: 51–77.

Contributors

Pascale-Anne Brault, professor of French at DePaul University, has published essays on the tragedies of Sophocles and Racine and on contemporary French literature and film. She is the cotranslator of several works of Jacques Derrida, including *The Other Heading* (Indiana University Press, 1992), *Memoirs of the Blind* (University of Chicago Press, 1993), *Adieu* (Stanford University Press, 1999), *The Work of Mourning* (University of Chicago Press, 2001), *Rogues* (Stanford University Press, 2005), and *Learning to Live Finally* (Melville Press, 2007). She has also coedited *Chaque fois unique, la fin du monde* by Jacques Derrida (Galilée, 2003).

Mark Buchan works and teaches mainly in Greek literature of the Archaic and Classical periods, with broader interests in literary theory, especially Marxist and psychoanalytic theory. His book *The Limits of Heroism: Homer and the Ethics of Reading* was published in 2004 (University of Michigan Press). He is currently working on a literary introduction to Homer's *Iliad*, as well as a series of essays on Greek tragedy and Latin love poetry. He has also coedited a collection of essays on Lacan and Antiquity (*Helios* 2006).

Peter Burian is Professor of Classical & Comparative Literatures, and Theater Studies at Duke University. His main scholarly interests involve ancient Greek theater and the classical tradition in the arts; his publications include numerous essays on all the surviving fifth-century BCE playwrights, as well as translations from Aeschylus and Euripides. He edits the series *Greek Tragedy in New Translations* for Oxford University Press, which includes his new translation of Aeschylus' *Oresteia* (with series coeditor and poet Alan Shapiro, 2003). He is a contributor to *The Cambridge Companion to Greek Tragedy* (Cambridge University Press, 1997), and recently published an edition of Euripides' *Helen* for Aris and Phillips Classical Texts (2007).

331

Mark Griffith is Professor of Classics and Theater, Dance, and Performance Studies at the University of California, Berkeley. In addition to wide-ranging articles on Greek tragedy and the satyr play, Hesiod, lyric poetry, early Greek education, and performance, he has also published *The Authenticity of Prometheus Bound* (Cambridge University Press, 1977) and critical commentaries on both *Aeschylus: Prometheus Bound* (1983) and *Sophocles: Antigone* (1999) for the Cambridge Greek and Latin Classics series.

Denise Eileen McCoskey is an associate professor of classics and an affiliate in Black World Studies at Miami University. She is the author of articles on topics ranging from women and slavery in the *Oresteia* to the problem of race in reading ancient Egypt. She is currently working on the book-length project, *Augustan Geographies: Mapping the Female Subject in the Early Roman Empire*.

Elaine P. Miller is an associate professor of philosophy at Miami University. She is the author of *The Vegetative Soul: From Philosophy of Nature to Subjectivity in the Feminine* (State University of New York Press, 2002), as well as articles on Kant, Hegel, Nietzsche, Beauvoir, Irigaray, and Kristeva.

Kirk Ormand, associate professor of classics at Oberlin College, is the author of *Exchange and the Maiden: Marriage in Sophoclean Tragedy* (University of Texas Press, 1999), as well as articles on Lucan, Ovid, and Clint Eastwood. He is currently at work on a book on the Hesiodic *Catalogue of Women* and an article on virginity in the Greek novels.

David Schur has taught at Harvard University, Miami University of Ohio, and Brooklyn College. He is the author of *The Way of Oblivion: Heraclitus and Kafka* (Harvard University Press, 1998), and he is especially interested in the theory and practice of close reading.

Charles Shepherdson is Professor and Director of Graduate Studies in the Department of English at the State University of New York at Albany and Senior Specialist with the Fulbright Program for 2006–11. He is the author of *Vital Signs: Nature, Culture, Psychoanalysis* (Routledge, 2000) and *Lacan and the Limits of Language* (Fordham University Press, 2008), and has written widely on contemporary continental philosophy and psychoanalysis. He was a Member of the School of Social Science at the Institute for Advanced Study in Princeton (1998–99),

Aristotelian Chair in the Liberal Arts at Saint Thomas Aquinas College (2004) and National Science Council Professor at Tsinghua University and National Taiwan University (2006–08). He is currently working on a book on aesthetics and emotion.

Victoria Wohl is an associate professor of classics at the University of Toronto. She is the author of *Intimate Commerce: Exchange, Gender, and Subjectivity in Greek Tragedy* (University of Texas Press, 1998) and *Love Among the Ruins: The Erotics of Democracy in Classical Athens* (Princeton University Press, 2002).

Emily Zakin is an associate professor of philosophy at Miami University. She is coeditor of *Derrida and Feminism: Recasting the Question of Woman* (Routledge, 1997) and has published articles in psychoanalysis, French feminism, and political philosophy. She is currently completing a book project titled *Tragic Fantasies: The Birth of the Polis and the Limits of Democracy*.

INDEX

DATE DUE

GAYLORD			PRINTED IN U.S.A.